Dethroning
the King

Dethroning the King

The Hostile Takeover of Anheuser-Busch, an American Icon

Julie MacIntosh

WILEY

John Wiley & Sons, Inc.

Published by John Wiley & Sons, Inc., Hoboken, New Jersey.
Published simultaneously in Canada.

For general information on our other products and services or for technical support, please
contact our Customer Care Department within the United States at (800) 762-2974,
outside the United States at (317) 572-3993 or fax (317) 572-4002.

Wiley also publishes its books in a variety of electronic formats. Some content that appears
in print may not be available in electronic books. For more information about Wiley
products, visit our web site at www.wiley.com.

Library of Congress Cataloging-in-Publication Data:

MacIntosh, Julie.
    Dethroning the king : the hostile takeover of Anheuser-Busch, an American icon /
Julie MacIntosh.
       p.   cm.
    Includes index.
    ISBN 978-0-470-59270-0 (cloth); ISBN 978-0-470-93958-1 (ebk);
    ISBN 978-0-470-93985-7 (ebk); ISBN 978-0-470-93986-4 (ebk)
       1. Anheuser-Busch, inc.   2. Busch family.   3. Consolidation and merger of
    corporations—United States.   I. Title.
    HD9397.U6B87   2010
    338.8'3663420973—dc22

                                                              2010032279

Printed in the United States of America

10 9 8 7 6 5 4 3 2 1

To my husband, Micah, for his limitless support and patience,
and to Miller, for arriving at exactly the right time

"It behooves a father to be blameless if he expects his child to be."

—Homer

Contents

Cast of Characters

Anheuser-Busch

Board of Directors

August A. Busch III: former Chairman, President, and Chief
Executive Officer
August A. Busch IV: President and Chief Executive Officer
Carlos Fernández González: Chairman and CEO of Grupo Modelo
James J. Forese: former Chairman and CEO of IKON
Office Solutions
Ambassador James R. Jones: former U.S. Ambassador to Mexico;
former Chairman of the American Stock Exchange
Vernon R. Loucks Jr.: Chairman of The Aethena Group; former
Chairman and CEO of Baxter International
Vilma S. Martinez: Partner, Munger, Tolles & Olson; later named
U.S. Ambassador to Argentina
William Porter "Billy" Payne: Vice Chairman of Gleacher Partners;
Chairman of Augusta National Golf Club
Joyce M. Roché: President and CEO of Girls Incorporated

General Henry Hugh Shelton: former Chairman of the Joint Chiefs of Staff

Patrick T. Stokes: Chairman of Anheuser-Busch, former President and CEO

Andrew C. Taylor: Chairman and CEO of Enterprise Rent-A-Car

Douglas A. "Sandy" Warner III: former Chairman of J.P. Morgan Chase

Edward E. Whitacre Jr.: Chairman Emeritus of AT&T; later named Chairman and CEO of General Motors

Executive Officers

W. Randolph "Randy" Baker: Chief Financial Officer

Robert Golden: head of Mergers and Acquisitions

Francine Katz: head of Communications and Consumer Affairs

Robert Lachky: head of Global Industry and Creative Development

Douglas Muhleman: head of Brewing Operations and Technology

David Peacock: head of Marketing

John "Jack" Purnell: former Chairman and CEO of Anheuser-Busch International

Gary Rutledge: head of Legal and Government Affairs

Thomas Santel: President and CEO of Anheuser-Busch International; head of Corporate Planning

Pedro Soares: aide to August Busch IV; former head of Anheuser-Busch Mexico

Other Key Players

Charles "Casey" Cogut: Partner, Simpson Thacher & Bartlett

Joseph Flom: Partner, Skadden, Arps, Slate, Meagher & Flom

Peter Gross: Managing Director, Goldman Sachs

Timothy Ingrassia: head of Americas Mergers and Acquisitions, Goldman Sachs

Leon Kalvaria: Global Head of Consumer and Health Care Banking, Citigroup

Kenneth Moelis; founder, Moelis & Company

Larry Rand: co-founder, Kekst & Company

Jeffrey Schackner: Managing Director, Citigroup

Paul Schnell: Partner, Skadden, Arps, Slate, Meagher & Flom

InBev

Executives and Board Members

Carlos Brito: Chief Executive Officer
Jorge Paulo Lemann: Director and key shareholder
Carlos Alberto da Veiga Sicupira: Director and key shareholder
Marcel Herrmann Telles: Director and key shareholder

Other Key Players

Francis Aquila: Partner, Sullivan & Cromwell
Douglas Braunstein: head of Americas Investment Banking,
 J.P. Morgan
Steven Golub: Vice Chairman, Lazard
Steven Lipin: Senior Partner, Brunswick Group
George Sampas: Partner, Sullivan & Cromwell
Antonio Weiss: Vice Chairman of European Investment
 Banking, Lazard

Grupo Modelo

Executives and Board Members

María Asunción Aramburuzabala Larregui de Garza: Vice Chairman
 of the Board, granddaughter of one of the company's founders
Carlos Fernández González: Chairman and CEO of Grupo Modelo;
 great-nephew of one of the company's founders
Antonino Fernández Rodríguez: Honorary Life Chairman,
 former CEO

Other Key Players

Joele Frank: Managing Partner, Joele Frank, Wilkinson
 Brimmer Katcher
Robert Kindler: Vice Chairman of Investment Banking,
 Morgan Stanley
David Mercado: Partner, Cravath, Swaine & Moore

Author's Note

The summer of 2008 is one many people wish they could forget. In the immediate aftermath of the collapse of Bear Stearns in March, the global financial markets briefly looked as though they might stabilize. By the time legendary American brewer Anheuser-Busch received a takeover bid from foreign giant InBev in June, however, lenders Fannie Mae and Freddie Mac were teetering on the verge of insolvency and concern was mounting that U.S. taxpayers might end up holding the bag on $5 trillion in mortgage liabilities. The government stepped in to rescue both entities; but just a few months later Lehman and AIG failed, Merrill Lynch was taken over, and Goldman Sachs and Morgan Stanley came pounding on the U.S. Federal Reserve's door in need of a life-saving favor. That New Year's Eve marked the first time I can ever recall hearing a unanimous sigh of relief that the year was over.

I'm one of the lucky few who spent that nerve-wracking summer thinking about beer. I covered InBev's takeover of Anheuser-Busch as the *Financial Times'* U.S. mergers and acquisitions correspondent, and while the newspaper industry wasn't exactly rolling in cash, I knew as the saga unfolded that I'd have a desk waiting for me in the newsroom as long as the two brewing rivals kept duking it out. Anheuser-Busch capitulated shockingly quickly, however, and since most of the world was distracted by the implosion of the U.S. housing sector and the disintegrating global financial markets, the companies' battle in the press was short-lived. That's one of the reasons I felt it warranted further treatment here.

Authors often attest that the books they write are nothing like what they first envisioned—that in the course of reporting one story, the undercurrent of a different and more interesting tale emerged. That wasn't the case for *Dethroning the King*. As the takeover fight unfolded that summer, it seemed as though each furtive conversation I had with a source hinted at a skeleton in someone's closet, and hardly any of it went reported at the time. With so much fodder at my fingertips—notes on what went on in the boardrooms of both companies, warped tales about the Busch family, and details on the drama that unfolded behind the scenes on Wall Street—I had a strong suspicion when I pitched this book about where the story was the juiciest. I just wasn't sure whether I'd be able to unearth enough details to make for a good read. The Busch family scions—and August Busch III in particular—don't wield the paranoia-inducing power they once did in St. Louis, now that their once-proud family company has been subsumed. But I still worried that I might be cast off like a pariah once I landed in Missouri.

Those fears proved to be woefully misplaced. People were eager to talk about their experiences. Anheuser-Busch played a huge part in the lives of countless Americans, from the company's employees, distributors, board members, and Wall Street advisors all the way down to the loyal drinkers of its Budweiser beer. Many of those people saw this book as their last chance to get something off their chests, a way to attain a level of catharsis and help lay the company to rest. Several said they'd been hoping someone would document Anheuser-Busch's collapse, and a few had considered trying to write books themselves before deciding they were still too exposed to the newly merged company or to former chief executives August Busch III and August Busch IV. People close to both companies told me separately that they had already cast the movie with help from their colleagues. One former Anheuser executive had struggled to decide whether the role of August Busch IV, tortured son and heir to the company's throne, should be played by Jonathan Rhys Meyers or Robert Downey Jr.

Former employees of Anheuser-Busch met me for breakfast, in their offices and at their local coffee shops in St. Louis, and even graciously invited me into their homes. Each interview was fascinating and colorful, but the time I spent with Anheuser's legendary marketing guru Michael Roarty tugged hardest at my heartstrings. Roarty had suffered a stroke a couple of years earlier, and I spoke with him in his living room, perched at the edge of his couch so I could hear him whispering from a reclining chair a few feet away. He labored to get the words out, but it was clear his recollections and sense of humor were as sharp as ever. After we finished, Roarty's graceful wife, Lee, patiently guided me through the lower two floors of their home so I could pore over hundreds of priceless photographs on display of the two of them standing with glitterati like Paul Newman, Frank Sinatra, Liza Minnelli, Lucille Ball, Joe DiMaggio, and former presidents George H.W. Bush and Ronald Reagan. It was an impressive display of the power big-spending Anheuser-Busch wielded in America. I drove away from Roarty's house grateful that I had decided to write this book, and remembering all the reasons I had decided to become a journalist in the first place.

Dozens of people close to both Anheuser-Busch and InBev spent as much as nine or ten hours apiece with me as I worked to form the structure of this story and to flesh out its intimate details. Some were happy to speak on the record, while others weren't comfortable seeing their names in print. I'm grateful to them all for the generous donation of their time and for their enthusiasm about the subject matter. On the way to my hotel from the St. Louis airport, my cab driver even offered to escort me to a section of the perimeter of Grant's Farm, the Busch family's ancestral country estate, where she had heard the security was weak. The popular local attraction had just closed for the season when I hit town, but she said I could probably sneak in if I wanted. I thanked her for her creativity and her eager complicity but politely declined.

My timing was slightly off in another respect as well, since I began researching this book while three months pregnant with my first child. Pregnancy and beer don't exactly mesh—not in American culture, at least—and I wondered how many glasses of cranberry juice I'd end up swigging as brewing executives and bankers invited me to meet them at bars once they finished up at the office. I was playing against type to begin with, as a young(ish) pregnant woman writing a book about the hostile takeover of a male-dominated brewer. I'd covered other macho topics in my career as a journalist, though, including automotive companies and the futures markets in Chicago. If you can hack it as a woman on the floor of the Chicago Mercantile Exchange, I rationalized, you can certainly stay afloat at the Anheuser-Busch brewery in St. Louis. I quickly found that my pregnancy helped humanize me to some of my more cautious sources. It made me seem more relatable. And since the saying goes that writing a book is the next-closest thing to having a baby, I suppose I've nearly had two. This book was a labor of love that burgeoned on both U.S. coasts. I first put pen to paper in a rented office in Manhattan's Financial District, right across Broad Street from the headquarters of Goldman Sachs. I penned the book's last few sentences three blocks from the ocean in Santa Monica, California, after moving across the country with my husband when I was eight months along, cartons of clippings and notes in tow.

It's easy to deal in superlatives when it comes to Anheuser-Busch, and the company gladly reinforced that image. It brewed America's favorite beer, its former chief August III was the most powerful brewer in the world, and its top staffers enjoyed only the best—sumptuous hotels, private jets laden with free Budweiser, and ritualistic gatherings studded with movie stars. Anheuser-Busch dubbed its flagship brand the "King of Beers" and spent more than half a billion dollars on marketing each year to make sure it became an American institution.

Anheuser-Busch's hostile takeover, which InBev attempted to make look "friendly" in the end, added two more superlatives to the pile. It represented the largest all-cash acquisition in history, and it marked the last giant merger that was inked before the global financial markets imploded. There were already indications that disaster loomed by the time the two companies first came together, and both sides made savvy moves that kept the deal alive when

September hit and banks started collapsing around the world. Merger activity had already plunged by then, and people who depended on big deals to stay busy at work were stuck watching the boring tennis match of barbs slung back and forth between Microsoft and its failed takeover target, Yahoo!

I ended up growing quite attached to some of this book's characters—even the ones I never had a chance to meet. Some were loyal to Anheuser-Busch, where one man's imposing views made life seem black and white for decades, while others were tied to the stark, competitive InBev, where the bottom line always dictates. After living and breathing each of these people every day for a year, though, it became impossible not to see even their most indefensible actions in a dozen shades of grey. When two companies that are as diametrically different as Anheuser-Busch and InBev are driven together, even the most simple relationships and decisions—even histories and legacies that have already been written—can quickly grow messy and complicated.

Prologue

They don't care what I think anymore.
—August Busch III

S ome men golf when they're looking to unwind. Others take their sports cars out for a drive or toss a few steaks on the grill. August A. Busch III liked to shoot things—ducks in the fall and quail in the winter.

He learned to love hunting from his father, who learned it from his father, and when he could take time away from the office, he would invite important guests to join him for a day of stalking waterfowl. He was a powerful man during the three decades when he ran Anheuser-Busch—powerful enough to compel some of his weaker-stomached subordinates to trudge into the marshes behind him, even though they'd have preferred throwing breadcrumbs to the birds rather than killing them.

The sun was slowly setting on August III's career in the early spring of 2007, when he and several Anheuser-Busch executives flew down to a plantation in Leon County, in northern Florida's Panhandle region, to hunt quail. He had retired as Anheuser's chief executive four-and-a-half years prior, had just stepped down as chairman, and now, with his son August IV newly in charge, retained only his position as a member of the company's board of directors. He was the most influential member of that group by far, but the transition to his son's regime had been messy and contentious, and August III was feeling marginalized.

The hunting group was eager to blow off some steam that year following the all-important Super Bowl football game. Everything had gone according to plan for Anheuser-Busch: More than 93 million viewers tuned in on February 4 to watch the spectacle, college-turned-NFL phenomenon Peyton Manning was named its most valuable player, and for a record ninth year in a row, an Anheuser-Busch advertisement won the *USA Today* Ad Meter poll that ranks consumers' favorite commercials. With their reign still firmly entrenched—thanks to an ad featuring beach crabs that worshipped in front of a Budweiser-filled cooler—the company's crack team of marketers breathed a sigh of relief.

That moment of respite was brief, however, for August A. Busch IV. He had only been running the company for a few months, and his father took issue right from the start with some of his decisions. August III wasn't the type to quietly voice his displeasure. He had torn so ferociously into his son that it had created an uncomfortable dynamic on the company's board of directors. He didn't approve of the alliances his son was striking with other companies, and he thought his new practice of inviting Wall Street bankers into confidential meetings was foolish. Anheuser-Busch had built itself from the ground up over the course of a century and a half. It didn't need to ink risky merger deals and rub elbows with fee-hungry bankers to survive.

As the group of hunting companions emerged from their bedrooms the morning after their arrival in Florida and prepared to head outside, a racket erupted from the plantation's formidable great room. August III, who had been using his cell phone to check in on things at the office, had hung up and exploded into a full-blown rage, ranting at no one in particular in front of the room's giant picture window and its view of the lake below. As the decibel level of his voice boomed higher and higher, it became apparent that his fury was fixated on two things: a beer distributing partnership the company had recently signed with foreign rival InBev, and his son's decision to invite a bunch of bankers down to an internal strategy session he had organized in Mexico just a week or two earlier.

Anheuser-Busch had been operating in a state of fear for months—everyone knew it was vulnerable to a takeover. By jumping into bed with the aggressive and growth-hungry InBev, even just on a deal to distribute its beers in the United States, he felt his son was asking for trouble.

"They've gone ahead and done this deal," fumed August III, who had strenuously opposed the joint venture. Anheuser-Busch was slipping out of his control, even with his own namesake in charge. "We're running scared, and here we are now doing a deal with these guys. We've let them inside the tent!" His hunting guests stared uncomfortably at their shoes, toeing the carpet, as the plantation's wait staff looked on in astonishment from the kitchen.

August III then shifted tack and blasted his son's courtship of Wall Street. By stocking what should have been a private meeting in Mexico with so many bankers, who had connections not just to each other but also to Anheuser's competitors and investors and the media, August IV had chummed the waters in a way that was bound to attract sharks, he contended. His protestations were so forceful that it seemed they would be heard in nearby Tallahassee, where his daughter and her husband ran a beer distributorship.

The last time August III had become so unglued over a threat to Anheuser-Busch had been in 1991, when President George H.W. Bush violated his "no new taxes" pledge and raised the excise tax on alcohol. August III thought he had played all his cards right: It was a Republican administration, one Busch family knew the other set of Bushes, and he and George W. Bush, the president's son, had even owned Major League baseball teams together. Those connections still weren't enough to keep the president from doubling the tax on a six-pack of beer overnight.

"All you did by bringing those bankers in there was send a telegraph wire out to InBev that you're ready to be taken over,"

August III snapped that day in the plantation house, turning in contempt toward the executives who stood off to th side to distribute some of the blame.

"You're putting up a FOR SALE sign. You're giving away too much information. All you did was get everybody in the world to sharpen their knives!"

He finally cooled off enough to head into the plantation's private reserve for the hunt, but the tirade had unnerved the group. They were already concerned that Anheuser-Busch had been left behind as its rivals ballooned in size. Life had been tense at headquarters for months, and everything came into stark relief that morning when they saw the worry and fear that flashed across August III's face.

"His point was that this is the beginning of the end, because now you guys opened Pandora's Box," said one member of the hunting group. "So while we thought maybe we were doing our due diligence, and I'm sure companies do this all the time, he said, 'You guys just brought this on yourselves.'"

Chapter 1

The Game Is Afoot

There's a shark in the water, and the shark is InBev.

—Anheuser-Busch executive

Wednesday, June 11, 2008, was forecast to be hot and sticky in St. Louis, with afternoon temperatures rising well above 80 degrees. None of the Anheuser-Busch executives who pulled into the parking lot of the soccer park in Fenton that morning expected to see much sunlight for the next 48 hours, however. After several decades of overpowering domination of the U.S. beer market, and a history of independence that stretched back more than 150 years, the company was under attack.

Anheuser's top staffers met often at the soccer park, one of several sites the company owned that were scattered around St. Louis. The Busch name was plastered all over town, in fact, on everything from the beer billboards that lined the city's highways and bus shelters to the plaques that marked some of its best-loved recreational sites. The

5

St. Louis Cardinals professional baseball team had called Busch Stadium home since 1953. Parents had been shuttling children for years to Grant's Farm, the Busch family ancestral home turned free-admission zoo. Students at St. Louis University congregated at the Busch Student Center, and visitors to the August A. Busch Conservation Nature Center in St. Charles, just outside the city, could even blast shotguns at the August A. Busch Shooting Range.

Less than three weeks earlier, the newspapers had picked up on something that prompted Anheuser-Busch to draw its own arsenal. Global beer giant InBev, the papers said, was preparing to lay siege to Anheuser with an unwanted $46.3 billion takeover bid.

Nothing was clear yet; InBev hadn't actually made a formal offer. The concept alone, however—and the fact that details in the newspaper reports were so explicit—set people afire at Anheuser's headquarters. Few companies on earth were more evocative of America, with all of its history and iconography, than Anheuser-Busch. Despite the forces working against it, from brewing rivals to alcohol tax–wielding politicians, the company had somehow made itself—and its key brand, Budweiser—as ubiquitous a part of American life as firecrackers and apple pie. If InBev decided to pounce and its takeover effort was successful, the glittering shrines Anheuser had built to itself in St. Louis could come crashing down, along with its supremacy as America's beer brewer of choice.

Most of America seemed to have never even heard of InBev. The company had grown from a tiny Brazilian brewing outfit into a globe-spanning megalith in an incredibly short period of time by normal business standards. InBev was now based in Belgium, but it was run by an intense, hard-charging group of Brazilians who had consistently gotten what they wanted as they pushed their company further and further up the list of global corporate powers. There could hardly be a more dramatic counterpoint to the gold-plated, history-laden Anheuser-Busch than cold, number-crunching InBev.

Arrogance and denial made some Anheuser-Busch executives believe that despite the missteps they had made over time, a takeover would never happen. The company—once the world's top brewer—had slipped into fourth place because of the insular, America-centric strategy it had espoused in recent decades, and it now appeared vulnerable.

Its corporate planning committee, though, had repeatedly run the numbers and determined that Anheuser-Busch was simply too expensive to buy. The concept seemed too illogical to entertain. How could Budweiser, a beer synonymous with American culture, ever be brewed by a Belgian juggernaut whose executives spoke Portuguese at the office? It was unthinkable.

As days ticked by with no official bid from InBev, sentiment among Anheuser staffers at headquarters arose that this was, yet again, just another one of the rumors that artificially boosted the company's stock price every few months. It was summer lightning, they thought—all flash but no rain. Still, something felt different this time. One newspaper report had included not just the price InBev was planning to offer but even the code names its Wall Street bankers were using for the project. A few members of the strategy committee—the 17 executives who mapped out Anheuser-Busch's future—were plagued by an ominous feeling about the whole thing.

Robert "Bob" Lachky, a well-liked executive who was famous in America's marketing circles for green-lighting Anheuser's "Wassup?!" ad and the Budweiser frogs, reacted at first to the takeover rumors with a defiant charge of energy. No bid from InBev had actually materialized, he reasoned, and even if one did, surely a company that pulled the kind of weight Anheuser-Busch did could fend it off. However, a conversation with one of his mentors—a former company executive—over the Memorial Day holiday weekend had abruptly spun him in the opposite direction.

"It's done. You're done," his former colleague had said.

"Come on, man, we can fight this," Lachky shot back, startled by the man's conviction.

"You're done," his mentor repeated determinedly, explaining that much of Anheuser's stock was owned by struggling pensions and hedge funds that would gladly take InBev's money. The markets were in the tank, and a bid from InBev would lock in badly needed gains for anyone who owned the stock. "This is a real offer. There's such sentiment right now that's going to be used against us," he said. "The fact that we're going to be forced to listen to it means that we're in, we're done."

In a way, some staffers were relieved to hear that InBev's long-rumored bid was on its way. "Maybe this is actually a good thing," they thought. "It's finally out in the open. We're in play now." Anheuser-Busch had been rumored as a takeover target for years, and battling the persistent speculation had been frustratingly distracting. Now, the company would know exactly which shark in the water was scouting an attack and how much it thought the company was worth. The take-over reports had already boosted the price of Anheuser's stock, which had gone nowhere since 2002, by more than 8 percent. If Anheuser could arm itself with the right data, it might even be able to convince investors it was worth more than InBev thought. The company was just starting to get back on its feet again after several rough years.

Positive thinking was only going to go so far, though, for a company that had done almost nothing to protect itself from the increasing threat of a takeover. Some sort of big change was starting to look inevitable. "The scenario you all hope for is that you can beat them off with a stick and be okay," said Lachky. "But you knew darn well they were going to come back again. This is a matter of time. They're either going to get us now or they're going to get us later."

Fear of the unknown had caused significant fissures within Anheuser-Busch since the reports of InBev's interest first hit. Staffers had been huddling in each others' offices at Anheuser's headquarters, which were perched on a sloping hill just west of the Mississippi River, for muffled but fervent debates about whether they'd all still be standing there in a year's time.

The company was refusing to comment on the rumors, in part because there was no actual bid on the table. How could it respond when InBev hadn't actually stepped forward to confirm or deny its interest? Still, that wasn't enough to appease the rank and file, who increasingly suspected that top executives knew more than they were letting on. The vacuum of information was causing a real credibility problem.

Douglas Muhleman, head of the company's brewing operations, faced a particularly frustrating quandary. Brewery workers were look-ing to him for answers, as their boss and as a member of the agenda-setting strategy committee. The fact was, he and the rest of the committee had little more information than their subordinates did about whether they were actually being hunted.

During a routine visit to the company's brewery down in Houston, Muhleman stood in front of several successive shifts of workers and did his best to calm the crowd as indignant employees ranted about the lack of information. The brewery's frustrated floor staffers, who weren't bound by the decorum that dampened criticism higher up the food chain, were getting hot under the collar. Hadn't they already been slashing costs for a year to make the company more competitive? And what did the Busch family think about all this? Didn't they control Anheuser-Busch?

"Guys, I'm down here and I'm trying, but I'm telling you I don't know anything," Muhleman said, looking out over a roomful of suspicious stares.

■ ■ ■

There had long been an unspoken assumption that it would be impossible for another company to buy Anheuser-Busch without the approval of Anheuser's domineering patriarch, August Busch III. August III, who was often called "The Third," was no longer CEO, having stepped down from active management six years earlier. His imposing presence on the company's board of directors, however, was still seen as a significant deterrent to would-be buyers.

The notion that Anheuser-Busch was actually controlled by The Third and the rest of the Busch family, though, was a commonly held misperception. The Busches were all bark and no bite from a financial perspective. They owned only 4 percent of the company—less than billionaire investor Warren Buffett, Anheuser's second-largest shareholder. The family still wielded a great deal of influence, and August III's son, 43-year-old August A. Busch IV, was now the company's chief executive, but they had nothing in their wallets to back themselves up.

"They were just the titular heads of this company," said one former executive. "They didn't have control. It was like a monarchy in Great Britain. These guys really didn't have the authority to do anything."

The people of St. Louis, where Anheuser-Busch had been based since it was founded, could be forgiven for forgetting that. Residents

there were emotionally tethered to Anheuser-Busch despite how antiquated and paternalistic the company and its ruling family had started
to look in comparison to the world's other leading corporations.
It wasn't just August III and August IV whose names and faces wall-
papered the town. There were so many Busches in the area that an
online search of the city's phone directory for the last name "Busch"
elicited an exclamation from the computer: "Whoa! Over 100 results
found." Some Busches were more notable—or notorious—than others. All who were part of the brewing clan knew what it felt like to
be important. "They've always considered themselves as part of a special class of people, and they were treated as such," said one former
Anheuser-Busch executive. "They were treated like royalty."

■ ■ ■

When Anheuser's top executives arrived at the soccer park that morning in June, they brought with them an electric current of fear and
apprehension. They were scheduled to meet with chief executive
August IV to put the finishing touches on a plan to slash and burn
as many costs as possible. Their goal just a few months earlier had
been $500 million, but with InBev now breathing down their necks,
it might have to be double that. The whole world was watching to
see whether InBev would make a move, and this was the best option
Anheuser had for keeping its investors happy.

They had never been known for cost-consciousness. For decades,
the aviation-loving Busch men and other staffers had hopscotched
around the country on the company's own fleet of sleek, leather-
outfitted Dassault Falcon corporate jets. It got to the point for a while
where even the wives of strategy committee members hadn't flown
commercial in years. To keep "Air Bud" running smoothly, the company had its own flight operations department with a staff of 20 pilots,
plus mechanics and other workers, all operating out of a spotless private hangar at the Spirit of St. Louis Airport.

When they weren't flying private, Anheuser staffers flew first-class.
"I want my employees at the front of the bus everywhere they go,"
August III used to say when he was CEO. "They should feel very

important." First-class flights were essentially company policy, and the perk stretched far down the pecking order. During The Third's tenure, the company even bought first-class tickets for young staffers who traveled back and forth between St. Louis and top business schools in Philadelphia and other cities.

Trips to New York meant stays at the glitzy Pierre hotel and $1,000 dinners. Visitors to St. Louis were treated to suites at the Ritz-Carlton. Still, the money Anheuser-Busch spent wasn't all for the home team's personal enjoyment—it also spent copious amounts of cash on its breweries, its theme parks, and even its Clydesdale horse operations to ensure that it had the best beer-making technology, the cleanest bathrooms, and the freshest paint jobs and flower arrangements available. For the 27 years he served as CEO, all of these costly efforts were undertaken to meet The Third's exacting standards, and many Anheuser executives were proud to work for a company that cared so much about quality.

The soccer park itself was a money pit. Anheuser-Busch helped build it in the early 1980s to house local youth players, and later bought it outright, spending two and a half years upgrading the facility to open it up to collegiate and professional teams. Because it was constructed on low ground, it was prone to flooding—and preventing and draining those floods was expensive. The irony was just too much. The Busches, who were avid duck hunters, would at points deliberately flood property on their massive farms to create the right environment for fowl during hunting season. However, the Anheuser-Busch–owned soccer park, which flooded on its own naturally, had to be pumped dry at significant cost.

August IV, who was known in aptly royal terms as "The Fourth," had been trying to right Anheuser's listing ship since becoming CEO a year and a half earlier in December of 2006. These weren't easy changes to make after decades of excess, especially with his father still on the company's board of directors. It was going to require real effort from his entire team.

Each executive showed up that day with a mental list of things he or she could offer up. Some were responsible for large segments of the company, like its brewing operations, its entertainment unit, or its giant marketing division. They weren't accustomed to being asked to take a hacksaw to their budgets. Still, this was not the time for idle contributions. They weren't panicked. They hadn't actually seen a bid from InBev. Even if one never materialized, however, it seemed likely that they would now spend the next several years fighting back one assault or another, whether from other rivals or from shareholders. The company needed to get leaner and meaner, and the group had two days to figure out how.

They filtered into a large conference room at the soccer complex and grabbed eggs and pastries from the breakfast buffet, milling about and chatting until August IV strode in and set his materials down at the head of the table.

The Fourth was a loyal Bud dresser, often sporting Anheuser-Busch–themed cufflinks or shirts with the company's logo embroidered on the front. He donned cowboy boots nearly every day, frequently in a preferred shade of green reptile skin, and on dressier business occasions he tended to pair them with an oddly tinged green suit. The boots afforded his five-foot-ten-inch frame an extra inch and a half or so, and he had Tony Lama, founder of his favorite boot maker, to thank for that—along, again, with Warren Buffett, who had owned Tony Lama's namesake company for the past eight years. The boost in height tended to help his cause with women but failed to prompt similarly adoring gazes from his strategy committee. They knew The Fourth had picked up the boot trick from his height-challenged father, and they weren't falling for it.

August IV had never liked coming in to his office at Anheuser headquarters downtown, but he had been skipping out even more frequently in recent months. He had set up an office and even a health room at the soccer park and preferred to work from there, citing construction on one of St. Louis's major highways as an excuse. He, after all, didn't pilot a helicopter to work every morning the way his father did. All the same, his decision to isolate himself from the rest of his troops illustrated how disjointed things had become for The Fourth at his own company, which, except for a brief stint, had boasted a Busch family member as CEO since its formation. The Fourth was feeling frustratingly ineffective and hamstrung by his father, and his increasingly distant attitude had rubbed off on the rest of the strategy committee. "The cat's away, the mice will play," one of them said.

"He increasingly was getting lazy about coming to the office," this person added. "He said, 'My war room is the soccer park.' But not really. We'd do meetings at his house, we'd do meetings at the soccer park, and because he flew a lot, we'd meet at Spirit, at the hangar. We'd have a lot of meetings there." It was reminiscent of times in the past when The Fourth, as the company's marketing head, would disappear from the office for days and force his deputies to track him down if work needed to be done. "He just never went to the office," the strategy committee member said. "He never did. And that was a shame, because I think that was one of his big mistakes."

With The Fourth now situated at the head of the table, the group got down to work. The day was scheduled to start with a presentation from two bankers at Goldman Sachs who had been counseling Anheuser-Busch for a while: Tim Ingrassia, who had just been appointed Goldman's head of Americas Mergers and Acquisitions at age 43, and Peter Gross, a top "relationship banker" who called upon Goldman's highest-profile clients. The two had known each other for nearly two decades, from back when they were both M&A bankers at the firm, and had stayed good friends even after their career paths diverged. Gross had been asked at the mid-point of his career to assume responsibility for Goldman's relationships with some of the world's biggest companies, and had since become a top banker for lucrative clients such as tobacco giant Altria. While Goldman had once been on Anheuser-Busch's blacklist, Gross had gotten his firm back in the company's good graces by doggedly making phone calls and knocking on doors in St. Louis. He and Ingrassia complemented each other well. Gross had the trust of August IV, whom he considered a friend. Ingrassia, the youngest of 10 children and a father of 4, didn't know Anheuser-Busch as intimately but was considered one of the best merger bankers in the business and had the deal-making savvy and stature Anheuser-Busch would need if it came under attack.

After rumors of InBev's interest had first hit in late May, Anheuser's board of directors held a meeting at which they lobbed a bunch of questions at the two bankers. Their main concern was whether InBev could actually finance a deal in the current environment, given that the credit markets were starting to disintegrate and Anheuser-Busch could

cost $40 billion or $50 billion. Just two months earlier, investment
bank Bear Stearns had collapsed and been sold to rival J.P. Morgan at a
fire-sale price. Could any company—even one as big as InBev—find
enough banks to loan them that kind of money?

The bankers laid out half a dozen bullet points, all of which
pointed to a clear answer: Yes, InBev probably had the capacity to
make a bid. With that established, the board's focus had immediately turned toward what it should do to prepare for that worst-case
scenario. With any luck, they hoped, the situation wouldn't devolve
that far. InBev would get cold feet, and Anheuser-Busch would
be left alone to fix itself.

Ingrassia and Gross were prepared to address that very issue—
fixing the company—that morning at the soccer park. They stood
up in front of the executive committee, their visual slides projected
on screens behind them, and launched into a presentation on what
Anheuser needed to do to thrive again and to protect its longstanding independence. The goal of the session was to work through the
company from top to bottom, discipline by discipline, to see how
many dollars they could come up with and how fast. Investors and
analysts on Wall Street were waiting for Anheuser's plan.

"If we don't do it ourselves, somebody else is going to do it to us,
and it's likely going to be them," Ingrassia told the group, referring to
the InBev takeover rumors. "What can we do, and how quickly?"

"The topic of the day was 'This is an emergency,'" one strategy
committee member said. "'We've got a problem here. We're about to
be taken over.'"

Still, it was going to be a challenge to get some Anheuser executives to change their entrenched views. The company had always made
certain arguably frivolous expenditures without a second thought.

The night before, after Ingrassia had returned late to his room at
the Ritz-Carlton, he flicked on the television and started aimlessly
surfing through the channels. One of the ESPN sports networks
caught his eye, and he paused on the station, blinking in disbelief.
It was covering a tournament in some incredibly arcane sport—it
could have been tiddlywinks for all he knew—and the competition was sponsored by Budweiser. He sat on the edge of the bed
and stared at the screen for a few moments, shaking his head, before

flipping to the next channel. Thanks to that incident, he had arrived that morning with an idea for at least one expenditure the group could cut.

The executives started to go around the table, one by one, detailing where they could eliminate costs. Marketing. Theme parks. Brewing. Packaging. Nothing was immune. The entire exercise felt surreal. They had been working to reduce spending for several years, but never on this level. This time, they were actually considering firing employees and cutting into retirement perks. It was going to hit St. Louis hard.

■ ■ ■

At mid-morning, with the Goldman team still plodding through its presentation, someone stepped in from outside the room and handed a note to August IV. He spent a brief moment reading it, his eyes darting across the paper, before rising from his chair and leaving abruptly. It wasn't unusual for The Fourth to duck out of a meeting to take a quick phone call, but this seemed different—it looked urgent, and he was not a man who was particularly prone to urgency.

Anheuser's other executives shot looks at each other from across the table, confirming that they weren't alone in their uneasiness. Not long afterward, a security guard who had been milling around outside in the hallway validated their fears. August had, in fact, been summoned for an urgent phone call, and the man on the other end of the line was Carlos Brito, chief executive of InBev. Anheuser-Busch and InBev had a partnership agreement, the executives knew, and The Fourth and Brito occasionally spoke for that reason. Still, there was no need for them to be discussing it now. As the minutes ticked away, it seemed clearer and clearer that this could mean only one thing. The cohesion in the room started to dissolve, and the executives began making private phone calls and gathering in small groups for hushed pow-wows.

A few moments later, Gross and Ingrassia, along with a small coterie of Anheuser's top staffers—men such as Chief Financial Officer W. Randolph "Randy" Baker, international head Thomas Santel, marketing chief David Peacock, chief legal officer Gary Rutledge, and internal M&A head Robert Golden—were summoned out of the room and asked to go join August IV in a back room a few steps away. They walked in to find The Fourth waiting for them, grave-faced.

Brito had just telephoned from Brussels to provide fair warning that he was about to send a letter proposing a takeover, The Fourth said quietly. Brito's heads-up represented a queer bit of Wall Street decorum—a way of politely patting someone on the back just before slapping him in the face. The InBev letter, which would formally confirm details of the bid, was on its way by fax. However, from his conversation with Brito, The Fourth already knew enough. InBev was proposing to buy Anheuser-Busch for $65 per share, or $46.3 billion, the same price that had been rumored.

There were a few hiccups and conditions: InBev wanted access to Anheuser's confidential financial information so it could be better-informed, and it hadn't provided many specifics on how it planned to actually pay for the takeover. There was no mistaking it—one of the worst fears of each executive sequestered in that fluorescent-lit conference room was now a harsh reality. InBev's bid qualified, in Wall Street parlance, as a typical "bear hug"—an attempt to make a hostile takeover by offering such a high price that the target simply can't refuse to consider it. Anheuser-Busch was being smothered.

The Fourth was astute enough to know that InBev's entreaty was a big deal. But he hadn't handled a situation like this before.

"Tell me what to do now," he instructed his advisors. "What do I do now?"

The group quickly hunkered down and started to map out a strategy, each staffer tossing in his ideas. They had to contact Anheuser's board of directors to get them organized, since the board would need to meet within a few days to set a course of action. They needed to loop in Anheuser's lawyers to set up a legal strategy, so they picked up the conference room phone to patch in Joseph Flom and Paul Schnell, two New York–based partners at the giant corporate law firm Skadden, Arps, Slate, Meagher & Flom, to brief them on the situation. Flom, a legend on Wall Street, had been Anheuser-Busch's legal counsel for decades and had an incredibly close-knit professional relationship with August III.

Because InBev was a foreign brewer looking to gobble up an iconic American company, the executives also knew they needed to get cracking immediately on a public relations strategy. Randy Baker put in a call to Lawrence Rand, a longtime partner at New York public relations firm Kekst and Company, who had been working with Anheuser-Busch behind the scenes for years in preparation for just this sort of event. Kekst advised a high-powered roster of companies and investment firms on how to handle public exposure, and it specialized in takeovers. The firm would need to brief Anheuser's internal PR staff on how to handle the situation, help them prepare materials for employees, shareholders, and the media, and start figuring out which buttons to push with politicians and community organizations.

Some of the men in that room, when they found a moment to catch a breath, decided that InBev's overture seemed eerily well-timed. The Brazilians had lobbed in this grenade of an offer just as Anheuser-Busch was trying to get the components of its cost-savings plan in place to unveil it to analysts. Was it just a coincidence? Or did InBev somehow know what they were up to?

Half an hour after The Fourth pulled his deputies out of their brainstorming session, the soccer park's fax machine sprang to life and spit out the offer letter from InBev, addressed to August IV. A few phrases jumped straight off the flimsy piece of paper. A merger of the two companies would be an "industry-transforming event," Brito said. "InBev is prepared to pay $65 per share in cash." Brito worked in a quick shout-out to Anheuser-Busch's beer wholesalers and its employees, said the merged company's North American headquarters would be in St. Louis, and said InBev would be renamed to reflect Anheuser-Busch's heritage. He was clearly trying to dampen Anheuser's ability to scuttle the deal by rallying popular sentiment.

International head Tom Santel, who had also been the company's strategic planning chief for the past decade, had been tracking InBev at the request of Anheuser's board of directors for nearly two years. Everybody knew that Anheuser was vulnerable and that InBev was a likely aggressor, but they hadn't been able to agree on a way to defend themselves. With InBev's fax now sitting there on the table, it felt as though the walls were closing in. "Seeing something like that in black and white, it suddenly becomes more real," Santel said. "It was like, okay, here we go."

The back room suddenly seemed stifling, so as a couple of the executives rejoined the larger group, several others stepped onto an outdoor deck alongside the building to continue their conversation. Another posse of Anheuser-Busch staffers who were congregated on a separate deck glanced over quizzically, trying to discern what was going on. After the men wrapped up their hushed discussions, they filtered back into the main conference room, hungry and scouting for lunch.

The rest of the angst-ridden strategy committee sat scattered around a few trays of food, picking over sandwiches and salads as they waited for the session to reconvene. It was obvious that something was up—August IV had disappeared, several other top executives had gone missing, and the two bankers who had been presenting to the group had vanished. They all knew what was coming. Their worlds were about to change. For those final few seconds before the boom actually hit, though, the uncertainty was still comforting.

"I do remember a fairly surreal feeling of being in this back room with August, knowing what was now definitively coming at us, and then walking back into this group of people who had no idea what was going on, who were sitting at a buffet getting food, with all the knowledge of what was coming their way that would change their lives forever," said one person who had been summoned out of the room by The Fourth. "Knowing that and grabbing something to eat, and thinking about how much this could radically change their lives and the city of St. Louis . . . I do remember thinking it was fairly surreal."

Roughly an hour after he left the conference room, The Fourth finally stepped back through the door. His agitated subordinates turned toward him and went silent in expectation.

"I just got a call," he said, his eyes flashing around the room to gauge his deputies' reactions. He briefly sketched out InBev's offer, gripping the company's fax in his hand, and then outlined what his team had planned so far in response. A few pockets of nervous chatter erupted as the group started to internalize what was happening.

"Are we going to fight this?" The Fourth asked, after giving the news a moment to sink in. He amplified his rhetoric a notch. "Are we going to stay together and fight this? What's the vote?"

Everyone in the room said yes. Loudly. What else was there to say? At the same time, their shell-shocked minds started to silently race—to warp ahead six months or a year, trying to picture Anheuser-Busch's future. They had put in 70-hour workweeks for decades. The company was their lives. What would it be like to no longer work for the most famous employer in St. Louis? To no longer feel quietly superior at Cardinals baseball games or to live in the only house on the block that was always stocked with free Budweiser? It was easy to bash The Third and The Fourth for their weaknesses, but they respected them, too.

"Most of these people are from St. Louis, and this is, like, the dream," one of the executives said. "They're the gentry class in their community. They grew up in south city with nothing, and here they are working at A-B. They're giving beer to their friends on the weekends and are the heroes of the neighborhood. Give that up? I'm not trying to be trivial, but this is how the psyche is in this town."

For many of the company's top executives, there also raged a more complicated internal battle. InBev's offer valued Anheuser-Busch at a much higher level than anyone else had in years. What would their piles of stock be worth at $65 per share, they wondered, running over the math in their heads. And what if Anheuser-Busch could get InBev to offer even more? That might mean a five-bedroom house in Vail rather than three, they thought—or maybe a 70-foot yacht rather than a 45-foot day cruiser.

"You're kind of going, 'Okay, at least we're worth something,'" one of them said. "You have that little part of you that's going 'Geez, the valuation is good. I don't like the way this plays out. The only way I'll get my money is if this place goes away.'"

"Isn't that terrible, though, and selfish?"

There was another factor adding to their guilt-tinged calculations, too. If they put their efforts where they had just put their mouths and actually fought InBev's bid, this could be the start of a years-long struggle to fend off one aggressor or another. And if they eventually prevailed, they'd still be stuck with the same ineffective management and paralyzed board of directors. It was, according to one executive, "a little sense of, not fear, but of fatalism, in that 'Okay, we fight this, and then the same management and board is still here. And they won't let us do anything.'"

The executives kept their mouths shut as these thoughts flew through their minds, ashamed by some of them and frightened by the lack of clarity on what lay ahead. One senior staffer let his bias slip, however. "We need to get that price up," he remarked off to the side. The ill-timed comment irked his more loyal peers, but they let it slide. Everyone was too stunned to care.

"We all knew it was possible because of the rumors," said one executive who was in the room that day. "But when the news finally came in, it was like a sock right in the stomach. It was hard."

InBev's formal entreaty sent wheels screeching into motion at Anheuser-Busch headquarters and, 900 miles to the east, up and down Wall Street. Emergency meetings were called as August IV began dialing down the list of people who needed to be put on alert. Once Anheuser and its lawyers determined that they should release InBev's offer publicly to keep shareholders in the loop, press releases were drafted and redrafted. The company's 14-member board of directors started checking in to determine when it could meet, and lawyers at Skadden, bankers at Goldman, and legions of other professionals who wanted to get in on the action dropped what they were doing and began clearing their schedules. Everyone was concerned, of course, that a company as legendary as Anheuser-Busch was falling prey to a foreign giant. There was also a tinge of excitement at the notion that they could be pulled into the highest-profile takeover battle of the year—and the largest all-cash merger bid ever.

■ ■ ■

After the beer executives' shock wore off that day, they bent their heads toward the conference room table and got down to business. Dave Peacock and Randy Baker, who had returned from their closed-door session with August IV more determined than ever, led the effort. If they had any chance of beating InBev back, they were going to have to convince Anheuser's shareholders that they had suddenly not only gotten religion on cost-cutting but could also execute on their plans. For a range of frustrating reasons, execution had been Anheuser's weak point since August IV had taken over as CEO in late 2006. Now they buckled down with renewed intensity, and the ideas came flying.

"It was totally surreal, because you're looking across the table at each other and you know it's not going to be the same," said Bob Lachky. "Nobody knew what was going to happen. For the first time in a long time, you saw people who had control of pipelines or fiefdoms suddenly being a little bit more open about giving up their goodies, because we had to do it for the common good. It was like 'Okay, I'll give up all my perks. My nice little Escalade.' Everything is on the table, from the most important budget items to the ones that were perks for top executives. Give it up, give it up."

It soon became clear that many of the cuts they were making were embarrassingly easy to identify. Anheuser-Busch had made such a substantial profit on every bottle of beer it sold for so many years that it had never needed to be strict on expenses. As one advisor put it, "Wildly failing at the management of expenses, their margins were ten points higher than Procter & Gamble's." Plenty of things could be done differently—or not at all—to generate more money, and InBev was bound to point them out if Anheuser-Busch didn't find them first. Anheuser had been floating along in its own little free-spending bubble for decades as the real world had developed around it.

As the group dissolved and headed home at the end of that first long day, they realized they had just become part of America's corporate history. It wasn't a part they wanted to play. Anheuser-Busch had always been the country's patriotic, conquering hero, not a fragile pawn susceptible to foreign interests. This, however, was an unmistakably *big* deal. The enormity of the moment even compelled some strategy committee members to stash away the documents that came out of the meeting for posterity and safekeeping.

Goldman's bankers jetted back to New York that night to start slogging away in preparation for Anheuser's board meeting, but most of the rest of the group met again on Thursday to finish the cost-slashing effort. By the end of their two-day sprint, they were closing in on $1 billion in pledged improvements, many of which would be in place by the end of the following year. Nearly one-third of that total would come through job cuts of 10 to 15 percent of the company's workforce. They hoped many of those cuts would come from early retirement and attrition, but with America's job market worsening every month, that many voluntary departures didn't seem likely. The company also agreed to raise beer prices and drastically reduce spending on machinery and other expensive improvements.

"Why hadn't we done this sooner?" the executives wondered, kicking themselves but also cursing the myopia and delusion that had always hamstrung their company. By waiting until InBev forced the company's hand, they knew they might have lost the ability to decide their own fate.

Anheuser's hubris and naïveté had led to its fall from grace, and it provided an apt comparison to the broader state of America at the time. After years spent downplaying or ignoring developments in other parts of the world, assuming that its supremacy was a constant, America's political and financial dominance were also at risk.

"I'll tell you what it represented," said one Anheuser advisor. "It represented everything that had gone wrong with American business in the last twenty or thirty years. I think these guys felt that the sun rose and fell in St. Louis. They were so dominant there that they totally missed what was going on in the world around them."

By the end of that day, everything already seemed to have spun out of control. Anheuser's share price jumped another 7 percent once the company had confirmed receipt of the bid, and investors started licking their chops and making wagers on whether Anheuser could fight off InBev. Everyone who had been huddled that morning in the soccer park's conference room had just become richer. But they didn't feel like celebrating.

"It was weird," one member of the strategy committee said, reflecting on the gut-wrenching day. "It was kind of like when you go to the doctor and you think you have cancer. But when the doctor finally tells you, you're still not prepared for it."

Chapter 2

Crazy and Lazy
at Loggerheads

The Busch family has cast-iron genes. They don't change an iota from generation to generation.

—Former executive William Finnie

Nicknames and caricatures have stuck with the Busch family's ruling men over time. August Anheuser Busch Jr., known as "Gussie," or "Junior," was the ebullient, beloved showman who charmed the masses into giving him a free pass for having 11 children with 4 different wives. August III, who was called "Augie" or—behind his back—"Three Sticks," was the calculating, inwardly drawn, power-hungry son who, after years spent waiting for his father to relinquish control, could bide his time no longer and took destiny into his own hands. And August IV, *his* son, who was usually referred to as "The Fourth," was the fifth-generation playboy who struggled to shed the cloak of his hard-partying past and who, despite being nicer and better-liked than his father, never matched his talent or met with his approval. In keeping with that tradition, it didn't take long for Anheuser's own Wall Street advisors to coin a pair of nicknames for The Third and The Fourth: "Crazy" and "Lazy," respectively.

August III won the genetic lottery on June 16, 1937, the day he was born into the wealthy Busch family of St. Louis and, as Gussie's eldest son, tagged with the first name "August." The name alone didn't secure him a seat on the company's throne. The monikers "August" and "Adolphus" were treasured family heirlooms, and they were sprinkled liberally among the offspring of gravel-voiced Gussie, who served as Anheuser-Busch's revered president and "second mayor" of St. Louis for 29 years. The Third's half-brother Adolphus, although he was nearly 15 years younger, could certainly have taken a shot at the company's top spot. Instead, Adolphus opted against binding himself for life to the all-consuming family business, leaving his more ambitious older brother free to scale Anheuser's ladder unimpeded.

Still, The Third's climb to the top was rocky and isolating. His steely, hard-charging demeanor was distasteful to those at Anheuser-Busch who preferred Gussie's sunnier brand of exuberance. Both men were singularly driven to succeed and to ensure that Anheuser-Busch remained the most powerful brewer in America. Rather than having that as the commonality that drew them together, however, their shared motivation was what ripped them apart.

Gussie, whose outsized personality made up for his slight stature, was a schmoozer and a charmer, a friend to U.S. presidents, and a face on the cover of *Time* magazine. Born in St. Louis on March 28, 1899, he was a barrel-chested soldier who loved cutthroat games of gin rummy, Winston cigarettes, and Silver Bullet martinis. Gussie's temper, though, could sour in a flash. The family he sired was disjointed and competitive. And both the start and end of his tenure as head of Anheuser-Busch were marred by sadness and controversy.

He started out in 1922 as a ninth-grade dropout at the brewery founded by his grandfather Adolphus, sweeping floors and cleaning vats. He rose quickly through the ranks and became president in 1946 when his older brother, Adolphus III, died prematurely after taking the reins from their father, who shot himself in the stomach to end a struggle with illness just two months after the 1933 repeal of America's Prohibition laws.

Gussie's talent as a consummate promoter proved evident well before he became president. The company's iconic Clydesdale horses were his idea: When Prohibition was repealed, he rustled up a team of the draft horses—which used to pull beer wagons in the family's native Germany—to haul the first post-ban case of Budweiser down Pennsylvania Avenue to the White House for delivery to President Franklin D. Roosevelt. Gussie's equally charismatic grandfather had once distributed pocketknives to work associates in lieu of business cards, and as he traveled the country 70 years later, Gussie passed out pocketknives of his own. When he left his own knife with one beer distributor or another, they would carefully place it in a glass display case or show it off to friends, demonstrating how a look through a peephole in the handle revealed a portrait of founder Adolphus.

"We used to give out replicas of Gussie's old knife," said John "Jack" Purnell, a longtime Anheuser-Busch executive who was hired when Gussie was chief. "Gussie could charm you—he could charm anybody. He had a natural flair for publicity."

With that flair, Gussie brought Budweiser, the company's flagship beer, to the country's thirsty, teeming masses. Adolphus had started to dream of selling beer across America not long after he founded the company, but Gussie had the foresight to build a brewery in Newark, New Jersey, on the country's east coast. The move was risky and expensive, but it boosted Anheuser-Busch's production, made it easier to ship beer around the country, and provided a platform for growth in the company's share of the U.S. market. By the time Gussie was forced out in 1975, Anheuser-Busch was the largest brewer in the world.

Gussie was best known, however, for his instinctive ability to connect with people. Anheuser-Busch's slogan, "Making Friends Is our Business," was very much his business. Eschewing planes and buses for his luxurious, Budweiser-stocked private railroad car, he peddled beer and visited distributors at whistle-stop trips around the country. To pep up purveyors in 1954, he invited 11,000 wholesalers, retailers, and barkeeps out to his imposing home, where he and his third wife, Gertrude, shook hands with a thousand guests each night for 11 straight nights. "When midnight came," he told *Time*, "my hand would be so swollen I couldn't move my fingers." He spent up to two hours on each of those nights soaking his hand in Epsom salts. All the pain was worth it—sales of Budweiser in St. Louis skyrocketed 400 percent after the event.

Gussie also branched into family entertainment in 1959 by opening the Busch Gardens theme park in Tampa, Florida, on the belief that well-run parks could broaden Anheuser-Busch's appeal. He, like previous generations of Busches, had always had a passion for animals. Grant's Farm, the compound where he and other Busch family members lived at various points in time, housed a menagerie of 1,000 animals on its 281 acres. He was an avid horseman, but Gussie also had some Dr. Doolittle-esque proclivities—the type that only extreme wealth can satisfy. He owned a camel and an elephant named Tessie, and took particular pride in his trio of chimpanzees, which he often dressed in cowboy attire. Adalbert "Adie" von Gontard, his cousin, dressed his own chimps in dinner jackets and had them sit at the table during cocktail parties, drinking Budweiser.

Gussie's most high-profile diversification effort, however, was convincing Anheuser-Busch to buy the St. Louis Cardinals baseball team when the team's owner was sentenced to jail for tax evasion in 1953. He won plaudits as a hometown hero for keeping the Cardinals in St. Louis, but the purchase was hardly altruistic—owning the Cardinals yielded a wealth of opportunities to promote Anheuser-Busch and its beer. He quickly rechristened their ball field Busch Stadium, and for decades afterward hauled a red beer wagon around the field with a team of Clydesdales to celebrate home games. "What was amazing was the reaction in the bleachers, where these guys making six or seven dollars an hour would rush to buy beer to toast 'Gussie' the billionaire," said Tom Schlafly, a rival St. Louis beer maker, in an interview with the local paper. "If Diana was the People's Princess, he was the People's King."

While Gussie Busch was ahead of his time in understanding mass marketing and promotion, the true architect of Anheuser-Busch's utter domination in America was his son August III, a mercurial, intimidating, detail-obsessed man whose ice-blue eyes turned even the smoothest Wall Street bankers into Jell-O. The Third, like the male Busch heirs before him, had been fed five drops of Budweiser beer just hours after his birth. Putting bloodlines aside, however, he wasn't your typical glad-handing Busch beer baron. He avoided crowds and public appearances whenever possible and preferred to spend his few moments of free time either secluded on his 250-acre farm near St. Louis or hovering above the masses in his Bell helicopter. People liked to joke that he kept the helicopter's rotor blades spinning outside while he ducked quickly into social functions. The Third appeared uncomfortable when he was forced to appear as a figurehead at ceremonial events and Cardinals games. And even in smaller, work-related settings, he often sequestered himself behind a phalanx of security guards or underlings to avoid being drawn into small talk.

"He was just cut from a different cloth, and was very private," said one person who worked for the company for decades. "In public, he was very, very impressive, but always all business. You never got behind the façade. He did have a lot of responsibility, a lot of which he took on himself. But he kind of thrived on that. He was just all business, all the time."

That hadn't always been the case. The Third's youthful antics suggested he might not develop into CEO material. He spent his teens and early 20s jetting around on adventuresome whims to ski and deep-sea fish, and seemed to spend more time on such diversions than on formal education, which was never assigned a high priority within the Busch family. He attended the University of Arizona for two years in the early 1960s but never graduated, earning a brewmaster certificate instead from the Siebel Institute of Technology, a brewing school in Chicago. Understanding the world of business, at least as it was lived outside his beer-subsidized life, didn't rank high on The Third's list at the time.

That all changed with shocking rapidity once he reached his mid-20s. A few years after his start at the company's bottom rung, August III flipped an internal switch so abruptly that it made personal reinvention look easy. He threw himself with vigor into a rigid self-tutoring program and covered every aspect of Anheuser-Busch's business, from marketing down to systems operations.

Such conversions became a habit for male Busch heirs over the years: Gussie's youth had been a wild one, and The Fourth would later handily improve upon his father's and grandfather's playboy reputations.

"Up through their mid-20s they're just wilder than hell, whether it's fast cars, fast women or, with August III, fast planes. They're out of control," said William Finnie, a former executive who worked for the company for 26 years, in reference to the Busch men. "Then, sometime in their late 20s, they take all of that energy and find out that business is just as much fun as this other stuff. So they throw all of their energy into the company with incredible results."

August III's self-propelled reformation in the mid-1960s was by far the family's sharpest, and it proved to be an early indication of the sheer force of his will and his competitive drive. From that point on, it was all work. Edward Vogel, who had been a company vice president at that time, said The Third had an "inferiority complex" because of his spotty academic record. Yet August III quickly began to prove that his sponge-like brain and unrelenting work ethic more than offset his lack of formal education. If anything, he became too hard-nosed and assertive for many of his colleagues' tastes.

■ ■ ■

The Third realized not long after starting work at Anheuser-Busch that it was due for modernization. He started advocating for change in a way that would later prove ironic when his own management style and perspective grew dated. Despite pushback from Gussie, August III started recruiting staffers from the top handful of U.S. business schools—the University of Pennsylvania's Wharton School, Harvard Business School, Columbia Business School, and Northwestern University's Kellogg School—to steer Anheuser-Busch into a more modern age. If Anheuser was going to knock off its competitors, it needed more intellectual firepower than Gussie's legions of old-school beer salesmen and brewers could offer. The Third's move to recruit a bunch of underlings also yielded a longer-term benefit. He surrounded himself with a cadre of loyalists—he dubbed the MBAs his "eaters"—who owed him their wealth and success. Those eaters rose through the ranks behind him, racking up hundreds of thousands of stock options as they went.

"August does not have a college degree, and he was up against not only Gussie but also all of the board," said Bill Finnie, who was a member of that group. "He really had to be good, and he knew he needed people that could help him look good."

Gussie, who espoused more of a "finger in the wind" corporate strategy, made no secret of his disdain for his son's growing ranks of MBAs. He didn't appreciate being told that the loyal staffers he had hired—many of them old-line beer salesmen and brewmasters with little business education—were outdated and insufficient. Still, the MBAs' computer models were saving the company money and pinpointing the best ways to expand. So while relationships between the old and new camps were rocky at points, Gussie grudgingly allowed spreadsheets to start making some of the decisions he would have made based on sheer guts and gumption.

"The old man, in his day, was great. But then scientific management took off," said Jack Purnell, one of the first six MBAs August III hired. "August III bought into that." The notion that The Third seized intellectual control of the company at roughly 30 years of age is striking, considering Gussie's vast experience and tenure. The Third was the right man for the task at that moment in history, just as Gussie had been when he injected Anheuser-Busch with life following Prohibition and the Great Depression.

"I think it was the right thing to do at the time," said Charlie Claggett, the former chief creative officer for one of Anheuser-Busch's longstanding ad agencies. "His dad was from a different era; he was an affable farm boy. August is much more of an engineer. He came in when the cigarette companies were eating Anheuser's lunch, threw out all of the good ol' boys and brought in Wharton grads."

With Gussie still technically in charge, The Third and his eaters helped Anheuser-Busch crush reams of smaller competitors in the 1960s by slashing brewing costs to a level its rivals couldn't match. That alone, though, wasn't going to beat Miller Brewing Company, which started coming on like a freight train at the end of the decade. Tobacco giant Philip Morris bought Miller from W.R. Grace in 1969, topping a bid from PepsiCo, and the move positioned Miller as Anheuser-Busch's most despised rival for decades to come. Milwaukee's Joseph Schlitz Brewing Company and Colorado's Coors Brewing Company, two other family-owned brewers, were also tough competitors. But neither had a war chest like Miller's. With new backing from its deep-pocketed parent, Milwaukee-based Miller was threatening to crush Anheuser-Busch under its thumb.

August III spent considerable time over the three decades in which Philip Morris owned Miller ranting that their rival was playing dirty—funneling money from its lucrative cigarette business toward Miller to make it a stronger competitor to Anheuser. Philip Morris had the right to redistribute money between divisions, and Anheuser-Busch could have employed the same strategy if it bought up a range of other businesses. But The Third loathed "cigarette money" and pretty much anyone whose hands touched it, and frequently lectured his colleagues about the dangers of smoking. Gussie was less shy than his son about drinking liquor and wine, and was known to enjoy a good smoke. When he ejected his father from the company, The Third immediately pulled the Winston cigarette dispensers out of the executive dining room at Anheuser-Busch headquarters.

"You couldn't have a pack of cigarettes," said former Budweiser ad man Charlie Claggett. "If they were Philip Morris brand, you'd be shot on the spot. But it was any cigarettes. He disdained the cigarette people because they weren't brewers, and brewing was what he was all about. They were just these tacky, rich, money-grubbing cabals who wanted to come in and steal his market share."

After being first to market in 1973 with a mainstream light beer, Miller enjoyed years of unobstructed dominance in that segment while Gussie waffled back and forth over whether Anheuser-Busch should jump in with a light formula of its own. "The old man didn't buy it, that 'Lite' was real beer—and he was still in charge in the early '70s," said Jack Purnell. "While the rest of us were really worried about it, including August, he wasn't. He thought it was just a momentary flash in the pan."

Gussie's age started to become a factor at the office in the early 1970s, which added to the challenges Anheuser-Busch was already facing. It was struggling to deal with the wage and price controls imposed by President Nixon in 1971, which had boosted the costs of its beer's ingredients, and rival Schlitz had come up with a novel battle tactic—a way to brew beer in just 15 days, less than half the time it took Anheuser, using new techniques that sped up the fermentation process.

Still, Gussie wasn't convinced that his son was ready to be chief. In 1971, at the age of 72, he named trusted deputy Richard Meyer as president of the company. Gussie remained CEO and chairman of the board, but the move was nonetheless historic: Meyer became the first person who wasn't a member of the Busch family to rise to such a lofty position. It served as a forceful reprimand for August III, who had put some of Anheuser's old guard on alert with his abrasive attitude and efforts to fill the company with workaholic clones of himself.

"The talk," reported *BusinessWeek,* "was that the elder Busch was teaching his chilly, tough-minded son some humility."

It didn't work. If anything, the move fanned the flames already burning within The Third's strident loyalists, who felt Gussie was past his prime. "The company was run like a corner grocery store," said Robert Weinberg, one of the first executives August III recruited, who was forced to resign after disagreeing with Gussie during a board meeting. "I couldn't give my secretary a twenty-five dollar a week raise without the old man approving it."

By 1974, Gussie was growing increasingly rattled by Miller's aggression and success. As Anheuser's profits and share price dropped through the floor, he started grasping at straws to turn things around by slashing the company's sales and marketing budgets and firing a slew of workers at headquarters, a shocking move that caused consternation within Anheuser's ranks. Concerns mounted that Gussie had lost his edge. After Gussie's lieutenant, Richard Meyer, resigned in 1974 to protest the job cuts, Gussie finally installed his son—who was already an 11-year veteran on the company's board of directors—as president.

The Third and his league of loyal underlings had a grand vision for Anheuser-Busch, and they were ready to unleash it on the market as soon as he became president. First, though, they had to wage war at home. Gussie was showing no indication that he planned to relinquish the CEO title. For a man in his mid-70s, he remained full of vigor and aggression—and that, for The Third, was the problem. The only thing now standing in his way was his own aging father.

So in May of 1975, The Third deposed Gussie with the same cool, detached efficiency that became a hallmark of his tenure. Fittingly, for a man whose life revolved around the brewery, 37-year-old August III seized control not in a heart-to-heart with his dad at the family dinner table but within the emotionally sterile atmosphere of Anheuser-Busch headquarters, through a dramatic and painstakingly choreographed boardroom coup. The power grab gave The Third a chance to show his remarkable ability to play one-on-one politics behind closed doors, a tactic he employed to great success for decades afterward with his own board of directors. He courted each member of Gussie's board individually to ensure he had the support of enough of its members, and secured commitments from a range of executives that they would resign if he was not elected CEO. Confident that he had the backing he needed, The Third then called for a vote on the matter by the board of directors.

The night before the board's scheduled meeting, Gussie summoned every director out for a face-to-face chat in the imposing "gun room" at Grant's Farm, one of many testaments on the estate to the family's longstanding fascination with firearms. As Walter C. "Buddy" Reisinger, a great-grandson of Adolphus Busch, strode toward the gun room's door, it swung open and another board member exited, shooting a wilted glance in his direction.

"Buddy, I only have one question for you," 76-year-old Gussie rasped, moments after Reisinger walked in. "How are you going to vote tomorrow?"

Reisinger, one of many family members who tried to broker peace between Gussie and The Third during the coup, confessed that he planned to vote for August III and then briefly outlined his position. The layers of internal politics and infighting were too messy to delve into. Among those issues was at least one tangible viewpoint: The board felt August III had a better grasp of the threat from Miller and how to address it.

"This should be the greatest moment of your life," Reisinger told Gussie. "You brought the company a lot of success, and you're still alive and can now turn it over to your son. This should be the best thing you could ever do."

Gussie wasn't swayed. When the vote came down the next day in favor of his son, Gussie—who had been emotionally ravaged just months earlier by the death of his eight-year-old daughter in a car accident—lashed out like a wounded animal at the directors and executives who betrayed him. The family split into factions based on their support or abhorrence of August's forced ascension, and Gussie's younger children by his third wife, Trudy, including The Third's half-brother Adolphus IV, were particularly upset.

"August has stabbed my father in the back," said Peter Busch, another one of Trudy's children, to a mentor of his at the time. After his 29 years as head of the company, Gussie was left with little to show for it other than his beloved St. Louis Cardinals. He remained president of the baseball team until he died on September 29, 1989, at home near St. Louis, at the age of 90.

"It was a tough time," said Michael Roarty, a legendary marketing executive at the company. "But I think the timing was right."

"Anheuser-Busch is a proud company, and the Busch family made it so," Roarty said. "Gussie was a proud man. But as time went by, August proved to be a great general. Many of the great things we experienced were directly attributed to August III. There's a tendency to forget that, but it shouldn't be forgotten."

When asked more than three decades later about the coup, The Third remained stoic and brief. "My father built the company," he said. "He was a visionary. He and I had years of a great relationship and I had great respect for him."

Yet from that day in May until Gussie's death more than 14 years later, the two men's relationship remained strained in the best of times and non-existent in the worst. They didn't speak for roughly a decade. Gussie hired Louis Susman, a St. Louis lawyer, to represent him on matters concerning the company, the Cardinals, and eventually, his giant personal estate, and Susman ultimately served as a go-between for Gussie and The Third.

At the time of his death, Gussie controlled a 13.5 percent stake in the company worth roughly $1.5 billion. For his work as executor of the estate, Susman was handed 2 percent of the trust income and 1 percent of the sale of Gussie's personal property and was soon worth millions.

In 2009, President Obama raised a few eyebrows by rewarding Susman with a job as ambassador to the United Kingdom, one of the country's most prestigious overseas appointments, despite his lack of foreign policy expertise. The promotion allowed Susman to move into

Winfield House, the London Embassy's opulent residence in Regent's Park, which makes Grant's Farm look like a stable. Many of those who spoke out in Susman's support cited the "diplomatic" experience he gained while brokering deals between Gussie and The Third, whose animosities seemed to be deeper-rooted than any harbored between the United States and the United Kingdom.

■ ■ ■

The Third's first few years in office weren't much easier than orchestrating the coup had been. After finally wresting control of the company, he turned to face a Teamsters strike—one of the most challenging environments in Anheuser-Busch's history. The union was threatening to walk off the job over pay negotiations, so The Third, who had no intentions of caving to its demands, staffed his white collar business grads on the breweries' production lines to try to keep the place afloat. The episode—The Third's baptism by fire—marked the start of his antagonistic relationship with organized labor.

"It was a disaster—an absolute disaster," said Bill Finnie. "The union people absolutely hated management in general and August in particular, and it was reciprocated. So August did not start off on day one on the right foot." Finnie spent the first six hours of every day cleaning soggy beechwood chips out of the brewery's giant metal tanks, crawling into them through a two-foot hole while grasping a toilet plunger and a rake. Then he and the other mid-level executives would spend four or five hours at their desks in the office. One of his subordinates, a graduate of the notoriously cerebral Massachusetts Institute of Technology, suffered that summer from a general lack of handiness and physical coordination. "He drove a forklift, and I think he had some pretty serious accidents," Finnie said. "It was pretty ugly. But at lunch, they'd bring us really fresh beer in gallon milk jugs, and it was the best-tasting beer you've ever had in your entire life." The company ultimately paid each of the white-collar workers a $1,000 bonus for their loyalty.

The union, to which August III had once belonged when he worked at the brewery, finally caved and agreed to the original pay package he had proposed. His hard stance made for the longest strike in company history, and it also proved the costliest. Production sank by half, and Anheuser-Busch's U.S. market share dropped from 23.4 percent in 1975 to 19 percent the next year. Miller, meanwhile, picked up speed and topped Schlitz as the nation's number two beer.

August III set out with a vengeance the moment the strike was over—not to punch Miller back into place with a nosebleed but to kill it. There was no questioning his level of determination. It was more a matter of execution. To rally his troops, and to provide them with a constant remainder of the height of the stakes, he had "ASU," which stood for his new motto, "A Sense of Urgency," printed on hats and T-shirts and engraved on pads of company paper that he then abundantly scattered around the Anheuser-Busch executive suites. One former ad agency staffer said he still got the chills decades later when recalling the inscribed notepads.

Chapter 3

The Colossus

It's hard to overstate how good a job he did in turning A-B into the biggest brewer in the world. He was like a colossus, despite his short stature.

—Chief executive of a rival brewer

August III didn't lower himself gently onto Anheuser-Busch's throne. After seizing control by force, he used it as a battle station, commanding his troops like a general at war. It was at this time, newly into his administration and with a bunch of challenges looming, that his peculiar personality and gruff management style hit full force. They weren't for the faint of heart.

The Third enraptured subordinates with his power, his unyielding drive to win, and the intensity and accuracy of his business instincts and ethics. But many of those same colleagues were also repelled by how brutally cold and judgmental he could be and by his bizarre relationship with his son, which left them fumbling to describe the mix of terror and admiration their boss simultaneously inspired.

"He was scary smart, and scary period," said Steve Kopcha, a former ad agency executive and copywriter of some of Anheuser-Busch's best-known commercials. "You just did not want to be around when he was angry. He's got these piercing blue eyes—I mean, he's scary. You could not con this guy at all. I had a lot of respect for August III."

One of The Third's former mentees called him a "cold son of a bitch" for kicking Gussie to the curb and for skipping the funerals of longtime employees, and then added that he was "really one of my heroes."

"He was a control freak of the first order," said a former advertising agency executive. "He demanded complete, abject loyalty, almost like a monarch would in the old days."

"He was a complete control freak," agreed Mike Roarty, with no hint of malice. "He marched to his own drummer." Roarty's wife, Lee, perched at his side, started ticking through a list of August's peculiarities—his claustrophobia, his fear of elevators, and his dislike of crowds—before Mike added: "In the 1980s, much of the innovation that came out of the company was dictated by August III. You can't deny his contribution."

That point yields little disagreement. During the years August III ran Anheuser-Busch, he *was* Anheuser-Busch. His life, in turn, was almost singularly defined by his work at the company. And he structured it so that his subordinates' lives could revolve around the office as well. The campus around Anheuser's headquarters downtown sported enough cushy amenities to eliminate most of the excuses an executive might use to leave the site: a health club, a fancy corporate dining room, and even a barbershop. Many insiders avoided these sites at all costs to keep from being cornered by The Third on the treadmill or while waiting in line for a breakfast table. But 60- to 70-hour workweeks were the norm even for those who ate their eggs at home—and usually with a few extra hours put in at night or on weekends. An Anheuser employee was never really "off duty."

"If you worked for August, you could expect calls any time day or night," said Charlie Claggett. "I remember once, there was something like thirteen inches of snow on the ground and we were supposed to be out at Spirit of St. Louis Airport at 8:00 A.M. The city was shut down, but it never occurred to any of us that that meeting wasn't going to happen. It was not even an issue. We knew it would start at eight, and if you weren't there, it would start without you."

Christmas and New Year's weren't immune, since The Third issued performance reviews around that time. In keeping with his extraordinary talent for being everywhere at once, he personally reviewed somewhere between 30 and 50 of his top executives each year. At their allotted times, the officers would filter one by one into the waiting area outside the conference room next to his office and then take their seats, clammy and sweating, as they waited their turn. Every 10 minutes or so, the conference room's current occupant would stumble out, wearing a facial expression that indicated how his review had gone, and the next person in line would step gingerly inside.

"You'd be in the bullpen waiting, and if they had issues with a particular person, it would take more than ten or fifteen minutes and things would get backed up," said an executive who underwent the process for many years. "You'd end up with three or four guys sitting in the bullpen, looking at each other like 'How do you think yours is going to go this year?' It was just weird."

The procedure, and the nerve-wracking anticipation that led up to it, made for some tense Decembers. But it also gave top staffers a few minutes of The Third's personal attention, and the troops further down in Anheuser's ranks always waited expectantly for word from their bosses on what August thought.

"Some people came out of there and it was beyond bad," the executive said. "But you'd get it straight from the top, good or bad."

The Third tended to concentrate his demands within his sales and marketing staff and the company's advertising agencies, which, with their ability to touch tens of millions of American consumers, were the lifeblood of the company's success. Marketers bore the brunt of the pressure around Christmas and New Year's, which always fell just a month before the make-or-break advertising spectacle of the Super Bowl.

"I felt bad for some of the marketing guys, because they really did get a lot of scrutiny," said a top executive from another part of the company. But no one was immune when The Third wanted something. He had been known to pick up the phone and call Henry Kissinger with requests.

In an attempt to inject The Third with some holiday spirit one year, a few executives from ad agency DDB Needham in Chicago hatched a plan. The Third had been flying them down to St. Louis every Friday for months in the early 1990s to hear new advertising pitches, and they were stuck traveling to meet with him in the company's airplane hangar just days before Christmas. To lighten The Third's mood, they decided to hire a trio of carolers—two women and a man dressed in full Dickensian garb—to hop on Anheuser-Busch's private jet for the trip to Missouri.

Once the group had settled on the plane, John Greening, DDB's worldwide account director for Anheuser-Busch, turned to address the carolers. "Listen, this guy has a 30-second attention span, so I want you to sing 30 seconds of three different songs and that'll be it," he said. The carolers nodded and contentedly nestled back into the jet's comfortable seats, wondering how they had gotten so lucky. Once the plane taxied to a stop at the company's hangar in St. Louis, Greening hurriedly shoved the singers into a closet.

"Let's get to work!" The Third said in a booming voice as he strode in moments later. After a few joking protestations about being dragged down to St. Louis just before Christmas, the DDB staffers told August III they had brought him a gift. Out from the closet popped the carolers, who launched into the first 30 seconds' worth of "Silent Night" as they had been instructed. As the trio quickly inhaled before moving into the next song, The Third sensed an opening and politely but firmly cut them off.

"That's great," he said. "Now let's get to work."

■ ■ ■

August III commanded a combination of arms-length admiration, respect, and terror from many of his underlings. As one former staffer in the company's marketing department liked to tell his colleagues, he had only two moods: pissed off and suspicious. It was tough to decide which was better.

He was adept at putting people on the spot—he actually seemed to relish it. He had an eye for detail and facts and he was usually right, which was incredibly intimidating. When he fixes his stare on executives, "their biggest concern is that he knows more than they do, even though the topic is in their area of expertise," former chief financial officer Jerry Ritter told *BusinessWeek*.

"If you weren't as well-versed in his business as he was, you didn't stand a chance," said Charlie Claggett. "You couldn't bullshit the guy. He was on top of everything. There wasn't a single, tiny aspect of the business he didn't know. You had to do your homework. If you didn't, or you were insincere, he could sniff you out and snuff you out. There was always this element of fear that permeated the place."

August III had a reputation for asking pointed, probing questions during meetings and presentations, targeting not just the person presenting the material but even the younger staffers who cowered in chairs along the wall.

"My mom always used to tell me this—the guy never asked a question that he didn't know the answer to already," said Walter C. "Buddy" Reisinger Jr., a former Anheuser-Busch staffer whose mother married into the extended Busch family. "But if he asked you a question, he really wants to know what you think, and you have 120 percent of that guy's attention. While he is talking to you, you own him. He is so focused."

"If you saw any A-B presentation slide, it'd have 4,000 numbers jammed on it," Reisinger said. "It violates every PowerPoint presentation rule. You could have 300 numbers on this thing, and he would say 'Uh, that cost per barrel for Bud Light at the Cartersville plant . . . Jimmy, didn't you show me something last week that was a tenth of a cent off?' It's frightening. He could do that time after time on anything, anywhere, and you're just trying to survive. The guy was 'on' 24-7."

That sort of atmosphere, where The Third's commanding knowledge of the business piqued the jangling nerves of his staffers, clearly led some of them to trip up. There was nothing to fear in making a mistake, The Third preached. Making the same mistake twice, however, was another story. His patience for underperformance usually didn't stretch that far.

He formed a policy committee of 9 or 10 top executives within the company, which was later expanded into the strategy committee, and governed discussions using the Socratic method. Staffers were required to present and back up their own views on key issues, and were often formally pitted against each other in staged "dialectics," with one team devoting weeks to preparing a "pro" view while the other evaluated the "cons."

"He's demanding," said one former strategy committee member. "He asked a lot of questions, he was intense, focused. Anybody who told you it wasn't a little intimidating every time they got up would be lying to you. And anybody who told you they got used to it would be lying to you. But at a point, you look forward to it because of the intensity and the challenge."

That challenge wasn't always overcome. The Third's rebukes were harsh and, occasionally, career-ending. He fired plenty of staffers over the years. Most left the company or, if they worked for an ad agency, were assigned by their bosses to other accounts or regional offices. "If you didn't do your work well, there was somebody else in line who could take your place. They had a lot of bench strength," said an executive who climbed to Anheuser's uppermost ranks.

The Third's legion of subordinates busted their tails every day to earn his respect, putting in exhausting workweeks and traveling for long stretches away from their families. These were salt-of-the-earth Midwesterners—people who tended to marry their high school sweethearts—and The Third demanded sacrifice. But he was compelling enough to get it.

"Mr. Busch is just a great leader; he was a guy you'd do anything for," one top executive said. "And if he patted you on the back, you felt like you could go for six more months because that's how much we all loved him and admired him. But he's not a man who gives love back. That was the tough part."

Helpful Anheuser ladder-climbers passed on certain pieces of advice to their less-experienced colleagues. Of utmost importance was that they knew their area of expertise inside and out, since it was a capital offense for a staffer to come up blank in front of August III on a subject he should understand. If that did happen, it was far better to tell him you'd return quickly with an answer rather than bluffing through a response. The Third's bullshit detector was finely tuned, and "if he finds out, it's not pretty," said one former executive.

It was important to have an abbreviated version of each pitch just in case he was running behind, because when The Third told someone he had two minutes, he meant it. He was known to take off his watch and set it on the table in front of him to draw attention to the time constraint.

And always, always look him in the eye, the company's senior staffers advised.

"I never got that instruction," mused one former executive. "But it never occurred to me to do anything other than that."

■■■

The Third's cross-examinations were particularly stressful during trips on the Anheuser-Busch planes. Executives traveling with August—and in some cases, even their wives—knew to mentally prepare for several unobstructed hours of his attention. He would often fly the plane himself on the way home, or at the very least, crack open a beer and take a break. "On your way down, though, it's your worst nightmare," said one former staffer. "You're in this thing for hours, and he's going to just torture you, peppering question after question. You weren't going anywhere. What are you going to do?"

August III also loved to show up unannounced. He staged frequent surprise white-glove inspections at Anheuser-Busch's breweries, theme parks, and wholesalers, and even at restaurants that poured the company's beer. The routine was simple: If the beer being served by a restaurant or shipped by a wholesaler was old, he would walk back to the beverage cooler and dump it all out. If a theme park's walkways were dirty, he'd have its general manager on a walkie-talkie within seconds, putting every staffer in the park on clean-up duty. To kick off his visits, The Third often headed straight for the bathroom—a tactic his father had also employed in his day. "When I visit one of our plants or any installation, I make a bee-line for the toilets," Gussie said. "Not because I need to make use of them . . . If the restrooms are unclean, if there is no soap or towels or tissue, you can just bet there will be something lacking also in many other phases of that operation."

The Third's desire for control and perfection drove him to be heavily involved in nearly all aspects of Anheuser-Busch's business. He once demanded that a television commercial be reshot because the horses in it were too skinny. His love for beer itself—the smell and taste of it, the way light filtered through a perfectly poured glass, and the way it was painstakingly made, from harvest to tap—made him a constant presence on brewery floors well past the end of his official tenure as CEO.

"He had an incredible passion for the product and the breweries and everything that had to do with the making of the beer," said one former executive committee member. "That was sort of his thing."

August III would ritualistically dig his hands into the breweries' hop bins, crack open the husks and inhale deeply through his nose, smelling them to gauge their quality. At brewery meetings, he liked to toss hops into hot water to make "hop teas," an acquired taste that even many beer aficionados find disgusting.

Dining with The Third at a restaurant meant sitting down in front of a lineup of the establishment's beers and spending the supper hour sipping and gargling to make sure they were fresh. After work, he liked to hit the tasting room on the brewing department's top floor. Even his office served as a beer-swilling laboratory. As a certified brewmaster, he was a member of the company's taste surveillance team, which tested beers from various Anheuser-Busch breweries every day to see if tiny adjustments to the process needed to be made. Anyone who ducked into his earth-toned office might encounter up to 50 numbered bottles lined up on his desk. He performed the same ritual many nights at home before his head hit the pillow at 8:30.

As one executive who used to scope out the company's breweries with August III joked, "The floors were always wet when you went on a tour with August. When he visited a brewery, you'd better wear shoes with rubber soles because before he got there, they were washing down everything."

There were complaints that the company's brewing operation was given carte blanche when it came to spending, even when it didn't seem necessary. "It was almost hilarious to go to a capital screening committee meeting," said one top executive. "Whatever brewing wanted, they would get. We had 300 engineers on staff at one time, creating projects just to do stuff." Still, it was worth every penny to August III.

At one time in the late 1970s or early 1980s, a group of ad agency staffers and marketing executives was running a series of focus groups out at a mall near St. Louis.

"I want to see one of those," August III said, and the marketers, of course, agreed. So The Third showed up at the mall that night as a group of consumers took their seats around a table, preparing to discuss Anheuser-Busch and its advertising. The Third and his cadre of marketers settled in a room off to the side, behind a plate of one-way glass.

The focus group caromed back and forth between various beer-related topics before settling on the concept of beechwood aging. A middle-aged man piped in with his two cents. "Oh yeah, I've been down at the brewery there where they've got those big wooden beechwood barrels. Yeah, the giant barrels, I seen 'em myself."

August III, stationed behind the glass, cocked his head to the side. "That guy is full of shit," he told the rest of the observers. "That's not what we have, that's not it at all." The man had clearly never seen any of the aging tanks at Anheuser-Busch's brewery, which were giant vats made of steel, not wood, whose bases were lined with beechwood shavings.

"I know, August, but that's what he thinks, so that's reality to him," said Steve Kopcha, who was running the focus group. As the group listened politely, the man continued spouting off phony bits of knowledge about the beechwood aging process until August III couldn't take it anymore. He got up, strode into the focus group's room with his hand outstretched in greeting, and said "Hi, I'm August Busch. Let me tell you how we do it."

"These guys are just sitting there with their mouths open," Kopcha recalled later. "For about an hour, he told them about beer and how you make it right. And I tell you what, there were ten new Budweiser drinkers for life. He sold a lot of beer that night. That's the kind of guy he was. If it wasn't right, he wanted it fixed."

For all of The Third's dedication to quality, however, and his efforts to pull everyday drinkers onto the "fanatic" side of the fence, Budweiser and Michelob haven't been viewed by the American public as premium beers since the 1950s. To many American drinkers and even more to drinkers in Europe, Bud and Bud Light are keg beers meant to be enjoyed five or six at a time in front of the television.

"People don't really care how you make the stuff," said Kopcha, echoing in blunt terms what Anheuser insiders try to skirt around more delicately. "They assume it's sanitary, and that's all they really care about."

"I wish I had a dollar for every time we tried to talk ingredients in a focus group, and somebody would say, 'Look, I don't care if it's made out of panther piss. If I like it, I like it and if I don't, I don't.' We could never convince August, although intellectually, he knew people were saying that."

August III's meticulousness filtered through the entire Anheuser-Busch organization, from its executive suites all the way down to the people who hosed off the Clydesdales or hauled cases of beer. Budweiser deliverymen during his era would routinely turn each can in their store displays so that the labels faced outward, and salesmen would stop by their local grocery on the way home from work to refill the beer cooler from the stockroom out back. It was that grassroots-level intensity that helped Anheuser triumph over Miller during The Third's first 15 years at the helm.

"We can second-guess, but you look at so many things that were so on and so right," said Buddy Reisinger. "There was no one who would outwork him, and no one who cared more about the place."

■ ■ ■

If there was one thing The Third loved nearly as much as brewing beer, it was flying. Anheuser-Busch was one of jet maker Dassault's top clients, and The Third, who started flying at the age of 15, relished the opportunity to rack up extra flight hours by taking the company's planes for a spin. Anheuser actually leased its fleet of jet aircraft and Bell helicopters from a company August III had formed, Ginnaire Rental, for several hundred thousand dollars per year and disclosed the cost in its annual statement to shareholders. Anheuser's fleet of pilots never minded the intrusion when The Third would assume the controls on the way home. "August was one hell of a pilot," said one former staffer. "And the pilots absolutely loved and respected him. He knew everything."

Rather than brave the St. Louis highway traffic and endure forced handshakes and small talk on the short walk from the company parking lot to his office, he also preferred to fly his helicopter to work each morning from his secluded farm in St. Peters, 40 miles to the east. He had a phobia of elevators, and flying to the office allowed him to descend just one flight of stairs from the roof each morning rather than having to hitch a lift up from the bottom of the building. The Third showed up each day by a quarter to seven, and his subordinates marked the promptness of their own more pedestrian arrivals by whether his helicopter was already perched ominously on the roof when they steered their cars into the parking lot. Anheuser-Busch operated on "Busch" time—events were dictated by The Third's arrival, not by the positioning of two hands on the face of a clock. Anyone scheduled to accompany him for a trip on one of the company's corporate jets knew to arrive at least half an hour early because "as soon as August gets there, you leave."

"Mr. Busch's omnipresence at the office—the helicopter ceremoniously on top of the building—always got you," said one top former executive. "Every day I'd drive to that office the years he was there, you'd see that helicopter and you knew your ass could be in that office at any minute answering questions—and not usually in a very friendly way. So it made you get there on time." Company staffers who were already in the building tried to ignore the thwack of the rotors each morning as the chopper settled on the roof right above their heads, but disregarding The Third's arrival was never easy.

"The helicopter used to come in over my head when I worked up on the ninth floor, and I found it very distracting," said another top former executive. "After a while, I took the bottles off my bookcase because I was sick of having them fall off."

Many companies would think hard before letting their CEOs helicopter to and from work each day, especially publicly traded companies with executives as influential as August III was. But August III was never bound to the laws of common men. Thanks to a mix of extreme wealth and a sheltered and provincial upbringing, he tended to circumvent life's harsher realities—or was never presented with the opportunity to face them in the first place. During one visit to New York for a business meeting, his security detail stopped traffic on busy Sixth Avenue as he exited an office building to allow him to get into his car. "This is a man who is not troubled by self-doubt," said the chief of a rival beer company.

One oft-repeated story concerned a trip by August III and a group of other executives to Barcelona. The Third refused to push back his usual dinner hour—which fell around 6 P.M., to make room for his early bedtime—even though Spaniards eat much later. They had to find a restaurant that would open early to accommodate The Third's wishes.

"Coming from one of the world's wealthiest families, he was not well traveled or well read," said one former ad agency executive. "He was extremely provincial in his viewpoints. Everything was St. Louis and hunting and fishing and the brewery."

Whether he was in or out of his element, however, strings were relatively easy for The Third to pull. On one particular Super Bowl Sunday, August IV hosted a party at his house with a few dozen friends and marketing executives to watch the game and, more importantly, to monitor Anheuser-Busch's exposure during the big event. The Fourth had a detailed rundown of when each Anheuser spot was scheduled to run, which said that right after the first series of commercials, the game's announcer would cue up a live aerial view of the stadium from the Budweiser blimp hovering above.

As the last scheduled commercial faded to black, everyone leaned forward in their chairs, waiting for the blimp shot. And then . . . nothing. No bird's-eye view from Budweiser's costly perch above. Just a bunch of sweaty football players prepping for their next drive down the field.

The Third erupted in anger and demanded to be connected with the head of the network immediately. There was no sense in starting at the bottom when he was paying wads of sponsorship dollars. Within what seemed like 30 seconds, August III had his intended target on the phone. And minutes later, the network abruptly cut to a shot from Budweiser's strategically placed airship.

"Forget that it happened period, it happened almost immediately," said one of the people who were in the room that night. "If you can do that all day long, to have someone say you can't eat dinner at 6, it's like, 'Bullshit. I'm eating dinner at 6. Look what I just did!' That's how things happened for them. It's his reality. He truly doesn't understand, because it's like 'When I ask for stuff, I get it.'"

"If you literally fly from St. Peters to the roof of One Busch Place, and then fly from that roof to Spirit of St. Louis airport . . . He's not even driving anywhere, except maybe from his house to the duck blind. It just didn't happen. As connected and as in-tune as he was with so many things, he was disconnected from reality. He wasn't delusional, he just had no idea what it was like to, like, drive in traffic."

He was very much accustomed to a life of wealth, but The Third wasn't obnoxious about it. He was "personally humble," said a former Anheuser staffer. "I never heard him say a braggy thing his whole life. 'Course if your name is Busch, you don't have to brag." The Third simply seemed to believe that bending the rules of "normal" life allowed him to be more efficient. And he was right.

"Could he have done all the things he did if he was a normal person and had a two-hour commute?" said another former employee. "Probably not."

August III made plenty of great decisions, but he was perhaps never more right than he was about his belief that Anheuser-Busch could win control of half of the U.S. beer market. Former Anheuser executive Frank Sellinger, who left the company to run Schlitz in 1977, spoke for many of Gussie's old guard when in 1980 he said: "I don't see any consumer product like beer having a 50 percent market share. You can't predict the likes and dislikes of the younger generation." That year, Anheuser-Busch controlled 28 percent of the U.S. beer market. By August III's last year as CEO in 2002, that number had swelled to 52 percent. More than one out of every two beers quaffed in America at the start of the new millennium was brewed by Anheuser-Busch.

■ ■ ■

The Third devoted far less time to family obligations than he did to his brewery. His own upbringing had been difficult, with so many half-brothers and sisters from his father Gussie's other wives, and those tenuous ties frayed further in the wake of his boardroom coup. He was semiestranged for that reason from Adolphus IV. Other half-brothers, meanwhile, struggled at points with legal troubles. Although the Busch family has seemed to have a propensity for getting into messy scrapes with the law, they've demonstrated an equally uncommon talent for bouncing back.

The family's fascination with—and prolific ownership of—guns turned deadly when Peter Busch, one of Gussie's sons, shot a friend at Grant's Farm in 1976, the year after August III's coup. Peter pleaded guilty to manslaughter. Billy Busch, another of The Third's half-brothers, endured his own stint of notoriety after getting tangled up in a 1981 barroom brawl in which he allegedly bit off part of someone's ear, as well as a child custody battle that wended its way all the way to the Missouri Supreme Court. Billy ratcheted down his profile in the wake of those scandals, investing in a giant Houston distributorship with his brothers Adolphus and Andy and, in mid-2009, forming a new company to brew and sell craft beer and other beverages.

Many of Gussie's kids and their spouses were involved with the business in some way or another, and most of them lived either in St. Louis or down in Florida. August III, though, the most powerful of the children, had the heaviest cross to bear. "He was pretty much raised on Grant's Farm, with a family about as dysfunctional as it gets, and then he was handed this behemoth worry," said one person close to the company. "He ran it exceptionally well, but that was his life."

The Third married Susan Hornibeck, a native of the Brentwood area of Los Angeles, on August 17, 1963, at All Saints Episcopal Church in Beverly Hills. It was as close as St. Louis would come to a royal union, joining together the Busch brewing empire with the daughter of a cosmetics distribution magnate. According to Susan— who, in a cruel twist for someone who married into a beer dynasty, was born with four kidneys—the two met while The Third was out on the West Coast to introduce Busch Bavarian beer. She was a lithe, blonde, 23-year-old tennis and volleyball player, and he just 24. They hit it off immediately on a blind date and were engaged six months later. Following a wedding reception held in her parents' backyard, she moved halfway across the country to The Third's

Waldmeister Farm west of St. Louis. By the fifth year of their marriage, Susan realized the relationship wasn't working. They tried to reconcile their differences for another year but got no results, so they split.

One of the most persistent rumors that arose during their divorce was that Susan had become romantically involved with marble-mouthed baseball sportscaster Harry Caray. Caray, who was hired in 1945 as an announcer for the Cardinals, served as the voice of the team for 25 years until a dispute with August III that was never publicly explained prompted the two former friends to part ways. Amid rumors that the argument involved Susan, Caray left St. Louis and eventually moved to Chicago to cover the White Sox and later, the Chicago Cubs. Susan consistently denied the rumors, calling her relationship with Caray "a friendship item, but not a romance item by any means." She said her dinners with Caray were friendly in nature, and attributed reported phone calls from her house to Caray to her card-playing habits. She and The Third used to get together with Caray and his wife, Marion, to play gin rummy.

Susan raised The Fourth and his sister, Susie, largely on her own after the divorce was finalized, while The Third generally saw them on weekends. Yet in an interview with the *St. Louis Post-Dispatch* years afterward, Susan nonetheless had good things to say about her ex, who had always impressed her with his "brains, and his personality, his sense of humor." She called Ginny, his second wife, a "lovely gal," and said she had spent Thanksgiving and Christmas with their family.

Virginia "Ginny" Lee Wiley, an attorney and former public defender who married The Third in 1974, five years after his divorce from Susan, was regarded by many in St. Louis as one of the few ball-busters who could handle marriage to The Third. Their relationship marked a stark improvement on The Third's marriage to Susan. "His second marriage was very different from his first," said Buddy Reisinger. "They were very close; they spent a lot of time together. He valued her opinion, and she's a very intelligent lady."

In 1980, when August IV and Susie were in their mid-teens and The Third and Ginny had two children of their own, The Third indicated that he realized his brutal work schedule had contributed to the collapse of his first marriage. "I learned in my 20s and 30s that it is important to have stability at home," he told a reporter over a hamburger and two Michelobs at the Pierre hotel in New York.

■ ■ ■

The Third demanded unquestioning loyalty from his staffers, and had a puzzlingly strong magnetism—even though his underlings knew that the closer they came to his inner circle, the more likely they were to suffer a blistering burn.

"He was a very, very powerful presence," said one strategy committee member. "He was very intense; he was very quick to judge people. You had to look at the paradigm in which he was raised, being born into a family like the Busch family. I'm sure you could probably find examples of him in just about any storied, moneyed families, in terms of how that type of upbringing shapes a person."

"If he trusted you, it was incredible loyalty. He would go to the ends of the Earth for people he thought had the best interests of the company in mind. If he didn't trust you, look out."

Those who couldn't help themselves worked their fingers to the bone to win an occasional mark of his approval. The further he progressed into his tenure, the less room he left for people to diverge from his tastes and viewpoints. Critics of the way The Third operated say that Anheuser's corporate planning staffers largely served as his sycophantic "validation committee."

"He surrounded himself with people he was very comfortable with," said one of the company's advisors. "This is not a guy who was going out on the street and is going to find someone very unlike himself to go spend time with. That's just not who this guy is. It was amazing to me how he could impact people with his persona. I looked at him and I just thought, 'This guy is just a bully.'"

The Third had a particularly strong level of distrust for the media. When one trade magazine published an article he didn't like, he launched an investigation to trace the leak. As part of the probe, he grilled a St. Louis dentist who was suspected of passing on information he had heard while drilling an Anheuser executive's teeth.

"His general philosophy was 'When the press asks questions, circle the wagons,'" said Harry Schuhmacher, a well-known chronicler of the beer industry who failed to snag a single interview with The Third despite years of trying. The first time Schuhmacher met The Third was at the dedication of a distributorship in San Antonio, where he walked up to introduce himself.

"Yeah, I've seen your paper," The Third said, and stalked off without another word, leaving Schuhmacher to wonder what The Third actually thought of his work. "Well, at least he's seen it!" joked the man standing next to him.

The Third's fear of having his trust violated grew particularly pronounced after a 1987 incident that rocked the company and led to the forced resignations of several top executives. During the bankruptcy proceedings of an advertising agency called Hanley Worldwide, allegations arose that three Anheuser-Busch officers—promotions manager John Lodge, wholesale operations vice president Michael Orloff, and sales head Joseph Martino—had accepted kickbacks and payoffs. The bankruptcy proceedings charged that Lodge had accepted $13,500 toward the purchase of a Porsche and included allegations that Orloff and Martino may have taken questionable payments.

Orloff and Martino maintained their innocence, and Lodge's lawyer said Lodge wasn't knowingly involved in wrongdoing. Although the company had a strict policy against employees accepting gifts from business associates, Martino, who eventually resigned, said such behavior was "part of the corporate culture" at Anheuser-Busch, and reports of other managers accepting gifts began to leak out. The firings of those allegedly involved didn't suffice for the image-conscious August III, who turned to Dennis Long, the company's second-ranking executive and one of his closest friends, for answers. As head of the brewery, all three men had reported to him. Long wasn't able to quell the pressure from August III, and he resigned, assuming responsibility for the executives' alleged infractions.

It was a painful pill for The Third to swallow. Long was his protégé, frequent traveling partner, and closest business confidante, and he had been one of the architects of the company's golden era versus Miller in the 1980s. He had been Anheuser-Busch's "inspirational leader," said one former executive, the perfect complement to detail-obsessed

August. The Third's determination to cut away Anheuser's cancer superseded his ties to his friend. "Augie does not forgive," said one former executive.

Life at Anheuser-Busch changed noticeably after that, and largely for the worse. The Third had seized control of 38 percent of the U.S. beer market, but he suddenly found himself lacking a CEO for his all-important brewery division and sporting a headless sales staff. To fill the gap, he announced that he would assume Long's former duties and act as president of the beer subsidiary.

Wall Street analysts expected him to quickly identify a new brewing head, and several names were circulated. Instead, August III told investors that he would hold both jobs for at least two years. He proceeded to do that and more. Nearly three years later, with The Third still pulling double duty, the *St. Louis Post-Dispatch* ran a column that read like a "Help Wanted" advertisement for Long's former position.

"He wasn't going to promote anyone into any position of importance within the company because he really, frankly, didn't trust anyone," said one strategy committee member. "That was a turning point. The minute he lost confidence in the people around him, it became a very difficult place to work. I could tell how much distrust there was of people in general because of the sting the company had endured, and Mr. Busch in particular."

■ ■ ■

That distrust only fueled The Third's unwillingness to delegate authority or to allow his views to be challenged. He was looking to circle the wagons and consolidate power, not to hand it to someone else.

"I had a client who used to say, 'Great men have great weaknesses,'" said Charlie Claggett. "I think there's a lot of truth in that. I guess that was August. One of his weaknesses was his strength also—his lack of trust. You had to prove yourself every day or else you weren't with him."

One former employee compared August III to Prussian king Frederick the Great, who had a difficult childhood under a brutish father and tended to confide in his beloved Italian greyhounds. "He talked to his pet dogs, but he had so much confidence in his own ability that he didn't need to talk to other people. He would just tell them what to do."

"You were not going to loosen up August III," said a former ad agency head. "He was a very narrow persona. He was constrained emotionally and intellectually. He mustered all of the resources and talents he had and was laser-focused on selling beer. And he learned how to do that really well."

Chapter 4

Selling the
American Dream

He's a very instinctive decision maker. He clearly understood that the advertising had to appeal to young males, drinking age males. He understood the importance of music to that group, of sex, of athletics and sporting.
—Roy Bostock, former ad agency head

People don't just drink beer. They drink the brand that lies behind the beer. And while many image-defining brands are expensive, like Mercedes or Gucci, even the very best beer is still an affordable luxury—a way for the common man to make a statement without breaking the bank. When someone walks into a bar and steps up to the counter to order a beer, the brand he shouts out says something about him as a person. August Busch III recognized that, and he exploited it.

"If you think about beer, in your own personal circle there are probably people who drink a different beer when they're in a bar than they do at home, when nobody sees them," said one former Anheuser executive. "There's a badge associated with the bottle you're holding in your hand when you're out in public or with your friends, and it's important. That didn't happen by accident. It happened because beer companies poured a tremendous amount of money into developing the image of their brands."

Anheuser-Busch didn't become the world's most famous brewer based on the superior quality of its products. Many beer connoisseurs disregard Budweiser for being "fizzy," "yellow," and "bland." It took a century and a half of exceedingly careful cultivation to turn arguably mediocre Budweiser into the King of Beers. Thanks to the billions of dollars in advertising spending that helped foment the cult of Budweiser, Americans love not only Anheuser-Busch beer, but beer in general. The mere sound of a pop-top aluminum can cracking open evokes memories of summer vacations, backyard barbecues, and thrilling sports victories. Beer is part of America's cultural fabric. And that's where The Third's brilliance was the most evident.

"He clearly knew that advertising was the brand," said Roy Bostock. "And therefore, as CEO, he was involved in the advertising up to his eyeballs. A lot of CEOs more often than not say the advertising is someone else's responsibility. Not August. He knew the criticality of advertising to the brands. Budweiser was created by the advertising."

And that was what InBev wanted to buy—all of the stress and sweat and tears through which Anheuser-Busch magically turned its middle-of-the-road beers into a patriotic movement. Budweiser, Brito liked to say, is "America in a bottle." And it doesn't just trump other beers, like Miller or Coors; it stacks up well against some of the world's most recognizable brands, period. Valuing a brand is an art rather than a science, but it was Anheuser-Busch's brands, not its brick-and-mortar breweries or bottling lines, that accounted for a huge chunk of the value of InBev's $46.3 billion bid.

Budweiser ranked as the 16th most valuable brand in the world in 2010, according to BrandFinance, which put Bud ahead of McDonald's, Disney, and Apple. The value of the Budweiser brand in dollars? In

May 2008, just before InBev made its bid, it was pegged at $17.2 billion, nearly 40 percent of the price of InBev's offer.

Gussie's Clydesdales and whistle-stop train tours hinted at Anheuser-Busch's eventual marketing prowess, but it was The Third who ultimately launched Budweiser's image into the stratosphere.

"Before August became CEO, the marketing department was really kind of Animal House," said one former executive, referring to the fraternity house environment depicted in the John Belushi movie. "It was fucking nuts." August III harnessed that raw energy and directed it into ads that targeted the right types of consumers. He understood that advertising needed to be one of Anheuser-Busch's most important products. It ultimately became even more critical to the company's success, some would argue, than the beer itself. During his tenure, Anheuser-Busch was able to take the vice of drinking alcohol—which had been banned in America just a few decades earlier, and turn it into something that conjured up happy images and drew people together.

The Third had no formal schooling in marketing, but it didn't take a master's degree to know who he needed to hunt—and how. With laser-like focus on its key consumers, the company consistently peddled two types of campaigns: "quality" ads that showed beer pouring out of a tap and Clydesdales tromping through powdery fields of snow; and the funny, irreverent ads aimed at younger drinkers.

■ ■ ■

August's big push into marketing started almost as soon as he hit the ground as CEO in the late seventies. Miller's growth rate was topping Anheuser-Busch's, Miller Lite was a smashing success, and the "Miller Time" ad campaign, which celebrated the camaraderie of blue-collar men, was a huge hit. John Murphy, Miller's president, had a voodoo doll that he named August and kept a rug decorated with Anheuser's "A&Eagle" logo under the desk in his office, where he would ceremoniously clean his shoes every morning. Miller's top executives asserted that they'd soon be number one, which infuriated The Third. "I'll never forget the look on his face," William K. Coors, chairman of fellow rival Adolph Coors, told *Business Week* at the time. "He said, 'Over my dead body.' And he meant every word of it."

August III sensed that advertising was the missing ingredient he needed to beat Miller and to push Anheuser's market share to 50 percent. When the Teamsters strike finally ended, he came on like a hurricane, firing staffers and making a critical move to install Mike Roarty as director of marketing. Roarty, an affable Irishman with a famously clever wit, was so instrumental during his 41 years at Anheuser-Busch that one of the three flags that often waved in front of the company's headquarters was Ireland's. "The American public doesn't want to hear about Germany," Roarty joked, slamming the Busch family's ethnic heritage.

Roarty was the comedic counterpoint to The Third's "straight man"—the very public face of Anheuser-Busch during the late 1970s and 1980s. He and The Third both had healthy egos, but that's where the similarities stopped. Roarty was a well-liked showman and creative genius who had a constant glint in his eye and was maddeningly late for meetings. "Michael is much more humorous than I am," Busch said. "He's a better speaker. I'm more direct, have a shorter fuse." But Roarty and August III clicked when it came to peddling beer, and the pair had a healthy respect for each other. Roarty used to keep a three-foot-high stuffed Clydesdale toy in his memorabilia-filled office and found it tough to keep a straight face each time The Third walked in and perched on it, sidesaddle, while trying to make a point. "He recognized the importance of network television and sports programming, of great creative and so forth, and he led it," Roy Bostock said. "And he had an ability to work with August III, which not everyone could do."

The first in Anheuser-Busch's string of advertising megahits came in 1979, when a team from ad agency D'Arcy presented The Third with a handful of pitches. By this time, The Third was hiring several agencies at a time and pitting them against each other to see who could come up with the best creative work. It wasn't cheap, but it produced some brilliant campaigns. One of D'Arcy's slogan ideas that year, the work of Charlie Claggett, was "This Bud's for You." The Third keyed in on it right away, and that tagline soon became one of Anheuser's most famous and heavily used salutes to the American worker.

"August picked it out of four campaign ideas, said, 'That's the advertising we want,'" said Jack Purnell. "And it turned out to be a bigger and better and one-up to Miller's 'Miller Time.' We saluted every worker you could think of over the next seven or eight years. We had salutes to umpires, we had salutes to all kinds of white collar and blue collar workers, salutes to female workers, you name it."

The Third wasn't much of a professional sports fan. His rare appearances at Cardinals' games tended to be uncomfortable for all involved. Still, he recognized the importance of sports media and spent astronomical sums to sponsor a vast assortment of sporting events, from World Cup soccer, NASCAR, and professional football's Super Bowl all the way down to small-town softball leagues. By 1985, Anheuser-Busch was the largest sports sponsor in the United States. A decade later, Anheuser started introducing team color–specific beer bottles and "fan cans" for Major League Baseball, the National Football League, and eventually even college sports, which got it into hot water over whether it was targeting underage drinkers. The company's utter saturation of the market prompted fans to inextricably associate Budweiser with sports. If you attended a sporting event, watched one on television, or listened to one on the radio, it was nearly impossible to get away from Anheuser-Busch.

"They wrote the book on sports marketing," said Charlie Claggett. "It was putting a Budweiser sign in every stadium in every town and devising local programs and promotions. I think it means a lot to people to have Budweiser as a sponsor. They covered every base, from the big national spots on the Super Bowl that reached millions of people to sponsoring whatever neighborhood they could get into." The company consistently topped its own ad spending records: In 1989, it spent $5 million on a series of six 30-second spots during the Super Bowl—twice as much as it had the year before—and the number kept going up from there.

Anheuser-Busch devoted so many hundreds of millions of dollars to advertising each year that it could afford to sponsor all of those neighborhood leagues and still lock up the exclusive advertising rights for key events. In 2006, it secured the rights to be the only Super Bowl alcohol advertiser through 2012, extending the chokehold it held on the world's largest single sporting event to a run of two dozen years. It reached a similar deal that year for advertising exclusivity during the NCAA college football Bowl Championship Series through

2010. By the time other beer companies decided to follow Anheuser's lead in sports marketing, they found it impossible to gain the same kind of access, and complaints from Stroh Brewing led the U.S. Justice Department to investigate whether it was legal for television broadcasters to let advertisers freeze their competitors out. Nothing came of the investigation.

■ ■ ■

The Third didn't just dictate Anheuser-Busch's overall marketing strategy—he commanded the group from the trenches. And while marketing is one of the more touchy-feely business disciplines, The Third presided over his marketing department with a sledgehammer. Getting an idea past him was never easy, and unlike many corporate CEOs who leave all but the most large-scale marketing decisions to others, he was the final arbiter on pretty much everything.

"When I saw him deal with his own people, and deal with the agency people who had been working with Anheuser and had built careers at the agency, he just bullied them," said one former agency executive. "It was a complete bullying attitude."

"August III could be very snap with his judgments, which was tough," said a former top marketing executive. "At times you could prove him wrong, and he'd be very complimentary afterward, but it was hell to live with him during the process."

Still, the heartache and stress were worth it for a crack at one of the world's largest corporate advertising budgets, and for a chance to run gutsy creative work nationwide that many other companies would tone down. Ad agency staffers battled for the chance to work on the Anheuser-Busch account despite the client's often irrational demands, and in the end, the spots they created were the type that swept the advertising industry's awards each year. Who wouldn't want to watch an ad he created air during the Super Bowl, rather than having it pasted on the back of a public bathroom stall?

Despite The Third's affinity for data-driven business school grads, his favorite way to test ad campaigns was to drag executives into the boardroom and fire around the table one person at a time, quizzing them on their views. The challenge, if your point of view countered The Third's, was to figure out how to present it gently enough to avoid getting fired.

Still, he was usually right. "He was instinctively good at creative work," said one former agency head. "In my judgment, he was stronger than The Fourth in that area or than virtually anybody else in the company. This is a guy who I didn't like, personally. But he had an ear for music, an understanding instinctively of what would appeal to young men—the target audience—and he knew that advertising drove his business. He wanted cutting-edge, leading stuff. He wasn't always right, but I can't pick an instance . . . where I thought he was wrong." Anheuser-Busch hit the advertising jackpot time and time again during the era of August III, which ultimately led to its victory over Miller in the 1990s during the era's so-called beer wars. It showed how a company could use advertising to separate itself from the pack without changing much at all about the product it actually brewed.

"There are certain things that are kind of commoditized about the beer industry, and image is the tiebreaker," said Bob Lachky, acknowledging that he'd be labeled a heretic for admitting that most beers are pretty similar. "Marketing was just intrinsically in our bones as a company."

The Third's triumph over Miller looked even sweeter after factoring in the war chest Miller had at its disposal. "August, if you think about it, was the David against Goliath," Charlie Claggett said. "If you imagine how intimidated he must have been when, as a young man, he's taking over this company and facing Philip Morris, with all of their market power and deep pockets. He doesn't know what to do, he's never been to college. And he's got to somehow face this giant and kill it, because if he doesn't, they're going to turn around and kill him. And by God, he did it."

The Third spared no expense on marketing, which ranked alongside the brewing operation as the two areas in which quality mattered to him most. He routinely demanded things people felt were impossible, refusing to compromise on the final product because of the finite number of hours in a day or the amount of money something might cost. As they shot and reshot expensive commercials and raced around the country on private jets, his staffers got the sense that money and time didn't matter.

"He let costs get out of control," said a former ad agency head. "But there was no question that he was going to spend what was necessary on advertising, in media, on promotions, and in production of the advertising to make it the world's best. And he did. It helped create some of the best advertising of all time."

■ ■ ■

The company's marketing dollars weren't spent solely on the consumer—Anheuser spent a good chunk of change making its own employees and beer wholesalers feel special, too. It operated what it called a "three-tiered" distribution system that consisted of the company itself, hundreds of distributors who served as regional middlemen, and the retailers who bought beer from those distributors. A critical part of the system's success was keeping the distributors happy. And one of the company's most tried-and-true ways of doing that was its annual wholesaler convention. The conventions technically served as a forum for sharing information and presenting upcoming ad campaigns. Anheuser-Busch's real agenda seemed to be hammering home that it was the biggest, most powerful brewer in the world. Its distributors— mainly men who were millionaires or on their way to becoming millionaires—would arrive dressed in black tie, their wives decked out in furs and jewels, to celebrate the success of the past year and pay tribute to the company that was helping them get rich. "The Third made so many of those wholesalers multimillionaires that they would have followed him anywhere," said one person who attended the conventions. "There was a huge amount of deference paid, a huge amount of respect. Nobody second-guessed a Busch decision, even in a three-tiered system, which is odd."

To mark the festivities, Anheuser-Busch would put all of its company-branded toys on display—its hydroplane, its race car, its hot air balloon—and use the power of its name and pocketbook to draw the attendance of Hollywood legends such as Lucille Ball, Frank Sinatra, Sammy Davis Jr., and Paul Newman. Marketing honcho Mike Roarty rubbed elbows with them all, and even co-emceed one evening's glamorous events in 1988 alongside Bob Hope and a bevy of showgirls who paraded in front of a curtain of dangling gold beads. When the conventions took place in California, the crowd and the nighttime performance roster were so thick with A-list movie stars that "you just got sick of it after a while," said one attendee.

"What we wanted to show was the big picture—to let people see that we're number one," said an aging Roarty 20 years later, as he reminisced at his home in an upscale suburb of St. Louis. "It was a great success, and it gave us an opportunity to say to our wholesalers: 'We're number one; make no mistake about it.'"

Two drawings of Roarty by Al Hirschfeld, the world's most sought-after caricaturist, hung carefully framed on the wall not far from where he sat, and his entire house was filled with photos of him hobnobbing with the rich and famous—a testament to the connections Anheuser-Busch had in entertainment, sports, and politics. A glint flashed in Roarty's eyes as he recalled filming a commercial with Frank Sinatra, one of several "Rat Pack" members he knew well. "We had a lot of fun, Frank and I," Roarty said, repeating that comment five minutes later in reference to Milton Berle. Movie stars, sporting legends, and powerhouse political figures were key to Anheuser's efforts to show distributors that their devotion to Anheuser-Busch was well worth it.

The conventions weren't always easy, however, for Anheuser's marketers. The Third liked to stage viewings of the year's upcoming commercial lineup in front of a packed convention hall to whip up excitement and send his salesmen home in eager anticipation. Each TV spot usually elicited thunderous applause as the giant screens at the front of the room went black. But that wasn't always the case.

During one of the company's annual conventions, the audience posted a muted reaction to an avant garde Budweiser commercial D'Arcy had produced. Gauging the crowd's disappointment, August III stood up. "How many of you dislike this advertising as much as I do?" he asked. As the comment elicited 5,000 collective "Boos," D'Arcy's advertising staffers shrunk into their chairs.

"I tell you what I'm doing right now," The Third said, motioning for D'Arcy's top executives in attendance to stand so the crowd could see. "I'm putting that agency on a plane tonight, they're going back to

St. Louis, and they're going to create new advertising for Budweiser."
As the crowd roared in approval, the chastised D'Arcy team marveled
at how deftly The Third had been able to turn the meeting into a
power-solidifying, tribal spectacle.

■ ■ ■

The Third held his marketers to incredibly high standards of both
performance and behavior. "It was a family-run business with a ton
of tradition and a ton of ego," said one former agency executive. "It
was slightly like working with royalty. There was a certain amount of
decorum that had to be practiced. You spoke when spoken to, you
made your point once, but you never made it a second time. Once it
was settled, it was settled." August III liked to put every new staffer
to the test right away, prompting some of them to compare it to boot
camp for the Marines.

Marketing was The Third's go-to tool in tough times, and it usually worked. Right before Christmas in 1976, he pulled a bunch of
marketing managers into a conference room, flipped on the overhead
projector, and slapped a transparency onto it that showed Miller's sales
coming on like a freight train. He pulled out a grease pencil, smashed
its soft point down onto the screen, and then dragged it out to the
right, extending both lines to show that Miller was soon going to
overtake Anheuser-Busch. He turned his icy glare out toward the men
in the room, staring them down one-by-one. "If these trends aren't
a whole lot different a year from now, a lot of you won't be in this
room," he said. Then he flipped off the projector, wished the group a
Merry Christmas, and walked out.

The Third had a talent for judiciously doling out special treatment
as reward for the stress, though his carrots were often calibrated to just
barely make up for the harshness of the stick. The company lavished
expensive but puzzlingly useless items on valued employees and ad
agency staffers. As a Christmas gift, one executive received a full set of
silverware emblazoned with the Anheuser-Busch crest. Another was
gifted with a giant statue of an eagle, meticulously carved out of white
alabaster, at his retirement party.

One of Anheuser's favorite perks, however, was a trip down to the company-owned compound on the Lake of the Ozarks, a snaking, 92-mile-long man-made lake west of St. Louis that teems with power boats, drunken partiers, and precariously balanced, bikini-clad women during the busy summer months. The Third would often invite up-and-coming marketers from various agencies out for a few days to the site, which was also used for company meetings and strategic retreats. It's a relatively easy three-hour drive from St. Louis, but Anheuser-Busch often shuttled people there by helicopter, sometimes piloted by The Third himself. On one jaunt that proved particularly frightening for his co-passengers, The Third deftly swooped down over a pasture and buzzed a herd of grazing livestock.

The lake compound's decor was maintained in 1970s fashion well through the 1980s and early 1990s, with its shag carpeting and Naugahyde bedspreads. "It was so Hugh Hefner," said one frequent guest during that time period. "It was just flirting with the period after disco—very luxurious, but had a dated look to it." Behind a square of living units lay the tennis courts and an elevated helicopter pad. A grassy space for volleyball and badminton sat off to one side not far from the pool, and several refrigerators stocked with cold beer were scattered around the property for easy access.

August IV was a big powerboat racer, and he loved to blow off steam by taking spins around the lake in the boats Anheuser-Busch moored at the compound, pushing them to bone-shattering speed as they smacked loudly across the water. "It was like a test to see what I could handle," said one of The Fourth's unwitting powerboat accomplices, who could feel his brain shaking in his helmet during one particular ride. If they started going too fast, The Fourth had instructed his passenger to touch the back of his hand.

"I said to myself, 'I'll be damned if I'm touching any part of him to slow down!'" the passenger said. So The Fourth pushed the boat to its limit. "We're going 110 miles an hour, knocking over guys in fishing boats with our wake. The wind and G-force is pulling at our faces. I thought: 'What a foolish way to die.'"

The Ozarks compound served as a testing ground for manliness and virility, at least for those who were unlucky enough to be subjected to The Third and The Fourth's occasional dares. From its executive suite on down to its brewery floors and delivery routes, the culture of Anheuser-Busch was heavily man centric. A person would have to be daft not to notice the locker room atmosphere, several former employees and advisors wryly joked. Anheuser-Busch sold beer, after all, not breast pumps. The fresh air of Missouri's great outdoors tended to bring executives' testosterone-fueled agitation to a head. Gary Prindiville, a sixth degree judo black belt and former police officer who worked in corporate security for Gussie, The Third, and The Fourth, performed more than a few physical acts of manliness in response to the Busch men's challenges.

On a sunny afternoon at the lake during The Third's tenure, a group of marketing staffers stood down at the water's edge where the powerboats were moored. Several of them were already a few beers deep on the day, and as they stood gazing out blearily over the lake, The Third turned to Prindiville and wagered that he couldn't swim to the opposite shore and back. Despite the group's beer goggles, it was clear that the lake measured a good distance across—probably more than half a mile. The entire lake, which is actually a dammed-up river, has more coastline than the state of California, and it teems with fast-moving motorboats.

No matter, Prindiville thought. He walked down to the dock, dove in, and swam the distance. He later dieted to lose 75 pounds and finished Hawaii's Ironman triathlon, again to prove his mettle to his Anheuser bosses.

The Third was a fit man himself, and The Fourth employed a particularly enthusiastic bodyguard named Bong Yul Shin, a charismatic Korean tae kwon do and judo grandmaster, who had a way of luring staffers into the health room at the crack of dawn no matter how bad their hangovers were. For a while, Mr. Shin and The Fourth were inseparable—he would even join The Fourth on jogging routes through sketchy areas of St. Louis or other towns in which the crew was traveling.

"Don't cheat yourself!" Mr. Shin would yell across the room as the yawning ad executives punched the air and sweated in their karate suits, shooting occasional glances off to the side to gauge whether they were impressing anyone.

More often than not, The Third's group recreational trips to the lake served as thinly veiled work events. The outings were often charged with as much tension and stress as the days staffers spent at headquarters, working away beneath the whirring blades of his helicopter on the roof. Anyone looking to practice judo at dawn had to add it to his already-thick early morning roster—even out at the lake. "We'd spend a lot of time preparing, and it was a tough go," said an advertising executive who attended several weeks' worth of planning meetings there over the years. The Third went to bed around 8:30 P.M. regardless of how late everyone else stayed up, and presentations started each morning promptly at 7:00. "By the time we had lunch," the executive said, "it felt like dinner."

The Third liked to multitask at the lake by listening to business presentations during meals. His subordinates obliged, of course, but they tended to leave the table hungry. John Greening, DDB Needham's top ad honcho on the Anheuser-Busch account, was summoned to dinner at The Third's house on the compound one evening in the early 1990s to present his agency's newest work. After exchanging pleasantries and quickly organizing their materials, Greening and Susan Gillette, the president of DDB's Chicago office, launched into their presentation. The Third, listening intently, tore into a pork chop his personal waiter had carefully positioned on his plate.

Forty-five minutes later, they finished their pitch, and Greening sat down to his own cut of meat, which by that time had gone frigid and was as tough as shoe leather. He motioned to the waiter. "This pork chop is kind of cold and tough now. Could you give me some barbecue sauce?"

The waiter paused, turned calmly, and bent down toward Greening's ear. "He doesn't approve of barbecue sauce," the man said, nodding in The Third's direction before striding back to the kitchen.

Charlie Claggett made only one trip down to the lake compound, but it yielded similar results. Bob Lachky, Claggett's main contact in Anheuser's marketing department, walked up to him one afternoon with a nerve-wracking request: "August would like to have dinner with you."

"Oh, great!" Claggett replied cheerily as a mild panic swelled up into his throat. He showed up at August III's living quarters that evening to find a handful of other marketers also waiting to take their seats at a long table. Andrew Steinhubl, Anheuser-Busch's top brewmaster, was hovering somewhat awkwardly in the adjoining living room.

"Andy, I'll be with you in a minute," The Third called out. "Have a seat on the couch." Steinhubl obligingly settled his substantial frame into the nearest piece of furniture.

Once the group settled around the dining table, a waiter pranced in and started delicately parsing out Cornish game hens, one by one, starting with The Third at the head of the table. Anheuser-Busch was pondering the launch of Bud Light, and in his characteristic quiz-show style, The Third started firing off questions. "What do you think?" he rat-a-tatted, sawing away ferociously at his game hen and shoving chunks of meat into his mouth as he worked around the table. "Do you think we should do this?" His dinner guests were too preoccupied with preserving their jobs to care that their own plates were still hen-free.

After another minute or so of speed-polling the group, August carved down to the last bits of flesh that clung to his hen's bare carcass. The waiter, meanwhile, who was still moving around the table at a comically slow speed, gently laid a hen to rest in front of the next hungry executive waiting to be served, just a few spots down from August III's seat.

"Okay, gentlemen, thank you very much," The Third said, brusquely excusing himself and then turning his attention toward Steinhubl in the living room. "Andy, let's go."

"And that was my dinner with August," said Claggett, chuckling about it years later. His plate was still bare when The Third strode out of the room that night.

■ ■ ■

Anheuser-Busch wasn't a place for people who needed frequent pats on the back for a job well done. It attracted those for whom merely being able to survive and, if possible, thrive in that type of environment was reward enough.

"Mr. Busch was the greatest field general you could ever work for," said Bob Lachky. "Yeah, it's easy to say he was tough and was acting irregularly. But you know what? When you got patted on the back by the man, you would go through a wall for him."

"To me, the biggest carrot was just succeeding," Charlie Claggett said. "You knew that if you took this particular hill, you were doing what other people were not given the opportunity to do. There was a big stripe you got to wear when you worked for that company. And they paid their executives really well."

That was certainly true. Thanks to Anheuser's reputation for doling out above-average salaries, the homes of its executives were scattered up and down the sloping hills of the nicest suburbs of St. Louis. Their children attended the best private schools, their wives drove luxury cars, and they served on the boards of the top area hospitals and arts organizations.

None of these creature comforts was a given, however. A good number of marketing staffers were either fired by August III or, if they worked at an agency, quickly yanked off the company's accounts after falling out of his good graces. "I was never asked to leave a meeting, ever," said one ad executive who worked with A–B for years. "I consider that one of the high points of my career. But the real high point is that we were able to get such great creative work out of such a dysfunctional environment."

■ ■ ■

Denny Long's dismissal during the graft scandal was probably the most controversial firing of The Third's era. However, D'Arcy, Anheuser-Busch's ad agency for 79 years, can lay claim to suffering the most dramatic and definitive beheading.

In 1994, *Advertising Age* reported that D'Arcy's media buying unit in New York had accepted business from Miller Brewing, Anheuser-Busch's arch-nemesis. There was probably no worse offense than this to August III, given how greatly he despised Miller and its parent, Philip Morris. William Melzer, managing director of D'Arcy's St. Louis office at the time, ducked into Charlie Claggett's office the morning the report came out.

"Do you know anything about this?" Melzer said. "Media buying for Miller?"

"Wouldn't happen," Claggett replied. "Why would we do that?"

"I guess I'd better call New York to check it out and see what's going on," Melzer said, turning on his heel and striding back into his own office.

The next time Claggett saw Melzer, Melzer was livid. "It's true— we did it," he said. "We bought media for Miller." Knowing how volatile The Third could be, the two debated which of them would confront their most important client with the news. The Third had already heard the reports well before Melzer reached him, however, and he went ballistic. It was going to take more than Melzer's efforts alone to calm the storm.

Roy Bostock, who was chairman and chief executive of the agency, quickly jetted to St. Louis from New York to contain the damage. He had met August III a few times before, once during a celebration of the 75th anniversary of Anheuser's relationship with D'Arcy that had been held at Grant's Farm a few years earlier. Bostock had gotten up on stage to present August III with a Clydesdale colt named D'Arcy. Conversation between the two men and their wives at the head picnic table had been torturous, and they hadn't exactly become fast friends since. Bostock was just the kind of Wall Street striver the provincial August III loved to hate. He passed down D'Arcy's decisions out of Manhattan, which bred people The Third didn't trust, and over the next decade and a half, he became a prominent force in corporate America, serving as chairman of Yahoo! during Microsoft's failed attempt to buy the company, as the chairman of Northwest Airlines, and as a director of Morgan Stanley during its battle to survive the 2008 financial crisis. August III's gruff style of intimidation, meanwhile, was just as off-putting to Bostock, who had taken it directly on the chin during the wholesaler convention at which The Third had publicly maligned D'Arcy's ad.

Bostock knew that from a profitability standpoint, D'Arcy's relationship with Philip Morris was far more lucrative than its relationship with Anheuser-Busch. Anheuser had even suggested at one point that D'Arcy should gladly handle its account at a loss because it helped D'Arcy improve its reputation.

Bostock met with August III and August IV to explain that D'Arcy wasn't buying media space directly for Miller—it was buying huge blocks of time for Miller's mammoth parent Philip Morris, which independently allocated the slots to its various brands. The practice had been common for decades, Bostock pointed out. D'Arcy also did media buying for both Procter & Gamble, which owned coffee maker Folgers, and General Foods, the owner of Maxwell House.

The Third peppered Bostock with angry questions but appeared to let the matter die. So when Claggett got a Saturday afternoon phone call from Bob Lachky that November, it stoked curious surprise rather than panic. "The Chief wants to see you out at the hangar tomorrow," said Lachky, who had been unwittingly roped by August III into helping manage the situation.

"What's it about?" Claggett asked. "I'll let him tell you," Lachky replied.

The next day, August III, U.S. brewery head Patrick Stokes, and Lachky pulled into the parking lot by the company's hangar at the Spirit of St. Louis airport at the same time Claggett drove in. The men gathered briefly out on the pavement to shake hands before heading inside.

"Go ahead, you go first," one of them said as they ushered Claggett toward the building, triggering a nerve that indicated something wasn't right. It felt like a Mafia hit.

They shuffled into a small room at the hangar, and August III launched into a brief preamble before getting to the punch. "We have to end our relationship," he said bluntly.

"What do you mean?" Claggett said.

"Well, you're not going to be our agency anymore," said The Third.

"Does that mean . . . so, you're taking the Budweiser account?" Claggett replied.

"All of it," said The Third.

"Michelob, Natural Light, O'Doul's," Claggett queried, listing the brands D'Arcy had managed his entire career.

"Yeah, all of it," The Third said again.

"Our business in Israel, Europe, Asia?" Claggett stammered, growing increasingly stunned as he internalized his own words. "Busch . . ."

"Charlie, *all* of it."

Claggett was speechless. Those accounts represented 80 percent of his office's revenue. Still, The Third no longer trusted the agency, and his trust was all but impossible to win back. With the meeting essentially over, he drifted wordlessly out to his car, plopped down in the driver's seat, and flipped on his phone to call Bostock in New York.

Bostock's response to the news made his loyalties clear.

"What a bunch of thugs."

The Third later called Bostock to lobby for détente between the two parties, at least in public, to keep Anheuser-Busch from being criticized for its decision. Bostock wasn't particularly eager for his agency's reputation to be dragged through the mud, either.

"Let's make this civil," The Third said. "Let's not make anybody look bad."

D'Arcy's loss led to a huge win for the Chicago office of Omnicom's DDB Needham, however, which won the Budweiser account. The day after firing D'Arcy, Lachky made a call to DDB's John Greening.

"John, I've made the sad call and now I get to make the glad call," Lachky said. "You'll be working on Budweiser, and we're going to come up there on Monday." The occasion was important enough to prompt a rare trip by August III to the agency's office atop the distinctive AON Center in Chicago, the city's second-tallest building at the time. That presented a problem for August III, who preferred meeting skyscraper-bound colleagues in their lobbies before heading to a destination closer to sea level.

He summoned enough gumption to step into the elevator with his bodyguard, Gary Prindiville, who told DDB's executives to maintain eye contact with The Third and to keep talking as the elevator sped to the top. The ad men turned to look straight at August III and started yammering on about whatever came to mind—Chicago's Blackhawks hockey team, the weather—until the elevator slowed to a stop and the doors slid open.

■ ■ ■

The Third made plenty of controversial decisions, but it was tough to question them when you looked at his results. Anheuser's share of the U.S. beer market doubled from 22 percent to 44 percent between

1977 and 1990, and four years later, Bud Light topped Miller Lite to become the best-selling light beer. August III made good on his quest to dominate America thanks largely to the power of propaganda.

"When I joined the company, we had 10 percent of the U.S. beer market," said Jack Purnell. "When I retired we had almost 50. And August III was the driving force."

Chapter 5

The Fourth Abides

I love my father. Take a walk through my house, and it looks like a father museum. Every picture on the wall is of my father, or me and my father—to the point where my mom comes over and says, "Where are all my pictures?" But he has been extremely tough on me. Maybe you can call it tough love.

—August Busch IV (Gerry Khermouch, Julie Forster, and John Cady, "Is This Bud for You, August IV?" *BusinessWeek*, November 11, 2002)

Some of the best ads during Anheuser-Busch's golden era in the 1990s were shepherded through not by August III but by his son, an up-and-comer in the Marketing Department who had a knack for picking irreverent winners. The Third was just as brusque with his own son, though, and even more begrudging with his praise, than Gussie had been with him.

On June 15, 1964, at 10 hours of age and just over 8 pounds in weight, August IV was fed his first few droplets of Budweiser beer.

And like his father, little August IV debuted at Anheuser-Busch at a very young age. That wasn't surprising, since the office was one of the few places in which the two could consistently interact. Ad agency executive Steve Kopcha remembered watching The Fourth bounce into Anheuser-Busch's boardroom, trailed by one of The Third's assistants, at the age of five or six—right around the time his parents were divorcing. As Kopcha and his team packed up their materials at the end of a marketing meeting, The Fourth plopped down in an oversized red leather chair and started spinning around in slow circles. "Well, Mr. Busch, I'll take him back now," The Third's assistant said, piping in after a few moments.

"Hell, no!" The Third replied. "Let him stay here and see how it's done." So young August IV stuck around for the next meeting—and got an early glimpse of what life might look like 30 years down the road if he played his cards right. By the time he was in second grade, he was sitting in on corporate strategy sessions.

"Here are all of the old big shots sitting down at the table, and one little five-year-old kid," Kopcha said. "And later on, he's the man."

■ ■ ■

The Fourth started working for Anheuser-Busch in his teens, driving a forklift and working to culture yeast. He traveled with his father on the company's corporate jets, even co-piloting them at times, to visit distributors and check in on breweries around the country. By his senior year in high school, he was working more than 15 hours a week at the brewery, some of them for course credit.

Susan Busch, whose six-year marriage to The Third ended in 1969, generally elicits praise for her efforts to rear their two children, August IV and Susie, on her own. "One of the benefits of August being raised largely away from his father is that he had a somewhat normal upbringing," said Bob Lachky. "She is a wonderful woman, just a wonderful person with a great personality."

Despite The Third's demanding schedule, the family's wealth and warped history, and even, according to Susan, "definite threats over the years" of kidnapping, August IV and his sister did relatively well while under their mother's control and tutelage and achieved more advanced levels of schooling than previous generations of Busches. Still, they suffered from their father's insular world view. The Fourth enjoyed an immensely privileged life, but he lived much of it in St. Louis and at the brewery, not mastering the broader liberal arts or traveling the globe to build his cultural acumen.

While out on a jog once with August IV, D'Arcy's Claggett turned to the young man to make small talk. "So, do you have any hobbies?" he inquired.

"Yeah, this is my hobby," responded The Fourth, who by that time had grown into a slightly taller version of his more compact father.

"Running?"

"No, working at Anheuser-Busch."

Claggett, who had just returned from living in London for a few years, asked whether The Fourth had done much traveling. He had been to Europe once, The Fourth replied.

"Both he and his sister Susie had pretty much spent their whole lives focused on the brewery," Claggett said later. "Wouldn't you think that if you had all of the money in the world, you'd want to broaden your horizons a little bit, get out to see what was going on?" It was certainly possible that The Fourth had such aims in mind but met with resistance from his father, who left the comforts of his farm and the city of St. Louis only when necessary.

Once The Fourth hit college, however—and slipped out from beneath The Third's physical restraints and the protection of St. Louis locals—he began to dabble more aggressively in the temptations of youth. His devil-may-care behavior started to rain repercussions on his record, his family, and the company.

He enrolled at the University of Arizona in Tucson, a rich kid on campus at his father's alma mater, and spent his freshman year in 1982 unmolested by controversy. That changed in an instant in the wee hours of the morning on November 13, 1983, when 19-year-old August IV's shiny new black Corvette flipped and crashed a few miles off campus on a curvy desert road, killing 22-year-old waitress Michele Frederick, who had been in the car's passenger seat and had flown through the sunroof. The Fourth, injured and dazed, was found hours later at his townhouse. Police found a Magnum revolver inside the wreckage of his car, along with a fake Missouri driver's license that put his age at 23. After a seven-month investigation that was swarmed by media coverage, local prosecutors determined they couldn't charge him with manslaughter and leaving the scene of an accident. It wasn't clear they could prove he had been the driver of the car, and they didn't have definitive evidence to show that he was under the influence of alcohol at the time of the crash.

Susan, who heard about the accident when she was contacted by the authorities, later said she was "absolutely devastated for young August. To have to go through something like that." She felt her son had been unfairly treated because "there is no just treatment for families with a name and money." When asked about the accident 15 years later, August IV said, "Somebody will always bring it up. I wish that weren't true, not only for me but for others whose lives were affected." He said alcohol was not involved in the crash.

The Fourth ducked out of the University of Arizona prematurely, just like his father had, and moved back to St. Louis to enroll at St. Louis University, where he started earning good grades in his business classes. He didn't stay out of the police blotter for long, though. Whether he hadn't absorbed enough lessons from the crash or whether, as his family claimed, he had a target unfairly slapped on his back, he got into another major scrape less than a year after being cleared of the charges in Arizona.

At 1:30 A.M. on May 31, 1985, August IV led police on a high-speed car chase through the Central West End of St. Louis, which ended when a detective finally shot out the tire of his silver Mercedes-Benz. He had sped dangerously close to an unmarked police car on a St. Louis highway, police said, and then took off after undercover narcotics officers in the car attempted to pull him over. A chase at speeds up to 85 miles per hour ensued.

After his tire was finally blown out, police found a loaded .38 caliber revolver on the floor behind The Fourth's driver's seat and took him into custody, charging him with two counts of third-degree assault, unlawful use of a weapon, and various traffic violations. The assault charges stemmed from the allegation that he nearly hit both officers who tried to approach his vehicle. Once they realized who they had arrested, however, the cops bent down and changed The Fourth's tire, chatting while they worked about how much they loved Grant's Farm. The Fourth said he hadn't ridden the train that circled the compound since he was 12 years old, which shocked one of the officers.

"You get me out of this," The Fourth said according to *Under the Influence*, a book on the Busch family, "and I'll fucking give you that train."

The Fourth's spokesman said the next day that he hadn't pulled over during the chase because the undercover officers were impersonating criminal types—he thought they were kidnappers. The police said they had taken chase because they thought The Fourth was a drug dealer who drove a similar car. After a three-day trial, 21-year-old August IV was acquitted, and his father stood up to personally shake the jurors' hands.

The indignities brought on by those public referenda on August IV's character and silver-spoon upbringing were overwhelming. Every citizen in St. Louis could already deftly weave a story about the scandal-plagued Busch family when called upon, and The Fourth's delinquencies made matters worse. They also made it harder for him to turn on a dime and devote himself to the company in the same way his father had. By 1997, The Third was telling the media that his son's past wasn't an issue anymore. Yet even during the takeover battle with InBev, 25 years after the Arizona crash, the *New York Times* decided to dredge up and rehash all of the sordid details yet again. "I wouldn't care too much about it," The Fourth told one of his advisors the day of the *Times* report, shrugging it off after so many years of badgering. "They'll be wrapping fish with it tomorrow."

While the heavily public scandals sullied The Fourth's reputation to a point where many would-be CEOs wouldn't have been able to recover, they failed to damage his standing enough to put his single greatest ambition out of reach, and he threw himself into the family business a few years after returning to St. Louis. The Fourth's professional "reformation" wasn't nearly as stark or all-encompassing as his father's—he never progressed to a point where anyone would consider him austere.

"He always had, and still has, personal demons," said Harry Schuhmacher. But he certainly made an effort to recover from the past and prove the naysayers wrong.

■ ■ ■

In many respects, the grassroots start of his career at Anheuser-Busch mirrored his father's. In one particularly critical way, though, The Fourth's approach differed starkly. Rather than having the foresight to build a team of loyalists and pull them up through the ranks as The Third had with his eaters, The Fourth let himself be led by The Third. "When I was there, the thinking was 'When is it going to click for August IV, and when is he going to build that kind of team?'" said one former staffer. "His closest people around him were his partying, socializing people who were not really telling him the truth." The Fourth took a more casual approach to leadership than his father did, and while it put his subordinates at ease, it also left them wondering whether he had the guts and drive to run a global corporation. Had he not been born with the name August Busch IV, some insiders said he might never have been a candidate for promotion to the top.

The Fourth worked hard, perhaps because he knew his detractors' talking points all too well. In 1991, he acknowledged how complicated it could be to sit in his chair. "Everybody thinks, 'It must be easy to be you,'" he said. "It's probably the hardest thing in the world to be me and to work under the pressure you have to be under. You have to do three times as good as the next guy to be considered to be doing the same job as he does."

August IV spent his first few years of official employment at Anheuser-Busch on the brewing side of the business. He worked for roughly a year as an assistant to legendary brewmaster Gerhardt Kraemer, spent another year as a line foreman, and spent three years as an apprentice brewer, even joining the Local Six branch of the Brewers & Maltsters union in a symbolic hat-tip toward the company's manual laborers. After dropping out of the University of Arizona, he finished a bachelor's degree in finance at St. Louis University in 1987 and then went to Europe to earn a brewmaster's degree from the heralded Berlin academy Versuchs und Lehranstalt für Brauerei.

Once his technical brewing education was deemed sufficient, The Fourth was pulled into an enviable position as an assistant to Mike Roarty. Many of the company's top executives over the years came up through the Marketing Department, and the move positioned August IV as the potential nucleus of the next generation.

Given August III's significant involvement in Anheuser-Busch's marketing efforts, The Fourth's promotion meant he'd be spending more time with his father. This set them on a collision course in a creative discipline in which decisions can be extremely subjective. The Fourth discovered when he began working for Roarty that he had a distinctive talent for marketing—and particularly for understanding the younger generations of beer drinkers whose habits and humor preferences tended to stump The Third. August IV instinctively sensed that the younger market wanted to see ad campaigns that were lively and irreverent, not ones with sappy ads that preached the merits of beechwood aging.

In February of 1990, The Fourth won his first big assignment at the age of 25 when he became senior brand manager for Bud Dry. It was a challenging post. Americans weren't sold on the idea of dry beers, which are brewed to have less aftertaste. But they were more profitable. The Fourth was charged with finding a way to spin Bud Dry into gold.

Under The Fourth's leadership, the company began running spots pegged on the phrase "Why Ask Why? Try Bud Dry," and the brand sprinted out quickly after its April 1990 launch, selling double the amount of beer Miller Lite sold in its first year in just nine months. Despite its auspicious beginnings, however, the dry beer category failed to gain long-term traction and Bud Dry ultimately sputtered and sank. That didn't derail August IV, however, who had already been named senior manager for the flagship Budweiser brand in the summer of 1991.

Budweiser's branding under his command took on a more casual, approachable flavor and gravitated toward quirkier humor, which proved incredibly successful. His efforts were noted by The Third, who promoted young August IV in 1994 to the high-ranking position of vice president of brand management, which put him in charge of all of the company's beer brands.

During the early years of his tenure as CEO, The Third demanded frequent, in-person updates from his Marketing Department and ad agencies to ensure that they were developing acceptable new ideas. Each week, he would peruse their new storyboards and assign them the green or red light. As The Fourth rose to increasing prominence within the Marketing Department, ad agencies began presenting their ideas directly to him. He would then take certain concepts upstairs and pitch them to his father behind closed doors.

The relay-style method seemed geared toward molding The Fourth into a stronger leadership candidate, but it also made life much easier for advertising staffers, who used August IV as a buffer against his father. The Fourth had plenty of experience handling his cantankerous dad, and he proved adept at blocking and tackling to keep the company's creative types free from too much outside interference.

"He would take the bullets, protecting us from the shots that might come from the 60-year-old men on the ninth floor," said one former marketing executive. "He could take five or six bullets and not drop dead, and I could only take two. He had a thicker suit of armor than we had on."

"I think that was all part of the seasoning process," said another former ad agency executive. "I think his dad wanted to see him in action. The Fourth had gut instincts, and he believed in them. He was not an empty suit or the owner's son. He was a presence and a factor on his own, and he fought for work that his dad wouldn't have approved in a million years."

The Fourth's greatest marketing coup may have been the Budweiser "Frogs" ad campaign, in which three bullfrogs croaked out the word "Budweiser" one syllable at a time. A team of creative staffers from D'Arcy pitched the idea in storyboard form to August IV and Bob Lachky in 1994. It had none of the traditional Anheuser-Busch visual gimmicks, but it was fresh and attention-grabbing, and it had the potential to turn the word "Budweiser" into a pop culture catchphrase. The Fourth caught on right away and served the concept up to his father.

"He took to the idea and brought it up to his father, but his dad didn't understand it," said Charlie Claggett. "Nobody was in that meeting. Apparently, they had kind of an argument about it, because it broke all the rules. It didn't have the 'pour shot,' a lot of things. And August III just didn't get it. He didn't understand why it was funny, why it was relevant to a younger market. But to his credit, he let August IV go with it."

The ad campaign wasn't just borderline bizarre—it was also expensive. No one knew up front how much it would cost to get three frogs to say "Bud-wei-ser," but D'Arcy's team sensed that it wouldn't be cheap.

"So we go and start talking to production companies in Hollywood, saying 'What are we going to do, how are we going to do this? We can't just take three frogs and nail their little webbed feet to a board and get them to say Budweiser,'" Claggett said. "The only way we could do it was to use animatronics, which is not cheap. To our horror, we came back with the price tag of $1.25 million, which was, 20 years ago, a lot of money for a 30-second spot that August III didn't even like very much. But again, this was a company that operated by instinct and feel, and August IV thought this was great. There was a lot of angst and worrying, but they said 'Okay, do it.' So we did." After a strong set of reviews in a few test markets, the ad made its national debut during the Super Bowl in early 1995 and is still listed as one of the best Super Bowl commercials in history.

The Fourth made it clear to his marketing colleagues that he knew their hard work reflected on him. He told several creative executives in the 1980s and 1990s that his ability to ascend to the top of Anheuser-Busch's ladder lay partly in their hands.

"The Fourth is a savvy guy and a sensitive guy," said a former marketer who worked with him closely. "Because of that, he would never come out and say, 'Will you help me be chairman of the company?' But he would say, 'My future is kind of determined by the work you guys do. I'll stay behind you just as long as you make me look good.' He didn't have to say it, because it was understood. It was kind of his job to lose. It was never like *Falcon Crest* or *Dallas*, coveting the job and thinking, 'I'll do whatever I can do get it.'"

Bob Lachky, who was 10 years older than August IV, suffered at points from the coincidence of being an equal to him in all but family name. Lachky was aggressively courted by The Third and eventually

hired out of DDB Needham in 1990 to be Anheuser's brand manager for Bud Light, but he spent more time than he wanted in that
position after August IV was tapped instead to manage the Budweiser
brand family two years later. The two didn't know each other well at
the time, but The Fourth took pains to reach out in an attempt to
mend fences.

"He came to me and said, 'Look, I know this was yours, and you
deserve this. I'm doing it because of who I am, I recognize that. But
let's work together,'" Lachky said. He and The Fourth became friends
that day. "Some people at times saw that as a weakness," Lachky said.
"It is truly one of his great traits. He clearly wanted others to stand up
and get recognized. I said 'August, I'll forever be indebted to you for
that.' I wasn't naïve. I was smart enough to know he was going to be
my boss one day."

"It's easy to bash him," Lachky said. "But I don't think there's a
step in that company that he didn't earn."

When The Fourth ultimately became CEO, he ended up with less
support than he needed. During his days in marketing, he had both a
talent for the work and a network of highly qualified and successful
people surrounding him. "They set it up so that he always had training
wheels," said one former ad agency executive. "He was set up so that
the people around him would make him ready."

With that support as a catalyst, The Fourth's tenure in marketing
produced a string of hits that marked Anheuser-Busch's best era. He
had a knack for identifying out-of-the-box ads that worked. In 1999,
four years after the "Frogs" campaign debuted, August IV pushed yet
another controversial spot onto the air that evolved into a similarly
memorable blockbuster.

"I can categorically tell you that 'Whassup?' would not have run
without The Fourth," said an agency executive who worked on the
aforementioned campaign, which featured a group of slacker guys
who tossed the slang term "Whassup?" back and forth to each other in
greeting. "His dad looked at it and said, 'I don't get this—what does
this mean?' And The Fourth said, 'It's funny, trust me.'"

"Well, are you going to run it on late-night?" The Third asked.
The company always ran its edgier ads later in the evening for older
viewers.

"No, Dad, I'm going to run it on prime time," The Fourth responded, which put The Third even more on the defensive.

"But The Fourth took all of it," the agency executive later recalled. "And he said, 'Guys, my dad approved this. But we've all got to hope that it works.'"

Legend among Anheuser-Busch marketers has it that one Friday, just two days before the first "Whassup?" commercial ran on network television, The Third and The Fourth were still debating whether the campaign would really work. The Third wanted more time to think about it before giving the go-ahead to the networks, but there was no time left if the company wanted the ad to run that Sunday. So The Fourth loaded some video equipment and a television into the back of a van, fired the engine, and drove up onto a well-known hill in St. Louis where a pack of Italian restaurants was concentrated. He pulled the truck up to the back of one of the restaurants and, with a manager's permission, showed the commercial to the restaurant's kitchen staff.

"They thought it was hysterical, and he said, 'Dad, I'm shipping it.' And the rest was history," said DDB's John Greening, who had been waiting for The Third's okay. "I remember thinking, 'Are we going to get the instructions to ship? Or are we just going to run some of the same old stuff?' The Fourth called me, or maybe it was an e-mail from somebody, and said, 'Ship it.' And it was like, 'Yes!'"

"We played it at the convention, and there were 6,000 wholesalers in this big hall in Houston," Greening went on. "We played the 'Whassup?' spot, and the whole place went crazy. I remember there was stuff falling from the ceiling, balloons, and we're all hugging one another like we had won the presidency or something."

■ ■ ■

The Fourth seemed to spend part of every day bobbing and weaving to duck his father's blows, but he enjoyed a certain level of job protection as the boss' son. Not everyone was as lucky.

"I had been fired at least three or four times," said Bob Lachky. "I said that in my exit interview kind of as a joke, but it was true."

The scariest such episode for Lachky happened in late 1997, when he tried to convince The Third that a series of ads in which a jealous lizard tried to assassinate the Budweiser frogs was a better fit for the upcoming Super Bowl than an ad that starred The Third himself, talking about the company's heritage. The Third had grown increasingly enamored with his own series of ads, which were controversial, given his astringent personality. "August Busch III has always seemed a little too tightly wound to appeal to the average beer drinker," one St. Louis reporter wrote in a newspaper column entitled "To Sell Beer Takes More Than a Glare." The Third had gotten decent feedback on his first set of commercials, however, and was pushing hard not just to film more of them but to have greater say in directing them and writing his own copy. Lachky, on the other hand, felt the Super Bowl warranted a new set of funny commercials that keyed off the successful but stale "Frogs" campaign. The situation quickly grew sticky for the marketing and film staff, who were anxious to keep The Third happy but also convinced that Louie the Lizard was a better headlining star for the year's biggest make-or-break event.

The debate hit a melting point just before Christmas when The Third was told his own ads weren't testing as well as Louie's. He gruffly insinuated that Lachky might as well pack his bags and leave. August IV stopped by to see Lachky later that day and found him despondent, lying flat on his back on his office floor.

"Buddy, don't worry. If you go, I go," The Fourth said in an effort to console his colleague, who was trying to sort out how to provide for his young children.

"August, don't even go there," Lachky said with a roll of his eyes. "Give me a break. You're not going anywhere."

"You'll be fine," The Fourth replied. "Don't worry, it's just temporary."

Sure enough, August IV convinced his father to review the positive feedback on Louie the Lizard over the holidays, and Lachky's job was still there when he returned. The stress and pressure had been almost unbearable, however, and Lachky found himself empathizing more with The Fourth's plight than ever before.

"August IV was going through this every day," Lachky said. "Can you imagine what that would be like, where every single day of your existence is getting through this kind of grind? I go through this three or four times in my career. He's been 'fired' every day of his life. Every single day, he's going through this."

"What people don't give him credit for is that the role he played, in terms of protecting people like myself and what we believed in, eventually wears you down."

The Fourth's dealings with his father were never easy. August III's life and behavior were not without their share of irony, and one of the greatest examples, perhaps, is that while he focused with razor-sharp intensity on never making the same mistake twice at Anheuser-Busch—and while he ridiculed, punished, and sometimes fired those who did—he repeated some of his father's worst mistakes at home. The tension between The Third and some of his half-siblings was well-chronicled, but when he married his second wife, Ginny, and had two children with her, he not only let a rivalry develop between half-brothers Steven and August IV but appeared to relish pitting them against each other.

"That's part of the whole father/son dynamic," said fellow Busch clan member Reisinger. "When Prince Charles was born, from the minute he was born every single person in England who supported royalty said, 'Okay, this is the future king. Prepare him. From the second the guy was born, they're preparing him and saying, 'You're the one, and we're going to make you ready and be there for you.'"

With August IV, Reisinger said, "It was always sort of like 'We'll see, we'll see.' No support, tear you down, tear you down . . . it's the extreme opposite approach. If you were told forever that you just may never be ready or you're not good enough, what are you going to think about yourself? That level of mental battering and torture is not good. Why that happened, who knows—but it's a whole different approach. It's unfortunate."

Steven was 13 years younger than August IV. The Third started to pull him into meetings and assign him roles within the company once Steven matured into a young teenager. Some Anheuser-Busch staffers thought the perceived rivalry between August IV and Steven would morph into the next Busch generation's battle royal. "There was a time where people would say to The Fourth: 'Hey, it's his mom going to bed with him every night, not your mom," said one former

Anheuser-Busch employee. Speculation was already running rampant in 1991, when Steven was only 12, that he might challenge The Fourth to the throne. "We just hope it doesn't come to that," The Fourth's mother said. In 2002, when Steven was 25, people close to the company said that August IV believed that his stepmother, Ginny, wanted Steven to take over the company. "For the past 12 years, The Fourth has said openly that his stepmother wants him to fail and her son Steve to run the joint," said one insider. "I don't know that it's true, but it's true that The Fourth feels that way."

Others, however, never saw Steven as much more than a distraction. He spent five years working as his father's executive assistant, rather than swapping into new roles at the company to broaden his expertise. When most up-and-comers were pulled into Anheuser-Busch's antiquated executive assistant program, in which they tailed a particular executive for years, half in mentorship and half in servitude, they'd stick around for one to three years before moving elsewhere to be molded for leadership. Steven's stasis in the job made his candidacy for a higher position less and less viable as time wore on.

"I never bought the Steven thing," said one strategy committee member. "He was never a factor. He was never a threat. He was just his father's sidekick. He would have been destroyed Day One."

Steven eventually started backing away from the business, and in October of 2006, less than a month after the board voted to install The Fourth as CEO, 29-year-old Steven left Anheuser-Busch altogether and purchased Krey Distributing, one of the company's most lucrative independent distributors, which was based near St. Louis and had been run by The Third's best friend from his school days. "I couldn't be happier with the career choice I've made," Steven told one local publication. "My brother is going to do a great job for us running the brewery. He's the guy that was groomed for it and is in the job, and it's a great fit. That wasn't something I was looking for." August IV's sister, Susie Busch Transou, who had rejoined Anheuser-Busch after completing an MBA, also left the company to run Tri-Eagle Sales, an Anheuser-Busch distributorship in Tallahassee, Florida, with her husband.

It was hard to blame The Fourth's siblings for backing away from the spotlight. Running the company was an incredibly heavy cross to bear, and just like other Busches who had avoided corporate work over the decades, they stood to be fabulously wealthy for the rest of their lives even if they never spent another day at Anheuser-Busch headquarters. Why take on the added burden?

Their departures eliminated an effective point of leverage for The Third, however. "When Steven left and his sister Susie left, I was very surprised. I think August III really loved hanging Steven, in particular, over The Fourth's head," said one former Anheuser-Busch employee.

■ ■ ■

In November 1996, a 32-year-old August IV was named vice president of marketing, which made him responsible for the entire brewery's marketing and sales activities and put him in a position to report directly to Patrick Stokes, the brewery's president. August III seemed supremely confident that his son would keep Anheuser-Busch ahead of the pack. Its advertising was winning back young beer drinkers who had been abandoning Budweiser throughout the earlier 1990s. Profits were rising again at a double-digit pace. And the company's stock was up.

"Budweiser isn't your father's beer anymore," The Third told a reporter just a few months after installing The Fourth as CEO. "I'll be retired by sixty-five. At that point, this is a younger person's game." Yet when the reporter said that insiders believed there was a 99 percent chance August IV was next in line to take over as CEO, The Third demurred. "I don't think anyone can say there's a 99 percent chance of anything in life."

Susie laughed at her father's cryptic remarks. "If my brother continues to perform as he has, it's 100 percent certain he'll have the job."

Two years later, a health scare put life and mortality into clearer perspective for August III. After feeling uncomfortable while exercising on a treadmill at his home on a Sunday in September 1999, Busch checked in with a doctor the following day and was told he needed a quadruple heart bypass operation. Trim and until then, seemingly fit, 62-year-old August III wanted to undergo the procedure as soon as possible. He was wheeled into surgery later that day at St. John's Mercy Medical Center and came out of the operation in good condition.

The incident immediately sparked questions over his succession plans. Anheuser-Busch told investors that no one else at the brewery had needed to assume The Third's responsibilities because there had been no emergency and the operation had gone well. Every senior Anheuser-Busch officer was required to let the board of directors know who could take over his or her position in case of an emergency, but a spokesman for Anheuser wouldn't divulge who would stand in for August III in such a situation. The Third recovered from the surgery's physical strain in his typically aggressive and efficient fashion. "I remember, maybe four weeks after his heart attack, he choppered into the soccer park and he looked great," said one former ad agency executive. "He always took care of himself. He was a fit person, and he ate right."

Still, it was clear to many Anheuser-Busch executives that a succession plan needed to be put in place, and their conviction stemmed not from their views on The Third's physical capacity but from a shift they noticed in his mental state.

"You could just see that period in the early 2000s, where he's getting older," said one former top executive. "Though nobody knows him well, he just feared mortality. His whole life, his whole soul, he had given to this company. To see it slipping away . . ."

The Fourth wasn't predisposed to oust his father in the same way his grandfather had been ejected. Thankfully, he didn't have to. Anheuser-Busch had been family-owned when Gussie was forced out, but thanks to a decision by The Third to list the company on the New York Stock Exchange in 1980, it now had legions of shareholders and answered to a stricter set of rules—one of which dictated that its chief executive should retire at or before the age of 65. The Third was set to turn 65 in June 2002, and while he was a powerful man, there was no way he was going to use that power to nullify the age requirement while under shareholder scrutiny. He owned just 3.4 million shares of Anheuser-Busch, less than 1 percent of the company's stock. He had no voting control over the matter. The Fourth would have to lobby the board of directors hard to win the CEO job, but at least he wasn't going to have to kick his dad to the curb. "Considering the history of my father and my grandfather," The Fourth said in 1997 in reference to the coup, "he knew he would retire by sixty-five."

Some former Anheuser executives said The Third's greatest fears were geared more toward becoming professionally obsolete rather than toward actually dying.

"I think he was facing his own mortality—not to sound overly dramatic—because of the mandatory retirement policy the company had," a former strategy committee staffer said. "I believe that if he could have worked until he dropped dead doing that job, he would have. There was no question he didn't want to retire." This executive once overheard a conversation between August III and Edward Whitacre, a longtime Anheuser board member and friend of August's, who was four years younger and who, at the time, was chairman and chief executive of AT&T. At the dinner table the night before a board meeting, the two lamented that they were being forced to retire just as they were hitting what they felt was the prime of their lives.

"August told me once: 'You know, guys like us, we never retire,'" the former executive said. "And I felt like saying, "What do you mean, guys like us? Guys like you!" He thought the wiser, though, smiled, and kept his mouth firmly shut.

Several years before The Third was due to turn 65, Wall Street analysts began to debate whether his son was the right candidate for the job. Many analysts assumed he was the most likely person to replace his father. "I wouldn't operate under the assumption that August the Third's successor would be someone other than August the Fourth," a Salomon Smith Barney analyst said in 1998. Still, others speculated that The Third might find a placeholder—rumored to be beer business head and August IV's boss Pat Stokes—to manage the company for a while until The Fourth was sufficiently able.

No amount of lobbying was going to change the impression by some investors that August IV was too young and inexperienced, and that promoting him at that particular time would be a stroke of nep-otism that could hurt the company's prospects. There were concerns about whether he was well-rounded enough, intellectually or manage-rially, to handle the top job. He had played a critical role in the compa-ny's marketing effort, but he hadn't operated Anheuser-Busch's dozen breweries, run its theme parks, managed its international businesses, or dealt with its network of opinionated distributors. And while The Fourth had tamped down some of the flames over the Arizona crash and his other legal troubles and was closing in on the age of 40, he had a naggingly persistent party-boy image. With a few more years under his belt, perhaps he would be more ready for the job.

Susan Busch in a 1995 interview called her son "an amazingly strong man" who was "doing very well with his life," and said she believed he was the heir apparent. "I would think so, yes," she said. "He's got the ability and he definitely has the desire, so I would think that he would be the next one."

When asked three years later what he would do if he wasn't named CEO, The Fourth indicated that he hadn't even weighed the notion. "What will I do? I don't know. I'm not going to consider that option right now." By the time 2002 rolled around, bringing with it The Third's 65th birthday, other Busch family members were also quoted saying that they expected The Fourth would claim the title. After all, The Third hadn't prepared any other candidates from within the family.

"August Busch IV is a little bit of a dark horse," one analyst said that year. "Wall Street doesn't know how bright he is, how good a leader he is. He's not a character who has been tested or tried."

On July 1, 2002, a month after August III's 65th birthday, he and the rest of the Anheuser-Busch board of directors announced that Pat Stokes, 59, would take charge of the company on a day-to-day basis as president and CEO. The Third would remain chairman of the board and would continue to serve on the company's agenda-setting strategy committee, which meant he'd still have purview over the entire operation. The implications of the decision were monumental, as Anheuser-Busch itself pointed out. For the first time in 142 years, the company would be run by someone who wasn't a member of the Busch or Anheuser families. The dynasty was coming to an end.

Stokes's promotion immediately sparked debate over whether The Third's decision to bypass his son meant that The Fourth might never actually measure up to his expectations and make it to the top. Most Anheuser-Busch watchers assumed The Third was just giving his son more time to get up to speed. "I think he thought that August IV was not ready yet, and so they gave him a number of other responsibilities," said former U.S. Ambassador to Mexico James Jones, who was a member of Anheuser's board at the time.

"I think he genuinely wanted to pass it down to his son, but I think his son just wasn't up to it," said Charlie Claggett. "August used to say, 'You're thinking with your heart and not your head.' And I think that was the weakness his son had. He just did not have that cut-throat willingness to cut somebody off at the knees if he had to, which is the way you have to run a brewery. Because let's face it, anybody can brew beer. It's just a matter of who has the most money and power, and who is willing to do what it takes."

BusinessWeek called The Third's decision to relinquish his operating titles but remain chairman of the company "a succession process as tightly orchestrated as any in the House of Windsor." Even though The Third had chosen a non–family member and denied his son the seat, the magazine joined cynics in taking him and the board to task for what it said looked like an "extremely temporary" aberration in the Busch family's succession legacy. "At a time when the image of the regal boss is more than just troubling, the Busch family seems somehow exempt from many of the rigors currently being imposed on the rest of Corporate America," it said. The Third and his board had allowed the murky succession debate to devolve to the point where they were damned if they appointed The Fourth as CEO and damned if they didn't.

The Fourth was promoted into Stokes's spot as head of the company's domestic beer operations, which would have been viewed as a plum new assignment had he not been in contention to be CEO. Instead, he was forced to address his cloudy future. "I don't take anything for granted in this company," The Fourth said the year after he was passed over for the job. "It's not a foregone conclusion that I'll go any further."

"The Fourth was young," said one former high-ranking Anheuser executive, who said the company faced a timing problem. "If you go back to 1990, he was way too young to be considered for president at that point. He hadn't done enough jobs at the brewery. So there was a gap there that just chronologically needed to be filled. Were people surprised? I was close enough to Pat that I wasn't surprised. August had a lot of confidence in him, and he was a smart guy."

The board installed Stokes with an almost implicit understanding that he would serve in the interim while August IV took more time to develop, said General Henry Hugh Shelton, a member of the board who helped make that decision. The goal was for The Fourth to be seen as a clear heir apparent by the time Stokes was ready to retire.

"Pat was there as the guy who could watch The Fourth ripen," agreed a former top ad agency executive. "He wasn't ready yet—the board would never have approved him when the heart thing happened, and then Pat stepped in. But listen, all of the strings were being pulled by The Third."

August III graciously insisted that Stokes move into his office when he became CEO. All the same, The Third shifted his own office just down the hall, and with the board's complicity, he kept both Stokes and his son on a tight rein starting in mid-2002. Stokes had never been prone to flights of fancy anyway. Rather than rising up through Anheuser's ranks by way of its more illustrious job functions, like brewing or marketing or sales, he came in through the back alley. He scored a major coup when he was named as August III's assistant not long after joining the company in 1969. Two years later, however, he shifted over into the company's purchasing division and spent the next decade and a half buying raw materials and deciphering Anheuser's web of transportation operations.

Stokes put those skills to good use after he was picked in the mid-1980s to run Campbell Taggart and Eagle Snacks, two struggling units Anheuser had been trying to build that were far removed from its brewing operations. After 15 years in brewing, Stokes became a baker and a pretzel vendor—and for the next six years tackled both units' production and distribution inefficiencies. He was never able to shine the tarnished Campbell Taggart into a company jewel, and Eagle Snacks never gained much of a presence against behemoth Frito-Lay. Stokes helped prevent further bloodletting in the wake of Anheuser's misguided acquisitions of those businesses. When The Third finally picked someone to fill Denny Long's seat as head of the brewery, he picked Stokes, pulling him back into Anheuser's big leagues.

Stokes didn't have his own crowd of "yes" men. He wasn't the type to advertise himself or spend time pressing the flesh to get ahead. "Pat was not known for being Mr. Congeniality," said a former executive who worked with him closely. "Let's just say that Pat's personality was not multi-dimensional."

August III relied on Stokes for guidance—at least, as much as he relied on anyone. They sat together in policy committee meetings, and because he was well aware of Stokes's mind for numbers, The Third liked to toss concepts his way in search of an opinion or analysis. "Pat had an incredible brain," one of his former colleagues said. "The guy knew numbers; he had a photographic memory. I wouldn't say August depended on Pat, but he would frequently seek Pat's opinion on things. So from that standpoint, I think people should not have been surprised."

"Stokes is an incredibly intense person, just as cold and analytic and hard charging as the Third," said Bill Finnie, another former colleague. "I think they are pretty much damn close to clones of each other." Those personality traits, plus Stokes's longstanding devotion to the company, made him an ideal CEO candidate for someone like The Third, who was looking to retain significant control over the business in "retirement." "During those days, I think there was an understanding between Pat and August III that Pat was going to run the company but August was going to watch after the beer," said a former top Anheuser-Busch executive.

"All the calls still got made by somebody named Busch," said another person close to the company. "Pat is a very smart guy and a capable executive. He's not an empty suit by any means. But he was just working in an environment that was not a democracy."

Stokes's appointment—and the way The Fourth tried to manage Anheuser's internal politics after he was passed over for the job—made things complicated at headquarters. The Third remained nearly as imposing a figure as he had before, and his position on the strategy committee gave him a view into everything the company was doing at its highest levels. The company's convoluted new management structure didn't bode well for morale or performance.

"It was just amazing how things started to fall apart when August didn't get that final nod," said a former strategy committee member. "He had the dynamic above him that was freaking him out, and every time he moved, it became a mess underneath because he wasn't paying attention anymore. He was looking up to manage his own situation and wasn't paying enough attention to what was going on down below. It was classic."

■ ■ ■

Anheuser-Busch also started to lose momentum against an increasingly aggressive Miller in the early 2000s, and its dominance of the U.S. beer market took a turn for the worse, dropping from the stunning high of 52 percent it hit during The Third's last year as CEO. Even if The Third had remained at the helm, there may have been nowhere to go but down. Miller was running harsh attack ads that were proving quite effective in reversing Miller Lite's decade-long slide against Bud Light. Drinkers' tastes, meanwhile, were changing, and more and more people had started to favor wine, liquor, and craft beers over mainstream brands like Budweiser.

As Anheuser's stranglehold on the market began to loosen, The Third, as chairman, with Stokes as his CEO, helped push through a few strategic moves that drew criticism from within the company's ranks. When Hurricane Katrina hit New Orleans in 2005 and prompted Anheuser's beer inventories to swell in hurricane-affected areas, the company had two options—it could cut prices to sell its beer off quickly or let it spoil on the shelves to protect its pricing power. Anheuser chose the former, and as the U.S. market leader, instigated a huge pricing war with the other brewers from which its market share never recovered. Its profit dropped by nearly a quarter in the third quarter of that year. "If this is successful discounting, failure looks preferable," one industry analyst quipped.

"He started a price war," said one strategy committee member. "He started cutting price to punish them, and took so much revenue out of the marketplace. And then blamed everybody else, blamed us, blamed the marketing guys, blamed August IV. There was just a lot of blame going around."

August III also pushed hard for Anheuser-Busch to hit back at Miller, a move many insiders felt was beneath Anheuser-Busch.

"That's when he started to turn on us, the marketing guys, saying, 'Nobody can talk to us that way! Attack!'" said Bob Lachky. "That's the point in time where we saw him change, where he became very aggressive, saying, 'It's marketing's fault that we can't grow.'" For the first time people could remember, August III was showing signs of being afraid, and he was lashing out in response.

Against the protestations of some of the company's top marketers, Anheuser-Busch counterattacked. It ran ads that portrayed Miller as the "Queen of Carbs" at a time when the protein-heavy Atkins diet had made "carbohydrate" a dirty word. And it shamelessly draped itself in the American flag while drawing attention to Miller's foreign ownership.

The Third's protectionist ads made some Anheuser-Busch insiders uncomfortable, particularly after he plastered the Busch Gardens theme parks with slogans and banners that shouted to unsuspecting park goers that Miller was foreign-owned. The propaganda seemed Big Brother-ish and out of place in an environment that was supposed to be about wholesome family fun.

"We were doing things that were crazy," said one former top executive. "Our theme parks were putting up signs that said, 'Drink American, not Miller,' and it was terrible. Consumers don't look at things that way. And someone who is a recent arrival in our country could take that the wrong way. It's just so wrong today. It's desperate. It sounds terrible."

One of Anheuser-Busch's advisors on Wall Street ran into the signs during a family trip to Busch Gardens in Tampa, Florida, three or four years prior to InBev's takeover bid.

"I was with my kids," the advisor said. "And in the men's room at Busch Gardens, they had all of these plaques up against SABMiller. 'It's not American. "SAB" stands for South Africa.' It was verging on racist craziness. I remember standing around the men's room going, 'What the hell?' There must have been ten of them."

August III was a student of his family's history. He often read old letters Adolphus had written about his days running the company, and he took them to heart, referencing at times how "My grandfather used to do this" or ". . . that." He knew that there were critical points in history at which Anheuser had nearly been lost—most notably, during Prohibition.

"He was always cognizant of the terrible trials the company had been through, and he just didn't want it to happen to him. He didn't want to lose the company," said one strategy committee member. "There was a lot of blame going around.

"He didn't trust anyone anymore. People can say Augie was going crazy—no. He didn't trust the team. He didn't want the thing to go down. He was going to solve it himself."

Anheuser's strategy committee meetings became contentious, as a growing number of the executives determined that the company needed to merge with a rival, or at the very least forge a strong alliance to stay competitive. The Fourth was still plugging away under Stokes as president of the company's all-important brewing division, trying to finally prove he was up to the task of being CEO. As the competitive landscape grew tougher and tougher, it became clear that he might have painfully few options at his disposal for ensuring the company's success by the time he was promoted. The Fourth undertook some efforts as brewery head to reverse the company's slide, bolstering Anheuser-Busch's brewing portfolio by adding new brands to its distribution system and trying to tap into the higher-end market. He also added non-alcoholic drinks from Hansen Natural Corp. to Anheuser's distribution chain and tried to get his father to consider buying Hansen outright or making other acquisitions.

And though The Fourth's view on the brewing industry was more global than The Third's, he also embraced some of his father's America-centric rhetoric to make his devotion to the company clear. At a wholesaler convention in March 2005, August IV whipped the group into a frenzy over the fact that Anheuser-Busch was the only major American-owned brewer standing in the wake of the MolsonCoors merger. To kick-start the troops into a patriotic fervor, he declared that the Miller commercials that targeted Budweiser were actually desecrating America. At the height of the crowd's excitement, he then strode to the chair where his father was sitting, paused, and knelt in front of him. The Third's eyes welled visibly with tears, and the over-the-top gesture pushed the wholesalers into rapture.

■ ■ ■

It had become clear by that time to many Anheuser-Busch insiders that August IV was bound to move into the CEO slot. The company's board had encouraged him to take a few steps in their shoes, so he had joined the board of package shipper FedEx in 2003. A few sections of his résumé still remained untended, however, and his image had as much to do with it as his actual competence. The Fourth still had a playboy problem.

A range of Busch men had built reputations for womanizing. August IV, though, significantly upped the ante, to the point where some Anheuser insiders wondered what he was trying to prove. He was known to walk into nightclubs and buy rounds of Budweiser for everyone in the bar, and was often seen patronizing St. Louis's trendier hotspots with a model or some other girlfriend on his arm—or frolicking at Lake of the Ozarks on one of the company's boats, surrounded by a bevy of bikini-clad women. His home, which had once been owned by hockey star Brett Hull, was described as the ultimate bachelor pad, with a huge hot tub and beer taps in the kitchen, and people reported that he often had women accompany him on business trips. One company advisor was once told by a prominent St. Louis businessman that August IV "came through our secretarial pool like Sherman through Georgia."

While General William T. Sherman left behind a trail of scorched forests and fields on his 1864 march to the port of Savannah, The Fourth was more apt to leave a string of broken hearts and spilled drinks. He was engaged at one point to a model from Missouri named Judy Buchmiller, but they rescheduled their wedding twice. "I'm very much in love with the girl I'm engaged to," he had said in early 1991. "We're still, hopefully, going to get married. We're very much in love. I want to marry the girl." Their engagement was called off for good later that year.

"I'll marry when the time is right," he said in 1997, when he was dating a woman named Sage Linville who had moved from California to be with him in St. Louis. "There's a girl I'm very much in love with," he said. "Sage Busch is an interesting name, isn't it? I'm not making predictions about that."

The Fourth, who shared his father's taste in blondes, toned down his party-boy antics in his 30s, although he certainly didn't abandon them. He logged plenty of hours trotting the globe in the company of Ronald Burkle, the California-based billionaire supermarket magnate and investor. The Fourth spent a good amount of time hanging out at Burkle's tony estate in Los Angeles, at points even putting in business calls to the company's advisors from his place, and Burkle described August IV in the early 2000s as his best friend. Burkle introduced The Fourth to Yusef Jackson, the son of the Reverend Jesse Jackson, at a party at his house in 1996, and Jackson and his brother Jonathan were later chosen to take over a key Anheuser-Busch distributorship in Chicago, prompting cries of favoritism that the Jacksons denied.

In 1998, a 34-year-old August IV told a reporter that while he was "not celibate, by any means," he was sharing his home with no female companions other than his three Rottweilers. His increased level of involvement at the company, The Fourth said, made establishing a personal life more difficult.

"If I don't start seriously working on a relationship, some ten years down the road I'm going to look back and say, 'Well, I made it in the company, but I missed something else,'" he said.

Eight years after making that statement—just in time, according to his synopsis—he finally did settle down. Amid persistent chatter that getting married was a requirement for him to become CEO, The Fourth wed 25-year-old Kathryn Thatcher, a native of Fairlee, Vermont, on the auspicious date of August 5th, 2006, in a nod, perhaps, toward a potential heir in the future. August's aunt, Beatrice Busch von Gontard, said at the time that she had always wondered how long the "August" name cycle would continue. "Where's the cut-off? Or do you be like Henry VIII and just keep going?"

The couple was carted away from their Bradford, Vermont, wedding ceremony by a team of eight Clydesdales pulling a bright red wooden beer wagon, which was festooned with white bows and sported a "Just Married" sign at the back. Its green-suited drivers, who perched on its steering bench next to a Dalmatian, pulled up outside the wedding reception site at the Hanover Inn across the border in New Hampshire for photographs. To the chagrin of some disgruntled locals, several of Hanover's best-known bars and restaurants agreed to feature Anheuser-Busch beers more prominently while guests were in town for the festivities.

The Fourth's decision to get married was "arguably as important" to his efforts to become CEO as his four years as head of the company's U.S. beer operation had been, the *Financial Times* said, because it dampened "the playboy image that had caused doubts about his suitability for the top job." According to *Fortune*, The Fourth had "long understood that he needed to marry in order to have his father, chairman August Busch III, and the board of directors take him seriously."

"That was always the quid pro quo," a former Anheuser employee told the magazine. "It was 'August, until you settle down and stop being the wild man, nothing is going to happen.'"

Even The Fourth's marriage, however—which was something his father ostensibly supported in concept—caused problems in the two men's relationship. "Some of the tension between him and his dad, I think . . . dealt with the fact that he did take off occasionally with his wife and go to the lake or wherever, to take a little bit of time off and away from the job to spend with her," said General Shelton. "When he got married, I thought I saw him adding a little more balance to his life, mixing a little bit of the social with the work, which I thought served him and the company very well."

The wedding left just one major box still unchecked—receipt of the board of directors' approval. That finally came in September of 2006 when the board announced it had chosen The Fourth as Stokes's successor and said Anheuser would be well served by his leadership.

There were reports of discord on the board about the decision. "He's a party boy, you cannot hide that," said industry writer Harry Schuhmacher. "There are too many people that know it. The hot tub in the living room, and dancing girls and parties all night . . . that went on throughout and still goes on today, I'm sure. And that's his nature. But Richard Branson is a party boy too. Does that disqualify someone from leading a large company?"

The board decided it didn't. And frankly, there were no other candidates who could match August IV's breadth of knowledge on the American beer industry. He could cite Budweiser sales statistics for small towns in Tennessee by memory, and he had literally grown up at the brewery. He wasn't the perfect candidate, but The Third hadn't cultivated any others. Compared with the company's next-best option—bringing in a consumer products executive who didn't understand the fickle beer market—The Fourth was deemed Anheuser's best choice.

"August IV has successfully prepared himself by leading the U.S. beer company through a period of great change and challenge," his father said in a press release dated September 27. "He brings with him the new thinking of his generation, yet appreciation for the great traditions and values of this company."

■ ■ ■

After 49 years at Anheuser-Busch, 68-year-old August III retired as chairman of the board on November 30, relinquishing a bit further his official hold on the group. Stokes, 64, who had been with the company for 37 years and had worked directly with The Third for more than 30 of them, took over as chairman.

Both men cut deals to remain highly paid consultants for the company, as per tradition for many of Anheuser's departing or demoted executives. August III agreed to consult part-time for six years, and Anheuser pledged to continue covering his business travel, office, and security expenses and even to continue leasing its corporate aircraft from his company. It also pledged to provide free draught and packaged beer to his house upon request. In December, he elected to be paid his $37 million pension, along with another $27 million in deferred compensation, in one lump sum rather than having payments spread out over many years. Stokes made a similar election and received $34.6 million in pension and deferred pay—bringing the amount Anheuser paid its two former chiefs that month to nearly $99 million.

After spending exactly half of his life working at Anheuser-Busch, 42-year-old August IV—who was literally born to be chief executive—took over on December 1 and brought with him an easygoing, approachable leadership style that contrasted sharply with that of his father's.

The mood at the company, though, was hardly euphoric. Investors and analysts were concerned about its heavy dependence on the United

States, where there were few opportunities for growth. Budweiser's market share had been slipping for years, and neither The Third nor Stokes had been able to stop it. Wine, craft beers, and imports were continuing to grow in popularity, and Anheuser-Busch was struggling to invent "beer occasions" that provided excuses for people to drink. Beer's total share of the alcohol market had dropped to 55 percent from its peak of 60 percent in 1995. The market was even topping out when it came to devoted beer drinkers. The human stomach is only so big, America's obesity problem notwithstanding, and Anheuser-Busch wasn't likely to convince many people to chug a case of Budweiser a day no matter how hard it tried.

The company's stale share price reflected these concerns, and investors were getting frustrated. It marked the toughest era for the company since The Third had taken the reins in the 1970s. August IV was staring a mountain of hard work in the face.

A few things changed when he took office. With the company under heavy pressure to rein in costs, he quickly decided to shutter Anheuser's ostentatious executive dining room. The luxurious eatery had served as a place of respite for Gussie and The Third for decades, but it was little more than a nerve-wracking poaching ground for many of their subordinates.

"He used to have breakfast in our dining room, which was like a bank dining room," said Bob Lachky, referring to August III. "It was gorgeous. [The Fourth] shut it down and made it a call center. He said it was ridiculous that only certain people in certain grade levels got to use it, and it was starting to separate the employees. Plus, I don't think The Fourth ever used it." Many of Anheuser's other top staffers also avoided the place like the plague. They weren't eager to get cornered and reamed out by August III as they tried to scarf down a ham sandwich. Still, most of them remember being summoned up there at one point or another.

One morning after his retirement, The Third helicoptered to the office and called down for breakfast, not knowing that his son had pulled the dining room's plug.

"And they said, 'But sir, we don't have the dining room anymore,'" Lachky said, recounting the story. "He goes, 'What?' And they said, 'Well, it's not here. It's closed. August IV closed it.' And he was like, '*What?*' He thought he'd come back to his old haunt, and it didn't exist.'"

A much bigger point of cost-related contention between father and son, however, involved The Fourth's decision to cancel delivery of a new $40 million Dassault Falcon 7X—Dassault's first fly-by-wire plane, which could make it all the way from St. Louis to China non-stop. The Third had been eagerly awaiting the aircraft for years, and Anheuser-Busch was scheduled to be the plane's U.S. launch customer. The Fourth strenuously objected to the idea, however, contending that it would send the wrong message to shareholders. He canceled the order, which made for one of the biggest rifts the two men's already-sour relationship ever suffered.

"There was a lot of consternation surrounding that decision," said board member General Shelton. "I don't know behind the scenes what went on, but maybe in retrospect, there wasn't as much prior coordination done before that decision was made to set it up so that it would not be a kind of 'In your face!' to his dad."

Those were minor cultural shifts, however. The Fourth faced a major battle against Anheuser's historic inertia if he wanted to enact meaningful change. While he was now officially CEO, some people on Wall Street suspected that he still might not be able to wield much control over the company with his 69-year-old dad still lurking behind the curtain and Stokes acting as chairman of the board. "Mr. Busch now has center stage for himself, but it remains to be seen if this is indeed his company and if he has the will—and the full support of the board—to move the King of Beers in the bold new direction it must go to deliver for shareholders," said analyst Carlos Laboy.

Stokes could have helped guide The Fourth through the transition. After 38 years with the company, he knew every button to push and had an ability to work with both father and son. But his continued presence seemed to help cement The Third's control.

"Pat was a good executive, he knew where all the levers were, and he was there ostensibly to help The Fourth," said one former top executive and strategy committee member. "But to put Pat in at chairman of the board was basically a transparent move to stay in control of what was going on."

"It was odd," the former executive said, summing up the environment within the company after The Fourth was put in charge. "It was his dad's way of keeping August at bay. By having Pat there, it was his dad's way of saying, "You're not quite ready. You have the title, but you're still not quite ready."

Former Anheuser staffers have mixed views on whether Stokes could have softened the blow of The Fourth's transition or whether he was equally hamstrung by The Third. "If there is anything I can blame Stokes for is that he didn't develop The Fourth," said Bill Finnie. "I am going to give him the benefit of the doubt, that maybe he could not have driven change. Stokes may not have been able to do a whole lot while he was CEO. But he sure could have made sure his successor would drive change. If Stokes had developed The Fourth, and The Fourth had not just had his own people but people with the same cojones that The Third had . . . it would have been a different story."

The Fourth did make several early attempts to promote new executives of his own choosing—he pushed hard to appoint one potential chief operating officer, but The Third disagreed and shot the candidate down. He did the same with several of his son's other nominees, and even targeted executives who were already with the company and who ultimately departed under pressure.

"He didn't trust anyone anymore," said a former strategy committee member. "His son said, 'Look, if you want me to be the guy, I should be allowed to pick my team and you should let me make some strategic decisions." The Third slapped many of them away, though, unchecked by a board of directors he had known for years, if not decades.

"If I can't have my team, how can you hold me accountable for performance?" The Fourth said in one newspaper interview.

The Third and The Fourth were polar opposites when it came to being able to trust and delegate. The elder was loyal mainly to people who provided commendable service to Anheuser-Busch. His son appreciated people who could be loyal friends, and was trusting to the point where it seemed that his father considered the trait a fault. The Fourth depended heavily on deputies and hangers-on, both at the office and away from it, and he struggled to differentiate between people who were truly competent at their jobs and those who were just good at being friends. The Third seemed determined not to let his son make certain mistakes—even if it meant constructing a workplace environment that allowed his son few comrades.

If August IV had asserted himself more strongly, he might have been able to avoid being professionally emasculated by his father. He never established his own nucleus of power to help him usurp his dad when the time was right. Right up until the time of InBev's bid in 2008, many people at Anheuser-Busch still saw themselves as "III guys" or "IV guys." The Fourth had strong support from the sales and marketing teams, but he never won the broader buy-in he needed from staffers in other key areas of the company—brewing, operations, and corporate planning.

The Fourth might never have been able to summon the sheer force of will he needed to outstrip his father's immense power, however. Stacked up against each other, The Third seemed to tower impossibly high over his son. "Mr. Busch never let go of the power base," said Bob Lachky. "August IV never really had a chance at building it, because his dad had rigid control. It was not for August IV's lack of trying. It was just blocked."

"I think he worshiped his dad," said Charlie Claggett. "I think he desperately wanted to please him, wanted to do the right thing. But that was the catch. Ultimately, I think his dad knew The Fourth was going to have to do to him what he had done to his father. In order to be a successful leader, you have to be able to make decisions on your own. You can't keep running to the old man all the time. You have to be willing to take risks and put yourself and your reputation on the line. I don't think he saw his son doing that, or maybe he saw him doing it, but not very effectively."

The stark personality contrasts between Busch CEOs were no secret to analysts and the media. "Mr. Busch remains a bit of a mystery as a leader, though he is viewed as outgoing and personable, especially compared with his father, who is regarded as stern and aloof," said the *Wall Street Journal*. As August IV's tenure got into swing, industry watchers sat back and waited with curiosity to see how the new arrangement at the top would play out.

The Fourth offered his dad at least one olive branch in an attempt to prove that their goals for Anheuser-Busch weren't mutually exclusive.

Not long into his stint as CEO, he invited The Third to attend a strategy committee meeting where each executive would be presenting his or her vision for the company's future. The Fourth wasn't obliged to include his dad, but The Third accepted the invitation and took a seat with the rest of the group that day to listen to their series of 20-minute pitches.

It quickly became clear that he didn't like what he was hearing. "Man, he was visibly—not quite angry—but visibly rejecting certain people's comments. People who had the audacity to say, 'We should buy Miller' or 'We should go do this,'" said one person who presented at the meeting. "He was just getting madder and madder and madder. It was so obvious it was a hostile environment for bringing in new ideas. And yet he was there, because he knew he controlled the board."

"The Fourth was reaching out to try and make sure his dad knew that 'I respect you,'" the executive said. "The Fourth was trying to get his dad to be a nurturer, to be a mentor. Mr. Busch would never be a mentor. He's not a mentoring type of person. He's not a person who says, 'My legacy is going to be to help the next generation.' Are you kidding me? He's the only generation that matters. That was the heart of August IV versus the coldness of his father, totally personified."

If there was ever a time for The Fourth to prove himself to his hard-driving father, this was it. "Mr. Busch is taking over at a truly seminal moment," wrote analyst Carlos Laboy. "As the August Busch IV era begins, A-B is not without options to recapture growth, but it is increasingly apparent to us that the current model is quickly running out of steam."

The Fourth spread his net wide in search of solutions, and investors were encouraged by the sense that he was more open to changing the company's strategy than his father had been. Yet even after ascending to Anheuser-Busch's highest perch and caving to many of The Third's demands, August IV was still laboring to win his approval. He said as much in a May 2008 *Wall Street Journal* interview that elicited a near-universal cringe.

"His love and respect will be when I'm ultimately successful," said The Fourth, admitting that his transition into the CEO spot had been "a very difficult, fluid situation." He had "never, ever had a father-son relationship" with his dad, he went on. "It's purely business." He concluded, "I honestly do believe if I failed in my professional life, it would be much harder to ever gain his respect."

He later regretted making those comments, which shook his advisors' confidence in him and looked embarrassing in hindsight—especially his admission that he had saved the few notes of praise he had received from his father in his briefcase. In his first decade of full-time work at the company, he had received only five. Industry watchers wondered what The Fourth's public relations team could possibly have been thinking in allowing the interview, and there were a few incredulous reactions as well on InBev's side of the fence. "We all sat around saying, Whoa. This is, like, a bizarre family drama we've stepped into,'" said one person close to the company.

The Third, as usual, stayed silent on the matter.

Chapter 6

The Hunter's Frozen Trigger Finger

Once the world became globalized, he was a fish out of water.
—Head of a rival brewer

There was a clear sense by the time August IV took over that Anheuser-Busch's golden era had ended, and he quickly grew paranoid that the company was vulnerable to a takeover or to the machinations of activist shareholders like Nelson Peltz, Eddie Lampert, and Bill Ackman, whose investment funds zeroed in on consumer-oriented companies that had grown fat or complacent. The Fourth had good reason to be worried. Rumors were rampant that one activist or another was buying up shares on the sly.

The company no longer had a handful of little brewers to chew up and spit out, and the huge profit margins it had enjoyed as it rode the market's wave upward over the years weren't enough to bank on anymore. Another lever needed to be pulled, and August IV, unlucky in his timing as the company's new CEO, was supposed to find it.

The biggest move he could make—one that would be much more hard-hitting than just slashing a bunch of costs—was executing a game-changing merger. There was a significant problem with that idea, though. That boat had sailed, with nearly every other brewer on it, while his father and Stokes had been in charge. All of Anheuser-Busch's major rivals had made huge consolidation plays of their own, with SABMiller and InBev aggressively leading the charge, and Anheuser had been left standing alone on the dock.

The most frustrating thing for The Fourth and his management team was that the problem they now had to fix—Anheuser-Busch's woefully inadequate global strategy—was a problem his father had spent nearly three decades creating. After The Third reached his life's goal and seized half of the U.S. beer market, Anheuser-Busch had run into a significant dilemma. What came next? The Third had trained his eyes so unflinchingly on crushing Miller in America that he seemed either blind to what was going on in the rest of the world or simply uninterested. That hubris—that callous disregard for Anheuser-Busch's global competition—now looked foolish and small-minded.

The Third had faced a critical choice during his tenure. If Anheuser-Busch wanted to keep growing, it needed to either expand into other countries or start producing other types of consumer goods, molding itself into a company more along the lines of Philip Morris. Rather than picking one of those avenues and sprinting down it with vigor, the risk-averse August III took baby steps in both directions.

■ ■ ■

In 1982, Anheuser-Busch made its first major foray into other types of consumer products, purchasing Campbell Taggart, the second-largest bakery in the United States, and creating the Eagle Snacks food unit. Anheuser's executives thought they understood the bakery and snacks businesses because they dealt in simple, store-delivered products. They figured their wholesalers would want to branch out and start delivering bags of pretzels and loaves of bread to the same stores that were already ordering beer. Campbell Taggart's profits plunged, though, and despite Pat Stokes's best efforts, the operation never really recovered.

"We felt we understood store door delivered products," said a former top executive. "We thought our wholesalers would like it, but it just didn't work out. It went into a cyclical down period, and we ended up holding the bag on something that fell far short of our forecasts." Jerry Ritter, Anheuser's chief financial officer at the time, admitted that the purchase of Campbell Taggart was made in haste and was overpriced, despite The Third's propensity toward heavily evaluating such decisions. August III even admitted he didn't understand the business as well as he should have. "We made our share of mistakes, but we are now quite optimistic," he said.

One of the few deals Anheuser-Busch did right as it attempted to diversify—its $1.1 billion purchase of Harcourt Brace Jovanovich's Sea World theme park properties in 1989—looked like a comedy of errors at first. Anheuser paid roughly 50 percent more than people had expected it would, and after the costly deal was inked, it became clear that the rights to Shamu, the famously recognizable killer whale character that drives attendance at Sea World each year, were still owned by a tiny California-based animation company. Anheuser had to shell out another $6 million, and a good deal of pride, to lock up Shamu.

To an extent, Anheuser's decision to dabble in areas like theme parks, bakeries, and snacks made perfect sense. Those businesses helped deflect criticism and attempted to minimize the risk it ran as a purely beer-centric company. As one former executive explained, "If you're in the theme park business, you can positively impact millions of consumers every day and tell them what a great company you are in a way that has nothing to do with alcohol."

Yet from a financial perspective, nothing else compared to the way Anheuser was minting money as it brewed beer. People simply weren't willing to pay the same markup on pretzels that they'd pay for beer. So Anheuser-Busch spun off Campbell Taggart and Eagle in 1996 and retreated back into its former role as a pure-play beer company, now with some theme parks on the side.

"The other companies weren't making the return on investment that the beer company was making, and held to that standard they didn't compare favorably," said one former executive. "It would have been hard to match the return on investment the beer company was generating. I don't care what business you were in. They were probably held up to an unrealistic benchmark."

All of the hours Anheuser's top executives spent chasing diversions like snack food and hot dog buns hurt the company where it needed help the most—brewing and selling beer in other countries. Unlike most consumer goods giants, Anheuser-Busch didn't employ a raft of worldly, well-traveled staffers who had strong views on its global growth strategy. Rather, The Third sometimes used the international unit as a place to park employees who didn't meet his standards elsewhere.

"There was nobody in the company that had any real foreign experience," said Rick Hill, Anheuser's former assistant treasurer, who is now an investment advisor to many former Anheuser executives in St. Louis. "Even the people in charge of international brewing were Americans; they didn't speak any foreign languages."

"As a young person looking to the future of the company, and looking at what other companies were doing internationally, their approach was just crazy," added Buddy Reisinger, his business partner, who worked for Anheuser-Busch for more than a decade. "A lot of times, it was totally discouraged. What the hell would you want to work overseas for?"

"I bet 90 percent of the employees came from south of Highway 40, out to 270, and to the river," Reisinger added, mapping out a patch of turf south and west of downtown St. Louis.

■ ■ ■

Anheuser-Busch missed out on several global expansion opportunities thanks to The Third's overly cautious insularity. He passed up repeated chances to cut deals that would have redrawn the global beer industry's map and protected Anheuser-Busch against takeovers. And he burned some bridges in the process that proved impossible to rebuild.

Anheuser–Busch tried repeatedly, for instance, to launch Budweiser in South Africa in the 1990s. Although local beer leader South African Breweries was the only company Anheuser trusted to brew Budweiser on site, SAB chief Graham Mackay wasn't interested. Mackay and The Third continued to see each other on occasion. Mackay visited Anheuser in the United States in the early 1990s, when South Africa was on America's blackball list for operating under the rule of apartheid. And on their occasional trips to South Africa, Anheuser's top international executives would usually visit with him.

On the most memorable one of those jaunts, which occurred when Anheuser was loosely considering SAB as an acquisition target, August III traveled to Africa with Jack Purnell and John Jacob, who was head of the National Urban League and an Anheuser board member. SAB didn't rank high on Anheuser's takeover list at the time because its sales were so heavily concentrated in one region, but Anheuser nonetheless felt a "get-acquainted" trip was warranted.

The trip helped reinforce that there wasn't enough chemistry between The Third and Mackay to serve as the backbone for an acquisition. Mackay was impressive and self-confident, but a bit too arrogant in Anheuser's view. "That doesn't mean he's a bad person," said one person close to the company. "I think he was justifiably self-confident. But anyway, that's the way he comes across. You're not going to see smiles." Anheuser's trio toured a few SAB breweries during its stay and even met for two hours with Nelson Mandela, who was angling to recruit more companies to invest in South Africa.

On the way back, the Anheuser executives were planning to stop in Munich so August III could give a speech at a huge brewers' conclave. But when their jet crossed into Zambian airspace, air traffic controllers said it lacked clearance to proceed and instructed it to either land or turn around. The notion of dropping into Zambia unannounced wasn't particularly appetizing, so they banked and returned to South Africa to secure the clearance they needed. Purnell, realizing they weren't going to make it to Munich that night, called his secretary in St. Louis from the airport tarmac and told her to summon Abercrombie & Kent, the ultra-luxe vacation provider, to book anything they might have available for the night between South Africa and Germany.

Abercrombie told the Anheuser executives to drop down for the night in Luxor, where half a dozen fez-topped Egyptians dressed in purple spilled out of a minibus to greet them when they landed. They bunked down that night in one of the city's grandest hotels, confident their trip had been a rousing success.

The feeling wasn't mutual. The Third hadn't made a particularly strong impression on his colleagues in South Africa. SAB's team had been planning to take its American guests to Soweto, a poor black township near Johannesburg where some of the key uprisings against apartheid had occurred. When The Third's ever-present security guards heard of the plans, however, they refused to let him go. So while the rest of the group, including other members of Anheuser-Busch's team, spent part of the day learning about the wrenching Soweto Uprising, The Third stayed back to keep out of harm's way.

Mackay thought his American counterpart was a shy, insecure, and somewhat strange man, and their run-in in Africa wasn't the only uncomfortable moment suffered between the two chief executives.

In the late 1990s, a minority stake in SAB that was owned by a company called Bevcon came up for sale. Goldman Sachs was running the auction process, and there was talk that whoever bought the small stake would garner a disproportionately large amount of control over SAB.

Anheuser-Busch expressed interest in a deal, so The Third and Mackay both flew their teams all the way to London for a meeting. Before Mackay and his deputies had even settled into their chairs, The Third, who was never one for customary pleasantries, launched abruptly into his proposal. He wanted control of the whole company if he did the deal, The Third said, snapping his fingers at one point to summon Purnell, who was standing behind him, in search of a missing piece of information. Control of SAB was more than Mackay was willing to grant, especially straight out of the gate, and he sat back in his chair, balking at The Third's audaciousness and reasoning to himself that there was probably room for negotiation. The Third wasn't interested in compromise. He assessed Mackay's response, thanked the SAB team for their time, and then left them sitting at the table, stunned, just minutes after the meeting had begun.

At the Munich brewers' conclave in 1997, The Third, as head of the world's largest beer company, admitted he had been late to the game on international expansion. "Due to the profit potential of the U.S. market," he said in his keynote speech, "we did not start exploration of the international market until 1980." He then pledged to focus on building international partnerships. "Our goal is to build Budweiser into a global brand," he said. "The globalization of American culture is also good for Bud."

He continued to drag his feet after acknowledging those missteps. SAB, on the other hand, didn't sit around waiting for the Americans to change their minds—it morphed from a backwater brewer in the developing world into a top global player within just a decade. After SAB won more freedom to expand when South Africa held its first its democratic elections in 1994, it hit newly developing markets in Eastern Europe hard—heavy-drinking territories like Hungary, Poland, and the Czech Republic—and moved its headquarters to London in 1999. In 2002, the brewer Anheuser-Busch had dismissed years earlier for being too South Africa–centric inked the audacious deal that hit Anheuser right in the gut—its $5.6 billion purchase of Miller. The move gave SAB immediate and sweeping access to the United States, the world's most profitable beer market, and rooted it deep into Anheuser's backyard. With that deal, SABMiller became the world's second-largest beer company behind Anheuser-Busch.

■ ■ ■

The Third continued to take tiny, defensive bites at the apple throughout the 1980s and 1990s. He weighed the possibility of a leveraged buyout in the early 1980s when buyouts were all the rage, but nothing happened. He cut a licensing deal in 1980 to have Labatt brew Budweiser in Canada rather than buying Labatt outright, leaving the Canadian brewer ripe for a takeover by Interbrew 15 years later. In 1986, he cut a similar deal with Guinness to brew and sell Budweiser in Ireland, allowing Guinness to later merge into beverage giant Diageo. Anheuser-Busch partnered up with Birra Peroni in 1993 to distribute Budweiser in Italy, with Kirin that same year to brew it in Japan, with Grupo Damm in 1995 to brew it in Spain, and with Kronenbourg in 1996 to brew it in France. By the late 1990s, it was obvious that the beer industry's growth was going to come outside the United States. The Third's rivals were snapping up assets left and right by then, and prices had skyrocketed.

"The company became sort of isolated, with some partial ownerships," said one former executive. "Some of these decisions should have been made in the 1980s and early '90s. The company had plenty of opportunities back then to reach out."

"We could claim globalization, but he did it on the cheap," said a person close to the company. "I think it may have been the case where having his name on the door made him less open to taking the kind of risks it would have taken to have gone global. A bigger thinker would have seen that coming."

"Part of it was that we were already the world's biggest brewer," this person said. "I don't think he ever saw the threat coming from the outside. I think he was always looking more toward the inside. For whatever reason, The Third didn't want to take that level of risk. It'll be one of those things he'll take to his grave."

Of all of Anheuser-Busch's missed opportunities, the most fateful was a chance The Third had to snuff out InBev before it was ever created. In the early 1990s, Anheuser decided it wanted to partner up with one of the two top brewers in Brazil in order to launch Budweiser in the fast-growing country. It interviewed top Brazilian brewer Brahma and its second-largest competitor, Antarctica, and eventually entered into negotiations with both to see which would offer the better deal.

Brahma was headed by a powerful trio of investment bankers— Marcel Telles, Carlos Alberto da Veiga Sicupira, and Jorge Paulo Lemann, the most famous banker in Brazil, who was as well known for the foiled 1999 attempted kidnapping of three of his children as he was for his professional successes. Two gunmen had unleashed a torrent of point-blank bullets at the driver of his children's sedan, but the heavily armored car saved their lives. Lemann moved his family shortly thereafter to Switzerland, his father's country of origin.

The reclusive Lemann and his two partners had taken control of Brahma in 1989 after selling Garantia, an investment bank that was known as "Brazil's Goldman Sachs," to Credit Suisse First Boston for $675 million. They funneled a fraction of that cash into their new beer endeavor. Telles became Brahma's chairman and chief executive officer, and the three men infused sleepy Brahma with their own competitive brand of banking culture.

Brahma's trio of bankers proved to be tough negotiators, so Anheuser-Busch went with the easier route in 1994 and bought a minority interest in second-ranked Antarctica instead. The partnership progressed along smoothly for several years until Brahma reappeared and stunned The Third and the rest of his team by making a bid to buy Antarctica outright. Anheuser-Busch analyzed the situation and concluded that the Brazilian authorities would never let the deal close for antitrust reasons—it would merge the country's top two brewers into one that held huge regional power and influence.

They were wrong.

Brahma won clearance for the deal and merged with Antarctica in 1999 to create AmBev. Under the trio of bankers' leadership, AmBev took off like a rocket.

The Third woefully misjudged what he was up against in Brazil, though he was given several chances to help steer AmBev's course. By the mid-1990s, growth-hungry Telles and Lemann had developed a sweeping vision for the future of the global beer industry, and they invited The Third to be part of the plan. Telles, who had spent some time with Lemann, The Third, and Purnell during a 1991 meet-and-greet trip to Busch Gardens in Williamsburg, Virginia, called to request another meeting, this time in St. Louis. He showed up at Anheuser's headquarters alone, clutching a bold proposition.

"Let's form the Coca-Cola of beer," he said to The Third and Purnell, explaining that if Brahma, Antarctica, and Anheuser-Busch merged, the combined company would have a lock on the North and South American beer markets.

"It was about a vision of the future in the Americas, where they would make a lot of the calls in other countries and we would make the calls in the U.S.," said Purnell. "It was a merger proposal; it was a "Let's get married, we can do better together than we can alone.'"

The Third and Purnell had never encountered anyone with such grand ambitions. Telles's supreme self-confidence—the sense of manifest destiny he radiated—was off-putting to the two St. Louisans, who still felt they were learning the ropes on the international front. Telles's pitch made it clear that he was way out in front of them.

"This proposal did not appeal to August," Purnell said. The Third couldn't stomach the concept of a tie-up that would put the Brazilians in charge outside the United States. So when Brahma and Antarctica decided to join forces, Anheuser-Busch backed itself out of the situation.

"That turned out to have been a fateful—I won't say 'fatal,' but rather a 'fateful'—decision," Purnell said. "We ended up exercising our "put" in Antarctica rather than joining their consolidated board. They then acquired Labatt in Canada, then went over to Europe, and then finally came back to make their offer for A-B."

■ ■ ■

The Third seemed to exert almost as much effort finding ways to avoid doing deals as he would have if they had actually happened. On the few occasions when transactions got close to the finish line, Anheuser's team would come back at the 11th hour and ask for a lower price or better terms. If they got what they asked for, they would turn around and ask for a little more—and then a little more, until the other party finally refused to budge and the whole thing fell apart.

"He was always trying to strike a deal that completely benefited A-B," said a former strategy committee member. "That killed more deals. There was always that little provision that tilted our way that absolutely prevented it from ever going outside the boardroom. That was a classic way of stopping everything."

"We couldn't roll the dice unless someone was willing to sell us a crown jewel at a low price, risk-free, which for some reason no one was willing to do," said former executive Bill Finnie, with an ample dose of sarcasm.

Rather than buying important assets, The Third and the rest of Anheuser's old guard fell into the habit of finding ways to justify standing still. There always seemed to be a reason why each of the assets simply wasn't good enough for Anheuser-Busch. It was "a cult of admiration," one company advisor said. "It was like a mutual admiration society." They'd criticize rivals for doing deals that belied their global ambitions, only to realize down the line that the deals had proven successful. "We didn't have long range corporate planning at all," said one former executive, who criticized Anheuser's corporate planning staff for being in The Third's back pocket. "We just didn't have it."

"We'd sit there and ridicule Coors for going into the UK, ridicule SAB for buying a stake in Miller," the executive said. "How do you keep criticizing people like this? How do you look at every deal like it can't work, it can't work, it can't work? It's working!"

Former director John Jacob stepped forward out of frustration during one meeting and asked, "How is it that we can never justify buying anybody, yet we belittle anybody else who has bought somebody? And then a year later, we sit here and realize that now they're making money?"

"He asked these types of pointed questions for about a year or year and a half until he gave up," said one of his former colleagues.

"We just coasted for fifteen years because we were so strong. And it caught up with us," agreed Bill Finnie, referring to the late 1980s and 1990s. "They really didn't have a strategy for about a decade or a decade and a half."

To The Third's credit, there were legitimate arguments against some of these deals. The decision to expand into nascent emerging markets wasn't a no-brainer. The two giant brewers that successfully did so—SABMiller out of South Africa and InBev out of Brazil—had no alternative. They started out there.

"When you have a business that was as profitable as his was, where the returns are as strong as his were, I'm not sure anyone would have been so smart to say, 'We've got to take over the world,'" said one Anheuser-Busch advisor. "We understand now why he should have, but it would have diluted his margins and diluted his returns. So it wasn't obvious. I think it's hard to criticize him for that, though it's very easy with hindsight."

The Third had his staffers run the numbers on a range of dealmaking possibilities over and over again. They considered everything under the sun. The verdict was usually the same. Why would Anheuser want to sink money into some risky foreign brewer when it could generate far more bang for the buck by investing its cash in the United States? International expansion didn't seem to make much sense at the time, at least in the short run.

"When evaluating other businesses relative to the U.S. beer business . . . almost any other investment paled by comparison," explained one former top Anheuser-Busch executive. "Now, there comes a point where you have to think beyond next year or three years and say, "In ten years, the map is going to be global, it's not going to be domestic, and these other companies are expanding. I need to position myself for that eventuality by making decisions today that might hurt the short-term return on investment, but are smart overall."

The Third had a strong aversion, in particular, to taking on too much debt, which would have been a requirement for any takeovers of size. The global financial crisis that started in 2007 showed the hazards of excess debt, and many companies whose top executives were less cautious than The Third became part of the wreckage. August III's aversion to risk, however—both financial and operational—limited Anheuser-Busch's growth opportunities. He preferred to reinvest the boatloads of cash Anheuser churned out each year back into his business.

"That's the part that just doesn't connect to me," said a former executive who watched The Third shelve a long string of potential transactions. "As smart of a finance guy as he was, he knew he had enough money to pull off these deals. A-B was flush with cash."

"A-B was not only better financed, it was the largest brewer in the world at the time," said beer industry scribe Harry Schuhmacher. "They could have easily stretched its balance sheet a little bit to get those deals done, but they were unwilling to do it."

Getting the numbers to work wasn't the only obstacle on the international front. The Third was a control freak of the highest order, and it was impossible to imagine that anyone could run an Anheuser-Busch operation abroad with the same oversight and intensity he showed in St. Louis. In many cases over the years, his rigid dedication to quality paid off. It didn't make it easy to find suitable takeover targets, though—or the people to run them.

"It was clear to me he couldn't go beyond the U.S." said Rick Hill. "He was not a very good partner with anybody. We would be a minority partner, but August could never say, 'You know the market better than I do, you run it.' He was a hard guy to deal with, I'm sure, for the minority partners. He was that kind of guy, though. He had strong principles."

Rather than contract brewing beer on location in Asia, for instance, Anheuser used to ship beer in sealed containers from the United States all the way to Japan. It gave the Japanese a taste of the real King of Beers, but the costs were huge.

"We never had any respect for anybody else's ability to make beer," said one former executive. "We didn't trust anyone. We didn't trust consultants, we didn't trust advisors. We only trusted one man's opinion on what we should do or shouldn't do."

■ ■ ■

While The Third had a talent for seeming to be everywhere at once, even he couldn't have it both ways when it came to global expansion. He couldn't possibly command operations in other countries the way he did in St. Louis, with his hands in every pot. Still, the alternative—easing back and letting someone else have day-to-day control of foreign assets—made him too uncomfortable.

The Third preferred to default to the same triggers that had always yielded growth for Anheuser-Busch—focusing on advertising and brewing consistent beer. The usual triggers weren't going to cut it anymore though. To compete in the new, globalized brewing market, Anheuser-Busch needed economies of scale—the cost savings big companies can generate relative to their smaller counterparts. While its rivals grew into brewing behemoths, Anheuser-Busch engineered its own destruction by becoming overly dependent on American consumers and turning its back on hundreds of millions of increasingly affluent drinkers around the world.

"We were quite aware that we went from being the largest brewer in the world to a company that looked up to InBev," said Douglas A. "Sandy" Warner III, the former chairman of J.P. Morgan Chase and one of Anheuser-Busch's most powerful board members. "I remember like it was yesterday sitting in the boardroom, and somebody saying, "Are we comfortable that in the process of the decisions we're taking . . . our relative size and scale is diminishing? Are we comfortable about that? Because that has implications. And we were. I think that was unanimous. We felt we were doing the right thing."

"The Third screwed the whole company up," said one Anheuser-Busch advisor. "Remember, InBev was 'this' big, SAB was 'this' big, and they were 'this' big," he said, spreading his hands farther and farther apart as he named each brewer. "Anheuser stayed that big. Remember, the first deal that AmBev, the Brazilians, tried to do was a merger with Anheuser-Busch way back when, and he threw them out. They then went and did the Interbrew deal. He never globalized. He turned down every single opportunity."

■ ■ ■

In 2004, Anheuser-Busch, whose employees had long boasted about working for the world's largest brewer, abruptly lost that title. AmBev, whose proposals for global domination Anheuser had shunned, announced that March that it would merge with Belgian brewing giant Interbrew in an $11.4 billion deal to create the world's top brewer by volume. SABMiller outstripped Anheuser in size not long afterward.

Anheuser-Busch's strategy committee, which had started debating the merits of a big acquisition years earlier, began to actively argue over whether they needed to merge with another brewer, and its meetings grew heated and contentious. "It all happened at once," said one committee member. "It was just amazing in those strategy committee meetings, because people were just blaming everybody."

Anheuser's executives started tossing around a range of options, all of which had been run over ad nauseam in the past. Some wanted to buy SABMiller. That would require a huge pile of debt—if SABMiller's Mackay was even willing to hop on board. Others focused on whether they could buy the rest of Grupo Modelo, the Mexican brewer in which Anheuser-Busch had already amassed a half-stake. However, the Modelo people disliked August III and much of the rest of the old guard at Anheuser-Busch. They even considered a merger with Dutch brewer Heineken, but dealing with the Heineken family was too complicated. The Third hadn't left his son a whole lot to work with.

He should have employed "an M&A strategy that had built up the business more and was more global," said one advisor to the company. "They were so limited in terms of international scope and the cost structure. It wasn't just The Fourth who did this. If anything, The Fourth came in and tried to be more forward-leaning, and The Third didn't want him to be."

"I got the sense that he was always trying to goad his father into doing more internationally, and his father would say, 'That's not your purview,'" said Harry Schuhmacher. "Your responsibility is the United States."

As Anheuser-Busch began searching for ways to play catch-up, China was an obvious answer. The Third had recognized China as a fast-growing and lucrative market, but his investments there had been cautious. Anheuser owned a tiny stake in Tsingtao, and it had also started brewing Budweiser locally in 1995 after buying a majority interest in China's Wuhan International Brewery. So in 2002, with Pat Stokes at the helm, the company decided to ramp up its exposure to China by cutting a deal to slowly raise its Tsingtao stake from 4.5 percent to 27 percent. The price Anheuser paid was rich for the limited amount of additional authority it won—the Chinese government remained Tsingtao's largest shareholder. Tsingtao was something people could hang their hats on in St. Louis, however, and it emboldened the company for when Harbin Brewery, China's fourth-biggest brewer at the time, came up for grabs in 2004. In an uncharacteristic move that indicated Anheuser-Busch had set aside some of its reticence, it won a month-long takeover battle for Harbin after SABMiller withdrew from the bidding. Victory didn't come cheaply, however. SABMiller already owned a significant stake in Harbin, and Anheuser had to pay off both SABMiller and Harbin's other shareholders at an inflated price to acquire the shares it didn't already own.

Even after showing aggression in the Harbin battle, Anheuser couldn't catch a break from those who felt it was already too far behind. "China was, like, an accident," one advisor to the company said. "A relatively small piece of the business."

"They just completely missed the boat when eastern Europe opened up, and when there was growth in Latin America," said Harry Schuhmacher. "They did have an early cue in China, but as far as the rest of the world, it really allowed SABMiller and then later InBev to just take all of those opportunities. That was just the culture. It was a Midwestern culture of conservatism, insularity and cronyism. It started to open up when August Busch IV rose through the ranks."

Unfortunately, The Fourth's efforts were too little, and way too late. By mid-2008 when InBev made its approach, the results of Anheuser-Busch's decades of expansionary paralysis were visibly clear. On a glass map of the world that hung in the lobby of the company's executive offices in St. Louis, an array of tiny lights scattered across the screen were meant to signify the breadth and reach of its facilities around the world. The United States and China were well illuminated, but most of the rest of the map remained pitch black.

Chapter 7

A Babe in the Woods

He was like Bambi, like a deer in the headlights.

—Advisor to Anheuser-Busch

A s The Fourth started to reach out to some of the parties his father had alienated over the years once he became CEO, it became apparent that he was operating with one hand tied behind his back, and his own father had fastened the knot. The Third hadn't fully loosened his grip on the company's scepter. A full year after his son took over, The Third remained an imposing presence at the company. He was still visiting wholesalers, causing confusion about who they should interact with at the mother ship, and he only moved out of his office at Anheuser-Busch headquarters at the end of 2007 when the board forced both him and Pat Stokes out of the building.

"A succession from a strong CEO, let's say Jack Welch to Jeff Immelt, is hard," said board member Sandy Warner in reference to General Electric, where he also served as a director. "In the case of

Immelt and Welch, which I've lived through, Welch hasn't been in the building once since he retired as CEO."

"August Busch III kept his office," Warner said. "Never moved his office. So it's hard to start when you succeed a brilliant, successful, long-term CEO. It's doubly hard when the guy is still on the board, still in his seat, still in the same place everybody has been used to for over 20 years . . . Then add to that that he's your father, and you've created an absolutely impossible situation."

"He knew that company from the lowest employee to the highest, and all of the procedures and processes. I think it was difficult to let go," said fellow board member Ambassador Jones. "I think there were some judgment calls and management decisions that The Third didn't agree with, and some he disagreed with more vehemently than others."

The Fourth had won the promotion he had always aspired to. When he pulled a business card out of his wallet and read the title, that's what it said—Chief Executive. He never felt like he was really in charge, though. It was maddening. As one former strategy committee member said, "I can't remember the titles we all had, because the reality was that August III was always there."

August IV was concerned that Anheuser-Busch was vulnerable to a takeover, however, and he was desperate to convey his growing sense of uneasiness and urgency to his colleagues.

During a meeting with The Fourth and Anheuser Chief Financial Officer Randy Baker in St. Louis not long into The Fourth's tenure, a high-ranking Citigroup banker named Leon Kalvaria ran through a list of dangers Anheuser-Busch faced at the hands of its rivals. Kalvaria's ties to the beer industry ran deep—he had advised Lemann, Telles, Sicupira, and the other Brazilians at AmBev during their merger with Interbrew, and had watched as the Brazilians asserted control over the operation and ousted John Brock, Interbrew's CEO. Kalvaria had also worked with SABMiller several times, both when it took a majority stake in Italy's Peroni in 2003 and when it bought Grupo Empresarial Bavaria, Colombia's largest brewer, for $7.8 billion in 2005. After working for so many years in the brewing space and spending so much time with its top executives, he knew what made each of Anheuser's competitors tick and where they had stashed any skeletons in their closets.

Kalvaria's warnings were enough to compel August IV to invite Citigroup, Goldman Sachs, J.P. Morgan, and some other Wall Street bankers down to Cancun, Mexico, a few months later, on February 7, 2007, to present their views to a group of Anheuser executives. August IV encouraged the bankers to get creative, hoping that they would help light a fire beneath his troops.

It had been nearly a year and a half since Wilma, a Category Five hurricane, had smashed into Cancun, wiping out cruise ship piers, flattening hotels, and washing away entire beaches. Much of the area had been rebuilt and was just starting to seem functional again. Rainstorms passing through town that week, however, had knocked down branches and soaked the grounds around the Ritz Carlton, where the beer executives were assembling. It made for a treacherous morning jog for Goldman Sachs's Tim Ingrassia, but he needed to clear his head ahead of what was bound to be an interesting gathering.

While Goldman Sachs now stood in Anheuser's good graces, its history with Anheuser-Busch was messy and complicated. The bank and the brewer had been close through the 1990s, but the trouble with Anheuser-Busch from Goldman's perspective was that it rarely executed the types of transactions that paid the best fees—large mergers and acquisitions. By mid-2001, when the German brewer of Beck's beer came up for sale in an auction Goldman was running, the two companies' relationship had waned, and Byron Trott, who later became a household name for being Warren Buffett's favorite banker, was working to maintain Goldman's relationship with Anheuser-Busch out of Goldman's Chicago office.

Anheuser submitted a first-round bid for Beck's, but the offer was so low that Goldman dropped Anheuser from the second round of bidding. August III was furious.

"He decided Goldman was a bunch of jerks, but really, they just didn't bid enough," said a person with knowledge of that deal. "The thought was that this would just blow over," said another person close to the saga. "But The Third can hold a grudge. What we heard in hindsight is that the message went out: Goldman Sachs is not welcome here."

It took that soured relationship years to recover, and in the interim, responsibility for covering Anheuser-Busch passed through several reluctant Goldman bankers before falling in the lap of Peter Gross. Gross had a reputation for persevering in the face of all sorts of difficulty, but Anheuser-Busch was a tough nut to crack. His firm had offended August III so deeply that the response when he called the company was: "Don't even bother calling here. No one will talk to anybody from Goldman Sachs."

Gross shifted strategies. He apologized to CFO Randy Baker for anything Goldman had done to upset the company and decided to focus his efforts on Anheuser's efforts overseas, including one particular burr in its saddle: its century-long battle with tiny Czech brewer Budejovicky Budvar, which also claims to produce the world's only genuine Budweiser beer. Gross even helped set up a meeting for August IV in Prague with the prime minister of the Czech Republic at the time.

Goldman wasn't able to solve the Budvar problem. But by spending so much time on a niggling issue—and by strategically avoiding run-ins with a still-bitter August III while doing so—he ingratiated himself enough to pull Goldman back toward relevance and into a relationship with The Fourth. The Fourth seemed to trust that Gross, after all the time he had spent on mundane issues, would offer the best advice he could.

■ ■ ■

The night they arrived in Cancun, Gross and Ingrassia joined another handful of bankers who had flown in from New York, along with roughly 20 Anheuser executives, for cocktails and dinner at the Ritz. Some of the bankers showed up expecting a relatively private audience with Anheuser's top executives, but they arrived at the Ritz's bar to find themselves surrounded by the same competitors they ran into at New York's popular watering holes. It was the first time some of them realized they would be making their pitches against so many competitors the next day. It had all the makings, in Wall Street parlance, of a "beauty pageant."

"It was all people I know, so nothing about it was awkward," said one of the bankers in attendance. "But I don't know if any of us thought necessarily that we were showing up to drink with each other."

The next morning, as they watched roughly a hundred of the company's top managers settle into their seats in the hotel ballroom, the bankers also realized they weren't going to be making intimate presentations to a selected audience of Anheuser-Busch executives. Large multimedia screens had been set up at the front of the room to make for easy viewing of PowerPoint slides, and it seemed like half the company had relocated to Mexico for the festivities.

The bankers made their 90-minute pitches one team at a time, and they each pounded on similar messages. The dispatches from Goldman and Citigroup were the hardest-hitting. Kalvaria and his Citigroup colleagues Jeffrey Schackner and John Boord spent a few minutes shooting down the notion that Anheuser-Busch should develop liquor brands, an idea that had consumed some of August IV's time, and then decried the excuses Anheuser had been using to explain why its business was flatlining. The company had been slapping away such questions rather than addressing them, blaming everything from their competitors' new can designs to the maturing U.S. market. During one board meeting, sales and wholesaling executive Evan Athanas showed a slide that indicated sales of Bud Light were suffering heavily against Coors Light. With little reaction from the audience, Athanas was just about to move to the next slide when board member James Forese interjected.

"Wait a minute—why is this happening?" Forese said, glancing around the room in wonderment to see whether anyone else was bothered by the company's flagging performance.

Coors had introduced a new, vented wide-mouth can for Coors Light, Athanas replied offhandedly—it was all a gimmick, really. The explanation seemed to suffice for many of the other executives in the room.

"It may be a gimmick, but our market share is tanking!" Forese said, perplexed as to why no one else saw this as cause for concern. "Shouldn't we dwell on this for a minute? We're getting slaughtered here!"

Citigroup's team reinforced that concern in Cancun. "If you can't grow the beer market in the U.S., why are Corona and Sam Adams making hay in your backyard?" they asked. Kalvaria focused on one slide in particular that showed that Mexico's Modelo was accounting for much of Anheuser's growth, and the dynamic in the room grew briefly uncomfortable—Modelo chief Carlos Fernández, a member of Anheuser-Busch's board, was sitting in the crowd. Then the Citigroup team pitched the deals they felt Anheuser should consider: They could buy the rest of Modelo, and InBev was a natural fit. InBev, however, which was swelling in size and already closely controlled by a small group of shareholders, wasn't likely to surrender its independence.

Goldman's Gross and Ingrassia were next, and they came out swinging. If Anheuser-Busch didn't make some significant changes, Gross said, it was just a matter of time before InBev came knocking. They had one and a half to two years before InBev would attempt a takeover, he and Ingrassia predicted, surveying the room to make sure the first few bars of their presentation were ringing home. It appeared they were. The dozen or so members of the strategy committee had heard this warning a million times. The rest of the room seemed startled. "If you stand on a perch as lofty as Anheuser-Busch, it's very hard to also consider yourself vulnerable," said one person who was there that day. So the bankers went on.

Even if InBev didn't turn predator, they said, Anheuser-Busch was still a sitting duck for activist shareholders. It was a wildly successful and well-positioned company that had let its massive advantages slip away in recent years. While Anheuser's executives blamed the company's stagnant earnings on the high prices of commodities, Coke and Pepsi—which were also in the business of wrapping metal around a liquid and selling it to customers—were growing, as were the world's other brewers.

"If InBev and SABMiller keep doing what they're doing, you're going to be picked off," Ingrassia said, while noting that for now, Anheuser-Busch still made more money and more beer than anybody else in the world. "If you don't take control of it, others will."

That day stands out in several Anheuser staffers' minds as the moment in which sentiment shifted. Anheuser's corporate planning committee had evaluated whether InBev could buy Anheuser and had ruled that the Brazilians wouldn't be able to pull off a deal. Those assurances had soothed some of the company's top executives. Others felt Anheuser's planning group was out of its league on this one, and still too beholden to The Third. Asking a group of subordinates to determine whether you're vulnerable is akin to "asking my wife if I'm handsome," said one of Anheuser's advisors. "If you only ask certain people, you're going to hear what you want to hear." With Anheuser in transition under a new CEO, the bankers made it clear in Mexico that InBev might pounce.

"I think that was an epiphany for a lot of people," said a strategy committee member who was hit particularly hard by the warnings. "There had always been a lot of work done around 'Who could possibly buy the company?' That it was outrageous that someone would come in and buy Anheuser-Busch. There was a certain level of thinking that it just wasn't possible, that no one could possibly afford it."

"That's when we began talking earnestly about how we needed to address the bigger picture," the executive said. "There was broad recognition across the management team that it was time for us to move forward and make some fundamental changes in the way we did things."

Those changes were going to have to involve buckling down like never before to slash the company's bloated costs. Several bankers had chastised the group for taking its eye off the ball and ignoring the need to keep costs low.

"A well-run A-B would have been bid-proof—that's what we told them in Cancun," said one of the bankers who presented that day. "They were the biggest, baddest guys in the biggest profit pool: the U.S. That's why everybody wants to be here. It's the biggest profit pool in the world."

"They were losing market share to their competitors, who didn't have all of the advantages they had. They lived in their little microcosm as the real world was developing around them. The company had so much money that they became fat and happy. And they underestimated the threats to their business and their organization."

Some of the bankers had deliberately avoided preaching that a big merger would solve Anheuser's problems—they knew it would look like they were shilling for business. Many of the company's staffers still felt like they had been slapped in the face by Wall Street honchos whose bonuses depended on their ability to conjure up deals.

"It was a very good discussion, because we were a very insular company and we had never really had that kind of frank discussion," said one strategy committee member. "But August brings these guys in, and each gives us a scenario that's worse than the other. 'You're going to be taken over if you don't do this.' Those guys all come in with a grin and say, 'I did the Cheerios deal,' and you're all rolling your eyes and going, 'We get it.' The message really angered a lot of us because all of these guys from Wall Street come in and tell you, 'You're doomed. You're going to be taken over. However, here's where we can help you! You should buy these guys, you should do this . . . the clock is ticking!' "

Such sniping and resentment was pointless to another top executive, however, who said Anheuser was already half-dead in the water by the time the group landed in Cancun. Anyone who first realized that InBev was a threat while sitting in that ballroom had been deluding themselves, the executive said. It had been clear for years. Whether the group from St. Louis cared for the bankers' persuasive tactics or not, they were right.

"It was arrogance that caused us to ignore them for so long."

■ ■ ■

That same arrogance allowed the fire that had been stoked in people's bellies down in Mexico to cool over time. After a few months passed and none of their competitors tried anything sinister, many of the company's executives returned to business as usual. "If you know a threat is coming, recognition is one thing. But you've got to then act on it," said one advisor to the company. "There's a big difference in life between recognizing a potential threat and truly addressing the possibility of it and acting accordingly."

"I think if we were to all look back, we would probably all agree we would prefer to have acted on some of these things sooner."

August IV did make a few moves in that direction. After Cancun, he hired Goldman and Citigroup and looped in Skadden, the company's longtime corporate law firm, to evaluate Anheuser's options and defend it against unwanted advances. The team kicked quickly into gear with a review that lasted roughly half a year. The Fourth also paired Anheuser CFO Randy Baker up with public relations firm

Kekst and charged him with a mission that was largely kept under wraps: preparing for a potential attack from an activist investor.

When The Third launched into his tirade at the quail hunting plantation in Florida, however, he had a point.

"I was very, very nervous about a whole bunch of banks giving their perspective," said one of the bankers who presented in Cancun. "I was worried they were having too many banks come to talk to them, and I was worried they'd be too honest with too many banks. Some of the banks not selected would be heavily incented to go and shop some of the information they had picked up in a fairly confidential environment."

The Fourth's inclusion of so many banks in Mexico did appear to come back to haunt the company once InBev made its play for Anheuser. J.P. Morgan, whose Cancun presentation didn't click with the audience, wasn't picked to work with Anheuser on its defense strategy. In the end, though, that suited J.P. Morgan just fine. When InBev started hatching its takeover plan roughly a year later, just as the financial markets were starting to disintegrate in the wake of Bear Stearns's collapse, it knew it needed to recruit one or two of the world's strongest banks if it was going to successfully rustle up $40 or $50 billion in financing. The first person InBev looked to was Jamie Dimon, the head of J.P. Morgan, who had just taken control of Bear Stearns and was emerging as one of the U.S. government's favored partners on Wall Street. Dimon was happy to accept such a lucrative piece of business.

"The Third was right," said one of Anheuser-Busch's advisors. "J.P. Morgan didn't get picked and then worked on the other side."

Randy Baker, the company's lean, square-jawed, and generally unflappable chief financial officer, was particularly furious about how the situation played out. J.P. Morgan had been Anheuser's go-to bank for credit for as long as many Anheuser insiders could remember, and just weeks before the firm allied with InBev, its bankers had been out talking to Anheuser-Busch to see how they could be helpful.

Given the two companies' longstanding credit relationship, J.P. Morgan was the bank Anheuser-Busch would have naturally turned to for money if it had wanted to buy the other half of Mexican brewer Modelo. The bank essentially abandoned its relationship to accept a more profitable commission advising InBev. Anheuser's board was livid. Citigroup indicated it was willing to help finance the company when it was hired for strategic advice, which replaced the loss of J.P. Morgan to a degree. J.P. Morgan was the strongest bank out there at the time, and after years of access to its credit, Anheuser-Busch suddenly found the door slammed in its face. With J.P. Morgan's former chief, Sandy Warner, as a key member of Anheuser-Busch's board, it made things even more awkward.

"J.P. had a long historic relationship with Anheuser-Busch and had done a lot of financing for Anheuser-Busch," said one advisor. "I think Anheuser-Busch thought it was incredibly disloyal that J.P. showed up on the InBev side. That being said, to be fair to J.P., they clearly were not asked to be an advisor. J.P. Morgan was incredibly upset that Anheuser-Busch didn't want to use them. And when InBev was looking for a balance sheet . . ."

■ ■ ■

The Fourth, chastised by his father's anger but not deterred, started making an effort in 2007 to show that he was receptive to merger ideas that would give Anheuser-Busch a bigger global presence. He had built up a relationship with Paul Walsh, the chief executive of alcohol beverage giant Diageo, on the board of FedEx. Walsh seemed interested in exploring whether Diageo and Anheuser-Busch could strike up some sort of deal, and the two executives held a series of quiet but deliberate conversations that centered around two different potential transactions.

In one scenario, London-based Diageo would sell Guinness to Anheuser-Busch in exchange for a stake in Anheuser of roughly 20 or 25 percent. Anheuser was lukewarm on the notion of owning Guinness, however, and while that deal was periodically discussed, it never gained significant traction. The two companies also discussed something that would have taken things much further: an all-out merger to meld Anheuser-Busch's beer empire together with Diageo's spirits and wine. Diageo owned some of the world's best-known brands, including Smirnoff vodka, Johnnie Walker whisky, and Captain Morgan rum. In certain aspects, combining those brands with Budweiser, Busch, and Michelob sounded like a brilliant concept.

Brewers and spirits companies have long struggled to find a magic solution that makes merging their businesses worthwhile. Beer and liquor are made, distributed, and marketed differently, so there aren't many ways to combine efforts and save costs. Plus, investors had been valuing liquor companies more richly than brewers, which made for a financial disconnect that was tough to overcome. Anheuser-Busch and Diageo couldn't concoct a recipe that worked.

The connection between the two companies remained alive enough, however, for Citigroup's Kalvaria to reach out to Walsh right after InBev made its takeover bid. Kalvaria asked to hear Walsh's point of view on the offer, listening for a sign that Diageo was interested in being a "white knight" for Anheuser-Busch—someone who could rescue it from InBev. Walsh knew Diageo couldn't offer nearly the same amount of cost savings as InBev could. He was not about to enter a bidding war he would almost certainly lose.

"Forget it," Walsh told Kalvaria. "I'm not going anywhere near this."

As they ran over the company's options in 2007, several top Anheuser-Busch executives continued to favor something even bolder: an all-out merger with global giant SABMiller, which was looking to stay ahead of the pack as the industry continued to consolidate.

That summer, August IV and David Peacock, his close deputy, met SABMiller's Graham Mackay for dinner at the Four Seasons restaurant in New York, which is housed on the ground floor of the Mies van der Rohe–designed Seagram Building on Park Avenue in Manhattan. The Four Seasons' Pool Room, a see-and-be-seen spot for New York's financial and media glitterati, was hardly a discreet setting for high-stakes merger discussions. The dinner was largely meant to help The Fourth and Mackay get to know each other, not to allow for furtive deal-making chatter.

The Fourth and Mackay spent the meal talking about their respective businesses, barely brushing over how they might fit together. After the bill was paid and August IV and Peacock headed out, Mackay and Kalvaria met for a drink at the Four Seasons hotel, where Mackay was staying. Dinner had gone smoothly enough to consider whether to push things further along, but there were some big questions that would need to be answered. What would it look like if the two brewing giants were hammered together? Where would the merged company be based? And who would run it? If Mackay remained CEO, August IV could perhaps run the company's business in the Americas. And despite the spotty history between The Third and Mackay, it might be worth handing August III a role as well. Rather than sticking to SABMiller's home base in London or moving to Anheuser's beloved but inaccessible St. Louis, they could split the difference and be based in New York. The concept was hardly even in its infancy, but Mackay and August IV indicated after that meeting that they were willing to pursue talks further, and the two companies spent more time analyzing a potential deal. It became one of the Anheuser-Busch strategy committee's most commonly talked-about options late that summer.

The key to the deal was how to handle Miller. The U.S. government's antitrust authorities would never allow a merger that joined the country's top two domestic competitors. Still, there seemed to be a simple fix—SABMiller would sell Miller to Molson Coors, the third-largest brewer in the country. It wasn't guaranteed to work from an antitrust perspective, but the companies' advisors felt it would pass muster. That was enough to perk up Anheuser's strategy committee and set its wheels in motion. "There was a flurry of analysis and activity around whether a merger with SABMiller would work or could work, and what it would mean," said one of the company's advisors.

Like most of Anheuser-Busch's dalliances with rivals, though, the SABMiller deal died on the vine. They were both big, proud companies that wanted to play the role of acquirer rather than target, and neither wanted to pay a premium for the other. The constant disconnect between August III and his son also threw cold water on the effort. The Third let The Fourth's management team spin its wheels to evaluate the potential transaction, but some executives never felt that the SABMiller option had any real momentum.

"In effect, I think August IV got pulled back by The Third, saying, 'Don't go down this route here,'" said one person close to the talks. "You had the whole palace coup going on, where most of the people The Fourth liked got fired—which was kind of also right around the end of those discussions," said another.

A strategy committee member agreed, referencing the stalled-out talks with both SABMiller and Diageo. "I don't think it was ever with a plan to go make a deal, because he could never get it past his father.

The bottom line was that nothing could be done without the approval of The Third or the board of directors. It was like, 'You can talk to whomever you want, but I'm not going to allow it to happen.'"

Meanwhile, SABMiller had also been talking about a merger with InBev, and some InBev board members seemed to favor a deal with SABMiller over one with Anheuser-Busch. SABMiller didn't fit quite as well with InBev as Anheuser-Busch did, but a deal with the South Africans could be much easier to execute than one with the unwilling Americans. InBev and SABMiller held a brief round of discussions, but the talks snagged on several significant issues. SABMiller was uncomfortable with the strong controlling position of the families that owned most of InBev and felt its shareholders wouldn't put up with such a structure. InBev, meanwhile, wanted to pay little or no premium.

"SAB's point was 'You know what, if you want to buy the company, give me a price. But we're not going to play with this,'" said one person who was involved in the talks. The discussions wandered off nowhere, and the idea was shelved.

By October of 2007, SABMiller had endured enough puttering around. Five years after buying Miller to get a U.S. foothold, it announced a groundbreaking deal to merge those operations in the United States into a joint venture with Molson Coors that would be called "MillerCoors." The deal joined America's second- and third-largest brewers to create a much stronger competitor to Anheuser-Busch, and was especially painful because Anheuser had scrapped talks with SABMiller only months earlier. Now, SABMiller was pounding down a second stake right in Anheuser's backyard.

Citigroup's Kalvaria quickly called Graham Mackay to see whether Anheuser could tempt him into abandoning the venture or integrating Anheuser into it. "Why did you do this instead of trying to push it further with us?" Kalvaria asked, before pointing out that SABMiller could have it both ways. Anheuser and SAB could still merge and then sell Miller to Molson Coors, just as they had discussed months ago. It might even make things smoother.

Mackay thanked Kalvaria for his interest but brushed the idea aside. The certainty of the Molson Coors deal was too valuable to sacrifice for the chance to play yet another waiting game with Anheuser-Busch.

After the MillerCoors venture was announced, Wall Street's legion of analysts and investors started handicapping which brewing giant would be next to make a major move, and many focused their sights on Anheuser-Busch. August IV had loosened the guidelines that limited the amount of debt Anheuser could take on, which gave it the financial flexibility it needed to be an active acquirer. By that time, though, it was looking more and more like a juicy target.

■ ■ ■

To address concerns about Anheuser-Busch's flagging superiority, The Fourth's team ratcheted up its focus on a cost-cutting program they dubbed "Blue Ocean." The effort to wring out waste first started in the company's brewing division under Doug Muhleman, a calm-spoken Californian with a fondness for nautical references. The Fourth soon implemented it more broadly, initially targeting cuts of $300 million to $400 million over a span of four years. Anheuser-Busch had always kept its interactions with Wall Street to a minimum during The Third's tenure, but with his son in charge, the strategy committee started considering whether to give analysts a detailed outline of their cost-cutting plans to prove they were moving in the right direction.

All of the fuss over saving a few hundred million dollars, however, indicated to some industry watchers that Anheuser-Busch was missing the point completely. The right response to SABMiller's dramatic move in the United States wasn't a paltry cost-cutting campaign. Across the Atlantic in Leuven, Belgium, InBev took SABMiller's move as a call to action.

In October 2007, not long after MillerCoors was unveiled, August IV met casually in New York with Jorge Paulo Lemann, the billionaire banker, spear fisherman, and former Wimbledon tennis player who had co-created InBev and was one of its most influential board members. Lemann, Telles, and Sicupira had steered themselves straight toward the top of the brewing industry since being rebuffed long ago by The Third.

Through their giant 2004 deal to merge AmBev with Belgium's Interbrew, the trio had taken a significant stake in InBev and three seats on the new company's board. The Brazilians and Belgians agreed to share control, but it wasn't long before InBev's Leuven headquarters started to look as though they'd been dropped into Belgium from Sao Paolo. Many of InBev's most important positions were soon filled by executives from AmBev's side of the deal.

The Fourth had forged a connection to Lemann through an important joint venture the two companies had struck just as he was taking Anheuser's helm the prior year. Their meeting in New York didn't seem particularly unusual to people on Anheuser's side, given that relationship.

The meeting held much more importance to people on InBev's side. Lemann, after referencing the deal SABMiller had just unveiled, suggested to August IV that day that their companies should consider a merger. The Fourth quickly demurred. He had plans of his own to resurrect Anheuser-Busch, and was eager to get back to St. Louis to focus on his cost-cutting campaign. Lemann's remark wasn't enough to formally register on Anheuser's radar screen. According to a regulatory filing it made a year later, "no acquisition proposals were made by InBev" in 2007 or early 2008. However, it rang alarm bells for some.

"To the extent you were on DEFCON 3, everything dialed up to DEFCON 4 or 5," said one person close to Anheuser-Busch. "There was no perception that anything was just innocent and casual. You sort of had the sense that there had been a change, which led to lots more preparation, lots more analysis. You could sort of feel that the odds were higher that something was going to happen than they had been."

The Fourth may not have felt Lemann's comment was anything other than an off-the-cuff remark. It had been quite deliberate, however. His quick dismissal of the notion of a merger suggested to InBev that it might have to consider more forceful ways of luring Anheuser-Busch into a deal. "They always said they wanted to put the two companies together, but just not then," said a person close to InBev.

Although August IV brushed Lemann aside that day, he did tell some Anheuser executives privately that a merger with InBev could be a great way for Anheuser-Busch to unlock value. "But I don't think that anybody on our side ever thought we would lose control of the company—that we would lose control at the board level," said an A-B executive, who posited that InBev began carving Anheuser-Busch up for eating soon after Lemann and The Fourth sat down.

"August IV was a babe in the woods at that meeting."

Chapter 8

The Old Gobi
Desert Trick

The basic concept was "Come clean, guys. We're all grown-ups here. What's going on?"
— Anheuser-Busch insider, on The Fourth's trip to Tampa

W hile The Fourth's encounters with SABMiller and InBev and the meeting he engineered in Cancun naïvely sent up a few flares, his instincts were right. Anheuser-Busch was vulnerable. He actually contributed to the problem just before his official start as CEO, however, when he pushed ahead with his joint venture with InBev despite warnings from his father.

The companies had first considered a deal to make Anheuser the exclusive U.S. importer of InBev's European brands back in early 2005, when Pat Stokes was chief executive. They spent roughly half a year working through the terms of an agreement before talks collapsed. They tried again the next year after Carlos Brito, who had been stationed up in Toronto during the first round of negotiations, was named CEO of InBev. This time, Brito dealt directly with August IV, who was just a few months shy of becoming CEO. Negotiations were held and information was exchanged, but yet again, the talks broke apart.

By late 2006, with The Fourth poised to become CEO, he and his team decided that finally inking the venture would rally distributors and help address the company's stagnating growth. The Fourth wanted the deal to be the first big initiative he pushed through as he transitioned into the top spot. He and his team ensured that the third round of talks with InBev was a success, and the tie-up was announced right after Thanksgiving.

The venture yielded plenty of benefits—Anheuser-Busch won the ability to offer U.S. consumers a broader variety of beers, like Stella Artois, Beck's, and Hoegaarden. The Fourth's eagerness to get the deal done, however, brought worrisome consequences.

Many joint venture agreements include a "standstill" clause that prevents partners from buying up shares in each other, attacking each other's boards of directors, or making other moves that could be viewed as steps toward an unsolicited takeover attempt. The Third had opposed the idea of a deal that did not legally protect Anheuser's independence, and it would have been perfectly reasonable for Anheuser-Busch to force InBev to agree to a standstill. That never happened, though. By the time the companies' third round of talks got underway in 2006, demanding a standstill provision to ward against a takeover wasn't a major concern for The Fourth.

In his defense, the joint venture was too small in scope to warrant a standstill agreement as a normal course of action. "I'm sure A-B could have raised it," said one company advisor. "I do think that would have been an interesting thing to bring up. But it also would probably have been outsized, relative to the scope of what that JV was."

"If A-B continued along the path they were on and InBev continued on the path they were on, I don't know if a standstill would have mattered at some point," the advisor added. "Public pressure (to merge the companies) might have been fairly significant nonetheless. But that said, a standstill is a standstill, and it would certainly have been helpful in a raid defense."

Curiously enough, despite all of the other efforts The Third undertook to limit his son's autonomy, he let The Fourth proceed with the deal rather than breaking out his veto. "His dad though it was a stupid deal, but he let his son go ahead and do it," said one person close to Anheuser-Busch. Though it wasn't evident at the time, The Third's willingness to acquiesce had significant bearing later on the company's future and on the success of his son's reign.

■■■

The partnership opened the doors to InBev's executives and let them walk right in to kick the tires and see whether Anheuser-Busch was worth buying—and for how much.

"It gave them an inside snapshot of how bloated the company was, because we had these guys following us around for a couple of years," said a former Anheuser-Busch executive. "They saw all of the executives coming in on corporate jets. They were just appalled at the excessive corporate overhead in the company."

"I think they were able to see the extent of what they could cut when they got in," the executive said. "Despite the worldwide economic meltdown, it gave them the strategy and the belief that if they could get the deal done, they could realize the cost savings."

The joint venture let InBev shack up for a while with Anheuser-Busch before deciding whether to marry it. It showed InBev where to make cuts and how to improve Anheuser-Busch's business. The companies' year and a half of cohabitation may have soothed The Fourth into trusting Carlos Brito, but it handed InBev a stockpile of ammunition on a silver platter. It didn't matter that The Fourth started trying to slash costs once he became CEO. With all of its miserly experience, InBev knew it could take any savings plan The Fourth concocted and top it.

"The gold-plated nature of the way A-B ran their business was not simply an invention of August Busch IV," one of the company's advisors said. "That had been in place for generations upon generations. Did InBev get a closer look at that and say to themselves, when they saw all of the aircraft and the hangar and everything else, that, 'Boy, there are a lot of costs we could cut out?' Yes."

The Fourth even invited Brito to one of the company's annual wholesaler conventions, where he had a chance to see for himself what Anheuser-Busch spent on discretionary items. August IV couldn't have chosen a more inappropriate guest to invite to his over-the-top party.

"That was August's naïveté, bringing the guy in," said one former Anheuser executive.

Under Brito, who had a Teflon-like resistance to the trappings of corporate wealth, InBev had never been a cushy place to work. The company earned its reputation as the "Wal-Mart of brewers" not long after it was created, and Stanford business school graduate Brito and his legion of American-educated MBAs took number-crunching and analysis to the extreme—to the point where critics argued that they were ruining the beer business.

Brito, a protégé of Jorge Paulo Lemann's, worked in an open floor plan office at a large table, surrounded by the staffers who reported to him. He decried anything that could be viewed as a symbol of professional status, and flew coach class on all but the longest airplane trips. As he liked to point out, most of InBev's beer-swilling customers didn't fly first class either.

In Anheuser-Busch's heyday, its executives bunked down at the sumptuous Pierre hotel, which is perched on New York's Fifth Avenue at the southeast corner of Central Park. Brito, however, abided by the same hotel policy InBev enforced for its whole organization, which meant that he wasn't staying at the Four Seasons while his underlings set up house at a local tourist trap. He stuck to a more pedestrian class of hotels—the kind in which it made sense to check behind the headboard for bedbugs, just in case. Before AmBev merged with Interbrew and the Belgians put their feet down on the matter, the Brazilians were even said to have bunked in pairs on some business trips to save money.

A married father of four and native of Rio de Janeiro, Brito's office uniform was casual and no-frills—a pair of blue jeans paired with a button-down shirt, sometimes tucked beneath a sweater. Jeans were the norm at InBev, and many members of the company's board even wore them during meetings. For an event of modest importance, Brito might upgrade to a pair of khaki pants.

Even Brito's name left little room for frivolity. There had been a handful of Carloses in his Jesuit high school class when he was young, which was bound to get confusing, so his teachers and classmates started using his blunt-edged surname instead. From that point onward into adulthood, the only two people who called him "Carlos" were his mother and, eventually, his wife. Compared to some of the larger-than-life personalities who commanded the beer industry over the years, Brito was a study in exercised restraint.

The one counterpoint to that, however, was his hunger for competition and desire to win. He habitually peppered his dialogue with jargony, business-themed catchphrases—the kind that are often mounted on office posters beneath a picture of a breaching whale or a waterfall. Despite his affinity for measurements and targets, Brito saw his job as a quest to understand what makes people tick—or in his case, what makes a person knock back one brand of beer on a Friday night rather than another. Like August III, he was a beer evangelist. He could wax at length about the proper type of glass in which each of InBev's beers should be poured, or about what the label badge on each bottle said about the person drinking it.

It was only natural for Brito to see his venture with Anheuser-Busch as fertile testing ground for a merger. To many on Wall Street, a merger between InBev and Anheuser had taken on an air of inevitability even before their partnership was struck. The debate had initially centered on which company would be the aggressor and which would be the target. As InBev swelled in size, Anheuser lost its right to claim the driver's seat.

Even after InBev surpassed Anheuser-Busch in size, however, Anheuser retained a key advantage. Its culture and history were soaked to saturation point with family heritage, Prohibition-era tales, pop culture references, and patriotic American spirit, which put InBev's dry, formulaic background to shame. That might be a non-issue in some industries, but brewers need to sell a "story" and a lifestyle, not just a can of liquid. InBev tried to project a rich image and frequently pointed out that its roots in Europe dated back to 1366. Behind closed doors, though, its executives knew their history left people lukewarm. They were self-conscious about it. Their offices in Sao Paolo looked more like those of a hedge fund than a brewer.

Anheuser-Busch was a dream takeover target for the Brazilians in many ways. InBev's growth rate was expected to start slowing, and they needed a new way to boost profits. "InBev was hitting a wall," one banker said. "Its growth was really challenged. And the beer industry is not exactly an industry with a big wind at its back. InBev clearly needed something to find something to feed that machine." Anheuser-Busch was the perfect candidate—it was full of waste that was easy to eliminate. From a cultural standpoint, Anheuser was the "anti-InBev," which also made it appealing. There was enough lore and legend associated with Anheuser-Busch to offset InBev's lack of rich history.

"From their early stages in the beer industry, they looked up to A-B as a great American icon, and would see it essentially as the fulfillment of a career goal to get a hold of what was the prize of the industry," said one person close to the company.

InBev cranked its machinery into gear once Lemann's meeting with The Fourth made it clear that he wasn't anxious to play ball. The two companies had plenty of connections that could quickly get messy if InBev grew too aggressive, so Brito wanted to avoid stepping into Anheuser's path with his guns ablaze. Instead, he assembled a loose plan that covered what the two companies would look like if they merged, how a deal could augment InBev's growth, and how much it could afford to pay.

■■■

By the time Monday, April 28, 2008, rolled around, this loose sketch had morphed into a concept that was ready to be presented to the company's board of directors. They were due to assemble one day prior to the company's annual shareholder gathering, which would be held on Tuesday at a hotel in Brussels, and while the board typically met in Leuven, the plan this time was to assemble at the Brussels offices of law firm Clifford Chance.

InBev's team of bankers and lawyers, who weren't bound to the company's frugal internal travel expense policy, curled up on Sunday night at the Hotel Amigo, an oddly named but luxurious hotel situated next to Brussels' famous Grand Place square, after spending most of the day preparing for the board's session. They wanted to make sure they were as well positioned as possible to answer the group's inevitable raft of questions. Brito, for whom the meeting would be particularly critical, even dropped by on the way back from a child's christening to check in on their progress.

On Monday morning, InBev's all-male board of directors—many of whom had long and appropriately worldly names that seemed to have been pulled from a *Mission: Impossible* script—settled themselves around a conference room table and prepared for the day's session. Their casual dress helped to set them apart from their business-suited bankers, PR handlers, and lawyers. A minor changing of the guard was set to occur following Tuesday's shareholder meeting: InBev had nominated Stéfan Descheemaeker, its Belgian chief strategy officer, to replace Allan Chapin, who had served on the board for 14 years.

InBev's interest in Anheuser-Busch was slated as a key topic of that day's session, and the company's advisors had done extensive work to assemble and distribute "decks" of material for the board that included a bunch of merger-related calculations and projections. InBev and Anheuser-Busch had been assigned code names, per tradition on Wall Street, to protect against the off chance that someone left one of the booklets in a Starbucks or was overheard chatting about it on the train. Anheuser was dubbed "Aluminum," and InBev "Nest." While InBev's machinations had progressed to the code name level of formality, however, the board's session that day wasn't served up as a make-or-break moment. InBev felt it had plenty of time at its disposal, and with August IV cool to the idea of a merger, it was especially in no rush. The board was still hoping to get Anheuser-Busch to comply without using force.

"It definitely was a decision point, and the outcome could be 'go,' it could be 'no go,' and it could be 'Let's think about it more, but no decision yet,'" said one person close to InBev. "Certainly, there were a lot of people there who thought it was the time to go. But there was also an extent to which the real desire from the very beginning was to not have this be hostile."

The likelihood of a friendly deal right off the bat, however, was low, as InBev's two closest advisors, Paris-based Lazard banker Antonio Weiss and New York–based Sullivan & Cromwell attorney Frank Aquila, told the board. They could hope Anheuser-Busch would change its militantly independent stripes and sit down for merger talks, but they needed to be prepared for a messy fight, given Anheuser's cultural significance in America. They would have to enter the process with that mentality to be successful.

The group spent part of its session debating which strategies would work better than others from a public relations standpoint. Nina Devlin—a partner at PR firm Brunswick Group who was later dragged into the news when her husband pleaded guilty to insider trading for stealing deal-related tips from her, some of which involved Anheuser-Busch—laid out everything Anheuser's shareholders and employees might care about if InBev launched an attack. Anheuser-Busch, to its loyalists, boiled down to a great deal more than just a pile of cash. It was thick with cultural significance, from the Clydesdale horses that marched in small-town parades to the Budweiser sponsorships that funded countless sports teams. If InBev bid for the company, lots of politicians and blue-collar workers would want to hear right away what its plans were for employees, the community, and the St. Louis brewery. InBev needed to decide which promises to make to Anheuser right up front and which ones to stash in its back pocket as bargaining chips for later, just in case the companies came to a point where they started debating Anheuser's actual price.

"They did not think these concessions would get them very far on price, but they thought it would get them a long way in terms of sentiment," one person close to InBev said. "They felt they wouldn't even be in a position to be negotiating price if they created a storm around all of these other things."

Some "sacrifices" were easy to make. Maintaining Anheuser's beer brewing formulas, for example, was critical. InBev didn't want to give loyal Bud drinkers an excuse to switch to something else. And changing InBev's boring name to incorporate "Anheuser-Busch" also made sense: It was a great brand. "The name was no big deal," said one advisor. "Brito would call it anything."

The debate over the location of the company's North American headquarters, and how to treat St. Louis in general, was more complicated. The Anheuser-Busch brewery there was expensive to run, and Brito was concerned that because some of the local workers' views were so entrenched, he wouldn't be able to make big changes without pulling the enterprise out of Missouri. If he moved the North American headquarters elsewhere and brought the best people from St. Louis with it, he could avoid being bogged down by so much baggage.

"I think Brito's reaction was like, 'Couldn't we just have it in New York City or somewhere?'" said one person close to the company. "To people in St. Louis, you might as well have it in Guam if you're going to put it in New York City."

Brito ultimately acknowledged that with the city of St. Louis already suffering heavily from the sagging economy, closing Anheuser's facility there would be too bitter a pill to swallow. One of InBev's political weak spots was its cold, ultracompetitive culture, and closing down the St. Louis brewery would only draw more attention to the cultural gulf that separated it from Anheuser-Busch. It could unleash a rain of political brimstone on InBev's head. Brito's team decided to stick with St. Louis, and focused instead on which facets of the business would stay there rather than shifting elsewhere.

Most of these arguments occurred between InBev's executives and their advisors rather than in front of the board. The directors were vocal that Monday in Brussels on certain issues as well, and drilled in on a handful of key questions. How realistic was the threat of a huge political outcry? And what impact could it have on their takeover bid? Could Anheuser-Busch actually block a takeover by using an outpouring of popular support to its advantage? And even if it couldn't, would the angst caused by InBev's takeover attempt affect its ability to sell beer in America? InBev didn't want to pollute its own well. The group had a healthy discussion, but left everything open for further debate.

"At that point, the timetable was looking pretty far out. In our view, it was still a couple of months down the road," said one advisor to the company. "It was more 'These are the things you need to think about and weigh.'"

To even get to the point where success was an option, InBev needed money. It couldn't possibly pay for the deal out of pocket, and the banking markets were getting worse by the day. InBev had loosely lined up a roughly $50 billion financing package with J.P. Morgan and Banco Santander, the Spanish bank, but that was only the tip of the iceberg. Those two banks wanted to distribute their exposure to other banks, especially in the risk-averse lending climate, and that process could take several more weeks at least. Thankfully, J.P. Morgan and Santander were two of the best-positioned banks amidst the rising rate of meltdowns at other institutions. That's why InBev had gone straight to J.P. Morgan's Jamie Dimon and Santander chief Emilio Botín when it began probing around for funds.

How much capacity did the global lending system actually have at the time for something like this, they wondered: $25 billion, maybe $40 billion? It certainly wasn't clear InBev could raise $45 billion or more. They were facing the worst credit environment since the Great Depression. They had to be careful, too—with each new bank they approached in search of funding, the risk increased that news of their plans would leak to the media. Anheuser's share price had already started ticking higher because abnormal options trading was showing increased risk of a takeover—word was seeping out within the banks InBev had consulted. InBev was already playing with fire, and it wasn't likely to have the luxury of taking several more months to cobble together a jumbo financing package.

As the board discussed the sketchy state of its financing that day, the directors' prejudice became clear: Jumping out of the gate with a bid before they had the money would be foolhardy. It could potentially ruin the only shot at Anheuser-Busch they might ever have. If they made an offer with weak financing, all Anheuser would have to do to turn shareholders against InBev would be to cast doubt on its ability to cough up the dough.

The board was scheduled to meet again in late May in China, so the directors decided to sit on things for a few weeks and take them up again on Asian soil. In the meantime, they gave their main investment bank, Lazard, the all-clear to start working more closely with J.P. Morgan to assemble financing for a bid. Perhaps they'd be able to secure enough commitments within the next few weeks.

"I think they expected to be talking more about strategy and getting the deal done, but the financing really almost hijacked it," said one person who attended the meeting in Brussels. "They were still working on it; there were concerns about it. I think it took up a much larger portion of the time than initially had been expected, which is why they sort of agreed to regroup. They needed to have a better sense of whether the financing would be able to be put in place."

■ ■ ■

The group reconvened for two days less than a month later, on May 21 and 22, in China. InBev's directors visited a few of its foreign operations each year to stay abreast of the business, and this qualified as one of those visits. They were a long way from home, so a range of key players and advisors dialed in by phone rather than showing up in person.

The company's bankers at Lazard presented the proposed merger pitch to the board yet again, and said that progress had been made on the money front. They hadn't cobbled together an entire financing package yet, but more banks were showing an interest.

The board was still uneasy. They had spent a great deal of time evaluating the holes in their case—anything Anheuser-Busch could use against them—and had worked hard to close them one by one. They didn't think, for example, that the merger would be viewed as anticompetitive by regulators in the United States or Europe. Yet they needed more than loose promises from a handful of banks to make the financing aspect of their bid bulletproof.

"Since there wasn't an antitrust issue, financing was the only thing we thought they could exploit," said one person close to InBev. And InBev just wasn't there yet with its banks. So again, the board decided to sit tight and wait.

That Friday, Frank Aquila, one of InBev's go-to outside lawyers, was sitting in his office on a conference call when an e-mail popped up on his computer screen that instructed him to dial in on another call immediately. He ignored it. Another urgent message popped up, and seconds later, his cell phone rang.

"Dial in right away," Antonio Weiss called out from the other end of the line.

"Well, I'm on a call, and I've got another in half an hour," Aquila said.

"Get the hell off your conference call," Weiss replied more deliberately. "Dial in right away. There's been a leak."

"Oh, people talk about this all the time," Aquila said. He wasn't particularly eager to excuse himself from the business he was attending to over yet another market rumor.

"No, there has been a credible leak," Weiss said, hanging on the last two words for emphasis.

A story that had just been posted on the *Financial Times*'s Alphaville web site was drawing a huge amount of attention, and for good reason. It claimed InBev was working on a $46 billion takeover bid for Anheuser-Busch, and said InBev might appeal straight to Anheuser's shareholders if August IV wasn't interested in a friendly merger. The story pegged the price at $65 per share, revealed the code names that had been assigned to the companies, and ticked off a list of attributes they would have if they were combined—all information that came straight from the materials InBev's bankers had presented in Brussels a month earlier. It even referred to an informal entreaty InBev had made toward Anheuser-Busch the prior October—the meeting between August IV and Lemann—and named J.P. Morgan and Santander as the banks that would help InBev pay for the effort.

What had transpired seemed immediately clear. Someone had taken matters into his or her own hands and leaked the information, either as a "trial balloon" meant to gauge the market's view on the deal or as an effort to jump-start the two sides. With InBev's plans now blown out into the open, its board—after months of stalling—would finally have to decide whether to pull the trigger. And Anheuser-Busch might be forced to consider an offer.

InBev altered its calculus the moment the news hit. Brito and the board had still been hoping to convince August IV to sit down for talks, but the leak made a discreet approach impossible. The board needed to make a decision fast. "There was nothing we could confirm; there was nothing other than a hypothetical," said one InBev advisor who explained the reaction in the company's camp. "We were just concerned about being so far on our back foot, worried that A-B would have now the opportunity to really start marshaling resources."

To complicate matters, Brito and many of InBev's directors and top executives were either stuck on long flights back to Europe or still spread around Asia following their board meeting. Some members of the group were shocked to realize that their unwillingness to commit in China might have sparked the leak. They had no choice now but to address the matter.

The board first had to decide whether to call the whole thing off. They could deny they had ever been interested in Anheuser-Busch, close the books on the idea, and maybe reconsider it at some point in the future. Their loans weren't in place, and with the markets in such a fragile state, there was no guarantee they'd get the money. No one wanted to blow their chance at such a coveted prize over market conditions that were beyond their control.

As long as InBev wasn't willing to play dumb and scrap everything—if it felt this was its best chance to affix the Anheuser-Busch jewel atop its crown—it was time to kick things into high gear. Media outlets and investors were already clogging the phone lines in InBev's communications office, and the company was saying it had no comment on the report. So were J.P. Morgan and Santander. To many market watchers, though, a "no comment" is an admission of guilt. If InBev really wasn't interested, it would simply say so right off the bat and extinguish the rumors.

At first blush, the market seemed to like the idea of a merger. It was a concept many Anheuser shareholders had already considered, given the consistent churn of the takeover rumor mill. Shares of Anheuser-Busch were up nearly 7 percent on the day, and while InBev's shares were down slightly, it had most of its own stakeholders under control. Rather than being owned by a bunch of day traders, the vast majority of InBev's shares were held by entrenched Belgian and Brazilian families and trusts that employed long-term perspectives and had representatives on the company's board.

It was something else, however, not the market's reaction, that largely guided the board's decision. InBev's phone started ringing on Friday afternoon with calls from banks all around the world. Merger activity was plunging because of the rough economy, and there weren't many opportunities to do deals or places to park money safely. Getting involved in what might be the biggest merger battle of the year was an imperative. "The issue about financing changed a bit as banks started calling up saying, 'Don't forget us, don't forget us. We've got cash,'" said one person close to the matter.

So InBev, which had worried one day prior that it might not be able to rouse enough lending power, found itself fielding calls from bankers who were offering to cram over the weekend to make speedy commitments. Their eagerness gave InBev the sense that finding roughly $50 billion in financing was possible. And it offered a window into which banks were advising Anheuser-Busch. According to sources, neither Goldman Sachs nor Citigroup phoned in to offer their services.

Over the course of that weekend, with many board members still scattered across Asia and its advisors in New York and Europe scrambling to adjust, InBev decided not to junk its plans. The board decided to use the rumors as a catalyst to put financing together and strike while the iron was hot—and before the markets fell apart further. They could afford to stay publicly silent for a week or two while they worked feverishly behind the scenes to scrounge up loans, Brito and his advisors felt.

"The view was that we were far enough along, and the response from the marketplace seemed to be very positive," said a person close to the company.

As an advisor to Anheuser-Busch put it, "They played their own game of chicken with their lenders. They were out in front of themselves on all of this, in part, I think, convincing their lenders that 'Look, it's going to happen, and it's going to happen without you. So you might as well be part of it.'"

■ ■ ■

On May 23, the same Friday on which InBev's advisors were yanked away from their desks because of the leak, August IV and Anheuser Chief Financial Officer Randy Baker started fielding some urgent calls themselves. Everyone seemed to have the same point of view: The Brazilians were on their way. It was only a matter of time.

Citigroup's Kalvaria called The Fourth from a Manhattan street corner to talk strategy. "These guys will come, and you've just got to get yourselves ready," Kalvaria instructed. "But don't precipitate anything."

Baker, meanwhile, suddenly became hugely popular on Wall Street as bankers at firms large and small started crawling out of the woodwork with offers to help defend the company. He hadn't seen the reports when they first came out. The first he heard of the rumors had been over the holiday weekend, when Larry Rand from the Kekst public relations firm pulled them up on his BlackBerry and called Baker from his backyard.

"We hear these rumors all the time," Baker said at first when Rand directed him toward the latest news. He had deflected so many take-over rumors that they were all starting to blur together, and plenty of them had involved InBev. His first instinct was that this one was no different.

"This one appears to be a little bit more substantial," Rand replied, scrolling through the text of the reports with his thumb. "They have code names—and a financing plan. It looks like a banker's coding on this. My gut tells me that this has got more validity than the others."

"Well, we're not going to comment," Baker responded as the news sank in. What could they say, anyway? They hadn't heard a thing from InBev. Before Baker and Rand hung up, their relaxing Memorial Day weekend plans now ruined, they agreed to collude with Anheuser's internal PR team and the company's lawyers at Skadden to prepare responses in case InBev came forward with an offer.

The worst part of the situation for August IV that weekend was the idea that he was supposed to sit around and wait for InBev to make the first move. He and some of InBev's top brass went back a long way. What was the point of building business relationships if they couldn't be called upon in a case like this? He wanted to know whether the reports were accurate, and felt he had the right to ask. So not long after the stories hit the papers, he drafted a brief but pointed e-mail to the InBev board member he knew best.

"He sent an e-mail to Jorge Paulo Lemann and basically said, 'These rumors are very disruptive. We should talk so we can put this all to rest,'" said one person close to InBev.

Given the seriousness of the matter, The Fourth might have expected to hear from his Brazilian colleague quickly. Lemann, though, who was still in Asia, employed a bit of coy brinksmanship. Rather than answering The Fourth right away, he instigated a subtle game of cat and mouse.

"Lemann did not answer for a couple of days, and then answered something like, 'I was in the Gobi Desert and out of touch. Just got your e-mail. I'm just getting on a plane back. It probably makes sense that we should meet,'" said one person close to InBev. "By the way, he was not as out of pocket as he made it seem." He was, however, on the other side of the world, so InBev's team knew he couldn't meet with The Fourth for a few days at best. Why not string him along a bit?

"Since we couldn't have the meeting for a while anyway, we thought, "Let's let things play out; let's see where things are and play the old I'm-running-around-the-Gobi-desert trick for a bit,'" joked one person close to the company.

Once Lemann and The Fourth finally connected, they agreed to meet in Tampa, Florida, on June 2. At the first session it held in the wake of the rumor reports, Anheuser's board had debated whether to reach out to InBev to ask for clarity. They had agreed it would make sense. "We said, 'Listen, let's find out what they want to do here, what they're talking about," said director James Forese. "We did it just because it makes good business sense to find out what's going on. Usually, you want to find out what your enemies are doing."

Plenty of people on Anheuser's side had reservations about sending The Fourth down to Tampa without backup. Lemann and his business partner Marcel Telles, who planned to attend as well, were sophisticated businessmen and strategists, and there was a huge imbalance of information between the two sides. The Brazilians knew exactly what InBev was up to, but August IV had nothing to offer them.

Some members of Anheuser's team weren't comfortable with the idea of meeting with InBev, period. It didn't matter who represented their side. They felt the leak had been deliberate—authorized, at least partially, by InBev's top decision makers. There were lots of reasons why someone at InBev, or someone working on the company's behalf, might have wanted the information to get out. It had already prompted merger arbitrageurs, who bet on merger deals and are often more anxious to see one transpire, to buy Anheuser's stock. Now, it was convincing August IV that he should meet with two of InBev's most powerful directors, even though they had the upper hand. It felt like Anheuser was playing straight into InBev's trap. The Fourth was CEO of the company, and the meeting had been arranged with the understanding that he would be Anheuser's representative. There wasn't enough negative sentiment to change that now.

The Fourth spent a good chunk of time in coaching sessions with Goldman and other advisors before leaving for Tampa, mapping out what might transpire and making sure he knew the right things to say.

When Lemann and Telles met him near the Tampa airport that Monday, the Brazilians weren't sure whether Anheuser's board actually even knew what The Fourth was up to. It wasn't clear the board had authorized the meeting, or even that it had approved the e-mail The Fourth had first sent to Lemann. Again, though, August IV was CEO of Anheuser-Busch. They had to assume he was speaking on behalf of the entire company. And according to board member Sandy Warner, he was. "August IV and the board were discussing every aspect of this," he said. "He was very good at keeping us informed. There was no issue there at all."

Lemann and Telles had a narrow tightrope to walk. InBev's financing still wasn't in place, so they didn't want to hint at a formal offer no matter how hard The Fourth pushed for one. They did want to convey, however, that there was truth to the takeover rumors. If August IV knew InBev was about to lay siege to his company, he might be willing to negotiate a friendly deal before things got messy.

When the trio sat down in Tampa, "August IV basically said, 'You know, you haven't even given us an offer,'" said a person close to InBev. "I think he was really trying to say, 'Hey, we're not for sale; go away.'"

It didn't work. After so much debate over whether to meet with InBev, and so much coaching and deliberation over how to approach the issue, August IV returned to St. Louis that evening with next to nothing. He had asked whether Lemann and Telles had a formal offer to make, and they replied that they didn't. Aside from that, their face-to-face had yielded frustratingly little clarity, and it had lasted all of 10 minutes. It was difficult for Anheuser's team to know whether Lemann and Telles had been cagey or whether The Fourth had simply misread them.

"My ideal result would have been for somebody else to have been sitting there with him who would be able to interpret what was said and what it meant," said one person close to the company. The meeting ended up in some ways being a nonevent, other than it established that there's something there. Clearly, there's something there. That was kind of the conclusion. Tampa showed that they were clearly working on something."

From getting nowhere with Lemann and Telles, August IV determined that InBev had a bid in the works but wasn't ready to act. Anheuser's team had already gauged that InBev would need to offer all or almost all cash if it really wanted to win, so they assumed Lemann and Telles had stayed mum because InBev hadn't been able to fill its coffers yet.

"Our conclusion at the time was 'These guys would love to do something, they're clearly trying to do something, and if they're successful we may hear from them," said one Anheuser advisor. "If not, we may not."

They did. Just nine days later, InBev stunned the group that had gathered at Anheuser's soccer park with a $46.3 billion takeover offer. In the letter InBev faxed to The Fourth that day, Brito made sure to include that "Jorge Paulo Lemann and Marcel Telles greatly appreciated your taking the time to meet with them on the 2nd of June in Tampa." It was like grinding salt in the wound.

Chapter 9

Mr. Brito Goes to Washington

I'm sorry. I'm from the Show-Me State. You'll have to show me.
— Christopher "Kit" Bond, U.S. Senator from Missouri

N early a week had passed since InBev made its offer, but the Brazilians hadn't heard a word from Anheuser's board. Politicians in Missouri and in Washington, D.C., had found plenty of time to take sides, however, and an uproar was threatening to build.

The situation had all of the dynamics of a potential political and media maelstrom. InBev's attack prompted visceral reactions around the world, but the tumult was ringing loudest, not surprisingly, in America. It was the summer before one of the most critical presidential elections in American history, and Senators Hillary Clinton and Barack Obama were duking it out in the primaries to determine who would face their Republican colleague John McCain at the polls in November. In Missouri, where McCain ended up beating Obama by only a few thousand votes—49.4 percent to 49.3 percent—the governorship was also up for grabs. The country was abuzz as politicians jostled against each other to do anything they could to rally constituents in their favor.

Thanks to InBev's bid, Americans who had brazenly endorsed the spread of their own country's tentacles into other nations were suddenly being forced to consider whether foreigners should be able to buy high-profile U.S. assets. Some claimed that no self-respecting American would continue to drink Budweiser if the deal happened. Others supported the globalization that led InBev from Belgium to Anheuser's doorstep, and realized they had to accept the good with the bad. When Toyota made its first foray into the U.S. car market, they pointed out, the indignation was so fierce that it seemed as though the Japanese were bombing Pearl Harbor all over again. Just a few years later, Japanese cars covered America's highways, and few consumers seemed to be giving it a second thought—particularly because many of the cars were actually built in America by American workers.

One Florida couple that had no connection whatsoever to Anheuser-Busch, other than having been to Sea World to see Shamu, created a web site called SaveBudweiser.com to generate support for Anheuser-Busch. "We're big supporters of the military," Wren Fowler, who started the site with her husband, told the *Wall Street Journal*. "Anheuser-Busch seems to be supportive, too. From there on, we only had Bud products in our house." It wasn't really about the beer, she said, it was about the cost-cutting InBev would enforce and the charitable donations it might eliminate. "I like the beer," she said. "But this is about something bigger."

Christopher "Kit" Bond, a U.S. Senator from Missouri, asked the U.S. Department of Justice and the Federal Trade Commission to review the proposed takeover, claiming that it was his responsibility to make sure the Bush administration considered the potential deal's impact on consumers and the market. In a letter to the U.S. attorney general, Bond said sentiment in Missouri that was adamantly opposed to the deal "intends to be active" and was "growing by the moment."

Democrat Claire McCaskill, the other senator from Missouri, expressed a similar level of angst.

Industry watchers waited to see whether presidential candidates would be drawn into the fray, and the media did their best to bait them. John McCain, whose wife, Cindy, was heiress to Phoenix-based Hensley and Co., the country's third-largest Anheuser distributor, stayed quiet on the matter—probably a wise move, given the hornet's nest it would have stirred up over his conflicts of interest. Cindy McCain, who was known to drive around Phoenix in a car with license plates that read "MS BUD," controlled somewhere between 40,000 and 80,000 shares of Anheuser stock, worth between $2.5 million and $5 million.

Barack Obama, who stayed mum on the topic for nearly a month, finally stated on July 7 that it would be "a shame" if Anheuser were bought by a foreign company. "I think we should be able to find an American company that is interested in purchasing Anheuser-Busch, if in fact Anheuser-Busch feels that it's necessary to sell," he said. It was at this critical moment that Obama first hinted he supported the government intervention in American business that became a hallmark of his early administration. Within months of his early 2009 inauguration, the U.S. government took ownership of General Motors and Chrysler to stave off the deepening recession and prevent heavy job losses for American workers.

President Obama, incidentally, appeared to enjoy using beer as a diplomatic tool. He held what became known as the "beer summit" at the White House during the summer of 2009—an attempt to unite a black Harvard professor and the white police officer who arrested him after they controversially came to loggerheads. And when the United States played England in the World Cup the following June, Obama suggested to British Prime Minister David Cameron that they wager the best beer in America against the best lager in Britain over the outcome of the match. The game ended in a tie, leaving everyone to guess which brand of beer the president thought was the nation's best.

■ ■ ■

InBev had been able to stay ahead of the media curve so far, but it feared falling behind as opposition to the deal threatened to build. InBev's team knew they couldn't let pro-American political sentiment spin out of control. That had happened in a few other instances recently, and the results hadn't been good. Dubai Ports World dropped an effort in 2006 to buy a company that operated American shipping ports because of the firestorm it generated on Capitol Hill, and Chinese companies had scrapped the attempted acquisitions of both oil company Unocal in 2005 and Internet router maker 3Com in March 2008, just a few months earlier, in the face of political opposition over potential national security risks.

The idea that a sale of Anheuser-Busch might have national security implications seemed ludicrous. Was anyone really going to try arguing that a beer brewer was vital to America's interests? Did it matter whether Budweiser was concocted by an American or Belgian company, especially if the beer was still produced in America by American workers?

InBev's team clearly didn't think so, but it wasn't worth finding out. They needed to put a softer spin on the story to get politicians and the media off their backs before the pressure grew too heavy. So Brito traveled to Washington, D.C., to fly the company's flag.

He was reluctant, initially. "Brito was of the view: 'Why should I waste my time? They're never going to like me, they're never going to support me,'" said a person close to InBev. He changed his tune when InBev's advisors argued that it was time to give the company a relatable public face and show it wasn't some out-of-touch foreign villain. They weren't necessarily expecting a boycott, but they did happen to be dealing with a country in which conservatives started calling French fries "freedom fries" when France opposed the invasion of Iraq in 2003—even though French fries actually come from Belgium, InBev's home turf.

"You could be this nameless, faceless foreigner, or you could be smart, articulate, bright, polished Brito," InBev's team told their CEO. "If you've got a guy like that who can talk on his feet and speaks good English," one advisor said, "why not showcase him and say, 'Hey, this isn't some weird guy from the barrio in Rio de Janeiro. This is a real guy, you know, Stanford Business School.'"

So that Monday, Brito went Washington, D.C. The goal was to demystify the company, to neutralize potential opposition, and to calm the representatives of Congress who were spouting rhetoric over the injustice of letting an American institution be acquired by a foreign rival. It was relatively clear that the most outspoken politicians would still oppose the deal, but shaking their hands in front of the cameras certainly wasn't going to hurt InBev's cause.

It wasn't an easy two days. Anheuser-Busch had burgeoned into an influential force in American politics over its century and a half of existence, and Brito was trying to combat all of the money Anheuser had spent over the years to ensure it was represented in the halls of Congress.

Missouri's politicians had always seemed to be pressed securely under Anheuser-Busch's thumb because it employed so many workers in the state—which, not coincidentally, has some of the most permissive alcohol laws of any U.S. jurisdiction. Passengers in moving cars there are free to drink alcohol legally, and there is no law against consuming an open container of alcohol on the street.

Anheuser-Busch also had significant pull on a national level. Its political action committee (PAC), which parsed out donations to candidates, was one of Washington's largest, and it ran one of the capitol's most active lobbying offices with roughly a dozen lobbying firms on retainer, including former St. Louis congressman Dick Gephardt's Gephardt Group, former White House press secretary Michael McCurry's Public Strategies Washington, and powerhouse firms Akin Gump Strauss Hauer & Feld and Timmons & Co. At the height of its political giving during the 2002 election cycle, Anheuser-Busch and its employees spent $2.3 million on candidates, with 57 percent of the money going to Republicans. A team of eight Anheuser Clydesdales even marched down Pennsylvania Avenue during President Bill Clinton's 1993 inaugural parade despite protests from health and anti-alcohol groups.

Anheuser-Busch also had help from like-minded groups like the National Beer Wholesalers Association (NBWA), based just outside of Washington, which represents more than 2,850 beer distributors across the country and is consistently one of the nation's biggest-spending PACs. The NBWA ranked as the fifth-largest PAC contributor to political candidates during the 2009–2010 election cycle as of mid-2010 after doling out more than $1.8 million—57 percent of it to Democrats and the rest to Republicans—during that time period. That put it ahead of other heavily active PACs like the American Bankers Association and the Teamsters Union.

The fact that Anheuser-Busch brews beer always made its lobbying efforts more challenging. It constantly faced opposition from groups like Mothers Against Drunk Driving (MADD) and others who said its advertising targeted underage drinkers. It was precisely because of that sensitivity over alcohol that Anheuser needed to wield such significant political influence. The company had already been through Prohibition once, and it was determined to push its roots deeply enough into Washington's soil to prevent shifts in public sentiment from wreaking havoc on its business again.

August III, like his ancestors, understood how the beer business and politics intersected and was diligent about staying ahead of the fight. At a time when pressure was growing in Washington to ban alcoholic beverage advertising entirely, he deftly handled criticism from MADD by throwing a bunch of money behind the effort to curtail drunken driving. "That slowly turned the focus to driving," said Charlie Claggett, who handled Anheuser's "Know When to Say When" moderation campaign. "It's not the beer that's the enemy, it's the fact that you get behind the wheel. That's the enemy. Get a designated driver and don't drive while drunk. Take care of yourself and your friends. It just changed the whole game."

The Third did the same to stanch frustration over discarded beer cans, endorsing the "Pitch In" litter pickup campaign and creating a recycling unit in 1978 that recycled more than 430 billion aluminum cans in its first 30 years. And when civil rights leader Jesse Jackson attacked Anheuser-Busch in 1982 over whether it had enough minority-owned distributorships, the boycott failed. The Third refused to meet with Jackson rather than pandering to him as other CEOs had, and decided to fight back by showing how the company's policies benefited minorities.

Anheuser-Busch also spent plenty of cash in Washington to help ensure that its burgeoning market share never became a political hot button. By the early 1990s, The Third's desire to control half of the

U.S. beer market had grown relentless. Many other CEOs, knowing that seizing half of their market could make them a target for public ire, might happily settle for 49 percent to avoid the controversy. Not August III.

"Mr. Busch, why?" Buddy Reisinger remembers asking The Third. "You hate the public stuff, you hate the government, the S.E.C. Why would you want to put an industry that's a functioning oligopoly . . . why would you want the government on your back? At fifty-share, a little bell is going to go off. Why is that the important thing?"

The Third, uncowed, pushed religiously onward. Hitting that magic number had become how he defined the next level of success, and the risk of having to run a political gauntlet to attain it was worth it. More likely than not, the dollars he spent in Washington would help smooth things over. And they did.

InBev, espousing that same notion, hired four of Washington's best-known lobbying and PR firms to calm tempers over its takeover attempt, including one run by former senators Trent Lott and John Breaux and another run by Joe Lockhart, a former White House press secretary. It started paying operatives from Mercury Public Affairs to call local politicians around the country to outline why it wanted to buy Anheuser-Busch and what the deal would mean for voters. And it sent two letters explaining the deal and the commitments it planned to make to key public officials in target states.

That Tuesday and Wednesday, several of Brito's new lobbyists escorted him to the offices of five Missouri congressional representatives and to a meeting with South Carolina's James Clyburn, the third-ranking House Democrat. The highly orchestrated spectacle, which drew a herd of reporters who followed at Brito's heels, was little more than an expensive and elaborately staged game. Brito wasn't going to convince any of those politicians to back the takeover—the sound bites they'd get for opposing the deal were too important for their next elections. And he certainly wasn't going to back down and scrap InBev's bid based on some minor agitation out of Missouri. His Washington jaunt was about face time, shaking hands, and kissing rings, not about demonstrable results.

McCaskill sat down with Brito and two of his aides at noon on Tuesday and offered them a choice between three Anheuser-Busch beers. Brito and McCaskill both grabbed Bud Lights, and she made a quick toast—"To Anheuser-Busch!"—before launching into a lecture on how hard it was going to be for InBev to win the hearts and minds of her Missouri constituents. The meeting adjourned after half an hour and McCaskill quickly huddled with Brito's attendant group of media scribes.

"They basically came to try to get me on board, so to speak," McCaskill told the reporters. "I said, 'Not going to happen.'" She was shameless in breaking out the rhetoric. "We do not have a 'For Sale' sign on our front lawn in America," she told the St. Louis Post-Dispatch in one interview, calling InBev's bid a "premium profit for hedge fund investors." Brito called his meeting with McCaskill "very, very help-ful." She issued a letter that day to Anheuser's board that called for them to reject InBev's offer.

Brito met with Kit Bond the following day and he, too, used the opportunity to voice opposition to the deal. It would mean job losses in St. Louis, a blow to the Missouri economy, and a loss of charitable contributions in St. Louis, said Bond, who couldn't resist tossing in a few of his own lines of cheesy politico-speak: "My Missouri constitu-ents say, this Bud's not for you," he said.

■ ■ ■

Brushing aside all of the pomp and circumstance, Brito's trip to D.C. actually helped both sides get what they wanted. He was able to promote InBev's cause and generate some press, and the politicians whose constituents cared about Anheuser-Busch were able to make it seem as though they were putting up a fight, even though it was clear there was little they could do to stop the deal. Brito only ended up needing to make one trip to the nation's capital. The political unrest sparked by InBev's bid didn't last long, but that wasn't because he had charmed his way into American beer drinkers' hearts. It was because they had too much else to worry about.

When InBev launched its attack on America's favorite beer com-pany, the country's baby boomers were just coming down from the high of living beyond their means for three decades. These Cadillac

Escalade and McMansion owners were suddenly facing overdue mortgage payments, empty 401(k)s, and unemployment lines. Regardless of how many cases of Bud were stacked in their four-car garages, they had little will to rally en masse for Anheuser—a company that had grown just as fat and delusional during the good years as they had. Anheuser's relevance in their lives, or at least the pride they took in drinking American-made beer, had diminished to a point where a hostile takeover of the company seemed on par for the course when so much else in America was already going wrong.

Given the madness that was unfolding in the markets and on Main Street, some of the news coverage of Anheuser's takeover battle that might otherwise have run on the front page of the world's biggest newspapers was relegated to their middle sections—or left on the cutting room floor. "It was almost like it got just a flash on CBS evening news," said board member General Shelton. "I really thought it would be viewed as a much bigger deal, but obviously it wasn't."

My concern is that across America, this is happening," he said. "Maybe it's not all bad—I'm a big believer in globalization and a world economy and things that could lead to peace long term. But I do worry when so many U.S. companies are going into foreign ownership."

At certain points in American history, protectionist rhetoric alone might have rustled up enough popular anger to ruin InBev's takeover attempt. But this was not a time for political or economic frivolity. People were too distracted by the credit crunch–related turmoil in their own lives to care about whether Budweiser was brewed by an American or Belgian company. That was the sort of philosophical debate people wasted time on when they actually had the luxury of time to waste, rather than spending it searching for a job or struggling to save the job they had.

So while InBev's takeover bid had brought with it two major types of risk—financial and political—one actually ended up helping to nullify the other. Americans who might otherwise have hoisted pitchforks in protest were distracted by the financial markets, which were threatening to collapse in shambles. And politicians found it tough to justify wasting time on Anheuser-Busch rather than addressing rising job losses, budgetary deficits, and disintegrating real estate markets. Yes, they'd ostensibly be fighting to save American jobs by endorsing Anheuser's independence. They'd also be helping to bail out a company that was run by multimillionaires and had been inefficient for years. It was already looking likely that they'd have to step in to float the wreckage of another iconic American company whose leaders had been too beholden to family interests, had gotten fat, happy, and lazy, and had ultimately run it into the rocks—General Motors.

Brito's public relations push was helpful, but InBev's ability to suppress public outrage had less to do with his efforts than with the complacency, resignation, and distraction of the American public. Protectionist sentiment, whether it was logical or not, just wasn't strong enough—Congress battled several months later over whether to include a "Buy American" provision in President Obama's $787 billion stimulus bill, but the fever over that issue also quickly died. The strongest words spoken against InBev, in fact, may have come from Stephen Colbert, the Comedy Central satirist who drowned his sorrows on camera in an effort to enjoy as much Budweiser as he could "before those waffle humpers change the formula."

"The big backlash some people predicted just really didn't happen," said Harry Schuhmacher. "You had some of it in St. Louis, but outside of Missouri, people appear not to know or care where their beer gets made. I think it's just an apathy on the part of people who drink light beer. They don't think about their beer. It's really just a nice, refreshing way to get ethanol into your system."

The cards were stacked against Anheuser-Busch. It could have produced a brilliant plan to slaughter InBev in the press, pulling out all of the protectionist stops and draping itself in the American flag, and much of it might still have fallen on deaf ears based purely on timing.

Curiously, though, Anheuser didn't come up with a brilliant counterattack. At first, it made a deliberate, and arguably foolhardy, choice to have no defense strategy at all.

InBev had assumed that its bid might spark a negative political reaction, and had nervously prepared for Anheuser to come out swinging as soon as the bid was official. Anheuser didn't have much of a leg to stand on from a financial or operational point of view, but it boasted a century and a half of American ownership and had legions of devoted Budweiser drinkers, union workers, and distributors at its disposal if it wanted to rally pro-American sentiment.

When InBev made its offer official on June 11, Anheuser scrambled to quickly issue a press release that said its board of directors would review the bid and decide "in due course." The merger battle appeared to be starting off with a bang. So after a quick gut check on Brito's part, InBev fired back almost immediately with the first rounds of a PR campaign it had painstakingly developed. Why give Anheuser-Busch time to gasp for air if everything was already prepped and ready?

InBev went live with a web site it had created to outline the proposal, and it started meeting with Wall Street analysts to argue its case. Brito wrote an opinion piece in the *St. Louis Post-Dispatch* where he reiterated the pledges InBev made in its offer—that it would keep all of Anheuser's 12 U.S. breweries open, for example, and maintain its North American headquarters in St. Louis. The company even began posting "interviews" with Brito online where people could watch him answer questions about the bid and what it would mean for Anheuser's workers, beer drinkers, and investors. It didn't matter that the person who interviewed Brito was Steve Lipin, InBev's outside public relations guru from the Brunswick Group, who had stepped in at the last minute to replace a former BBC journalist whose British accent—when paired with Brito's own foreign inflection—sent the wrong message. How would that have looked to people in St. Louis, InBev's team wondered? It was better to have the questions posed by an American, and InBev knew that most of the people who would watch Brito's interview online didn't know Lipin from Adam.

Like many of those who advised InBev on its Anheuser-Busch bid, Lipin had a long and lucrative history with the company and was incredibly loyal to Brito. When he discovered that the caterers at his daughter's Manhattan bat mitzvah didn't offer InBev's beer brands, he arranged for special accommodations. He couldn't be seen hosting a huge party where the bar was stocked with Stroh's rather than Stella Artois.

After firing off its initial press release, however, and making InBev think things were about to get ugly, the entire Anheuser side lapsed into silence. For the next two weeks, it was hard for Brito and his colleagues to get a sense of what Anheuser was thinking, even through back channels. They waited fruitlessly for a signal—any sort of overture that might indicate that their American rival was willing to talk. They weren't expecting a decision from Anheuser's board right away. Based on the wording of its response to InBev's offer, it seemed clear that the board wanted to show it wasn't in a rush. This was now the biggest all-cash takeover bid in history, however. In such high-profile merger situations, even the most confidential details tend to get spread around behind the scenes between banks, law firms, media outlets, and PR handlers as everyone jockeys to stay in on the action.

■ ■ ■

The vacuum of information from Anheuser-Busch's camp began to worry InBev. Anheuser-Busch was either taking a shockingly casual approach to the bid, which was certainly possible given the arrogance it had displayed in the past, or there was something else absorbing its attention behind the scenes.

Elements of both were at work. An undercurrent of delusion had always run up and down the chain of command at Anheuser-Busch, right until the day InBev's bid came in. Some staffers had grown frustrated over the company's myopia, but many still had a hard time believing that Anheuser-Busch—the American icon, maker of the King of Beers, and reigning conqueror of the U.S. beer market— could possibly be takeover bait. Even though the Busch family no longer technically controlled the company, the sheer force of The Third's personality alone had always been sufficient to ward off threats in the past. They had no reason to believe he was willing to sell this time around.

It wasn't the first time Anheuser-Busch had overestimated its relevance or power. "I think they were slow to take it seriously," said one person close to Anheuser. "They were in denial. I'm just not sure The Fourth understood, and I'm not sure anybody really wanted to tell him from within his circle of advisors. They had just received presentations in front of the board saying 'These guys couldn't afford us, we're too big.'"

Another, more deliberate move on Anheuser's part also slowed its reaction time, however. Its public relations team had cautioned the board against preparing any sort of defense strategy before InBev made

Gussie was a Dr. Doolittle of sorts—he owned a camel and an elephant and took particular pride in his trio of chimpanzees, which he often dressed as cowboys.

August Busch III, Marcel Telles, and Jorge Paulo Lemann during a fateful 1991 meeting in Williamsburg, Virginia, when Anheuser-Busch and Brazil's Brahma were considering a tie-up and both brewers were No. 1 in their countries.

August Busch IV, chief executive of Anheuser-Busch at the time of the takeover, holding a Clydesdale's reins in 1991 when he was a senior marketing executive.

Source: Time & Life Pictures/Getty Images

August Busch III, Jorge Paulo Lemann, and Marcel Telles inspect the canning line at the Anheuser-Busch brewery in Williamsburg, Virginia.

Former Anheuser–Busch board member Edward Whitacre

Source: Getty Images

Timothy Ingrassia, Americas Mergers and Acquisitions Head, Goldman Sachs

Source: Copyright © PatrickMcMullan
.com

Douglas A. "Sandy" Warner III, former lead independent director of the Anheuser–Busch board

**Joseph Flom, Partner, Skadden,
Arps, Slate, Meagher & Flom**

**Leon Kalvaria, Global Consumer and
Health Care Banking Head, Citigroup**

**Peter Gross, Partner,
Goldman Sachs**

Antonio Weiss, Vice Chairman of European Investment Banking, Lazard

Source: Copyright © Stéphane Gizard

Robert Kindler, Vice Chairman of Investment Banking, Morgan Stanley

Source: Jeff Connell, Wagner International Photos

Frank Aquila, Partner, Sullivan & Cromwell

Carlos Brito, Chief Executive Officer of InBev, lifts a Stella Artois in Leuven, Belgium, to toast InBev's 2007 results.

Source: AFP/Getty Images

InBev directors Carlos Sicupira, Jorge Paulo Lemann, and Marcel Telles

Source: Webb Chappell: Wonderful Machine

Jorge Paulo Lemann, Marcel Telles, Jack Purnell, and August Busch III peer into an Anheuser–Busch brew kettle in Williamsburg, Virginia, in 1991.

Source: Copyright © MaxImages@gmx.com

María Asunción Aramburuzabala, Grupo Modelo's Vice Chairman of the Board, with husband Tony Garza, the former U.S. Ambassador to Mexico, and former First Lady Laura Bush.

Source: U.S. Embassy in Mexico

Carlos Fernández González, Chairman and CEO of Grupo Modelo

Source: El Universal, Compañía Periodística Nacional

Don Antonino Fernández accepts a personalized soccer jersey in April 2010 as the Mexican and Spanish national teams announce plans for a friendly match in Mexico City.

Source: LatinContent/Getty Images

"Anheuser-Busch is a 'we' company. It is team management. It is honesty and integrity. It is creativity and ingenuity. It is the application of management science. Above all, it is people, common sense and hard work. We don't know the meaning of the words: It can't be done."

—*1987 Annual Report*

an actual bid. Kekst felt it would reflect bias and make the board vulnerable to shareholder lawsuits. Some companies have no qualms about firing off a speedy rejection to an unwanted takeover attempt, but Anheuser took an especially—and perhaps overly—cautious route.

"You really can't create, and ought not to create, a defense strategy that's off the shelf," said a person who favored Anheuser's line of thinking. "It says that companies are predetermined, if they get a bid, to knee-jerk to do that rather than to evaluate the bid. You're biased." Because of the delayed start, Anheuser's board didn't consider a major media battle plan until June 25, a full two weeks after InBev's offer rolled in.

InBev and the rest of the world waited that entire time for Anheuser to draw its battle axe. Surely a legendary American company like Anheuser-Busch would have a wealth of options at its disposal. But Anheuser never bit.

"We were very surprised that they did not poison the waters in some way," said one InBev advisor. "We expected more of an antagonistic response, and thought they would start marshaling their parties to say what a bad idea this was. That's when we really realized that they were going to be disorganized and slow-moving. We would ask around and say, "Are they talking to people? What are they saying?" And people would be like 'Yeah, no, not really.'"

Several members of Anheuser's board made it clear that they were willing to fight if there was a chance of turning popular sentiment against a deal. In June, they asked for a report on the ammunition they had at their disposal. The board was running through a laundry list of tactics it might try to use to save the company: a "Pac-Man" defense in which Anheuser-Busch would spin around and make a bid to acquire InBev; a "scorched Earth" campaign where it would break itself into pieces and slam InBev in the press to sabotage its takeover effort; a deal with another brewer; and even a deal with a private equity firm. If they opted for one of these alternatives, the board wanted to know, how badly could they publicly malign InBev without hobbling themselves? And what were InBev's pressure points? Politics? Patriotism? Penny-pinching business practices? If they were going to dig into the trenches, they needed a big pile of mud to sling.

At the board's request, Kekst prepped a PR campaign for Anheuser to use if it decided to go ballistic on InBev. Larry Rand and his partner

Thomas Davies passed out a set of pitch books at the board's June 25 meeting, and Rand launched into a quick rundown of how Anheuser-Busch could run advertisements and opinion pieces in U.S. newspapers to roil the masses and compel the Teamsters union, beer distributors, and state and national congresspeople to enter the fray. He showed a proposed ad that echoed the same altered slogan Kit Bond had slung at Brito in Washington: "This Bud's Not for You." If the board really wanted to go to the mattresses, Rand said, they could inflict real damage upon InBev—and he was ready for battle.

The board was nonplussed. Kekst's "hard core" PR campaign wasn't nearly as combative or inventive as they had expected it to be. Was running a few pithy newspaper ads and boring op-eds really the best they could do? Anheuser-Busch was an American institution, and this had the potential to be one of the messiest takeover battles in corporate history. Surely there were more aggressive ways to incite public anger over the bid and rustle up support for Anheuser's independence.

"That seems kind of anemic," one of the directors told Rand. "What if we really wanted to fight this thing? What do we do? It doesn't look like you guys have really even thought about it."

"I see a bunch of these one-liner tactics," said another, glancing down at the pitch book in front of him, "but what would you actually say? Where are the messages?"

Rand and Davies exchanged rueful glances as the rest of the room looked on expectantly, basically nodding in agreement that the pitch seemed tone-deaf and out of touch with the harsh realities of the situation they were facing.

"That's how it resonated with all of us in the room," one Anheuser advisor said. "We thought, 'This is literally one of the biggest takeover attempts ever, and this is what you show up with?' It was like he had hardly spent any time thinking about it. Everyone was totally underwhelmed by it, and it was just like 'You've got to go back and do some more work.'"

Kekst, however, had actually showed up with quite a bit more. Rand's team had ginned up a series of proposed advertisements and taglines that aimed straight at InBev's jugular—exactly the sorts of specifics the board was looking for. However, none of it ever saw the light of day. Randy Baker, who was spearheading Anheuser's public relations effort, had reviewed Kekst's materials prior to the board's meeting and pulled Rand aside.

"We don't want the board to see all of this stuff," he told Rand, instructing him to pull the harsher sample ads and talking points out of his pitch book. By the time all of the offending pages were removed, Kekst's "scorched Earth" campaign was about one-fifth its original size, and even less formidable.

"No one really wanted to engage the board on anything very aggressive," said one person on Anheuser's team. Baker seemed gun-shy about presenting certain information to Anheuser's directors, and because all of the communications efforts went through his office, the decision was ultimately his.

"Management was really controlling all of the information flow to the board," said one person close to the company's PR effort. "He was really, really trying to keep a very close control on things. Basically, things would go into his office, and that was kind of it."

If the company's ultimate aim was to fight, it had already dropped the ball on a huge opportunity due in part to its disjointed PR structure. Because InBev's financing wasn't knitted together at first, Anheuser could have fired back with vigor, using those initial few weeks to hamper InBev's attempts to recruit more banks. That didn't happen, though. Anheuser had stayed silent, giving InBev time to assemble the money it needed to make an all-cash bid.

Aside from buying the other half of Mexican brewer Modelo, furthermore, the company's defensive options were looking pretty unappealing. The board was already frustrated that August IV hadn't done more, financially and strategically, to shore the company up against a takeover.

"A year before, we had directed management to prepare defenses in case there was a run made at us," said Ambassador Jones. "We didn't have any indication that anybody would do that, but you had to be prepared for it. And somehow, this came up and it seemed like preparations hadn't been made as we had thought."

"Some members of the board thought that August IV hadn't led the way he was supposed to, but nobody knew for sure," Jones said. "Once we got into a hostile takeover situation, we had to just concentrate on our business."

There was no way they could simply reject InBev's offer without offering up an alternate plan. A Pac-Man defense wouldn't work because Anheuser had no interest in owning InBev. It would be nearly impossible for a private equity firm to compete with InBev, given the horrendous credit environment. And a scorched Earth campaign could really come back to haunt them. What if they weren't successful in driving InBev away, and they ended up sitting across the table from the same people they had been slamming in the media to negotiate a deal? Anheuser ran the risk of irreversibly poisoning its own well.

Some board members had favored an attack on InBev when they walked into that June 25 board meeting. It seemed they had no choice afterward but to lay low. Op-eds and snarky newspaper ads weren't going to cut it. At the end of that day's frustrating session, they opted against launching a scorched Earth attack and told Kekst to destroy its most aggressive materials. Instead, Anheuser's management decided to play up the company's Blue Ocean cost-cutting plan and publicly prod at the valuation of InBev's offer to suggest it was too low. It was a weak-kneed approach, and they knew it.

Anheuser's public relations campaign turned into even more of a tag-team effort from that point on. Several advisors, including Joe Flom and the company's bankers, tossed their hats into the ring with Randy Baker, Dave Peacock, Anheuser communications head Terri Vogt, and Kekst to serve as a de facto PR committee.

"Ultimately, the PR effort was something that all of us kind of then jumped in on," said one person who was involved. "There was just the sense that we had an awful lot of people looking at this, and I think everybody felt that we had all done the drill before, working on raids, and we could handle this stuff." Peacock, a marketing man by trade, played a particularly heavy role in the effort, in part to offset a lack of involvement by August IV. "The Fourth in many ways was very distant from a lot of this stuff," said one company advisor. "It was really done by Peacock, by Randy, by all these other guys."

It was an inopportune time for Anheuser-Busch to experiment with its outreach effort, however. The company's PR push was threatening to become even more disjointed at a time when sending a cohesive message was critical. Investors and the media were already wondering why Anheuser was taking so long to respond to InBev's bid. *Advertising Age* ran an article entitled "A-B Losing the PR War to InBev," where it slammed Anheuser's "reactive, bunkered-down posture" and said it "appeared to be struggling to get its side of the story into the press."

"This is not complicated stuff—it's PR 101—but they don't seem to be doing even that," the article quoted one PR executive as saying.

■ ■ ■

There was at least one legitimate reason for Anheuser-Busch's public silence, however. It was cranking away furiously behind the scenes to identify alternatives to InBev's offer. There were a few possibilities—a deal with another suitor, for example, or some sort of tie-up with a big private equity firm. Anheuser had already decided to unveil the latest details of its Blue Ocean program to investors sooner than it had planned to help its cause. Only one option really looked viable: a purchase, at long last, of the 49.8 percent stake in Mexico's Grupo Modelo that Anheuser-Busch didn't already own.

A deal to combine Anheuser-Busch and Modelo, which brewed Modelo, Pacífico, and Corona Extra, one of the world's most popular beers, made sense for a whole host of reasons. They could cut plenty of costs by joining hands, and it would significantly broaden both companies' global footprints. Most importantly, there was a good chance that Anheuser-Busch and Modelo, combined, would be too expensive for InBev to swallow given the perilous state of the lending markets on Wall Street. Welding Modelo onto Anheuser-Busch could boost Anheuser's price tag by $10 billion or $15 billion.

"This was a totally feasible, realistic defense, because not only would it improve the stock price, the size of the company would be out of the zip code where InBev could finance a deal," said one Anheuser-Busch advisor. Even if InBev were still somehow able to bid for both Anheuser-Busch and Modelo, it would make it nearly impossible for them to pay fully in cash. Sending InBev back to the drawing board—and making it either beg a bunch of struggling banks for more financing or issue shares of stock in a rough market—could ruin its effort entirely.

So rather than hearing gossip about how Anheuser-Busch was progressing with the evaluation of its bid, the few scraps of news InBev heard in those first few days after making its offer involved the name "Modelo." It was worrisome. InBev's advisors professed that they could handle the Modelo threat. Yet some actually feared they couldn't. The financing markets weren't stable, and making a bid for Anheuser alone had been risky. Cobbling together enough money to buy Modelo on top of Anheuser-Busch could be nearly impossible. InBev had somehow barrel-rolled under the credit market's garage door just as it was closing shut. The chances that it could perform the same trick again—with much more cash at stake—looked slim.

The situation threatened to get particularly sticky for Lazard's Antonio Weiss, whose banking relationship with InBev over the years had been critical to his success as a merger specialist on Wall Street and in Europe. Weiss, a well-mannered banker and Yale graduate with perfect diction and a toothy smile, had been based in Paris for about eight years. He spent his daytime hours in the world of finance, but he also had one foot in the literary world as publisher of the *Paris Review*, the highbrow American journal. He had once apprenticed for the *Review's* well-known founder and editor, George Plimpton, who helped him win the affections of his eventual wife.

Weiss, a native New Yorker who clocked loops in his soccer cleats around the Central Park Reservoir as a boy, had advised Interbrew on the 2004 merger that created InBev. He was now, uncannily, facing off against the other two banks that had been involved in the deal— Goldman Sachs had also advised Interbrew, and Citigroup had been seated on the other side of the table, counseling AmBev. Weiss's fortunes had been tied to InBev for nearly a decade and a half. Back in 1994, when he had been a young vice president at Lazard with only a year or two under his belt, the firm was hired to represent Interbrew in the potential sale of Canadian brewer Labatt. Interbrew had been called upon as a potential "white knight" bidder to buy Labatt and save it from less desirable suitors, and a team at Lazard was assigned to the deal. The takeover eventually transpired, and as 1995 rolled around, a good deal of post-transaction clean-up work needed to be finished. Interbrew wanted to boost its stake in Mexican drinks company Fomento Económico Mexicano SA de CV (FEMSA) and sell some assets, and it wanted Lazard to manage the process. The team that had advised Interbrew on the Labatt deal, however, had suffered some turnover, and Weiss was suddenly pulled into the middle of the process. "You'll be sufficient," Interbrew told Weiss, voicing confidence in the young banker despite his lack of proven experience. Weiss never forgot. From that point on, he and the company that ultimately became InBev had a symbiotic relationship—each, over time, helped boost the other's fortunes and cachet.

Weiss valued InBev as his most important client. The company was also now working with J.P. Morgan, but Doug Braunstein, J.P. Morgan's head of investment banking, was there more to pull together InBev's financing package than to offer strategic advice. Braunstein did happen to have a connection to Anheuser-Busch board member Sandy Warner, however, thanks to Warner's former role as chairman of J.P. Morgan Chase, and his position as a bit of an insider appeared to rankle Weiss at times. "There clearly was growing friction between the two of them," said one person close to InBev. "There was a point in the process where Antonio didn't even want to talk to Doug, and basically said to Steve Golub [his Lazard colleague], 'You know, look, you deal with Braunstein. I'm not going to deal with him.'"

It was clear that Weiss was the banker Brito and his fellow Brazilians trusted most. And with so much on the line—not just InBev's money but also the reputations of everyone involved—a strategic misstep could prove disastrous. Wall Street's deal-making machinery tends to move in just one direction—forward—and as companies and their advisors get caught up in that momentum, they can lose the ability to retrace their steps or to walk away from a deal. If Anheuser-Busch struck up a deal to buy Modelo, it wasn't clear that Weiss could still advise InBev in good conscience to stick it out and press onward with the takeover. The deal would be much more difficult to close, the companies would be harder to successfully combine, and the debt required to finance the transaction would bury InBev for years.

Something had to be done to keep the pressure on Anheuser-Busch and force it to focus on InBev's offer, not on Modelo. The InBev team wasn't sure how serious the two companies' talks had gotten. To further muddy the waters, questions were starting to surface over whether Modelo had a contractual right, as Anheuser's partner, to block InBev's takeover attempt. InBev's lawyers didn't think the claim was valid, but all of the legal running-around had thrown a handful of sand in the gears.

There was one matter on which InBev was confident, however, and that's what it decided to use as a tool to regain the market's attention. Some of Anheuser's shareholders were bound to revolt if it tried to buy Modelo rather than taking the $65 per share offer already on the table. To ignite that group of investors, and perhaps compel them to lobby against Modelo before talks progressed any further, Brito made yet another courtesy call to August IV on June 15 and then sent out another carefully worded press release.

InBev, which had the "greatest respect for Grupo Modelo and its management," it stated, had read reports suggesting that Anheuser may have approached Modelo about a deal. In light of those reports, InBev wanted Anheuser to understand that its offer was for Anheuser's current assets and business only, not for its business combined with some or all of Modelo. In other words, InBev was threatening consequences if Anheuser-Busch tried to pull a fast one and ink a deal with Modelo. Its intent wasn't to convince Anheuser to stop the Modelo talks, which InBev knew was unlikely, but to get Anheuser's shareholders to rally against them. They were staring at a quick and easy pile of cash for their stock. Why take the risk on a deal with the Mexicans?

Crafting that letter, and pretty much everything else that involved Modelo, was a tortuous process. InBev had "relationships everywhere" in the beer industry, as one advisor put it. It felt the opportunity to rile up Anheuser's shareholders, however, was worth the effort.

The warning was successful in seizing back the market's attention for a day or two, but it didn't illuminate anything new or novel for Anheuser-Busch or its stockholders. If Anheuser was going to buy the other half of Modelo, which it had repeatedly opted against in the past, it already knew it had only one shot do it right. Winning shareholders' trust was going to be a steep challenge. And that was only after assuming The Fourth could convince his own board that buying Modelo was their best option.

Chapter 10

Angry Bedfellows

They didn't like each other—that was clear. They held the Anheuser-Busch people pretty much in disdain. They felt they were much better operators.

—Person close to Modelo

Thankfully, Anheuser–Busch had been keeping the idea of buying the rest of Modelo on ice for decades. The Fourth and his deputies understood the concept intimately, since it had been considered countless times over the years and then stuck back on the shelf in each instance. Part of the reason for the company's paralysis was that the five Mexican families that controlled Modelo had never been willing to sell. Anheuser, however, had never put a compelling offer on the table. Now, The Fourth was eager to convince Modelo that it was time to set the companies' fractured history aside and get serious.

Anheuser's board was already well aware of the Modelo option. During a meeting two weeks earlier, when they had first convened to address the rumors of InBev's bid, they had discussed whether a deal to merge with Modelo could keep InBev at bay.

So in an attempt to salvage both the company's independence and his reputation, August IV told Tom Santel, the head of Anheuser's international business, to pick up the phone as soon as the ink dried on InBev's offer and call Carlos Fernández González, The Fourth's counterpart at the Mexican brewer.

Fernández, Modelo's 41-year-old chairman and CEO, had been expecting the call and had done some prep work in advance. On June 10, the day before InBev's offer came through, Fernández had met with Robert Kindler, a top banker from Morgan Stanley whom Fernández had summoned to his family office on the picturesque Paseo de la Reforma in Mexico City. Kindler caught a 1 A.M. Mexicana Airlines flight that morning out of New York's John F. Kennedy airport in order to be there on time, a tough pill to swallow even for a road warrior who had spent countless hours traveling as an investment banker and, before that, a corporate attorney. To rub an extra bit of gravel in his bleary eyes, there was no driver waiting to pick him up when he landed at the crack of dawn. He had to hitch a ride to his hotel with a few bankers from UBS who also happened to be arriving in the country's smoggy capital on business.

Fernández wanted to prepare that day for what Modelo felt was inevitable: a bid by InBev for its partner and majority owner, Anheuser-Busch. Once InBev made an offer and the fireworks started, Modelo wanted to ensure that it could stay relevant and maintain some negotiating leverage rather than getting trampled.

"We knew it was coming," said one person close to Modelo. "I mean, everyone in the world knew that InBev was making a bid. There was no secret to it—months before that, not just then."

Kindler and his team at Morgan Stanley, which included bankers both in New York and on the ground in Mexico, had agreed to advise Modelo several weeks earlier after David Mercado, a partner at Cravath, Swaine & Moore, the white shoe firm where Kindler had once practiced law, called to see whether Morgan Stanley had any conflicts that would prevent it from taking the assignment. By hiring Kindler for advice, Modelo had aimed straight for the top—he was one of Wall Street's highest profile and best-connected strategic minds.

The Queens-bred Kindler wasn't your typical Ivy League banker, though. He had an aversion to neckties and preferred to brag about his stand-up comedian brother Andy rather than talking business.

Kindler's team hadn't been given much of a head start, but it didn't take long to grasp Modelo's strategic options. The Mexicans had hashed through the scenarios for a deal with Anheuser-Busch numerous times, and they had their priorities clear. By the time Santel called Fernández, Modelo had primed its pump and was prepared to hear what he had to say.

■ ■ ■

Anheuser-Busch's relationship with Modelo stretched back to March of 1993, when Anheuser paid $477 million for a 17.7 percent stake in the company. At the time, the deal pegged Modelo's equity value at $2.65 billion.

Modelo had already ballooned by then into Mexico's biggest brewer, and the venture represented an effort by Anheuser, which controlled 44 percent of the U.S. beer market, to find better ways to grow as opportunities in the United States became tougher to come by. The deal was celebrated north of the border as an insightful way to boost Anheuser-Busch's exposure to a rapidly expanding new market. And while the companies' pact had holes in it that came back to haunt both parties over the years, the investment proved to be one of Anheuser's smartest strategic plays. It secured the right to boost its stake in Modelo to just more than half of the company when the deal was first signed, and while it took a few years and at least one threat of arbitration, that's what Anheuser eventually did.

"That was a great acquisition—a $1.6 billion investment for 50 percent of Modelo, later worth something like $13 billion," said Jack Purnell, who orchestrated the deal as head of Anheuser-Busch's international business at the time. "That's the reason I'm still thought of well around the company." Don Antonino Fernández, the Mexican patriarch who had been CEO of Modelo at the time of the deal, emerged looking decidedly less victorious, and the perception that Modelo had allowed itself to get hoodwinked only worsened as the years passed.

Modelo had faced several threats in the early 1990s that made it amenable to the deal. The North American Free Trade Agreement (NAFTA) was undergoing final revisions in Washington, and many Mexican companies were concerned about how they would compete against U.S. products that might flow into their market if both countries slashed import taxes. Modelo was also expanding and building new breweries, and its aversion to debt made it eager to find cash to fund those efforts. Mexican beverage maker Fomento Económico Mexicano SA, or FEMSA, furthermore, had already sold a 7.9 percent stake to Miller. If Modelo's biggest rival was going to tie up with the second-biggest brewer in the United States, the best way for Modelo to top it was to ally with No. 1 Anheuser-Busch.

Anheuser-Busch had plenty of reasons to need Modelo, too. Despite their differences, both companies shared a particular history. They had swelled into the 500-pound gorillas in their respective markets by expanding and improving their own businesses, not by acquiring others. It took scrappiness and fortitude to do that successfully, and both companies had struck upon winning recipes.

More importantly, however, Anheuser had buried itself in a pile of efforts to sell Budweiser abroad that added up to relatively little. It needed a better way to snag some foreign growth for itself, and Mexico's thirsty crowds were pushing beer consumption upward by 6.5 percent a year. The Third's archrival, Miller, was moving much more aggressively to take advantage of this type of global expansion.

When The Third finally pulled the trigger and bought into Modelo, it marked a refreshing change for Anheuser staffers who had grown tired of chasing their tails on deals that never happened. The tie-up took several messy years to come together. Negotiations were plagued by stops and starts. Agreements were reached in principle, and then disputes arose over agreements. August III and Jack Purnell jetted down for meetings with representatives for the families that controlled Modelo in cities ranging from Guadalajara to Cabo San Lucas. And The Third turned repeatedly to his beloved dialectics to determine whether the investment was worthwhile, pitting teams of executives against each other to debate the matter. Purnell and his staffers conducted three separate month-long reviews on the Modelo deal over a span of two years.

"There were problems over control initially," Purnell said, which was hardly a surprise given The Third's historic tendencies. "August was very much a hands-on manager, not a big delegator. He wanted control, but later on, after taking a trip to Mexico, got comfortable not having control." August's willingness to let Modelo take the driver's seat was atypical, since his inability to cede control had torpedoed most of the other deals Anheuser-Busch had considered. Part of his decision stemmed from the political situation during that era in Mexico. The companies felt Modelo might be able to deal more effectively with Mexican President Carlos Salinas and other top politicians, who were heavily enmeshed in the business sector, if it remained under Mexican control.

The debate over who would pull Modelo's puppet strings, once resolved, gave rise to another sticking point in the talks. If the Mexicans were going to stay in charge of their own business, August III thought it only seemed fair that they should get less money for the stake they were selling. Disagreements on pricing stalled the talks for a long time, but "eventually," Purnell said, "they came around to our price." Modelo's willingness to take a lower offer finally got the deal done. The fact that Anheuser had secured sweet financial terms for itself wasn't lost on Modelo. Angst about the partnership within Modelo's controlling families intensified during the first few years of the tie-up as Anheuser increased its ownership at prices that looked cheaper each time Modelo's performance beat expectations.

Using options that were set to expire at the end of 1997, Anheuser bought up chunks of Modelo until it owned just more than half the company—but not without a battle. In late 1996, three years into the agreement, Anheuser announced that it planned to pay $550 million to more than double its stake to 37 percent. A dispute over the purchase price stalled the deal, however, and Anheuser warned its investors that if the two parties couldn't reach an agreement, the issue might tumble into arbitration. Three months later, Anheuser finally made its purchase—but at a cost of $605 million, a 10 percent increase over its initial plan. It then paid another $550 million the following month to buy its remaining 13.25 percent stake, bringing its total ownership to 50.2 percent. Through all three transactions, the amount of cash Anheuser sunk into Modelo totaled $1.63 billion.

From a financial standpoint, the investment proved lucrative and critically important for Anheuser-Busch. Without the profits it reaped from Modelo, it would have endured even harsher rebukes from Wall Street analysts and investors as its own business in the United States slowed. A variety of terms in the agreement stacked up in favor of Modelo, though, and provided some reassurance to its controlling families even after Anheuser-Busch seized majority ownership.

The most valuable cards in Modelo's hand involved control. The original deal with Anheuser gave Modelo sole decision-making capability, not only over how its operations were run but also over the amount of money it paid out in cash dividends each year. Those dividends went straight to Modelo's controlling families and to the company's other shareholders, including Anheuser-Busch.

"There were theoretical hooks in the agreement, but the reality is that Modelo had the biggest hook," said one person close to Modelo. "It was entirely under Modelo's control how much cash stayed at Modelo or went out to the shareholders. And from Anheuser's perspective, the only thing they really cared about was the dividend because they had no control. Historically, there were a lot of disputes about that. Anheuser really couldn't control what Modelo was doing."

A different problem drove Anheuser's beer wholesalers to the edge, however. U.S. distribution rights weren't included in the 1993 agreement—which meant that although Anheuser-Busch had invested heavily in the company, someone else imported Modelo's beers. Anheuser tried to win the rights to import Corona, but in 1996, Modelo tied itself for another 10 years to its original distribution partners in a move that looked suspiciously like an effort to swat Anheuser away. Modelo brushed Anheuser back yet again when those agreements expired, leaving Anheuser's distributors still competing against Modelo's beers in the United States rather than selling them. "That was a real point of contention with Mr. Busch in the 2000 decade," said a former top executive at Anheuser-Busch. "How come we don't have rights to Modelo when it was a growing brand—how can we not have rights for all of our wholesalers?"

The Third, despite his intense powers of coercion, never found a way to shoehorn the Mexicans into submission.

"These guys were expecting to buy the company in the first years of our partnership, and they were doing everything they could to upset us," said one person close to Modelo. That's one of the reasons the families that owned Modelo set up a controlling trust to manage their interests—to make it clear that they had no plans to sell. The Third and his team's rude and persistent entreaties angered Modelo's Mexican patriarchs.

"They were not going to sell their souls to us after the way we treated them," a top Anheuser executive said. "He would just get livid, he would threaten, he would cajole, he would do everything he could to try to make them do it," the executive said. "That's not the way you negotiate a deal."

■ ■ ■

Money and control weren't the only thing that drove Anheuser-Busch and Modelo to the wrestling mats. The more time the two companies' executives and family members spent with each other over the years, the less it seemed they could stomach the personal interaction. Some executives in St. Louis felt Modelo wasn't trustworthy—that they didn't play by the same rules of business conduct Anheuser did. Modelo insiders, meanwhile, saw the Busches, and August III in particular, as patronizing and rude.

"August III they despised," said Harry Schuhmacher. "He was just so arrogant."

One particular tale that reared its head during the InBev take-over battle was legendary at both companies. In the early 1990s, when the two rivals were still negotiating their original deal, a group of Anheuser-Busch executives flew down with their spouses to Cabo San Lucas, a vacation spot on Mexico's Pacific Coast, for a weekend of deep-sea sport fishing. The group convened at the docks one morning with Modelo's top executives and their wives, packed what they needed into a couple of fishing boats, and motored off with their hired crews in search of marlin.

August III's boat hooked a good-sized fish not long after setting out, and Valentín Díez, a senior vice president of Modelo at the time, took the chair and began fighting to reel in the fish. More than an hour later, August III glanced over at Valentín, who was covered in sweat and still laboring behind the reel, and suggested that someone else should relieve him for a while. Then The Third's cell phone rang, and he turned away to answer the call, rejoining the group moments later to announce that he had to return to the United States for an urgent matter. Something clearly ranked higher on his list of priorities than the opportunity to bond out at sea with his potential Mexican business partners.

The Third's boat mates agreed to turn around and head in, but their captain wanted to hand off the rod—and the valuable marlin still attached to it—to another boat first.

"Out here?" The Third said quizzically. "No way. That's too dangerous with two boats out here in the open sea, rocking and rolling the way we are!" The boats were indeed caught in some sizable swells, and several of the women on August III's boat, including his wife, Ginny, had been struggling to keep their breakfast down since they first tossed in their fishing lines. The wife of Pablo Aramburuzabala, a key Modelo controlling shareholder, had been up on the bridge with the boat's captain for 40 minutes, lobbying half-jokingly for the group to cut its lines and turn back to dry land.

It quickly became clear that August III and the captain were threatening a standoff. The captain wasn't ready to give up on his marlin, nor was he thrilled about having his judgment overruled by a brusque, ice-eyed American while out at sea. It was safe to say that the captain hadn't met many men the likes of August III.

The Third turned to Purnell and quietly instructed him to take hold of the fishing rod and yank on it, hard. Purnell did as he was told, and the line predictably snapped, sending the marlin reeling into the depths with a shiny new hook embedded in its cheek. With no prize left to fight over, the captain angrily grabbed the steering wheel and pivoted his boat toward shore.

Once the group hit dry land, word quickly spread that The Third had rudely offended his counterparts at Modelo by forcing them to return early—and by making little effort to dispel the notion that he had more important things to do back home. According to Purnell, the truth was distorted. "They were not mad at us at all," he said. "In fact, Pablo's wife was very happy with us, and Pablo was too. Everyone was kind of laughing at it."

That wasn't how it came across to the Anheuser-Busch and Modelo executives who heard about the trip in the days that followed, however. And as time wore on, their beliefs about what happened mattered more than those held by the executives who were actually on the boat.

Relations between the two companies defrosted slightly after Carlos Fernández became CEO. After spending almost six months with Anheuser-Busch as part of a development program, he had returned to Mexico with a decent sense of what made Anheuser-Busch tick. He even built up a strong relationship with The Third, and with The Third's encouragement, he developed a straightforward relationship with August IV as well.

Fernández didn't particularly click, however, with various members of The Fourth's management team, and it was plainly obvious when the companies' takeover talks kicked off in 2008 that he and the rest of Modelo still harbored a general level of distaste for much of Anheuser-Busch's leadership.

Fernández and The Fourth represented an almost humorous exercise in contrasts. Carlos, who was two years younger than August IV, was a conservative, Catholic family man who had married the daughter of one of Modelo's elder statesmen and relished the time he spent with their five children. "One of the most obviously striking things is the difference in capacity between the Modelo son and the Anheuser son," said one Modelo advisor. "They couldn't be more different in personality and temperament. Carlos goes home every night to his wife and their bazillion kids and is a happy, sound, measured guy."

Fernández made a practice of responding with a polite "thank you" to every e-mail that dropped into his inbox, regardless of its level of importance. It was an endearing and gracious habit, and it wasn't atypical for a man of his cultural background. It got him into hot water, though, once Modelo became enmeshed in its talks with Anheuser.

"The lawyers freaked out on him about that," said one of Modelo's advisors. "Even when he gets an e-mail with newspaper clips, he writes back 'Thank you.' And you're like, 'Don't do that!'" Modelo's lawyers didn't want someone to refer to Carlos's response as "proof" that he had read a particular e-mail if, in fact, he hadn't.

Fernández espoused the same conservative values his family and the other Modelo families had always upheld. His job wasn't an easy one—he had to cater to the five family branches that co-owned Modelo while also managing the brewery and representing its interests in Mexican business and politics. The circle of wealthy corporate families in Mexico is relatively small, and their fates tend to be inextricably braided together. His straight-arrowed devotion to Modelo at an early age also set him apart from The Fourth, whose more casual attitude toward work bled well into his 40s. And while Carlos and August IV were both young CEOs, Carlos had been branded as Modelo's heir apparent in his late 20s when he was promoted to the company's board. August IV still hadn't convinced certain detractors that he deserved the CEO's job even after it was awarded to him.

Still, Fernández and The Fourth got along relatively well. August IV knew not to wear certain parts of his temperament—the partying and womanizing, namely—on his sleeve. "I think August could hide that side of him pretty well when he wanted to," said Harry Schuhmacher. "There are stories, and things get out, but if he needed to play the good boy he could. He was a Tiger Woods tragic character, where he could have this outward appearance of a sober executive and then also have this other side of him."

■ ■ ■

On paper, Fernández and August IV also shared one thing in common. Fernández's connection to Modelo came through his family. In his case, it began with his uncle Don Antonino, the longtime Modelo CEO who had sealed the company's original agreement with Anheuser-Busch. Carlos began tagging along at Don Antonino's side during visits to the company's Mexico City brewery at age 12. By high school, he was working there part-time, hauling sacks of grain and absorbing as much information as he could. Don Antonino, who had fought as a Nationalist in the Spanish civil war and had no sons of his own, commanded broad respect in the industry throughout his 30-year tenure and was a valuable mentor to his young nephew. Fernández returned the favor by holding Antonino in the deepest respect.

He kept a portrait of his elder hanging on the wall of the sleek board-room in their family's offices—pictures of various family members were pretty much everywhere—and he liked to shuffle guests into the room and direct them reverentially toward the piece of art.

Fernández was elected to Modelo's board in 1996 to fill the vacancy caused by the unexpected death the year before of Pablo Aramburuzabala, his father-in-law and a key controlling shareholder, at age 63. Just a year later, at only 30 years of age, he was named chief executive of Modelo to replace his uncle Antonino.

Both Carlos and August IV faced significant pressure, as leaders of a younger generation whose elders were still a strong presence at their companies. Carlos sat down several times over the years with The Fourth to share his experiences in dealing with Modelo's older scions, hoping that it might help to improve the frigid dynamic between The Fourth and his father. August IV's tether to his company's governing board of directors was much shorter than Carlos's. And August IV had no like-minded fellows-at-arms who were as strong a presence as María Asunción Aramburuzabala.

María, a striking woman of 45 who had inherited her father's stake in Modelo upon his death, was in many ways an ideal business partner for Carlos. She was his sister-in-law, the granddaughter of one of Modelo's founders, and the richest woman in Mexico. And while Carlos's skills were strong on the operating side of the business, her savviness lay more in the area of finance. However, they operated with similar intentions when it came to Modelo's future.

When she inherited her father's Modelo ownership, María had been unemployed and raising two children, and had almost no business experience. She decided to throw herself into the family business rather than letting others control her fate, and from an office the size of a broom closet, she made two of Modelo's bankrupt yeast companies profitable within a year of taking them over. María proceeded to build a reputation as a savvy businesswoman who rivaled the men in her family, and in 2000, she outmaneuvered a competitor to win control of a 20 percent stake in Mexican media giant Televisa.

Known by the nickname Mariasun, she was married to Antonio "Tony" Garza Jr., the son of a Texas gas station owner who served as U.S. ambassador to Mexico under President George W. Bush.

Garza was tight with Bush, the former governor of Texas, who first appointed Garza as Texas's 99th secretary of state before naming him head of one of the United States' largest embassies. The "golden couple's" 2005 wedding drew the attendance of former First Lady Laura Bush and kept breathless gossip columnists enthralled for months on both sides of the border.

By 2009, the year in which *Fortune* magazine named her the world's 26th most powerful woman at the age of 46, María was serving as a member of several major companies' boards of directors and living in a palatial home in Mexico City with Garza, who decided to abandon Texas politics for a career as a lawyer and consultant. The choice was certainly a defensible one, given the size of his wife's beer fortune. She shared her windfall with her mother and sister, but there was clearly plenty of cash to go around. María's name was frequently tossed into the same sentences as Carlos Slim's, the Mexican tycoon whose fortune has ranked larger at points than those of either Bill Gates or Warren Buffett.

"We really didn't know her until she took her dad's spot on the board, and then she kind of ballooned," said one former Anheuser-Busch executive, who wistfully described Aramburuzabala as "foxy." "She's a sharp dresser, and has a smart business head on her shoulders. She really is something."

It wasn't all praise, though, for the two young minds behind Modelo and their families. Economists have railed since the 1990s against the policies that allowed a handful of Mexicans to become billionaires by controlling giant, monopolistic pieces of the country's telephone, cement, silver, and beer markets. The beer industry, however, has brewed fortunes for dozens of families around the world over the past two centuries. María wasn't even the richest person whose wealth was tied up in the drama that unfolded between InBev and Anheuser-Busch. In 2007, just before the global banking system collapse decimated inheritances worldwide, a *Forbes* magazine list of the world's richest people pinpointed four characters with even larger bank accounts who also played roles of varying degrees in the saga.

Two of those were somewhat tangential. Jack Taylor, founder of St. Louis-based Enterprise Rent-A-Car, ranked with his family as the world's 37th-richest person with $13.9 billion, ahead of three Russian metal tycoons and corporate raider Carl Icahn. Taylor, who was 84 the year the list came out, built his fortune on rental cars. His son Andrew, who took over as CEO of Enterprise in 1994, was a member of Anheuser-Busch's board and a company shareholder when InBev launched its takeover attempt. Julio Mario Santo Domingo, the Colombian patriarch of his own wealthy family who was born the year after Jack Taylor, ranked 132nd on the list that year with $5.7 billion. The Santo Domingo Group controls a broad portfolio of companies, but one of its key holdings at the time of InBev's bid was a 15.1 percent stake in InBev rival and potential party-crasher SABMiller.

Not much further down in the *Forbes* tally, his name interspersed between those of telecommunications tycoons and financiers, sat InBev's Jorge Paulo Lemann with a fortune of $4.9 billion. Lemann's business partner Marcel Telles ranked 432nd with $2.2 billion, followed finally by Mariasun. Her estimated $2 billion estate sat tied for 488th with the estate of Carlos Sicupira, the third member of InBev's Brazilian triumvirate.

■ ■ ■

Fifteen years into their tumultuous partnership, with InBev knocking on the door, Anheuser-Busch and Modelo were forced back to the negotiating table for a new round of talks. The high stakes both companies were now facing made their earlier warfare look like a series of sandbox spats.

For Anheuser-Busch, this literally meant everything. A deal to merge with Modelo—or at the very least, a near-deal that could be used to threaten InBev into making a higher bid—was its only realistic defensive option. Modelo, meanwhile, sensed blood in the water, but it knew its bargaining position was precarious. The talks with Anheuser-Busch were likely to produce a binary result—Modelo could either execute a huge financial coup or suffer a monumental loss in power and leverage. If the Mexicans played their cards right, they might finally win retribution by selling the company at a high price to a desperate Anheuser-Busch. If not, they could have to watch helplessly as Anheuser's half-stake fell into the hands of InBev, whose strict operating style might make it an even tougher partner to deal with.

The first phone call Fernández got from Anheuser-Busch during the takeover fight actually came from August III. The Third reached Carlos on his cell phone on Saturday, May 24, the day after news of InBev's interest first hit the papers, to see whether it was true that Spain's Banco Santander was lending money to InBev to help in the effort. Carlos was a member of Santander's international advisory board, and his family had long been one of the bank's major shareholders. With those connections, The Third thought he might know whether the Spanish were involved.

The Third was clearly upset by the takeover rumors, and it didn't help when Carlos expressed surprise that he had first heard news of InBev's plans through the media. Carlos was spending time that day with his family, and had no more information about Santander's involvement than anyone else. He had heard about it for the first time from the papers as well.

"Can you find out?" The Third asked. Carlos wasn't privy to that sort of information, however. There was nothing he could do to help.

Once InBev made its bid official, August IV's team wasted no time in firing up talks with Modelo. Tom Santel called Fernández to request a meeting just hours after reading InBev's fax during the strategy committee's session at the soccer park. On Thursday, June 12, the very next day, he hitched a plane to Mexico City, leaving instructions for his corporate planning team on how to handle the second day of the session without him. He spent Wednesday night prepping for the biggest pitch of his professional career.

Santel arrived at Fernández's family offices bearing a formal presentation, a copy of which he handed to Fernández as he launched into his pitch. And the pitch was big.

Anheuser-Busch wanted to buy the rest of Modelo, Santel explained. The company understood that to get Modelo on board, it was going to have to pay a higher relative price for Modelo's assets than InBev was offering for Anheuser's own business. Modelo's growth prospects were stronger than Anheuser's, and both companies knew it. So while he didn't have a number set in stone, Santel said Anheuser-Busch was willing to consider a deal that valued Modelo at roughly $15 billion, which ranked well above the prices paid for other beer companies in recent years.

Fernández was shocked to hear the Americans propose such a big number straight out of the gate. The suggestion that they should pay a rich price for Modelo, however, was just fine by him. He knew that Anheuser-Busch's back was against the wall. August IV and his team had limited time to negotiate a deal before InBev grew more aggressive.

The value Anheuser-Busch was willing to assign to Modelo, which soon settled at $15.2 billion, wasn't uncovered on Wall Street during the companies' talks. Had it been, it would have surely prompted jaws to drop—and could have sparked enough outrage from Anheuser-Busch shareholders to nullify the negotiations before they progressed any further.

"They came up with a rather large price to pay for Modelo," one Anheuser-Busch advisor put it bluntly. "It was a huge fricking price."

Modelo's controlling families had wads of cash, however. That wasn't their primary concern. It was a different point in Santel's presentation that day that really perked up Fernández's ears.

"You, Carlos, would be CEO," he told Fernández.

Fernández leaned in to make sure he was understanding things correctly.

Carlos, Santel explained as he continued, could be put in charge of all of Anheuser-Busch Modelo—both companies combined—if he was willing to go through with the deal, while The Fourth would shift into a more ceremonial role with less power over day-to-day operations. That meant Fernández could steer the company in whichever direction he and the other Modelo family members chose.

It also meant that August IV was willing to hand Anheuser-Busch over to the Mexicans—at significant expense—in order to evade the Brazilians. Such a risky move was likely to spark a war among Anheuser-Busch investors over the right course of action. InBev's offer was already on the table, and its financing was coming together more tightly each day. A deal to combine Anheuser-Busch and Modelo could preserve Anheuser's "independence," at least optically. It would have to go off without a hitch to boost Anheuser's value to the point where it met investors' expectations.

August IV's offer to cede control was an effort to address those concerns. He wasn't likely to convince dubious shareholders that he was the right person to perform such a monumental task. He didn't have much operational experience, and he had none whatsoever in executing a merger. If shareholders knew that Fernández was going to be in charge, they might be willing to stick around.

Fernández was dubious. "What do you think about that, personally?" he asked Santel, who had sat on Modelo's board for more than a decade and knew the two companies' relationship well. "And what about the other members of the strategy committee?"

"Everyone enjoys working with you," Santel reassured him. "They'd be happy to." And he meant it. "God, he'd be a great boss to have," one strategy committee member said later, summarizing his thinking at the time. "He'd make us look like a multinational company, with August still there as a titular head."

The two companies' bankers and lawyers were briefed on the meeting within hours of Santel's departure from Mexico City, and The Fourth called Fernández soon afterward to confirm that he supported the terms that had been outlined. "I'm more than happy to work with you on the future of Anheuser-Busch," The Fourth said.

Months later, however, interpretations differed as to exactly when August IV and his team first agreed to let Carlos be chief executive— and whether Carlos pushed for it himself as a condition for starting talks.

"It was absolutely clear that Carlos was going to be the CEO and run the business" from the very first meeting, one of Modelo's advisors said. "So from Carlos's perspective, that actually had some appeal."

"Carlos would have never gone to his board and everybody else if that wasn't on the table," another Modelo advisor said.

People on Anheuser-Busch's side of the fence saw things a bit less clearly. While August IV and Santel may have suggested that Carlos could be CEO or co-CEO during the early stages of the companies' talks, they say, The Fourth never explicitly admitted that his team made the offer right from the start.

"No one would admit they had promised him the job," said one of Anheuser-Busch's advisors. "I bet he was promised the job. But no one will own up to having guaranteed him on day one that he would have that job."

"I'm not aware, and I don't believe that it happened, that August would have offered him that," said Sandy Warner. "There was no commitment at that moment. There was never any commitment to Carlos."

Even Santel wasn't able to clear up which promises were made to Carlos.

"I think there was some confusion there," he said. "I recall there was confusion on who said what to whom."

"We were certainly willing for him to run the whole international show. That was one of my jobs, but I'd be happy to have him do it, too."

Regardless of when the suggestion was made and how firm a commitment it represented, there was no question that Carlos's reputation exceeded The Fourth's when it came to operating a beer business. If the two executives had been pitted against each other and asked to whip up an inventive marketing campaign, The Fourth would have had a big edge, but Carlos was viewed as one of the better operators in the beer industry, even by executives within Anheuser-Busch.

"If you look at Modelo, it basically grew market share and was a tightly run company with very low expenses," said a person close to Modelo. "And that was all Carlos." If Anheuser-Busch was considered the U.S. beer market's "category killer" in 2008 with a 48.5 percent share of the market, Modelo warranted a different term entirely. By the end of that year, it controlled 63 percent of the Mexican market for domestic and exported beers.

Handing control to Fernández seemed like the responsible thing to do, and it looked like the best way to enlist the full support of the Modelo families. It could also be a way for August IV to escape the rigid, stifling box in which he had been suffocating since taking his current job. If either he or Anheuser's board had doubts about his leadership abilities now that he was 18 months into the gig, this was their chance to hand his crown to Fernández under the auspices of the deal. The Fourth would never have to admit he wasn't cut out for the position.

"When the card got played for Carlos to be CEO . . . and August to have a ceremonial role, at that stage in the game it was pretty smart because August was probably like, 'I'm done, I can't take it anymore,'" said a former Anheuser-Busch executive.

"I sense that he had . . . some feeling of kinship and responsibility to the other managers and employees," said one advisor to the company. "With just getting out of the limelight or stepping aside, it wouldn't have been that the company was lost on his watch, and it wouldn't have been that the people who mattered to him—the employees and managers—were toast. That was a much better result than InBev, even if he was not going to be CEO under either circumstance."

"It really created a much better company," said a person close to Modelo. "And Augie [IV] was a disgustingly awful CEO, so it actually was better."

To put less of a strain on its finances, Anheuser wanted to use its own stock to pay for as much of Modelo as possible. Companies that sell themselves are often turned off by the notion of accepting stock as payment, but under the structure Anheuser-Busch was proposing, the Modelo families could end up owning about 15 percent of the company—four times more shares than the Busch family did. That would make them the most powerful group of Anheuser-Busch share-holders by far, and they'd be controlling an even bigger company.

The proposition of owning the single largest stake in the company, combined with the notion that Carlos would be in charge, helped Modelo come around pretty quickly to the idea of accepting stock as currency. With Carlos at the helm, the value of their shares would depend on his leadership, not on August IV's. It was a much more palatable concept.

Santel's proposal in Mexico City was just an early-stage foray. Carlos and María knew it could take weeks of negotiations to strike up an actual deal. The tone his visit had set was unmistakable, though. Anheuser-Busch looked desperate—at least, that's how The Fourth's team had telegraphed it by making such a generous proposal right up front. They were offering Modelo the moon, not just by handing away control of the company but by proposing to pay a huge price to do so. It seemed backward, frankly. During merger negotiations, companies tend to lobby hard to either win control or to pay a lower purchase price, not to sacrifice control and pay extra to boot. The offer sounded too good to be true.

Kindler and Cravath lawyer David Mercado thought as much. Modelo was willing to kick off formal talks based on what Fernández heard from Santel that day. As the company sprang into action, the two advisors issued their first of many warnings.

"This is all very interesting, but you'd better stay close to InBev," Kindler cautioned. "You're just a 'stalking horse'"—an option used by a takeover target to lure higher offers from other parties. If that were true, Modelo could get dumped by Anheuser-Busch at the 11th hour and be stuck with InBev as its new half-owner. Given the history between the U.S. and Mexican brewers, such a move was certainly not out of the question. "The Mexicans had chips on their shoulders— they were waiting to be insulted," said one Modelo advisor.

Even if Anheuser-Busch was truly intent on a deal, the sheer concept that its board of directors would ultimately agree to hand the CEO's spot to Fernández still seemed shocking.

"I could not see the Anheuser-Busch company merging with Modelo and allowing a Mexican national to become CEO of the American gem," said one of Modelo's advisors. "I couldn't see it. I became a believer as people kept telling me, but on our initial briefs, we were like, 'Okay . . .' "

■ ■ ■

To protect itself in case Anheuser-Busch planned to use it as a pawn, Modelo knew that it needed to get cozy with InBev, too. The Mexican brewer had to look out for its own interests first, and it needed to try to preserve its rights in case InBev took over. That could require some rough negotiating tactics. If Fernández and his team agreed to turn their backs on Anheuser-Busch and supported InBev's bid, they would undoubtedly improve InBev's chances of success. And they might be able to win more freedom from InBev in exchange. They could use the threat of such a move as leverage against both sides.

InBev's Marcel Telles had actually reached out to Fernández, whom he had known for some time, just a few days after InBev first offered to buy Anheuser-Busch. Fernández was at home with his family when Telles called, but he stepped aside for a few moments to listen to what Telles had to say. InBev had great plans in store for Anheuser-Busch, Telles professed, and it wanted to build a strong partnership with Modelo. A few weeks later, the two men met at Cravath's law offices in midtown New York to discuss their companies' structures and family traditions.

Cravath's Mercado had a long history with InBev. He was a Texas-born, fluent Spanish speaker who specialized in Latin American deals and had worked closely with the Brazilians in the past—including on the 2004 deal to merge AmBev with Interbrew. Kindler and Mercado had come to know and trust each other long before that deal, which happened roughly around the time the more senior Kindler left Cravath for his first job in banking, as global head of mergers and acquisitions for J.P. Morgan. Kindler wasn't the only lawyer on Wall Street who had jumped ship for the banking side of the M&A business, with its splashier headlines and bigger pay packages. As the Modelo situation was proving, he still had plenty of chances to work with his old colleagues.

He and Mercado pulled in another one of their frequent collaborators—public relations maven Joele Frank—to advise Modelo on strategy and media tactics once things got rolling in mid-June. Modelo realized that things could get sticky if a deal with Anheuser-Busch neared the finish line. There would be countless investors to appease and dozens of reporters to lobby—not to mention the very families that controlled Modelo, who needed to be corralled for critical discussions and votes. A few members of Congress were bound to take note and start asking questions if the Mexicans took control in St. Louis. And if talks fell apart, Modelo was going to need a bulldog to press its case behind the scenes and keep the media on its side. While the documentation that lay behind it looked somewhat shaky, Modelo believed its original agreement with Anheuser gave it the right to veto a takeover of the company. At the very least, Modelo thought it could forcefully adopt that stance and become a burr in InBev's saddle, making life in Brussels painful until InBev agreed to some sort of compromise.

Mercado and Kindler had known the boisterous Frank for decades and had worked with her on plenty of deals—Mercado had even been staffed, as an associate just five years out of Yale Law School, on Frank's first-ever transaction: an $820 million hostile bid in 1989 by Vitro, the Mexican glass maker, to buy Florida-based Anchor Glass Container Corporation. Vitro spent 66 days battling to subsume Anchor Glass, whose biggest customer, interestingly enough, was Anheuser-Busch.

On Sunday, June 15, four days after InBev bid for Anheuser-Busch, Mercado put in a phone call to Frank and caught her in the middle of her son's graduation ceremony at Stanford University in California. Oprah Winfrey was the university's graduation speaker, and her speech made headlines, largely because she had endorsed Barack Obama in the upcoming presidential election after a career spent staying out of politics. Frank ended up with less time than she had expected for reveling in her moment as a proud mother.

"You have to be in Mexico City now," Mercado told her bluntly. "They want you there now." It was an abrupt flash back to reality, but Frank knew this was her best chance to get involved in what was shaping up to be the year's most exciting takeover battle. Anheuser and InBev were already working with other communications firms, and Modelo was the next-biggest player tied up in the fracas.

She left her family earlier than planned on Sunday and flew from San Francisco to Los Angeles to catch a connection to Mexico City. She didn't have much time to get up to speed, but reams of coverage of the budding war over Anheuser-Busch had been in all the papers. Frank spent the flight to Mexico scouring packets of media clippings that detailed The Fourth's checkered history, the warped dynamics of the Busch family, and the tainted relationship between Anheuser-Busch and Modelo. There were lots of bases to cover.

Mercado seemed just as concerned about the prospect of trying to negotiate with InBev, however, as he was about Modelo's talks with Anheuser-Busch. Based on the work he had done with InBev's Brazilian honchos in the past, he knew that swimming in both companies' shark tanks at the same time could be dangerous. The Busches tended to wear their prejudices on their sleeves, and the messy history between the two companies was already out there. Talks with InBev's steely crew, on the other hand, could be trickier to navigate. And the stakes for Modelo were incredibly high.

"Mercado knew InBev really well, and he was really, really concerned," said one Modelo advisor. "He just kept saying, 'You've got to understand these people. What we're doing is really going to be nasty.'"

Chapter 11

The Board: August, August, and Augusta

You've got this perception on Wall Street that we're dysfunctional. Well, maybe. But every company looks dysfunctional at a time like that, don't they?
—Former Anheuser-Busch marketing ace Bob Lachky

O n the night before Anheuser-Busch's first takeover-related board meeting in St. Louis, the teams from Goldman Sachs and Skadden touched down relatively late. It was late enough that the best place they could find with a kitchen that was still open for dinner was an old Italian restaurant in a sketchy warehouse district just off the banks of the Mississippi River.

The place was nearly empty when the small group of bankers and lawyers sat down, but the questionable digs didn't bother Skadden's Joe Flom, who launched an impressive attack on a massive surf and turf platter. Flom, a man in his mid-80s who, "dripping wet out of the shower, might weigh 105 pounds," according to one colleague, pounded down substantially more than his diminutive frame seemed it could handle. But he had as aggressive an appetite for a good takeover fight as he did for food, and he was gearing up for battle. He needed all of the energy he could muster.

Flom's work for Anheuser-Busch far predated the creation of InBev, as did his close relationship with The Third, and the Brazilians' hostile bid appeared to have set his blood to boil. His aptitude for defending vulnerable corporate clients had grown legendary over the years. He had a knack for finding alternate takeover suitors or, at the very least, wringing more money out of bidders' pockets when they appeared to be bone dry.

Flom had been a key figure on Wall Street since the late 1970s, when he and rival corporate attorney Martin Lipton were considered the best in the takeover business. Flom was particularly well known in deal-making circles for the "Jewish dentist" defense, which he concocted in 1975 while defending dental equipment maker Sterndent against a hostile bid from Magus Corporation. Flom decided that attention should be drawn to the fact that Magus was part-owned by Kuwaitis, and started loudly proclaiming that if the deal occurred, Sterndent's clients—many of whom were Jewish dentists—were bound to take their business elsewhere. The scare tactic worked well enough to give him time to find another bidder for his client, and the episode showed how a well-run public relations campaign could bolster traditional legal takeover defense measures.

"His first instinct was to show a good, strong defense," said one Anheuser-Busch advisor. "If you do that, you're going to be able to negotiate or find something else. Flom's theory has always been 'You give me enough time, and I'll find a solution.'"

"At the end of the day," said the advisor, "Joe always has an incredible instinct for moving things around so you can maximize value." Flom was getting to be somewhat long in the tooth, however, and wasn't as intimately involved with Skadden's day-to-day practice as he used to be. That was where Paul Schnell, another top Skadden M&A attorney, came in. The two spearheaded Skadden's team of advisors to Anheuser-Busch, with Schnell handling many of the particulars.

Anheuser's directors were accustomed to meeting 9 or 10 times a year. The Busches traditionally hosted dinner for the group in St. Louis on the night before each of their gatherings, which had always given the board's members plenty of time to catch up on anything that had transpired in the last month and a half.

But they were about to start getting to know each other much, much better. On May 29, six days after news of InBev's interest hit the papers, the board had met to discuss the rumors. Gossip had been swirling for months that the Brazilians were on the prowl, and the board knew InBev was big—and getting bigger. It was clear that Anheuser-Busch needed to keep growing to avoid being consumed. But few of the board's members believed that the company was already within InBev's reach. "I don't think anyone on the board felt that it was as close as it was—that InBev would be able to amass enough capital to buy Anheuser-Busch," said General Shelton. "That part of it caught us by surprise."

With so much uncertainty suddenly facing the company, the board had a solid docket of issues to cover that day. Goldman's team outlined how InBev might try to finance a bid at the rumored $65 per share, the company's executives laid out their progress on their Blue Ocean cost-cutting plan, and Skadden made the first of many presentations that covered the board's duties to shareholders. They mulled over the potential for a deal with Modelo, and debated whether to try to meet with InBev to hear things straight from the horse's mouth.

But when the board disbanded that day, the ball was in August IV's court. Barring any overtures from InBev, they planned to let him and the rest of Anheuser's management push ahead with their cost-slashing efforts and restructuring plans. And as the days ticked by with no word from Belgium, Anheuser's directors began to hope the takeover threat had dissipated. Maybe InBev couldn't cobble together the financing it needed, or had thought twice about the wisdom of sparring with its joint venture partner.

They weren't off the hook for long. When InBev faxed in its offer, everything dropped right into their laps, and their collective nightmare began. Many people who serve as corporate directors would relish the chance to bid for a rival company, but few are eager to be placed under a microscope on the receiving end. Suddenly, a raft of investors and news anchors turned their focus toward Anheuser's 14 board members to gauge how they might react. And their judgments weren't pretty.

■ ■ ■

Anheuser's board of directors during the fight against InBev constituted a significant improvement on its governing bodies of old. Past directors of the company had included a deputy U.S. defense secretary who resigned in an insider trading scandal and a wealth of cronies and St. Louis–based supporters of the Busch family. Facing a barrage of criticism from shareholders, The Third had taken some halfhearted steps late in his tenure to flesh out the group with a few people who seemed more independent. But The Fourth said he wanted to push those efforts further to "bring new board members on that have a diverse point of view."

The Fourth, however, had not appointed a single new board member since becoming CEO. All of the directors he answered to were installed by his father with the exception of James Forese, a former chairman of IKON Office Solutions and IBM executive, who was elected in 2003 while Stokes was in charge. "They were trying to change the board, and I was the last member to go on as sort of the 'next generation,'" said Forese, who spent several weeks at the company with both The Third and The Fourth when he was appointed, learning about the business.

The convoluted relationship between August III and August IV wasn't the only thing that made for complicated dynamics within the group. Nine of its members had served for at least a decade, which led to complaints that they were too heavily entrenched in August III's camp. Several served together on the boards of other companies. The Third, for one, sat on the boards of AT&T and Emerson Electric with three other Anheuser directors, and he and fellow director Edward E. Whitacre Jr. had known each other for decades. The Third had been one of the AT&T directors who approved a controversial $161.6 million pay package for Whitacre in 2007, the year he retired.

The heaviest criticism tended to center around the financial relationships between certain directors. Anheuser-Busch paid for tens of millions of dollars in auto rentals and other services each year from Enterprise Rent-A-Car, which was run by board member Andrew Taylor, although Anheuser argued that the amount it paid wasn't big enough to represent a conflict of interest. The company used the services of some firms that employed its board members and made donations to others. Pat Stokes came under fire because his son owned a lucrative Anheuser-Busch beer distributorship.

Four directors were considered insiders: Stokes, the two Augusts, and Carlos Fernández, Modelo's CEO. Everyone else was considered "independent," despite some of their longstanding business and personal ties to each other. Close relationships can yield certain benefits in the boardroom. But they can also lead directors to strike allegiances that pollute their decision-making abilities with insider politics. "There was a lot of cross-stocking of the board," said beer industry scribe Harry Schuhmacher. "They were all friends, and they were all on each others' boards. They all kind of looked after each other. That helped to insulate the company from the real world."

Accordingly, Anheuser-Busch was awarded a grade of "F" in corporate governance from The Corporate Library—the worst score possible—in April 2008. It was taken to task for potential conflicts of interest between its board members and the advanced age and tenure of certain directors, among other things. Anheuser's score from RiskMetrics, another shareholder advisory firm, was higher, and the Corporate Library boosted its grade slightly to "D" in June. But it was still nothing to be proud of.

When August III was questioned at the outset of the InBev battle about the ties between board members, he said the directors at issue didn't sit on any committees that could pose conflicts. "Second thing is, there's a great advantage to being able to communicate with the person who was running Emerson, the person who was running AT&T," he said. "Think of the cross-pollenization and communication that we had on planning, finance and other matters." He closed with a sweepingly broad statement: "As far as integrity is concerned, people who are running major companies in this country today would never touch something that was a conflict of interest [except] in a few publicized cases. So I don't think there are any questions with overlapping or cross-pollenization of boards."

Most of Anheuser's advisors say its directors got too much flak for their apparent conflicts. There were lots of connections between members of the group, they admit, but that didn't detract from their professionalism. "The board as a body, contrary to what everybody believed was going on, was actually doing their work very diligently," one company advisor said.

Nevertheless, the directors took a bruising in the media for ostensibly being beholden to August III, and it served as a major point of frustration. To counter the persistent criticism, Anheuser-Busch's board went to great lengths to do everything by the book during its battle with InBev. They were advised to meet in person as often as possible, and they obliged, knowing their every move would be viewed under a magnifying glass. But rather than convening at headquarters, where they knew they might be spotted by employees and the hungry local media, they agreed to sequester themselves within Anheuser's private airplane hangar at the Spirit of St. Louis airport.

Anheuser-Busch had used the hangar over the years for everything from run-of-the-mill marketing meetings to high-drama negotiating sessions between warring baseball team owners back in the days when it ran the Cardinals. Like everything Anheuser owned, it was done up in rich style—filled with aviation-related Anheuser-Busch mementos and sporting gleaming floors that were clean enough to throw a picnic on.

Trappings at the hangar still weren't as cushy as the ninth floor executive suites at headquarters, but meeting at the airport brought benefits on another level: The board and its advisors could be stealthily shuttled to and from the site on Anheuser's sparkling fleet of corporate jets. They tended to arrive hungry, since Anheuser stocked no food on its aircraft despite their formidable supplies of free beer. But it was tough to complain.

Each time they landed at Spirit of St. Louis, the board and its advisors would walk through the hangar and into a small waiting room on the ground level, where they could plop down on a set of sofas to wait for their colleagues. They had a view of the tarmac from there and easy access to the adjacent coffee room and a tiny bathroom, which allowed them a few moments to relax as they waited for The Third's helicopter to float into view on the horizon. A stairway led up to the boardroom on the hangar's second floor, which was situated down the hall from a small kitchen.

Board meetings usually followed the same format each time— again, to leave no room for critique. The entire board would sit down for its main meeting first, along with a range of Anheuser-Busch executives, bankers, and attorneys. When that session finished, the executives would leave, often taking the bankers with them, and The Fourth would have a few minutes to make comments before exiting the room. The Third and Pat Stokes would then take the floor before leaving as well, turning the session over to the independent directors and their lawyers. A company secretary who stood sentry outside the boardroom would force everyone else to leave the second floor and go downstairs to wait it out. They weren't even allowed back upstairs to grab food from the kitchen. "If you were downstairs and went upstairs to get a bagel, they were like, 'No, you're not allowed upstairs,'" one advisor said, "which always seemed kind of silly."

Good corporate governance always warrants a certain degree of precaution, but Anheuser's board was much more fearful than most about all of the different ways they might get sued. If they wanted to buy Modelo instead of dealing with InBev, for instance, all they would need to do was sufficiently explain that they felt the Modelo plan was better for shareholders in the end. "Skadden said we could go ahead from a legal standpoint and do it," said one advisor.

"But there's always this question mark about what will happen if you go and make an acquisition and fend off a bid, and then the shares trade down. That's what scared them. Getting sued. Very few companies will do an acquisition in the face of an offer."

The board also knew that Anheuser-Busch's shareholders included some high-powered and influential investors, the most famous of whom was Warren Buffett, the so-called Sage of Omaha. Just two months earlier, Buffett had teamed up with family-owned candy maker Mars to buy Wrigley, the world's largest gum manufacturer, for $23 billion. The deal, which Goldman Sachs helped engineer, gave Buffett a more than 10 percent stake in Wrigley, and it helped prompt a later bid by Kraft to buy Cadbury—two other companies in which Buffett had major stakes.

Buffett was influential enough that his utterings tended to sway opinion on Wall Street just as much as former U.S. Federal Reserve Chairman Alan Greenspan's once had. And Buffett happened to have a significant connection to InBev that tweaked nerves at Anheuser-Busch. He had served on the board of Gillette with Jorge Paulo Lemann and called Lemann a good friend. With his money on one side of the deal and his friends on the other, it was tough to tell how Buffett felt about the proposed transaction. If he publicly endorsed InBev's bid, it might not be worth Anheuser's effort to fight anymore. But he was Anheuser's second-largest shareholder, with a stake of nearly 5 percent, and he didn't usually come out in favor of hostile takeover bids, which could bode well for Anheuser's case. Buffett often kept quiet about his investments, however, and many industry watchers assumed he would stay out of the Anheuser-Busch fracas altogether.

"We all wanted to know where Buffett stood," said one person close to InBev. "Both sides wanted Buffett on their side." But on July 11, a month after InBev registered its official bid, he confirmed in an interview that he hadn't been involved in the matter, and would be "making no news on that subject."

Another wrinkle added to the board's paranoia about lawsuits, and while it shouldn't have had much of an effect on the directors' behavior, it did. Both August III and Enterprise's Andy Taylor had been personally sued, as former directors of St. Louis's General American Life Insurance Co., after the company collapsed on their watch and was forced to sell itself to MetLife in 2000 for $1.2 billion. They and other directors, many of them prominent St. Louis figures, agreed to a $29.5 million settlement more than two years later. They admitted no wrongdoing, and the payment was covered by insurance, but the fiasco had put August III and Taylor through the legal wringer, and they were hell-bent on ensuring that it never happened again.

August III and Taylor focused their lines of questioning during many of the board's meetings on legal scenarios that were incredibly unlikely. The Third, in particular, raised so many legal concerns that he appeared to sway the board toward undue fear as well. "I think that was done to get some of his fellow directors to be more concerned than they had a right to be," said one person who heard The Third's incessant queries. The board's lawyers pointed out that in the lawsuit-ridden United States, getting sued was almost a matter of course for any board whose company underwent a merger. Some infamous law firms start drawing up documents and searching for plaintiffs the day a deal is announced.

August III, however, was also soliciting opinions from others. "He was taking it from third parties," said one Anheuser-Busch advisor. "He'd raise the most horrible and rare potential results as possibilities." He was "crazy-focused on the legal side of things," said another. The behavior pattern fit perfectly with The Third's longstanding habit of scuttling potential deals by pricking as many trial balloons as he could before they got off the ground.

"I remember he said, 'I'm not going to spend the rest of my life in depositions,'" said another advisor. "He was very hung up about that. It was an issue every time."

That fear seemed to serve as an equally cumbersome millstone around Taylor's neck. As one advisor put it, "He was involved in some deal with August that led to shareholder litigation, so that was his only concern."

■ ■ ■

Goldman Sachs had started working with Anheuser-Busch's management on its restructuring efforts not long after the gathering in Cancun, and it had officially signed on to advise the company on the InBev situation on May 27, four days after the leaks first erupted and just prior to the board's first meeting. Two weeks later, Citigroup had solidified the terms of its own engagement with the company. But Goldman's ability to capture the flag first paid off handily. Although the board hired both banks for advice, it wanted only one of them to speak on its behalf during the critical talks with Modelo and other parties—and it chose Goldman.

"Would Citi have liked to have been in all the rooms and negotiations? Yeah," said one person close to Anheuser-Busch. "But I think the company realized that was going to be too many chefs" in the kitchen. "Citi was brought in because, I think, the board wanted to not necessarily have a bank that could be accused of only being on management's side."

Being relegated to a secondary role wasn't an easy pill for Citigroup's Kalvaria and Schackner to swallow, but they handled it gracefully. They were, after all, one of just two banking teams that were actively advising on one of the biggest takeover defenses in history. Citigroup was set to earn up to $30 million in fees, plus another $2 million for the quarter, for advising Anheuser-Busch, and Goldman had up to $40 million in fees coming its way.

The board erected a Chinese wall between Goldman and Citigroup in the boardroom, again in the interests of being cautious. Bankers from different institutions often combine forces on certain tasks if they've both been hired to advise on a deal. But Anheuser's board asked the two banks to make all of their presentations separately, using separate sets of analysis, to make it clear that they had solicited enough independent advice. The Goldman team would stand first to outline its case to the board, and Citigroup would follow. Both teams reached the same general conclusions and provided similar recommendations throughout the process, but Anheuser's directors felt they could never be too careful.

Anheuser had also considered whether to hire a bunch of other banks as co-advisors to tie them up and prevent them from helping to fund InBev's takeover. Because of the conflicts of interest, no bank that was actively counseling Anheuser-Busch would be able to assist InBev as well. Yet the board opted not to go that route, which didn't improve the odds of its takeover defense.

The board met twice in late May and early June—once on May 29 and then again on June 13, once they had InBev's proposal in front of them and could review the bid. "Ladies and gentlemen, this is a very serious offer," The Third said when he addressed the board that day, confirming the obvious. Anheuser's directors had known InBev was serious the moment its bid came in at the rumored $65 a share, which was higher than many of them expected its initial foray might be.

"I was surprised that they picked such a big number," said lead director Sandy Warner. "Once $65 was on the table, that was a pretty good price."

But things didn't really fire up in St. Louis until the morning of Thursday, June 19, when the teams from Goldman, Skadden, and Citigroup shuttled in on "Air Bud" from the Teterboro, New Jersey, airport and assembled at the soccer park to prepare for the board's scheduled meeting the following day. After a comprehensive dry run, part of the group left to grab dinner together while others headed to the Four Seasons hotel downtown to finalize their materials and get a decent night's sleep. The next day's session at the airport would be the first in which both banking teams would present their views to the board.

■ ■ ■

Meetings at the airport hangar allowed August III and, when he also flew in, August IV, to land their helicopters outside and stride straight into the waiting room minutes later—which is exactly what The Third did the next morning as he made his usual ceremonial arrival. He often showed up a minute or two after the rest of the crew assembled. "It was always a staged entrance," said one advisor.

The Third and the rest of the company's directors filed up the stairs to the second floor of the hangar and settled into their places around the makeshift conference room's giant U-shaped table, which didn't match the grandeur of the horseshoe-shaped boardroom table down at headquarters. Whether out of seniority or decorum, The Third always sat at the top of the horseshoe next to Pat Stokes and The Fourth while the rest of the board scattered up and down either side—always in the same seats. By the time Anheuser's other executives and advisors claimed the chairs that ran along the walls, the room was usually packed.

The Third slipped out of character that morning and started spinning animated stories as his colleagues readied for the meeting—a rarity for someone who wasn't prone to small talk. St. Louis was awash in the worst floodwaters in 15 years, and with the Mississippi River threatening to crest near record levels, the basement of his farmhouse was soaked. Water damage didn't present the same quandary for August III as it did for St. Louis's poorer residents, but his visible agitation still gave him a more relatable quality that morning.

There had been a major defection from the board's ranks just a day earlier, which also prompted some chatter as the meeting kicked off. When the negotiations between Anheuser-Busch and Modelo had started eight days prior, the two brewers' boards of directors had been heavily intertwined. The Third and The Fourth were both members of Modelo's 20-person board, as were Tom Santel; Anheuser's legal head Gary Rutledge; Pedro Soares, who tended to act as a "body man" for The Fourth; and former U.S. Ambassador to Mexico Jones, who had served on Anheuser-Busch's board since 1998. Meanwhile, Carlos Fernández, who was chairman of his own board at Modelo, had been an Anheuser-Busch director since 1996.

That changed quickly, however. If Modelo wanted to adopt the best negotiating stance it could, Fernández needed to be free to talk to both Anheuser-Busch and InBev and to play them off each other. There was no way he could do that and still serve on the Anheuser-Busch board of directors. It would represent a clear conflict of interest.

A key item on the Anheuser board's agenda that Friday was an update on its negotiations with Modelo, so Fernández had resigned from his position the day before. When Anheuser announced the decision on Friday in a press release, analysts and investors speculated that Fernández had realized it was time to put Modelo's needs over Anheuser's. The two companies had been begrudging bedfellows to begin with. He now needed to switch gears entirely and focus on securing the best future—and the most money and independence possible—for Modelo.

"That's why Carlos resigned," said a person close to Modelo. "He couldn't be on the Anheuser-Busch board and be talking to InBev. He just couldn't. And we wanted both Anheuser-Busch and InBev to know that we were talking to each of them."

That left Anheuser's board with 13 members. And despite the commonalities that stemmed from their interwoven pasts, they hadn't all arrived that morning with their battle-readiness set to the same level.

Hugh Shelton, or "The General," as he was often called, joined the board in November of 2001 at age 59 after retiring as chairman of the U.S. military's Joint Chiefs of Staff. "He knew a lot of soldiers who drank a lot of beer," one advisor said, and he had certainly faced more pressure during his two tours in Vietnam and while serving under Presidents Bill Clinton and George W. Bush than he ever did at Anheuser-Busch. He had even been knighted by Queen Elizabeth II. Highly technical business matters weren't Shelton's area of expertise, however, and he was relatively restrained during the board's sessions. "This was not his kind of battle," another Anheuser insider said.

Two women served as directors of Anheuser-Busch. One, Joyce Roché, had known The Third from their work together on AT&T's board, and had been a director of Anheuser for 10 years. She spent most of her time working as the head of Girls Incorporated, a non-profit, but she had been a personal care executive before that and was Avon's first African-American woman vice president.

The other female director, an attorney and former president of the Mexican American Legal Defense and Educational Fund named Vilma Martinez, had served on the board for 25 years—more than half of August IV's lifetime—and was the longest-tenured director aside from August III. Almost exactly a year after the InBev takeover rumors hit, President Obama named Martinez as the U.S. ambassador to Argentina.

Roché and Martinez conducted themselves professionally, and despite the length of time they had known The Third, seemed quite supportive of Anheuser's new management team under August IV. Martinez was more willing to challenge August III's viewpoints than most of her colleagues. "Sweet, bright, and tough as nails," one person close to the board said, in reference to Roché. "She would have fought."

Shelton and Ambassador Jones, who was also a former chairman and CEO of the American Stock Exchange, ranked in that category, too—and they had their reasons. Anheuser-Busch had long been a huge supporter of the American military, for example, which made Shelton proud. He knew there was no way the Brazilians and Belgians would throw so much money toward the U.S. armed forces. They also valued Anheuser's legacy as the last major American-owned brewer, its family-owned history, and its philanthropic endeavors. "I didn't want to sell to begin with, because I thought we had a very good company that was really not only responsive to shareholders but to employees and the communities we served," said Ambassador Jones.

A clear fissure ran down the middle of the board, however, separating a handful of the most business-savvy members, who were generally the most plugged in with August III, from the rest. A few factors helped delineate between the two groups, and one was how important Anheuser's paycheck was to each director's overall lifestyle. The fees the company paid, which usually totaled somewhere between $88,000 and $114,000 a year, mattered more to Shelton, for example, after three decades of service in the U.S. military, than they did to the astronomically wealthy Ed Whitacre or Andy Taylor.

Another factor reeked of elitism—the board's balance of power also loosely pitted those who were members of the exclusive Augusta National Golf Club, host of the legendary Masters Golf Tournament each year, against those who weren't.

Augusta is famous for its pristine links and high-powered membership roster, which has boasted bold-faced business and political names including Warren Buffett, retired General Electric chief John "Jack" Welch, Microsoft founder Bill Gates, retired Morgan Stanley head Philip Purcell, auto magnate William C. Ford, legendary IBM chief Louis Gerstner Jr., and August III's brewing rival Peter Coors.

The Georgia golf club is also infamous for the people it doesn't include—women. Women's groups and the media have repeatedly skewered Augusta for having no female and few African-American members, and Tiger Woods, a Masters winner and honorary Augusta member, said during one round of controversy that the club should admit women. Augusta, however, maintained throughout that time that it did not restrict based on race, gender, religion, or national origin.

The figurehead of the Augusta group on Anheuser's board was Augusta's chairman, William Porter "Billy" Payne. The well-connected Payne, who helped Atlanta win its bid to host the 1996 Olympic Games, had a great deal of influence among golf aficionados. He was relatively inactive on Anheuser's board and rarely spoke during deliberations. When his jet arrived late for one critical board meeting, he stepped nonchalantly down the stairs with a newspaper tucked under his arm, his wife two paces behind him, dressed in a yellow suit and toting her Kindle, as the rest of the group watched. "I don't remember anything about him in meetings. I don't remember him saying a word," said one of Anheuser's advisors. "But he was a fun guy to talk to around the danishes when there wasn't a meeting going on."

The "Augusta connection" on Anheuser's board mattered more because of the other directors it involved. Three of the board's most influential members belonged to the golf club—former banker Sandy Warner, former telecom chief Ed Whitacre, and Vernon Loucks, a former healthcare executive. While their golfing buddies spent the early summer of 2008 on Augusta's Bermuda grass tee boxes, these three played key roles in dictating the future of Anheuser-Busch. "There was a split between those who were members of Augusta and those who weren't—almost a split along those lines," said one of the company's advisors. "I was told, 'Follow Augusta.'"

Sandy Warner served as the leader of the group of independent directors, after having rotated into the role according to the board's practice. Warner fancied himself a deal maker to an extent, and not without reason. After being named as the youngest CEO in J.P. Morgan & Co.'s history, he helped engineer its $30.9 billion sale to Chase Manhattan Bank in 2000, creating one of the few banks that emerged intact from the global financial crisis of 2007 and 2008. Warner had also been a director at General Electric for 16 years and had more recently joined the board of Motorola. He was generally regarded as an honest broker who did his best to navigate Anheuser's sticky issues.

Ed Whitacre's pedigree was similarly lustrous. He had come a long way from his hometown of Ennis, Texas, a small burg at the edge of a railroad where his dad had worked as a railroad engineer. Whitacre got his start in the telecommunications industry one summer during college, when he—the first member of his family to make it to a university—begged for a job hammering in fence posts and measuring telephone wire for Southwestern Bell in Dallas. Nearly three decades later in 1990, he took over SBC, the smallest of the Baby Bells, and transformed it into a giant by acquiring companies ranging from other Baby Bells to Ameritech, which he bought in 1999 for $62 billion. In 2005, SBC bought AT&T and adopted its name.

Like August III, Whitacre still had plenty of backwater in his blood despite rising to such heights in corporate America. He hated using computers and e-mail, hadn't started golfing until his mid-40s, and professed that his favorite activity was using his tractor to dig holes and crush trees on his suburban San Antonio ranch. At six-foot-four, his friends and colleagues called him "Big Ed."

Whitacre was not a shrinking violet—he had a strong sense of his own abilities. That self-confidence became apparent after the Anheuser saga ended when he agreed to become CEO of recently bankrupt automaker General Motors to help lead it out of the U.S. government's debt, despite acknowledging when he initially became the company's chairman that he knew nothing about cars. Whitacre had already popped up on national television by that time as the star of a GM ad campaign that offered a 60-day satisfaction guarantee for car buyers. The commercials were reminiscent of the 61 commercials Lee Iacocca filmed for Chrysler following its government bailout, but they were not nearly as successful. The public's reaction actually harked more to the lukewarm reviews August III had received for his own commercials at Anheuser-Busch.

Whitacre was a leader in the Anheuser-Busch boardroom, but that was because he commanded reverence, not because his behavior was outwardly estimable. He didn't talk much, but when he did, the board listened. Whitacre's muted behavior irked some Anheuser insiders who felt that he should have been more vocal, given the depth of his experience. "He was conspicuously quiet in the board meetings," said a person who attended the sessions. Other board members, like Sandy Warner, Jim Forese, and The Third, would ask questions periodically or make substantive comments. "But Whitacre was silent," this person said, "which made you feel a little bit that he had already kind of figured out where he wanted to go with it. I was actually disappointed that a guy as well known and well thought of as him wasn't more vocal in stating what he thought of things and being more open and up front about it."

InBev, unbeknownst to Anheuser, had accurately pegged Whitacre and Warner as two of Anheuser's most financially sophisticated directors and was tailoring its outreach efforts to them. After so many years at the helm of public companies, both men understood the concept of fiduciary duty, which dictated that their primary responsibility was to preserve or increase the company's value to benefit its shareholders. With that mandate in mind, InBev felt

Warner and Whitacre couldn't ignore an offer of $65 per share when the company's stock had recently been trading in the low $50s.

Warner and Whitacre were broadly viewed as the board's most powerful members—not counting "insider" August III. To help temper The Third's influence, the board opted to have the pair represent the entire group at critical points. "We designated them to go do a lot of the work for us," said fellow director Jim Forese. "We said 'Hey, Sandy, you and Ed take the lead here.' Which is what you normally do when you've got a complicated situation."

Several other directors also helped flesh out the group's inner circle. Vernon Loucks Jr., the former chief executive of healthcare company Baxter International and founder of healthcare-oriented management firm The Aethena Group, was a deal-savvy director who held significant sway because of his background and longevity on the board. Loucks had become an Anheuser-Busch director in 1988, the same year as fellow Augusta member Whitacre, and was a thoughtful and rational businessman who was used to being on the "inside"— he was inducted while at Yale University into its secretive Skull and Bones society. He had served on more than a handful of other boards in recent years, including the boards of Quaker Oats and St. Louis–based Emerson Electric, and had actually undergone a few mergers of his own. Baxter bought American Hospital Supply Corp. in 1985 and later spun off several divisions, and Aethena had formed an alliance with an investment firm in 2001. Loucks, however, wasn't seen as someone who would agitate for a fight. "He wasn't a spear-carrier," said one person close to the matter. "He would go with what made the most sense."

Enterprise's Andy Taylor wasn't a member of Augusta, but he was still considered to be in the loop. Since The Third had bowed to criticism and slowly eliminated most of the St. Louis acolytes who once populated his board, Taylor was the group's sole remaining local connection aside from the two Augusts and Stokes. "He's a buddy of August III, from St. Louis, and was concerned about St. Louis, but he certainly was not against selling the company," said one Anheuser advisor in reference to Taylor, who wasn't overly vocal in most of the board's meetings. As one former top executive put it, "The only people who mattered in this whole damn thing were Sandy Warner, Andy Taylor, probably Vernon Loucks, and Ed Whitacre."

Another director who pulled a good amount of weight, however, was Jim Forese, the one member who had been named during Pat Stokes's tenure. Forese asked astute, probing questions, and he seemed willing to entertain a fight with InBev if it made sense. He also had an interesting connection to the bankers at Citigroup: His son, James A. Forese, had a heavy-hitting job as co-head of the bank's global markets unit, which managed all of its sales and trading functions, and sat just down the hall from Leon Kalvaria. Some of James Sr.'s effectiveness on the board of Anheuser-Busch, however, was tempered by the fact that he hadn't been on the scene as long as the rest of his colleagues. "I wish, quite frankly, that he had been a little stronger, because I think his heart generally seemed to be in the right place," said one company advisor.

■■■

Those four or five "outside" directors held the keys to Anheuser's future. Only one man, though, made a habit of seizing control of the boardroom and steamrolling the debate, and that was August III, the group's consummate insider. He encouraged other board members to speak their minds, and at points would call on people he felt were too quiet. The ability he had to cajole them into adopting his point of view was both awe-inspiring and, to those who had differing views, maddening.

"No one overtly ever wanted to take The Third on," said one Anheuser insider. "This guy was so used to everybody in and around St. Louis, and certainly at Anheuser-Busch, just genuflecting to him. His whole life had been everybody kowtowing to him. The fact that his nickname was The Chief—he wouldn't even know how to deal with somebody unless they bent to his will. God knows what he thought of anyone who didn't."

The Third's small ownership in Anheuser-Busch hardly seemed to matter. The imposing force of his personality was enough to overpower anyone else in the room. "This was a family-controlled corporation where they only had 4 percent of the stock," said one company advisor. "I mean, the force of personality to let that happen . . ."

Goldman Sachs's Tim Ingrassia had never met The Third before the first board meeting he attended. It was clear as the former chief jumped down from his helicopter and stalked into the boardroom, even before he spoke, that he possessed a strange kind of magnetism. "Watch this guy work the room," Ingrassia said, leaning over toward Peter Gross as they waited for the meeting to start.

August III sat down and began canvassing the group, looking from one person to the next. He'd catch someone's eye and then— there it was—he'd wink or nod in his or her direction. And damned if that person didn't immediately sit up straighter or adjust his tie. The Third, whether consciously or not, was quietly establishing himself and asserting his superiority.

As Gross and Ingrassia watched the scene unfold, The Third turned unexpectedly toward Ingrassia and gave him a little wink as well. Ingrassia sat up in his chair and puffed out his chest before he could catch himself.

"You're doing it!" an incredulous Gross hissed at his colleague.

The Third knew how to work a room, but he seemed to feel it was more effective to lobby people individually if he was looking for a certain result. There weren't many places to hide in the airplane hangar, but he was skillful nonetheless at pulling people into the coffee room or hallway for furtive pow-wows. One advisor compared him to Lyndon Johnson during Johnson's days as a highly effective Senate Majority Leader in the 1950s, when he was photographed several times giving other senators the "Johnson Treatment"—leaning so aggressively into them while making a point that they nearly toppled backward.

"That, right there, captures the man," the advisor said. "He spoke very rarely in open forums, but would talk to them in the bathroom, in the copy room, holding small conferences at the end of hallways. This whole thing played out in the airport hangar over a course of weeks. It was not happening out in front." The Third was a behind-the-scenes coalition builder, and his preferred style of negotiation was one that sapped power away from others. When bilateral deals are cut one-on-one, no one else knows the context of the talks or the nature of the result. The Third seemed to understand the value of leaving other people guessing as he strategized and polled for votes.

"He's a consensus builder, but he does it behind the scenes," the advisor said. "A lot of what he did took place behind the scenes. I don't think he left a lot to chance, let's put it that way. I don't think he would walk into a room without knowing what people thought beforehand."

The Third has often been described as a "charismatic" figure, but begrudgingly. "The Third is the most impressive person on the board," said one person close to the company. "He was hugely charismatic, intelligent, powerful. Whether his powers were being used for good or evil, as some might say, he was impressive as an individual. He had his hands around everything. You knew he was working everyone."

Others argue that his success had less to do with charisma and more to do with sheer intimidation. "When The Third was challenged, he wouldn't even look at you," one advisor said. "This guy was a classic schoolyard bully. If he could intimidate you, he would intimidate you, and he would bust the crap out of you. If you kind of pushed back against the guy, he would pretend he didn't hear it and wouldn't take you on. He literally didn't want to deal with somebody unless he could intimidate them. And I was just so disappointed that that's who the great August Busch III was."

"The Third was, for such a long period of time, the head of that company, and he really ran that company with a fairly iron fist. The board was essentially people he knew well," this person continued. "Those were really long and strong relationships. So when he came into the room, he cast a pretty big shadow. I didn't really find him to be charismatic or to be very candid. I found him at times to be much more rigid and agenda-oriented than others, and at times I regretted that because it was not the most helpful dynamic. He was so unbelievably opinionated about any issue that came up."

■ ■ ■

The board's independent directors made some efforts to distance their decision making from The Third's influence during the InBev takeover battle, to varying degrees of success. "It was clear that while he had a lot of background and knowledge that was important—and we didn't want to lose that—he wasn't controlling it," said Jim Forese. And with a few notable exceptions, The Third tempered himself during the actual board meetings. He had an unnerving habit of passing notes to the corporate planning and finance people who usually sat behind him along the wall.

One Anheuser advisor was less distracted by the note-passing than by The Third's "transparent" agenda. "The thing that was distracting was that he had a very, very strong point of view and was trying to kind of push it on the board, and had a very strong view also on what he thought of his management team."

"The Third would basically try and bully whoever was presenting at the time into conceding whatever point he wanted them to make."

He was never seen lobbying for support from one particular board member, however: his own son. The two rarely seemed to communicate at all. On the day InBev made its bid, The Third filled a reporter in on the secret to how he was able to operate as an Anheuser director once his son became CEO.

"[Our w]orking relationship boils down to communication," he said. "It's all in being open, and talking to the board and to the CEO who, in this particular case, happens to be my son. But hell, he was in there for twenty-something years before he came up with that job. So he's seen all the deals and done all the jobs, so it's not very hard to communicate."

Others beg to differ. "They didn't communicate much, except if you call communicating on a daily basis getting your ass chewed," said one strategy committee member.

"One thing I will never forget," said a company advisor, "is that I was sitting in a board meeting . . . right behind The Fourth and The Third, and looking at one head of really dark hair, one head of kind of grey hair, them both wearing their cowboy boots. And just thinking 'My goodness, it's a shame they're not closer friends.'"

The contrast between the two men in the boardroom could hardly have been more pronounced. They could barely even make eye contact, and August IV had a way of looking as though he was asking his dad for permission to speak. They didn't break into battles in public—the friction between them was always subtle and indirect. When The Third ducked into the airplane hangar's tiny bathroom at one

point, not knowing his son was already in there, it made for a suspense-
ful few moments for everyone who was standing outside imagining the
forced confrontation.

"I never saw The Third and The Fourth say a word to each other,
which I thought was remarkable," said one person who worked to
defend the company. "The Fourth really had nothing to say. He rarely
said anything."

"Just watching him in the board meetings—the discomfort was
palpable. I felt for the guy. He was cordial and amiable, probably
a guy you would enjoy spending time with. It was almost one of
those Greek tragedies. He was put on a throne that maybe he never
wanted to be on and didn't feel comfortable sitting on, surrounded
by people who had different agendas. There were a lot of sharp
knives all around him."

For a few rough months in particular, the person who brandished
the sharpest blade against The Fourth was his own father. When
August IV started as CEO, the two had pledged to the board that they
would make their relationship work. They had a monumental falling-
out, however, in April of 2007, right after the first annual shareholders'
meeting of The Fourth's tenure, and it isn't clear their relationship ever
fully recovered.

August IV was scheduled to make his first major briefing to
investors at the meeting, which was held at Sea World in Orlando,
Florida. As he prepped in the days leading up to his big moment,
The Fourth showed his father a deck of slides that were meant to
accompany his presentation. The Third gave his stamp of approval.
When The Fourth briefed the crowd the next morning on the company's performance, though, he left several of the slides out.

August III went absolutely ballistic. He felt he had been tricked
by his own son, and was concerned Anheuser's shareholders had been,
too. Some of those slides had contained information investors should
have seen, The Third angrily contended, and he didn't want to be
accused of concealing it.

The Fourth claimed that his presentation had simply been too
long. He and his staff had made a few changes the night before to
pare things back, and it wouldn't have made sense to call his dad and
wake him up just to say he had eliminated some slides from the deck.

The Fourth had no obligation to show his dad the changes. August III was just a regular board member—he wasn't even chairman of the company any longer—and there was no need for the board to sign off on August IV's slides. These were the types of things The Third believed fell within his domain, however, both as the company's former CEO and as its current chief's dad.

"Whenever you have a former chairman or CEO who remains on the board, there is a bit of tension there," said General Shelton. "It just happens in this case that it's a father and his son."

Rather than hashing the matter out with his son in private, The Third made his rage so clear to Anheuser's board that various members of the group ended up trying to referee the argument. It didn't work, and the problem compounded upon itself as The Third grew even more irritated by a range of other successive issues that involved The Fourth. The tension grew so thick that several directors were forced to sit down with both of them to warn them to keep their eye on the ball—the company—and make sure that their disagreements didn't affect its performance.

"We did some things to try to make it work," said Sandy Warner, one of the board members who attempted to mediate between father and son. "We could have done a better job."

"We got August III to agree to leave the building, to take his office and move it somewhere else," Warner said. "We got Pat Stokes to do the same thing. Those are little things. It was hard. But you know, we'd have worked through that, too. That wasn't at the root of this."

"When the split occurred between The Third and The Fourth, I think the board was disappointed and didn't know exactly how to deal with it, other than the fact that The Fourth was the CEO and we had to support The Fourth," said Ambassador Jones. "But I think that was a big disappointment to the board members who respected August III and had high hopes for August IV."

"There was a constant trying to patch that up, and trying to make it work," Jones said. "It never seemed to be the same after that."

Carlos Fernández, the anointed son of another family dynasty, found himself pinned in a difficult spot a couple of times when the dynamic between The Third and The Fourth was at its worst. Fernández had forged a surprisingly tight bond with The Third over the years, despite his elders' distrust of the man. He and August were brutally honest with each other. Carlos felt comfortable cutting it to August straight, in a way his dutiful subordinates and the rest of the board wouldn't.

"How would you feel about running Anheuser-Busch?" The Third quietly asked Carlos during one of his trips to St. Louis. Things were rough at the time between father and son, and Carlos assumed The Third was making his comment out of spite. He brushed it off, saddened that the two men's relationship had deteriorated to such a point. It proved not to be an isolated incident, however. Once or twice more, during dinner with the board of directors the night before a meeting or while visiting his farmhouse, The Third again floated the idea of having Carlos take the reins.

■ ■ ■

The spat over the shareholders' meeting cooled from a boil to a simmer after a few months, but the volatile dynamic between August III and August IV remained evident as the InBev saga intensified. The Fourth, who seemed unwilling to challenge his father's dominance, receded further and further into the wings as the fight progressed. He rarely made presentations on the company's operations or other management issues, and he became increasingly out of touch and distant. If there was ever a time when Anheuser-Busch needed to run like a well-oiled machine, it was that summer. Unfortunately, too many of its internal gears were rattling loose to make that a possibility.

"If he said four words any time we were in a board meeting, he said a lot," said one Anheuser advisor. "I can't remember The Fourth ever asking a question," said another. "I think he was frightened. I have seen in my life fear in a lot of situations. There was fear in his eyes. Fear of saying the wrong thing. Even when it was his program, he didn't advance it. Even if he embraced it, Randy [Baker] handled a lot of it; Dave [Peacock] handled a great deal of it."

The strangest thing about their dynamic was that The Third had convinced the board of directors to install The Fourth as CEO. That would suggest that he had a certain level of confidence in his son. Few things he did seemed aimed at bolstering his son's ego, however, or catalyzing his ability to lead the company. With Stokes presiding as chairman and Warner heading up the group of outside directors, The Fourth was left to represent Anheuser's management. Unfortunately, August III and the board didn't appear to have a particularly high level of respect for Anheuser's team of top executives.

The Fourth decided in June to hire Ken Moelis, a well-connected Los Angeles–based banker, as an extra advisor—thanks in part to his close friendship with Ron Burkle. Burkle was a key client of Moelis, who had stepped down as the top banker at UBS in 2007 to start his own bicoastal firm.

Moelis was ostensibly there as an advisor to the company, and was listed as such on its press releases. His real task, though, seemed to be counseling and protecting The Fourth. "August was, quite frankly, probably feeling a bit under siege, not only from InBev but from members of his own board at times," one advisor said. "It probably didn't seem like a bad thing for him to have a couple of extra friends around to talk to." Moelis attended several board sessions, but he never presented in any of them and stayed largely out of the fray. "Look, when we can be helpful reinforcing something you think is important, just reach out to me and tell me," he told his fellow bankers at one point.

"Ken was very quiet in the background, and I think got paid a very modest amount of money," said one person close to Anheuser. August IV was incredibly loyal to his friends, and it didn't surprise the rest of Anheuser's team in the least to see him hire Moelis. They figured Burkle had asked him to pull Moelis on board, and he was happy to extend the favor. The relationship proved symbiotic. Moelis's firm received publicity for being associated with such a high-profile takeover defense, and August IV gained an advocate and counselor. It was hard to blame The Fourth for wanting someone in his corner of the ring.

"It's not like The Fourth was leaning back and Ken was whispering in his ear," said one advisor. "But I got the sense that Ken probably had some late night conversations with The Fourth to give him comfort that he wasn't observing any screw-ups."

Pat Stokes, who had been the chairman of Anheuser's board for a year and a half when InBev came knocking, did his best to keep the group running in an orderly way. His was a tricky cross to bear, however. Stokes was one of The Third's original whiz kids from Wharton and had been his right-hand man for years. Yet he had shifted some of his allegiance over to The Fourth to straddle the impossible divide between the two men and preserve his own career and integrity.

"I put Pat in the Randy [Baker] category, of having mastered the ability to be a professional but to not get trapped," said one person close to Anheuser. "He was clearly The Third's guy, but I thought he carried himself well."

"Pat Stokes, God bless him, he figured out how to manage the family situation," this person said. "He was a surprisingly impactful person in a very quiet way, because he was one of the few people who had the credibility to not be cowed by The Third."

■ ■ ■

With Stokes at the steering wheel, the board sat down together on June 20 to compare Anheuser-Busch's options. A few executives explained to the group that they had found ways to save $1 billion in annual costs during their two-day session at the soccer park—much more than first anticipated. Those measures, plus a hike in beer prices, would probably boost the value of the company's shares by a few dollars apiece. Still, as Goldman and Citigroup weighed in with their views on the plan, it became clear that slashing costs alone wasn't going to push Anheuser's shares above the $65 floor set by InBev.

Cost reductions combined with a deal to buy Modelo, on the other hand, certainly might, if combining the two companies boosted their growth a few years down the road. It had been only eight days since the Modelo talks first started, and just one day since Fernandez resigned, but a deal to buy the rest of the Mexican brewer was already clearly in focus as Anheuser's best defensive play.

That meant that Anheuser actually needed to wrap something up with the Mexicans, though. Having Modelo as an option wasn't useful unless the likelihood of a deal was legitimate, and the talks were already running into snags. The board wasn't as sure as The Fourth seemed to be about the notion of allowing Carlos Fernández to be

CEO. If they were going to entertain paying the huge price The Fourth and his team were eyeing—$15.2 billion—they weren't eager to also cede leadership of the company. How could they explain that to shareholders? It would look like they were paying Modelo to steal Anheuser-Busch's keys.

Goldman and Citigroup both ran through projections on how worthwhile a Modelo deal would be at certain prices, and they compared the rich price Anheuser had proposed to other beer deals that had been done more cheaply. The deal could put Anheuser-Busch at risk if it wasn't executed well, they pointed out. If the board wanted to fend off InBev, continuing those talks was its only real option. So the board gave the Anheuser-Busch executives who were spearheading the Modelo talks a green light to continue.

By the time the board met again five days later, on Wednesday, June 25, it had let two weeks tick by without making a response to InBev's bid—a painfully long time by Wall Street's standards, at least, if not by St. Louis's. Anheuser-Busch had issued a second press release on the 16th to reiterate that its board would announce a decision when it was good and ready, and investors had been waiting since then for an answer. They were finally about to get one.

Anheuser CFO Randy Baker stood up first that day to outline the latest stage in the Blue Ocean cost-cutting scheme, and Goldman and Citigroup then presented their conclusions on InBev's bid. Both keyed in on the same things. The bid was opportunistic, they said—InBev was preying on Anheuser-Busch at a time of weakness. With Blue Ocean, they might be able to boost the company's stock price toward $65. And if they pulled out all the stops by acquiring Modelo and maybe even spinning off the company's entertainment division, Anheuser was probably worth $67 or $68 per share. InBev's current offer simply wasn't enough. If InBev's team wanted to lock Anheuser-Busch down, they'd have to go higher.

"The company knew it certainly had more than $65 in value," said one advisor. "They had worked the numbers. But it came down to execution risk. The question was the ability of the current management to execute on those plans."

The answer to that question wasn't clear. For now, though, the bankers said, the board had a strong enough rationale for rejecting the bid. It wasn't a recommendation they made lightly: Judging a take-over bid as inadequate can be risky for a bank. Kalvaria and Schackner had spent time discussing their potential inadequacy opinion the night before on conference calls with Citigroup's attorneys.

The board held a meeting by telephone the next day, once every-one had returned to their home bases, to confirm its rejection of the bid and to run through its next steps: moving more forcefully down the road with Modelo and rallying shareholders around the company's new Blue Ocean effort. Anheuser had a highly anticipated conference call with investors and analysts coming up on Friday, and Randy Baker and The Fourth were prepping to use the opportunity to unveil their new cost-slashing plans to the world.

The board agreed unanimously over the phone that InBev's $65 per share bid was simply too low. Whether or not various directors wanted to sell the company, it seemed clear they could get more. There was no indication of what InBev would do next. While it might drop the effort in the wake of Anheuser's rejection, it could also try to circumvent the board and convince Anheuser's shareholders directly that a takeover was the best option. Still, the board's convic-tion was strong that day in late June.

"It was a relatively easy rejection," said one Anheuser insider. "To be candid, I don't think there was ever great doubt with the first bid that we were going to reject it," said another. "I don't think there was great controversy. It's just standard practice in M&A—the first bid somebody makes, you reject. The question is, what do you do with the second bid?"

In a press release issued later that day, Stokes said InBev's bid did "not reflect the strength of Anheuser-Busch's global, iconic brands Bud Light and Budweiser, the top two selling beer brands in the world." Warner, as lead independent director, added that the offer wasn't com-petitive "with alternative plans the company has developed in recent months," a nod to the Blue Ocean scheme Anheuser was about to unveil. To show that they weren't stonewalling to shareholders' detri-ment, Warner added that the board would "continue to consider all opportunities that build shareholder value."

The board's independent directors, anticipating that their rejection of InBev's offer might be the start of a very public war rather than the end of it, had agreed the day before in St. Louis to hire law firm Simpson Thacher & Bartlett for additional advice. Speculation had been building that the group would hire their own legal counsel, and for good reason. Things were starting to get messy, particularly when it came to the company's entanglements with the Busch family.

Adolphus Busch IV, The Third's estranged half-brother, had shocked Anheuser's executives, the press, and even members of his own family the prior week by issuing a public letter that called for Anheuser to negotiate with InBev. Adolphus directed some of his plea straight to the board, reminding them to remember their obligations to shareholders.

"When Anheuser-Busch became a public company, the Busch family and Anheuser-Busch management understood that future decisions had to be made in the best interests of all shareholders," Adolphus wrote to The Fourth and the rest of Anheuser's board. "InBev's offer provides the opportunity for Anheuser-Busch brands to compete globally. I believe that as directors you have a fiduciary duty to commence negotiations with InBev in order to bring about this deal."

Andrew Busch, another half-brother of The Third, then said exactly the opposite a day later, coming out in support of August IV, the board, and the company's efforts to "remain a strong company headquartered in St. Louis."

Adolphus owned less than 1 percent of Anheuser's shares. Still, 1 percent of the company would be worth $460 million if Anheuser accepted InBev's offer. These were powerful sums of money, even for a family padded with generations of wealth.

The situation was shaping up to be more than some of Anheuser-Busch's directors had bargained for. After years spent acquiescing to The Third and hearing little pushback from investors, they were caught in a hail of crossfire not only between Anheuser and InBev— which would have been bad enough—but between Anheuser and its own founding family. "You think of these guys as board members— would you want to be dragged into this?" said one former executive. "When they saw the family thing, they figured, 'I don't need this.' Whitacre didn't need it, Taylor definitely didn't need it. He's running his own company. They didn't want to get the board sued, because they'd seen that before."

One former Anheuser staffer said that Adolphus's letter was like waving a red flag in front of a bull to The Third, whereas others contended that Adolphus was being used by InBev and called his letter a red herring—the same type of unpredictable slop that tends to crop up in many high-profile takeover fights.

"When this stuff happens, God knows who gets up who owns stock and might say something," one Anheuser insider said. "The fact that there was a 'Busch' after his name . . . at the end of the day, the Busch family owned a very small amount of stock in the company. So a Busch family member who held a very small amount of stock, coming out saying something, got the credit that deserved—it got a headline but substantively didn't [involve] enough stock for it to be determinative."

"I think it probably pissed him off a fair amount, but The Third never lost his cool," said one advisor.

■ ■ ■

When the independent board members started to push in favor of hiring their own lawyers, the initial plan was to hire well-known New York M&A attorney Ed Herlihy from law firm Wachtell, Lipton, Rosen & Katz. There, again, Anheuser's Augusta connections came into play. Herlihy was one of the country's top bank merger experts, and he had been hired by J.P. Morgan's Jamie Dimon to lead the bank's fire-sale purchase of Bear Stearns. He was also an avid golfer and a member of the exclusive country club. "We looked to see who was on the board, and we saw the Georgia connection," said a top attorney at a rival firm. "We obviously knew who at Wachtell they must have been talking to."

Skadden felt it had matters under control and wasn't keen on hiring anyone else. It argued that bringing in another law firm might draw unwanted attention and prompt questions about why such measures were needed. The outside directors, however, wanted a separate set of advisors who would protect their interests as they looked more closely at buying Modelo. When the idea of hiring Wachtell was nixed over potential conflicts of interest, they turned to Simpson Thacher &

Bartlett's Charles "Casey" Cogut, another well-known M&A lawyer. Cogut and the rest of his team mounted up after it became clear that the board was going to reject InBev's bid.

"Skadden had been resisting separate counsel for various reasons," said one person close to the matter, but "there was still a notion amongst the independent directors that they wanted it, and this was a good point of demarcation."

The board's decision to hire Simpson Thacher rallied the troops over at InBev, who felt it validated their strategy of targeting certain members of Anheuser's board. InBev saw the move as an indication that Warner, Whitacre, and the other independent directors would drive Anheuser's decision making from that point on, rather than insider August III and his son.

■ ■ ■

InBev's team got wind that Anheuser's board was meeting that Wednesday, and since they hadn't heard an offer to fire up negotiations, the Brazilians readied themselves for rejection. They weren't about to cry in their coffees—they had assumed it would come to this, and they quickly authorized their advisors to move into their second planned phase of attack. Anheuser-Busch didn't know what was about to hit it. Or perhaps more accurately, it didn't know it was about to get hit so soon.

On June 26, just a few hours before Anheuser's board agreed by phone to turn down InBev's bid, InBev filed suit in Delaware on a critical matter that had huge repercussions: whether Anheuser's entire board of directors could be removed without cause all at once. The filing wasn't so much a traditional lawsuit as it was a request to clarify a key point. InBev believed that the whole board could be ejected simultaneously through a written shareholder vote, but it wanted to make sure the courts agreed before it took any additional steps. The lawsuit was a major shot across the Anheuser board's bow—a warning that InBev might launch an effort to eject them against their wishes. InBev wanted them to feel the threat of what was coming next.

Years earlier, when takeover rumors first started dogging the company, Anheuser-Busch had grown worried enough about its security to institute some hefty anti-takeover protections. It decided to stagger its directors' tenures, which meant only a fraction of the board would come up for election each year, and it installed a "poison pill" shareholder rights plan, which would make a hostile takeover prohibitively expensive by flooding the market with new shares of stock if a bidder tried to vacuum up too large a stake in the company.

Anheuser's staggered board remained in place until 2006, when in response to a trend in corporate America toward increased shareholder rights and transparency, the board followed in the footsteps of many of its corporate brethren and "destaggered" itself. It had already let its poison pill provision expire two years earlier. The move to destagger helped appease the shareholder rights' groups that were constantly harassing the company, but it was done in a way that left a loophole InBev could exploit.

When a Delaware-based company destaggers its board, it usually adds legal language that says the board cannot be completely removed without committing some sort of infraction. In this case, though, that language wasn't included. As one person close to InBev put it, "It was somebody's oversight."

Anheuser's board begs to differ. "Were we aware of what we were doing? The answer is yes," said director Jim Forese. "You don't have that kind of high-powered board not know what it was doing." Members of the board opted to destagger their terms and not to entrench themselves in their jobs because they wanted to improve the company's corporate governance, he said. They had no regrets.

General Shelton, however, admitted that while the board knew what it was doing, the fact that they might all be ejected together may not have registered until it smacked them in the face. "We all knew that was a possibility when we signed up for it," he said. "But until you get put in that situation, I don't think the reality of it is driven home quite to the extent that it is when you say, 'This could get ugly pretty quickly.'"

Ambassador Jones seconded that perspective. "It could be considered a mistake, I suppose," he said. "We did it because we were trying to do a number of things that put us in line with the then-concepts of good corporate governance."

"I don't think we envisioned InBev at that time, or a hostile takeover, because we thought we had a very good company and that wouldn't be an issue."

Whether it was an oversight or a noble but naïve move to boost shareholders' rights, the board was highly vulnerable. Unless they challenged InBev's lawsuit and somehow won, which they quietly believed was unlikely, InBev would be able to call for a special vote to replace them with an entirely new slate of directors. To make matters worse, InBev would only need a bare majority of Anheuser's shareholders to vote in favor of any new board members it proposed, a low hurdle compared to the two-thirds majorities required by some other companies. InBev had found the holes in Anheuser's defensive armor, and it was tearing at them.

"The road to Hell is paved with good intentions," said one company advisor. "In an era where people are looking for quick hits, if you have a staggered board, don't end it. If you don't have a staggered board, there's no way you're going to be able to put one in. A staggered board is a real lifesaver."

■ ■ ■

If the Busch family had still been in control of Anheuser-Busch, however, there would have been no need for debate over poison pills and staggered boards at all. Their votes would have determined Anheuser-Busch's fate.

Most family-owned companies establish two-tiered shareholding structures once they become publicly traded, which provide a way for families to maintain voting control even if they reduce their economic stake. The technique worked well for candy maker Mars, which had stayed solidly independent, and for publisher Dow Jones, whose controlling family members decided to sell to Rupert Murdoch's News Corp. It would have been logical to assume that the Busch family had voting control of Anheuser through its own dual-class system.

Yet no such structure existed. The entire Busch clan held a combined financial stake of less than 4 percent of the company, not nearly enough to influence the result of a shareholder poll. Even if every family member opposed a takeover and they convinced Warren Buffett to follow suit, they would deliver a mere 9 percent of the company's votes. Control of Anheuser-Busch's fate, in other words, had slipped into the hands of the hedge funds and cutthroat speculative investors who had been buying up chunks of Anheuser stock from more traditional "mom and pop" stockholders since InBev's bid became public. Those cash-hungry investors were exactly the type who might vote to upend Anheuser's board if InBev pressed forward with its new plan.

J.P. Morgan's team had been stunned to hear that the Busches lacked voting control over the company they had founded. When InBev's advisors sat down for the first time in May with Doug Braunstein and Hernan Cristerna, one of the firm's top European bankers, Cristerna was particularly taken aback.

"Wow, I've always thought the family really controlled the company, or at least had significant influence," he said during at meeting at Lazard's offices in New York. "With these numbers, I'm surprised they weren't taken over years ago."

Anheuser's board considered putting a poison pill back in place as a roadblock against InBev, but decided it would be too glaring an effort to concentrate their power.

"I think the board was pretty united that it was important, given the family history and the fact that people thought it was a family company, to have state-of-the-art corporate governance," said one person close to the board. "People didn't want to do anything that could be viewed as unfriendly to shareholders. It's all about winning the hearts and minds of the shareholders, and you want to seek the high ground."

They had already lost one critical mind and the money that came with it—Warren Buffett's. While they couldn't be 100 percent certain, Anheuser-Busch's advisors believed he was rapidly unloading his more than 35 million shares of stock at prices right around $60 per share. "Buffett was unloading his stock as fast as could be," said one of the company's advisors. "We had a pretty good guess pretty early. You tried to work backwards on where trades were coming from, so we had a pretty good guess." Buffett seemed to have decided it was smarter to lock in the gains he had already made on Anheuser's shares rather than waiting to see if InBev would make a higher offer.

Anheuser's board knew that the details of Buffett's stock sales, which ended up totaling nearly two-thirds of his Anheuser-Busch holdings, wouldn't be made public until he filed papers with the Securities and Exchange Commission at the end of the quarter. That meant that they had until August to get their plans for the future squared away before news of the sales hit the wires. It would be impossible to negotiate with InBev after that point.

"That was not going to be a great backdrop for a price negotiation," the advisor said. "It was 'Wait a minute. If Warren Buffett is willing to sell at $60, why would I raise my price from $65 to $70? If the Sage of Omaha is selling at $60, is there any value there?'"

"Fidelity was selling its stock, too," the advisor said. "It's just that when Fidelity sells its stock, it's not viewed as a message to the world. When Warren does, people read into it."

■ ■ ■

Even though that Thursday had only marked the first significant step in Anheuser-Busch's defense—its rejection of the bid—things were already looking dire. The board had no way of clawing back some of its old protections without angering investors, no one in Washington was coming to bat for the company, and there was no more hope that Buffett would publicly oppose the deal. The board was looking increasingly vulnerable to a coup each day—and this time the threat was coming from outside, not within. Anheuser knew that InBev had a strong chance of winning its lawsuit. "I predict we would have lost that battle," one advisor said, "so the board would have been up for election." Still, that didn't mean they were about to concede publicly.

That's exactly what happened the following day, however, when August IV made an enormous tactical blunder on the company's heavily anticipated Friday morning conference call. Randy Baker and The Fourth spent most of that morning's session taking investors through their plans to expand and accelerate Blue Ocean. All of the cuts the strategy committee had unearthed during its meeting

at the soccer park were laid bare for Wall Street and the city of
St. Louis to digest. Some, like reducing the company's energy usage
and its spending on equipment, weren't a big deal, whereas others were
tougher to swallow. Anheuser-Busch planned to offer an early retirement program with hopes that 10 to 15 percent of its 8,600 salaried
employees would take the bait. If that didn't happen, the company
might have to make the job cuts itself. After years of avoiding such
tough decisions, Anheuser-Busch simply had no choice.

There were plenty of skeptics on the call that day. It wasn't clear
that The Fourth and his team could really follow through with their
leaner new strategy. Cutting jobs and eliminating waste had always
made people within Anheuser-Busch uncomfortable—it was against
their culture. Why should anyone believe things were different now,
especially with a quick $65 per share in cash as the alternative?

"Blue Ocean should probably have been implemented sooner,
but it meant cutting jobs and trimming costs, and these are all
tough things for a company that is so entrenched in its hometown
to do," said one company advisor.

"It was low-hanging fruit," said another. "It was pretty easy to do,
but this team didn't have the history of organizational change, cost-
cutting, and restarting growth. They hadn't done it before."

■ ■ ■

When the question-and-answer portion of the conference call kicked
off, the analysts who had been given permission to talk politely lobbed
in a few softball questions about the restructuring. Inevitably, though,
the queries soon started to focus more directly on the status of InBev's
attempted takeover. The Fourth deferred several times at first to Baker.
Then he started answering more of the analysts' questions on his own.

Roughly halfway through the Q&A, one analyst asked about
InBev's lawsuit. Was it clear to Anheuser-Busch, he wondered, that
its board couldn't be ejected all at once without cause? The answer
should have been cut and dry. Anheuser's official stance was that it
was confident the directors couldn't be removed all at once, and that
it planned to let the court decide. Instead, The Fourth committed

a monstrous gaffe. Yes, he told listeners on the call, InBev did have the power to eject the entire board if it could get more than half of Anheuser's shareholders to vote in its favor.

The call came to an end a few minutes later and the operator thanked the participants for their time. Just as everyone was about to hang up, August IV interjected with a plea for another few seconds of airtime.

"Wait, wait, wait. Can I make one last statement, please?" he called out. "Can we correct my statement about director removal and say we will challenge InBev's claim in their lawsuit that they can remove directors without cause? I was wrong on that statement, and that is the correct answer. Thank you."

The Fourth had tripped like a fool when he should have been more focused than ever, and it hadn't escaped the media. He wanted to take those words back almost as much as he wished he could wipe clean the promise he had made to the company's 600 distributors at their annual conference in April. Anheuser-Busch, he had vowed to a packed room, would never be sold "on my watch." That wasn't a commitment he was sure he could keep anymore.

It wasn't clear that August IV was the right man to lead Anheuser-Busch, and that huge mistake, made in such a public forum, didn't boost anyone's confidence in his ability to lead under pressure. It was tough to imagine a way that the board could reject InBev outright without making a change at the top.

"The board was in a tough position. If they were going to fight like cats and dogs, they were going to have to say 'We believe in this management team, and they're going to deliver you this value in time with very low risk,'" one advisor said. "As a board member, that's what you have to get your head around to say 'No.' That, or they would have had to bring in new management."

Yet while there were whispered debates between small groups of insiders over whether The Fourth should be replaced, the subject was never broached by the board of directors.

"That's one of the things you consider in a takeover battle—do you replace him?" one advisor said. "But it never really was a subject of conversation."

Chapter 12

The Montagues
and the Busches

You had to go through the motions. If you didn't go there, you weren't going to get Brito to up the bid. From the company and the bankers' point of view, the more real it looked the better.

—Anheuser-Busch advisor

A t 8 A.M. on Wednesday, June 18, three days after InBev fired off its warning letter over Anheuser's dalliance with Modelo, Morgan Stanley's Rob Kindler and several of his colleagues sat down at the downtown Manhattan headquarters of Goldman Sachs, a monolithic, maroon-marbled building at 85 Broad Street, for their first meeting with Goldman's Ingrassia and Gross. By this stage, the Anheuser-Busch board had explicitly instructed Goldman not to involve Citigroup in meetings or phone calls related to Modelo. Ingrassia and Gross felt bad about the slight, since their working relationship with Kalvaria and his team was strong. The board, however, had made up its mind.

"The Bud board and management team had a point of view that there had to be a single voice talking to the other side, and for whatever reason, they wanted that to be Goldman," said one of the company's advisors. "I don't think it was a lack of confidence in Citi. I don't think it was evil in any way. I think it was that 'We're just going to have one voice on this. We're going to make it simple on us, and we're going to make it simple on the other side.'"

By the time they met that morning, the parties had only been negotiating for five days. Before things progressed any further, Modelo's team wanted to make itself clear on a few points. They had no intention of accepting any bid that wasn't richer than InBev's bid for Anheuser-Busch, a stance that Kindler reiterated to Ingrassia and Gross. Modelo's higher-growth beers like Corona and Pacífico sat in a category above Anheuser-Busch's tired, old brands like Budweiser and Michelob, Kindler explained, and Modelo deserved to be paid accordingly.

Modelo, conversely, was happy to take as much stock as Anheuser-Busch could offer as payment for the takeover, because its five controlling families believed that combining the two companies would boost the shares' price over time. There was one critical reason for the families' confidence in the deal, which led Kindler to his third point: Carlos had to be put in charge. With Carlos at the helm rather than the young Busch scion, the Mexicans felt their investment would be safe.

■■■

Kindler and his team then headed back down to Mexico City that afternoon to prepare for a meeting with Carlos and Mariasun. They all assembled the next day at Carlos's family office, just as they had eight days earlier. This time around, though, the talks weren't speculative. Modelo's controlling families were now closely monitoring every development, and Carlos was due to present his views on the proposed takeover to Carlos's uncle, Don Antonino, at their office later that day.

With a loose offer from Anheuser-Busch on the table, they started hammering out the details.

Carlos and María approached the concept from different angles, but they both favored selling to Anheuser-Busch. María felt the time was right from a financial perspective. The Americans were offering a very rich price—a price they might never see again—and she favored accepting the offer before the pressure on Anheuser-Busch wore off. Carlos, meanwhile, was staring at a chance to run the entire company—to seize operating control of one of America's crown jewels. He wasn't eager to go down in history as the man who traded his family's legendary company to a rival. If he could be CEO of all of Anheuser-Busch Modelo, the controlling families' new investment in the company's stock would be under his tight purview. They would own the biggest stake in what would be a much bigger company, and Carlos would be running the show.

"From an operating perspective, which is the budgets, business plan, distribution, all of that—that would be controlled by Anheuser-Busch," one advisor in the negotiations said. "But on the other hand, Carlos would be the CEO of Anheuser-Busch. So there was a lot of elegance in that transaction. He could basically say, 'Look, I personally made sure that Modelo stays in Mexico and keeps its name, and that can't be changed.'"

"From Carlos's perspective, this was pretty straightforward," this person added. "I'm going to get a premium, but I'm also going to run the company. It's going to be called Anheuser-Busch Modelo, and life is great."

Six months before InBev's bid, The Fourth had acknowledged in an interview that Anheuser was batting the concept of a deal with Modelo back and forth. "There are . . . a lot of opportunities out there in working with Grupo Modelo and Carlos Fernández," The Fourth said. "He's a superstar. [T]heir ability to come along with us, if we can convince them that a certain opportunity would make sense for both of us, would I think be a very interesting proposition."

Like August IV, however, Carlos answered to a higher boss. Ninety-year-old Don Antonino wasn't as controlling or megalomaniacal as August III, and he hadn't continued to wield his power as obsessively after retiring. From the moment talks started with

Anheuser-Busch, though, Carlos and María had known he'd be the lynchpin who would either fasten their bargaining effort together or let it fall apart.

Don Antonino had been made the company's "honorary life chairman" in 2005 when Carlos was named chairman of the board. He was the keeper of the company's flame and its revered patriarch. More importantly, though, he held Modelo's purse strings. The families that controlled Modelo did so through a series of complicated trusts, and Don Antonino, simply put, ruled those trusts with a blocking vote. He couldn't unilaterally set new courses of action for the company. He could, however, vote "no" and send a deal with Anheuser-Busch straight to the scrap heap.

The key to winning Don Antonino's support had more to do with pride and nationalism than with numbers. He was certainly happy with the rich bid Anheuser-Busch had put on the table, and he was fine with the idea of putting his nephew in charge. To really convince Don Antonino to give his blessing, though, Carlos knew he would need to preserve as much of Modelo's independence and Mexican roots as possible. Antonino sported a high social and political profile in Mexico, and his values were concentrated more heavily in those areas than on extracting the last possible nickel from Anheuser-Busch.

"He's already a very wealthy man," said one person close to Modelo. "His motivation was not just 'Can we get a great premium?' His motivation really was preserving Modelo."

Carlos, María, and their advisors agreed to insist that Modelo would be awarded at least three seats on the merged company's board of directors, two of which they would occupy, and to require that its operation in Mexico remain there as a separate entity under the same name, with a governing board chaired by Don Antonino. So far, they had gotten little pushback on those points from Anheuser, which agreed that it was in everyone's best interests to keep Modelo's structure intact. "We both wanted Modelo to look the same down in Mexico," said international head Tom Santel. "We weren't going to plaster our logo all over the place. We wanted them to keep running it." That would prove key to winning Don Antonino's support, and it could also help suppress the notion that

Carlos was surrendering the family business to the Americans. In fact, Anheuser-Busch wanted a commitment that Modelo's controlling families would stick around as major shareholders after the deal occurred. "We did not want them to throw the keys on the table and walk away," said Santel.

The proposed deal's structure was uncannily similar to that of another deal done between a giant U.S. company and a Mexican target: Citigroup's acquisition of south-of-the-border bank Banco Nacional de Mexico (Banamex). It wasn't a coincidence. Anheuser-Busch and Modelo deliberately copied the structure of the Banamex deal, down to the separate board of directors that Banamex maintained after the acquisition.

Carlos outlined the transaction to Don Antonino in the boardroom of their family offices later in the day on the 19th. He always tried to catch his uncle in the mornings when he could—given his advanced age, Don Antonino preferred to spend his afternoons reading at home. His view, as he expressed it that day, was that the merger would benefit Modelo's families by giving them a controlling stake in a much more powerful brewer. The deal would create a bigger, better company for both Anheuser-Busch and Modelo. To Carlos's great satisfaction, Don Antonino granted his blessing to move forward.

■ ■ ■

North of the border, in St. Louis and New York, the Modelo option was sparking hope for Anheuser's team. Company staffers and strategy committee members who had been tasked on the potential transaction, which had been assigned the Shakespearean code name "Project Montague," were clocking long hours in the hopes that they could save their company by finally closing a deal that had never worked in the past. If they could bring the Modelo transaction to within feet of the finish line, they believed, it would be pulled across with the support of August III and the board.

Responsibility for hammering out the Modelo deal had fallen to The Fourth, who had never before handled a task of such mission-critical nature. He, however, then delegated much of the work to a range of subordinates. While Anheuser's corporate planners had gen-erally been stuck under The Third's heavy thumb in the past and had consistently endorsed the courses of action—or more appropriately, inaction—he favored. Now, after decades of extreme caution, the team was now hurriedly putting together a proposal that seemed to heavily and even desperately favor Modelo. With the whole world watching, the situation was putting some of the board's members ill at ease.

As discussions between Modelo and Anheuser grew more intense in late June, and as the Anheuser-Busch board became increasingly uncomfortable with how The Fourth and his deputies were handling the matter, Sandy Warner stepped forward to put an end to the game of telephone and serve as a more direct line of communication between Carlos Fernández and the Anheuser-Busch board. Warner had known Fernández for a long time, and with so many issues up in the air, he felt it was time to start making more decisions at the board level.

"He sort of said, 'Let me be in on some of these phone calls,'" said a person close to the talks. "He was gradually losing his patience with the whole situation."

Warner's shift into a more active role coincided with a critical decision by the board that sent Modelo reeling. While The Fourth and Santel had clearly suggested that Fernández could take over as CEO, the board still wasn't keen on the idea. They were worried that they might look reckless for offering to pay such a high price for Modelo while also relinquishing control of the company, all to avoid talking to InBev. That didn't seem to provide for a great deal of "independence" on Anheuser's part in the future.

"I think people just thought that it was over-reaching, with this premium, that the guy also runs the company," said one advisor. "To be fair to Modelo, they probably felt that we were in a position where they were key to us staying independent."

The board's other concern was that putting Fernández in charge wasn't the easy fix to Anheuser's "CEO problem" they were looking for. The Fourth seemed fine with the notion of installing Fernández as CEO or co-CEO. "The Fourth, I don't think by himself, had any issue with Carlos playing a very big role," said one Anheuser advisor. "The Fourth was in no way standing in the way of that and was very open about it. I think The Fourth was pretty supportive of it all the way through."

"The bottom line is he's a really nice guy who should have never been CEO of a company like Bud, and every director knew it," said another person close to the company.

Yet Fernández, the best-positioned candidate to replace The Fourth, was too much of an unknown quantity for some members of the board—even though he had served with them as a director for years. Some felt that while he would be a boon to the company's management team in general, he wasn't ready to be CEO of a global corporate giant with decidedly American roots and culture. A few argued that he should move to St. Louis first to get to know the company's operations and prove himself. If that went well, he could ascend to the CEO's spot a few years down the line.

"Carlos is a terrific guy, but he's not a U.S. CEO—on top of the details, running a business day to day," said a person close to Anheuser. "And he's not a figurehead."

Once the board determined that it wasn't willing to throw its weight behind Carlos as the company's designated savior, it decided that The Fourth had to rescind his offer. He needed to inform Carlos Fernández that the CEO spot was off the table.

It wasn't going to be an easy message to relay, given the history of antagonism between the companies, and The Fourth knew it would require more than a cell phone call from outside his local Starbucks. He had to do it in person. "I think he felt he had a personal relationship with this guy—he wanted to look him in the eye," said an Anheuser-Busch advisor. "That was the way he did things," said one of his former deputies.

So August IV's team reached out to Modelo to schedule a meeting with Fernández on Tuesday, June 24, without disclosing its nature. To accommodate their busy schedules, the two CEOs chose a regional airport situated near the U.S.-Mexico border in Texas, right on the line between Missouri and Mexico City as the crow flies. They agreed to fly in on their private jets and convene, in true Anheuser-Busch form, at an airport hangar that had space available for a meeting.

As usual, August IV traveled that day with Pedro Soares, his omnipresent right-hand man. The Fourth, like his father, employed a small army of people to perform business and personal tasks for him that ranged from the sundry to the substantive. And amidst his entourage of secretaries and hangers-on, there was always one person it seemed he couldn't live without—his head handler and personal attaché. Evan Athanas had helped The Fourth in that capacity for a while before shifting into a vice president's position, and Soares, another executive, had then moved into his place.

"This is a legacy of The Third, who always needed somebody to make him feel like he was a bit of royalty," said one person close to Anheuser-Busch. The Third's traditions of forced subordination and hierarchy stretched across the entire company, from the huge number of personal secretaries Anheuser-Busch employed to the executive assistant training and apprenticeship program The Third had long espoused.

"August Busch, and it spanned from III to IV, ran the company like it was in the 1950s with chiefs of staff and little people running around," said a company advisor. "August IV did what his father did, and he used to have chiefs of staff."

Soares was a competent executive in his own right, having run Anheuser-Busch's operations down in Mexico for seven years. He was one of several Anheuser executives who served on Modelo's board, and he spoke fluent Spanish, which helped Anheuser's cause south of the border. Soares's welcome presence tended to help off-set Modelo's distaste for many of Anheuser's other executives.

The greatest impact Soares had, however, stemmed from his ability to keep August IV on message. He would often speak in The Fourth's stead during meetings, and he interacted with the company's advisors on his boss's behalf. At times, Soares would even pull Anheuser's bankers aside as they prepared The Fourth's remarks to the board to make sure things were being captured the right way. He traveled with The Fourth to Mexico, sat in on most of The Fourth's meetings with Fernández, and was part of nearly every Modelo-related phone call that occurred.

"Everyone should have one," joked one person close to the company in reference to the role Soares played before softening his stance. "I never had any evidence other than that he was a competent, informed business person who was willing to play the role of aide-de-camp, Gal Friday, and conscience to some extent. This is the guy who made sure that August woke up in the morning. He provided the sorts of backbone of professional support August needed, and August needed it. August needed a full-time confidant, conscience, motivator.

"August was not a hard-working, detail-oriented guy. He needs somebody, like a doppelgänger. Pedro was August when he needed to be."

That was the type of thing that unnerved the company's board of directors, however. The Fourth's need for wingmen had presented problems in Tampa, and it came into play again that day in Texas.

Fernández arrived with a single lawyer in tow, and after the men greeted each other and sat down, it was Pedro Soares who started talking. The Fourth had pushed for an in-person meeting with Fernández to relay the bad news, and the two men had a relatively strong relationship. When the time came, though, he had Soares deliver the blow to his Mexican colleague rather than handling the matter chief-to-chief.

When The Fourth debriefed Anheuser's directors at their board meeting the next day—the day on which the board decided to reject InBev's $65 per share offer—he even made a deliberate and somewhat bewildering point to tell everyone that Pedro had done a great job in relaying the message to Fernández. He was kind to praise Soares in such illustrious company, but the whole thing seemed odd. As one person close to Anheuser phrased it, it was as if he had set up a meeting with a fellow CEO to discuss something critical and then sent his secretary in to explain the scenario.

■ ■ ■

As Soares laid everything out to Fernández that day in Texas and watched Fernández's eyes grow dark with anger, The Fourth looked ashamed. Ashamed that he had offered to subordinate himself to a rival, and ashamed that he now stood there in front of Fernández, a man he had come to know and respect, to retract the offer. He had grown so constrained by his father and the board of directors that it seemed like he wasn't even at liberty to quit.

The news completely blindsided Fernández, who had assumed Anheuser-Busch wanted him to pack up and fly to Texas for a productive deal-related meeting, not to slap him with a demotion.

"This is not in the spirit of the deal we have been discussing," he retorted, frustrated that he was going to have to go back to Modelo's controlling families to relay the news. One of the main reasons they had agreed to negotiate a deal was because Carlos was going to be in charge.

"If someone is going to run this company, it needs to be someone who has a good track record," Fernández said, turning toward The Fourth. It was crystal clear, Fernández felt, that he had delivered better as Modelo's chief than August IV had as CEO of Anheuser-Busch.

Soares and The Fourth did their best to diffuse Carlos's anger during the short amount of time they spent with him that day, but they weren't particularly successful. "Carlos had to fly to Texas in his private jet, land, do all this kind of crap . . . it was incredibly insulting," said one person close to Modelo. "Pissed was not the word, if I can remember."

"I don't think Carlos would have bothered flying to Texas to be told it wasn't going to happen," said another. "I think he went under the pretense of 'We've got stuff to talk about, my family to your family, big deal, only principals, etcetera. And that was when this message was delivered that 'You're not going to be CEO, but maybe we can figure something else out—head of the Americas or something.'"

Fernández was livid on the flight home, and spent a good amount of time talking with his lawyer about whether Anheuser-Busch's decision would be a deal breaker for Modelo's family owners. It had been less than two weeks since the start of their talks, and the Americans were already retracting one of the deal's key components. What was next?

Sandy Warner quickly called Fernández to apologize, and he tried to explain the board's rationale. The cost of the transaction was already so high, Warner said, that having Carlos be CEO of the merged company sent the wrong message to Anheuser-Busch shareholders. They'd be giving up too much. However, he laid out what he hoped would be a sufficient consolation prize: Within less than a year, Warner said, he was certain that Carlos would be appointed CEO. It just couldn't happen right away.

Warner acknowledged that he spent a good deal of time talking to Fernández about the role he could play at the merged company. "I had discussions with Carlos about how capable I thought he was, and said that working with August IV, the Anheuser team and the Modelo team, he had a real future in this company," he said. "If he still wanted to work—and that wasn't a given—but if he still wanted to work, there was a lot of work to do, and he and August would make a great team. He's a young guy, and a lot of things can happen."

Tim Ingrassia then called Morgan Stanley's Kindler to try to douse the fire further. "We can't be viewed as paying you a premium and having you take us over," Ingrassia explained. "That just won't work." Ingrassia then voiced the same pledge Warner had made to Fernández.

"Look, nothing is committed," Ingrassia said. "But I would be shocked if a year from now, Carlos is not the CEO of this company. We just can't commit to him."

"What credibility do you guys have?" Kindler fired back, unimpressed by the olive branch. "You've got to be kidding me!"

Carlos reflected on the uncomfortable entreaties The Third had made to him in St. Louis—his furtive admissions that perhaps Carlos was a better CEO for Anheuser-Busch than his own son. He was now starting to doubt The Third's true intentions, given how clumsily he and the rest of Anheuser's board had just backtracked.

Somewhat counterintuitively, however, the Anheuser board's decision suggested to Kindler for the first time that Anheuser was seriously considering the transaction, not just using it as leverage against InBev. The Mexicans took a small bit of solace in knowing that Anheuser's board was actually weighing the terms of a deal and sorting through governance issues, not just treating the notion of buying their company as a joke.

■ ■ ■

Carlos and María were angry and frustrated that Anheuser-Busch had retraced its steps, but after decades of bad blood between the two companies, they weren't surprised. "Modelo was not looking to be sold," said one person close to the company. "All of these family members are independently wealthy. It's like 'You came to us, we didn't go to you. We're very happy down here; we have a great business down here. And now, you basically renege.'" Loose promises that Fernández might take over in a year or two weren't enough to substitute for Modelo's loss of certainty up front. It was going to be much harder now to strike up a deal that would meet Don Antonino's approval.

It quickly became clear that without a guarantee that Carlos would be in charge from Day One, there was no way Modelo's controlling families would accept so much stock as payment for the deal. They didn't want their fates and their fortunes tied to Anheuser's board and August IV. So they decided to flip the terms of the deal and demand a mostly-cash transaction. A cash takeover would be tougher to finance, but if Anheuser wanted it badly enough, it was possible. And it was the only option that gave Modelo's controlling families enough certainty that they'd be paid appropriately for their stake. Their ties to Anheuser-Busch would be limited once they got their payout, and Carlos, who had reached the end of his rope with the gang from St. Louis, could separate from the company and go his own way.

"We came back, after much debate because our guys were so pissed off, and we said, 'You know, we'll still do the deal,'" said a person close to Modelo. "But we're not going to take anywhere near the amount of stock we were going to take in the first deal. We don't trust your management team. We were happy to take mostly stock if Carlos was running it. We're not taking a bunch of stock if The Fourth is running it." Modelo's game of hardball was morphing into yet another grudge match between the two rivals.

When Modelo set its new proposal in front of Anheuser-Busch a few days later, it discovered that while Anheuser's board didn't want Fernández to be CEO, they also weren't keen on the idea that he might pack up a briefcase full of cash and head off into the sunset once the deal went through.

"There were a lot of negotiations about what Carlos's role would be," said a person close to Modelo. "We went back to them and said, 'We'll do this for mostly cash, we'll take a little bit of stock, and Carlos is gone.' And that totally freaked them out."

"No, you don't understand," Ingrassia told Kindler. "Look, the board will never approve this unless they know that Carlos is on board."

After more rounds of back and forth, the companies finally agreed to push forward with a mostly cash deal through which Carlos would become the merged company's international head. Don Antonino and some of the other families' members weren't as eager about the deal in its new form, but the elements they valued the most were still intact.

"Nothing was ever going to happen if we didn't have the structure where Modelo would stay as a Mexican company, in Mexico City, called Modelo," said a person involved in the talks. "That was fixed in stone."

Still, Modelo was wary enough about Anheuser-Busch's capabilities and motives to shift its backup talks with InBev into high gear. It had become clear that whichever two companies struck up an alliance first were going to leave the third out in the rain to get soaked. It was still possible that a deal between Anheuser and Modelo would be scrapped and InBev would win the war. Don Antonino's support wasn't 100 percent guaranteed—nor, for that matter, was an endorsement from Anheuser-Busch's own board. Modelo wanted to have agreements in place ahead of time that gave it free rein over how it spent its money and distributed its beers worldwide.

So Modelo decided to negotiate hard behind the scenes with InBev as well. The Modelo team sat down several times in late June and early July with key InBev advisors to press their most important points. "At the same time we're talking to Anheuser-Busch, we of course are talking to InBev, because we had to hedge our bets," said one person close to Modelo. "We had to use one against the other for negotiating leverage."

"Proof positive that we were virtually sure we were a 'stalking horse' is that we were playing both sides," said one person close to Modelo. "We were having as many meetings with InBev as we were with Anheuser-Busch."

In exchange for greater freedom, Modelo was offering to set up a more consistent formula for paying out its dividend, which would provide more certainty for InBev than Modelo currently afforded Anheuser-Busch. Modelo knew that a steady stream of dividends would prove useful to InBev as it labored to pay off its debt following an acquisition of Anheuser-Busch's size.

InBev's point of view, according to one advisor, was that "Modelo had negotiated a pretty bad deal for themselves in the original transaction, and there was hope that this could be used to say, 'You can have a better deal in some way,' and sort of pit them against Anheuser and put them in favor of InBev." Modelo and InBev started working to draft agreements to this effect in early July, but the two companies reached an impasse. Modelo wanted to make sure that InBev, like Anheuser, would have no ability to take control of the company, and it also wanted the right to sell itself—both its own stake and the stake that would be owned by InBev—to a third party if it so chose.

Modelo's controlling families weren't pushing hard to sell, but they wanted the chance to change their minds a few years down the road, and they believed SABMiller was an interested buyer. One person close to Modelo said SAB's advisors were "all over" Modelo in late June and July trying to gauge the prospects of a deal, though a person on SABMiller's side contended that it wasn't considering Modelo seriously at the time.

InBev, however, wasn't willing to enter into a deal that might let Modelo sell its stake to SABMiller. InBev professed to the Mexicans that it would love to buy their entire company, but simply couldn't do so while it was also trying to acquire Anheuser-Busch. The sheer size of those two companies combined was too much for InBev to digest all at once. That was the reason Anheuser-Busch was considering it as a defense tactic.

"Their view all along," said a Modelo source, "was, 'We're happy to let you run independently. You're never going to hear from us. We want you to be on the board of our parent company. All we really want is two things—first, that you give us the cash; and second, that you don't sell to anyone else.'"

■ ■ ■

On Tuesday, July 1, Anheuser's board was scheduled to meet for a major update on the Modelo talks. Investors had taken a few days over the weekend to digest the details of Anheuser's cost-slashing plan and to gossip about August IV's mistake on the call, and the company was finally enjoying a little bit of the momentum that comes with leading the news cycle rather than reacting to it. It didn't last long. InBev issued a press release that morning—another disclosure that was uncannily timed to coincide with an Anheuser-Busch board meeting—in which it announced that the financing for its bid was now set in stone.

That didn't provide an ideal backdrop for the meeting, but Anheuser's team still had reason to be positive. Carlos Fernández and his crew had come around to the idea that he wouldn't be CEO, and with Anheuser willing to make more of its payment in cash, the potential for a deal was looking good. August IV and the rest of his team were prepared to crank away over the Fourth of July holiday weekend to get the transaction down on paper as quickly as possible.

All they needed was the board's blessing to continue, and they got it that day. Goldman, Citigroup, and Anheuser's own executives all presented their views on Modelo and outlined how the deal might affect InBev's bid. Goldman was confident that the transaction would preserve Anheuser-Busch's independence. Anheuser's executives were racking up their third straight week of late nights with those same prayers in mind, scrambling to get the deal done before InBev made its next move. They all understood they were treading a fine line. If they wanted to keep Anheuser-Busch independent, they needed to engineer a deal that would drive InBev away without actually making its bid impossible. That sort of defense tactic could get the board sued.

The Third, given his historic distaste for acquisitions, was never going to be an easy sell. He had even shown signs of buyers' remorse over the initial stake he had purchased in Modelo—one of the best things Anheuser-Busch now had going for it. Anheuser's team, however, now believed they were heading into the holiday weekend with a mandate for inking a transaction. They sensed that The Third and the rest of the board, who made plans to meet on Monday, supported their efforts to mold the deal into finished form.

"August III just likes being in control of things, and plenty has already been written and said about his hesitancy with respect to risks in the world and international," said one person close to the company. "He's a tough guy, and he's quite skilled at killing things.

He was, at the margin, always going to be a challenge. But I think we all thought it was achievable, and he was certainly allowing it to move forward. He hadn't killed it yet, I guess I'd say."

The Fourth and the rest of his team, however, were dangerously close to becoming pawns in a chess game they didn't want to play. To sign a deal with Modelo, they had to negotiate hard with the Mexicans. There was a chance, though, that Anheuser's board was saying one thing and thinking another for strategic reasons—that some directors opposed the deal and merely wanted to use Modelo as a bargaining chip against InBev.

If that was the board's real motivation, the Modelo talks were nothing but a farce, an act Anheuser's team had to keep up in order to pressure InBev. They would have to pretend they were dead-set on a deal and push it toward completion even if the board had no intention of approving it.

"They had to offset Brito's bravado, him saying, 'I'm not moving beyond here,'" said one Anheuser-Busch advisor.

"It's a bit of a bluff. But we knew that he wasn't going to call it."

Chapter 13

A Seller from "Hello"

The Third, I think, had decided that he liked the price, and he let them muddle along with Modelo. But he was never going to do the deal.

—Anheuser-Busch advisor

A ugust IV didn't end up spending that Fourth of July weekend the way he had expected he would just a month or so earlier. His family's name had been emblazoned on millions of cases of beer sold that weekend, the holiday on which Americans drink more beer than on any other occasion. Ahead of the previous year's July Fourth, the Beer Institute—a lobbying organization he chaired—had helpfully pointed out that when Thomas Jefferson and America's other founding fathers weren't distracted by their work on the Declaration of Independence, many of them had been brewers with a "vision to establish beer as an economic force for the nation's future."

The Fourth's own vision for the future now looked unnervingly hazy. Rather than celebrating America's Independence Day the way the

Institute had said he should—with barbecues, fireworks, and a cold beer—he spent it scrambling for ways to protect the independence of his birthright.

To make matters worse, he and the rest of Anheuser's board awoke on the morning of Monday, July 7, to learn that InBev had just lobbed in another grenade as part of its siege. It was pushing ahead with its audacious move to forcefully eject Anheuser's entire board, and had released an alternate slate of nominees it had finalized over the weekend. If elected, those directors would launch a new review of whether to accept the merger bid—and it was likely they'd vote yes. The board of Anheuser-Busch had unwittingly become part of the story.

InBev's advisors were proud of themselves for assembling a cast of nominees they felt would intimidate Anheuser-Busch. Their goal was to lure former captains of iconic American companies, but they considered their ability to secure two candidates, in particular, as a major coup.

The big win from a psychological standpoint was Adolphus Busch IV. His public plea the previous week for Anheuser to negotiate with InBev had stunned Anheuser's team, and InBev had twisted the knife even deeper that morning by placing his name near the top of its list of nominees. Adolphus had offered to help Brito in whatever way he could when he had released his letter to Anheuser's board, and Brito was glad to take him up on it. His willingness to go to bat for the Brazilians was like "manna from heaven," said one person close to InBev. "We knew Adolphus was around, but no one thought that Adolphus would do this," said another. For all of InBev's contentions that it wanted to play clean and keep things friendly, it was more than willing to use the Busch family's fractured history against it when the opportunity struck.

"When they put Adolphus up at the top of the page, with all of these other guys who were well known, you start to say, 'Oh my God, these guys have played the ultimate card putting Adolphus in there, because that is an absolute punch in the gut to Mr. Busch [III],'" said one former Anheuser executive. "No way was he ever going to allow another guy from the family, an estranged family member . . . that was the ultimate low blow."

Henry "Hank" McKinnell, the former chairman and chief executive of giant drug maker Pfizer, also agreed to join InBev's roster at the request of Lazard's Steve Golub, who had advised Pfizer on its $90 billion deal to buy Warner-Lambert in 2000 and on its $60 billion purchase of Pharmacia in 2003. McKinnell was a well respected leader in the drug industry and just the type of high-flying corporate leader InBev was looking for. He had, however, been abruptly replaced ahead of his scheduled departure from Pfizer amid questions over his performance and an uproar over his pay.

As for the rest of InBev's slate, Ernest Mario had run pharmaceutical giant Glaxo Holdings. John Lilly had been CEO of Pillsbury. Others had been top executives at Nabisco, Guidant, and ArvinMeritor. Some of Anheuser's board members had professional ties to their proposed replacements—Anheuser's Vernon Loucks, for example, served as an advisor to one private equity firm alongside Mario—and investors were now debating whether InBev's slate was a better fit for Anheuser than its own board. The move was aimed at luring Anheuser into merger talks, not at actually ejecting its entire slate of directors. InBev, however, looked prepared to wage that battle if necessary.

Anheuser's board members weren't panicked when they arrived at the airplane hangar that morning—the release of InBev's nominees was a logical next step in the wake of its lawsuit. "It's a normal tactic. No big surprise," said Jim Forese. The development did spark some debate over how likely they were to keep their jobs, however, and there was no denying that it made that day's already-important meeting seem even more critical.

The board was planning to debate the Modelo option yet again that morning as it decided how to handle the attempted hijacking of its ranks. Things had changed significantly, though, since the previous week. Anheuser-Busch and Modelo had finally come to terms on a deal, after decades of maddening stops and starts.

The teams on both sides of the border were pumped. They had worked feverishly over the extended weekend to cram everything together, from details of the deal itself to the press release and press conferences they would use to announce it to the world. A team of Anheuser executives had holed up with Goldman's bankers in the meeting rooms at Skadden's offices to negotiate with Kindler, Mercado, and the rest of Modelo's team. After a spirited set of talks, they were ready to go. And the deal had the blessing of Modelo's controlling families, who had been rounded up for conference calls several times in recent weeks as terms of the sale kept changing.

The two companies' PR staffers were trying to figure out the best way to announce the deal. Should it be rolled out in Mexico City? That had been the thought at first. Or maybe in two cities on the same day, one in the United States and one in Mexico? The Fourth could start the day with an announcement down in Mexico, the companies decided, and then he and Fernández would fly to New York for round two. All Modelo's side needed was the all-clear from Anheuser's board.

"We had fully negotiated a deal," said one Anheuser-Busch advisor. "We had a deal that was done."

■ ■ ■

The board was planning to tackle a couple of issues that Monday, but its clear priority was deciding whether to pull the trigger on Modelo. The acquisition's terms had already been recut several times as various board members—and often, The Third specifically—had raised concerns about one point or another and asked that they be addressed.

As the directors settled back expectantly in their usual chairs, waiting for the Modelo pitches to begin, Tom Santel stood up to assemble the management team's presentation materials. August IV remained in his seat, and he stayed there as his deputy launched into the opening bars of their pitch in favor of the deal. A few people in the room were surprised to see The Fourth behaving so passively, given how important that day's presentation was to his company's independence. To others, though, his decision to let Santel take the lead was par for the course. "I've seen enough of him, and heard enough, to know that his doing less rather than more was not surprising," said one company advisor.

August III, like his son, also lived up to his reputation that day. He had walked into the airplane hangar with a strong sense of how the board's meeting would end before it even began.

As Santel finished up his pitch on why the Modelo deal made sense, The Third started rifling through a pile of documents in front of him. Rather than showing up that day with a pen and a blank pad of paper, he had asked several of Anheuser's executives and bankers— most of whom were already scurrying frantically over the weekend to nail down the Modelo deal—to pull double-duty and run separate sets of numbers that he could analyze on his own. By the time the last of Anheuser-Busch's advisors arrived on Sunday evening, The Third had already summoned Santel and M&A head Bob Golden out to his farm for a full briefing session, where he asked them to present their calculations on Modelo. He had run the two men ragged all weekend with demands for information and had requested details from Goldman, Citigroup, and Skadden as well.

"He actually got a lot of data and pulled it all together," one advisor said, "such that by the time he got to the meeting, he already had it all. He had all of these pre-done questions he had already thought through. And look, to be honest, that's a good board member. He was the most prepared board member. He was more prepared than The Fourth. He worked three times harder."

"He has a reputation for this even from when he sat on other boards," another advisor said. "When he sat on Whitacre's board [at AT&T], there was always separate analysis done for him because he always wanted to see different types of analysis than what was being done as a matter of course."

Santel's presentation was less than polished—his team had rushed to cram everything together by Monday while also catering to The Third's demands for face time, and he had worked virtually nonstop except to sleep. Still, he was pumped. He thought his team and Modelo had hammered together a strong deal.

None of Anheuser's executives, therefore, expected The Third to spring out of the gate with as much force as he did at that moment, when he launched into a pointed series of questions about Santel's assumptions and financial projections, using the information they had helped him gather over the weekend as ammunition. They were stunned by the chilly reception.

"Tom Santel had been sort of his fair-haired boy, and it was kind of surprising that he took such vigorous issue with what Tom had just presented," said Ambassador Jones. "I do remember that Tom Santel was both surprised and very disappointed."

It was no surprise that The Third was hesitant about buying Modelo. He had never favored the idea. "The way InBev and SAB had had all of these opportunities to grow is that he never wanted to do any acquisitions," one advisor said. "His being anti-deal in general was not, I think, new to these people."

As The Third ticked aggressively down his list of concerns, taking issue with the deal's high price and the risks it involved, it dawned on Anheuser's staffers that his efforts to fix and fine-tune the Modelo proposal in recent weeks may have been aimed more squarely at nixing it. They had essentially negotiated two different deals back-to-back to meet his demands, and he still wasn't happy. "We got one deal done, he kept trying to get us to get more stuff to see that the deal was killed, and we kept getting everything he wanted," said one executive.

"The Third just ripped the thing apart," said one person who watched Santel's pitch get torn to shreds. Modelo was the fly The Third couldn't swat gently out of the air, so he was now slamming his fist down onto the table to kill it.

■ ■ ■

InBev's team took great care to unfurl a takeover strategy that gave its bid the highest possible chance of success. It spent months hemming and hawing over the particulars—everything from the state of the financing and political environments to how much it cost to feed and brush Anheuser's 250 Clydesdales.

The Brazilians ended up having the unlikeliest ally imaginable— one who was able to sway Anheuser's board much more effectively than any of InBev's best-laid plans.

August III, as his son was discovering that day, had a new set of priorities. While The Fourth and his team worked frantically to structure the company's defense that June, his father had quietly indicated to a few startled Anheuser insiders that he would support a sale of the company to InBev. The 70-year-old former chief appeared to have determined that a deal was inevitable, and he was focused on getting the best price possible.

Virtually unrecognizable in wrinkled shorts and ratty sneakers, The Third had crept up two weeks earlier on Citigroup's Kalvaria, who had just landed at the company's airplane hangar and was about to grab a car into town for a meeting at Anheuser-Busch headquarters.

"Hello, Leon. Come here, let's go talk," The Third whispered brusquely, all but dragging the startled banker into the hangar's tiny ground floor bathroom. Kalvaria had thought he was a janitor.

The Third stepped into the bathroom's single stall, shut the door behind him and sat down on the toilet. "What do you think, can you get me $70 per share for this company?" he said, his voice echoing out from behind the stall door. "Can we get them to pay $70?"

"There was no bigger seller than August Busch III," said one person close to the Anheuser board's deliberations. "From the first moment, he appeared to be a seller."

In fact, The Third had started badgering people over how much InBev might pay as early as the very first board meeting held during the crisis.

"The secret that never came out was that The Third was a seller from absolutely day one," said another person close to the company. "I can't describe it, but from that first board meeting it was obvious that he was a seller. And to some extent, it was obvious that some directors and The Fourth were going to play the role of devil's advocate. Most of the board just wanted to make sure they were good fiduciaries and made the right decision."

"I think The Third was a seller from 'Hello.'"

It's a revelation that would have shocked Anheuser's investors, members of the Busch family, and the entire city of St. Louis, had they known at the time. It's what ultimately drove the nail into the Modelo deal's coffin and torpedoed Anheuser's efforts to save itself from foreign control.

No one in the press or on Wall Street picked up on it, perhaps because the board and its advisors knew their bargaining position would be ruined if The Third's willingness to sell became public. For all anyone outside the airplane hangar knew, Anheuser's legendary former chief was still operating in his normal state—stubbornly refusing to consider the deal and doing his best to strike it down.

Anheuser's executives had known from the start that he would be the toughest member of their audience that day—he didn't seem to have much faith in them. Yet some were still blindsided by the strength of his opposition to the Modelo deal. "There were a lot of people on the management team who really viewed The Third as pretty hostile," said one Anheuser insider. "He was hostile to this stuff all the way through."

"He was clearly just looking to ultimately negotiate a deal with InBev. That could reflect, more than anything else, that he didn't feel comfortable with the management team we had and didn't have a level of comfort in the management team running the business, implementing our restructuring, and integrating a large acquisition. And when he saw InBev come with cash, he just wanted to get the best deal he could out of InBev and go home with his money."

The Third's eagerness to sell even appeared to affect his relationship with Sandy Warner during the takeover fight's latter stages. "My impression is that before InBev even appeared, [Warner] had been a proponent for taking over 100 percent of Modelo, from way back," said one Anheuser advisor. In late June, after several weeks of talks between the parties, Warner had continued to seem open to exploring a deal with Modelo. He knew Modelo well after serving for so long on Anheuser's board, and knew it was a major contributor to Anheuser-Busch's results.

"It would have given us, I think, a very interesting portfolio," Warner said. "A lot of efficiencies. It was an interesting deal. But very expensive."

Warner's willingness to jump into the Modelo talks appeared to create some distance between him and The Third. "Warner was officially the lead director and liked doing stuff like that. He seemed to enjoy being in the middle of it," said one advisor. "And I think he was much more of a proponent of the Modelo deal. I'm not sure I ever knew precisely where Whitacre was on the spectrum of things. But what was really clear was that Whitacre was still trusted by The Third. Warner was not trusted by The Third. I think he thought Warner was supporting The Fourth and supporting [his close deputy] Dave Peacock and this concept of doing Modelo, and not selling the company."

After The Third wrapped up his barrage of questioning that day, the Modelo matter was opened up to the full board for debate.

The tides of the meeting, however, had irrevocably shifted. Once The Third had sufficiently skewered Modelo in front of the entire board, there was no way Anheuser's exhausted executive team could contain the damage. He held too much sway over the group.

"It got to the full board, and basically the notion was . . . given the price, given the risks, how could you do [Modelo] without engaging to some degree with the other guys to see what was there?" one advisor said. The meeting devolved into a series of smaller group discussions over what the company should do about InBev, and the Modelo transaction's momentum evaporated.

"What do you think InBev could really pay?" the directors quizzed each other, tossing out numbers based on their bankers' recent presentations. InBev might not have the ability to finance a deal priced at $72 or $75 per share in cash, the bankers had explained, and the notion of taking some of the payment in stock was a non-starter. Still, $70 per share in cash was probably doable if Brito wanted Budweiser badly enough. August III adopted his signature modus operandi and started cornering people one-on-one as the others looked on anxiously, considering what they would say when it was their turn.

"What's the number? What's the number?" The Third asked Tim Ingrassia.

"What's *what* number?" Ingrassia queried.

"The number. You know, the number. What number can we get?"

Some of the directors might not have had a particular view going into the meeting on what InBev might pay. After The Third acted as a single-party whip, however, lobbying them as a group and then badgering them one by one, pricing became the main topic of concern.

"He's just an oddly charismatic guy," said one person who was there that day. "He's a caricature on the one hand, and on the other hand, he's just got this ability to bend a room to caring about what he thinks and what he says. If it was 13 to 1 for a moment on a straw poll before an official vote, I wouldn't bet against him if he was the one. He knows how to get things done."

With the group's attention sufficiently redirected toward InBev, Anheuser's executives and bankers filtered out of the room to allow the board to whittle itself down to its independent directors. August IV, the first board member in line to exit, then stood to offer his point of view.

His perspective was clear: After all the years Anheuser had spent as a powerless half-owner of its Mexican partner, he favored finally taking control of Modelo. The statement wasn't overly rousing. Several people in the room were disappointed that The Fourth never made an impassioned pitch for the plan on which his team had worked so hard. "I think some of the board felt that as the process went on on InBev, August IV could have been more assertive," said Ambassador Jones. "He kind of shrank back from asserting himself on the deal and did not provide some of the leadership that the board expected from him." Part of the reason for that, Jones mused, may have been "because August III was taking a strong position on some of those issues."

After The Fourth stepped out of the room, Stokes tossed in his carefully worded two cents—he had reservations about the Modelo deal but seemed neutral to favorable on the idea. And then he handed the floor to The Third. Now that the time for decision making had come, The Third let up on his full-court press. Leaving the independent directors thinking that his view was overly polarized might actually backfire in his face. So he briefly reiterated why he believed the deal didn't make sense, and then turned the matter back to the board.

"When it came time to count noses, he summarized his concerns but was much more diplomatic and basically said, 'If you folks think this is something we should do, we should do it,'" said one person who was in the room. "[I]f you guys think this is what makes the most sense for the company, I'm not going to lay down in the road in front of it.'

"But he may well have said that fully knowing what was going to come out of the other guys," this person said—knowing, in other words, that other key board members would vote in favor of reaching out to InBev. "On Saturday and Sunday, he had been laying down in the road in front of it."

■ ■ ■

Whenever The Fourth was ejected from the boardroom, he would slink off into a little anteroom at the hangar that housed the fax machine and printer and start jabbing away on his BlackBerry, like a kid playing with his Game Boy outside his father's office. At one point during the independent directors' deliberations, The Fourth turned to the advisors seated next to him.

"What do you think they're talking about in there?" he said, only half-joking.

The Fourth had seemed increasingly dazed and out of sorts over the past few weeks, but his colleagues were nonetheless stunned to hear such a comment coming from the CEO of a major corporation. No one said much then, but several of them recounted the moment later in exasperation.

"What do you think is going on in there?" one of them said incredulously. "I don't know. You're the fucking CEO!"

August IV's spacey behavior unnerved some of Anheuser's executives and advisors, who knew there had never been a more critical time for their CEO to be on the ball. During one board meeting, he leaned over to one of his advisors to ask how the Busch family was going to sustain itself financially if the deal happened.

"If we sell the company, how are these guys ever going to get their dividends going forward?" he asked.

"It was like a trick question," the advisor said. "I said, 'August, if they sell the company they'll have cash. They can go decide whatever they want.' It was just bizarre. People were looking at him like, 'Where the hell did that question come from?'"

"I used to wonder if August was on drugs in the meeting," the advisor said, voicing a question that was echoed by several other members of the team. "Because he would just sit there, like, completely out of it. At points, it seemed like he might be falling asleep.

"The Fourth was slowly falling apart," said another. "He was in a physical and mental haze for weeks. Pedro's job was to get him dressed so he could show up for things he had to be at."

■ ■ ■

Once Stokes and The Third had exited the boardroom, Joe Flom took the floor and made it clear to the independent directors that he was up for a fight if they wanted one. He didn't push them in one direction or another, but he said they had the legal flexibility to turn InBev down if they wanted to. "He talked about their fiduciary duty," said one person in attendance. "They didn't have any duty to sell the company, there was this other terrific transaction out there, and yeah, it might get attacked, but there were good reasons that would uphold the action."

"It was like the last stand—we'll get them on the beaches."

The board felt that Anheuser-Busch's standalone plans could beat InBev's $65 a share offer, especially if Modelo was added in on top. They were uneasy, however, about hopping into bed with the Mexicans in the wake of The Third's performance that day. After letting the debate run on for a while, the oracle-like Whitacre finally interjected to offer his perspective.

"I just don't understand how we do this other transaction, with all of the risks entailed in it, without having some communication with the guys who put a very big bid on the table to see if they won't do better," he told the board. "Then we can decide what to do."

It was tough to argue with that logic, even for anyone who might have wanted to. If Modelo were offering itself at a bargain price for a limited time, things might have been different. However, Modelo's demands kept rising. How could the board explain its decision to shareholders without at least asking InBev for a higher bid? It would seem blindly irresponsible.

Some members of the board worried that they might lose Modelo altogether if they reached out to InBev. The Mexicans and their advisors were bound to be furious. Still, they decided, business was business, and their job was to get the best deal possible for Anheuser's shareholders. To lessen the affront to Modelo, they could keep InBev on a short leash by requiring them to come back quickly with a response.

With a unanimous show of hands, the directors agreed that Anheuser's best choice was to ask InBev to raise its bid. They needed to see the Brazilians' best and final offer in order to make the right decision, which meant there was no choice but to break the silence.

Just one question remained: Who should make the overture? Such a critical phone call, after weeks of stonewalling, would require a deft approach. Anheuser needed to carefully open a dialogue with its now-bitter rival and extract a higher bid using the threat of an alternative deal as leverage. If Anheuser overplayed or underplayed its hand, either by inflating the Modelo transaction's prospects or by revealing that the board was wary about it, InBev might not take the bait. "I won't accept a dime less than $70," Ambassador Jones told the group, voicing a sentiment some other board members shared as well. But at $65 per share, InBev's current offer wasn't even that bad, given how poorly Anheuser's shares had been trading.

August IV was the obvious candidate for the job. The board had serious misgivings, however, about whether he should handle such a sensitive task. His trip to meet with InBev's executives in Florida had created more ambiguity than it had cleared up. It would be inappropriate to crack open the vault and call upon August III to help, and dipping a step beneath August IV in the ranks to recruit a second-tier executive would also look strange, especially since most of those executives favored the Modelo deal. So the board turned inward and ruled that Warner and Whitacre should team up with The Fourth to make the call.

"It was the three of them for adult supervision," said one Anheuser advisor. "There was no way anyone would trust him."

With the board now settled on a course of action, it came time to summon their CEO. A member of the group ducked outside the room, motioned to the secretary who was standing guard in the hallway, and asked her to find August IV to request that he return to the boardroom. When he strode in a few moments later, Warner debriefed him in front of the group.

The news must have been hard to swallow. The Fourth had labored for three weeks straight to secure the Modelo deal and save the company, and he was now being flatly overruled by his own board. He had never held much sway with the directors, but this was a punch in the gut—especially since his own father had helped steer the board's decision.

Still, August IV held himself high. "Once the evaluations were all done, I don't know that he had any big disagreement with it," said Jim Forese. "He was actually quite professional about it," said another person who was in the room. "And he was certainly, in those dealings from then on, quite professional. I don't think he was shocked."

He was distracted enough, however, to neglect relaying the board's decision to the rest of his team. The company's bankers and executives had all been sitting in a separate area of the hangar, expecting that someone would come out to issue some type of pronouncement and perhaps bring them back into the boardroom to discuss matters further with the entire cast. Instead, they looked up and saw The Fourth's helicopter firing up its rotor blades. A moment later, one of the Anheuser-Busch jets started taxiing away from the hangar toward the airport's runway.

They exchanged puzzled looks, wondering whether the board's executive session had adjourned, what had been decided, and whether the departing plane was a New York–bound flight that was leaving some of them stranded in St. Louis. It was strange that no one had filled the bankers in, but even more disturbing that Anheuser's anxious executives had been left in the lurch. The board's unceremonious dissolution suggested that Modelo was definitely not a "go," since the clueless people in the room were the ones who had been managing those talks.

"The fact that the whole management team wasn't brought back in is a little bit of how they treat people," said one advisor.

Once most of the directors had disappeared, Sandy Warner finally summoned the group back into the boardroom, where he sat them down and announced that they had decided to contact InBev to request a higher offer by Wednesday.

"These are serious people, and they've offered a serious price," he said, as board chairman Pat Stokes stood off to one side. "Let's see what the best we can get out of them is. We're going to go back to them and see if we can get more."

By then, the news wasn't a complete surprise. Everyone had just witnessed The Third's vocal opposition to the Modelo deal an hour or two earlier. It left them shell-shocked to hear that the three sleepless weeks they had just spent on Modelo were being dragged out further so that the board could dip its toes in InBev's waters at the last minute.

Tom Santel, after spearheading the entire effort, was particularly taken aback. "I was shocked at that—that they were going to check with InBev first," he said. "It just seemed, really, an odd thing to do, to check with an outside party before you did something."

"We were trying to save the company," he said. "We thought we had a very attractive means to keep our company independent, to grow it with an attractive deal and to really create an exciting future for ourselves and get the one deal we thought we'd never be able to get. There was a lot of disappointment."

At Warner's request, the bankers in the room huddled before boarding their jet back to New York to write a script that would help guide the conversation he, Whitacre, and August IV would soon have with InBev.

Anheuser's team of dejected executives, meanwhile, trudged out to their cars and agreed to meet up at the Fox and Hound, a chain sports bar just outside the airport, to drown their sorrows. They were driving home, which kept them from commiserating too fully. After working like dogs to push the Modelo deal to the brink of an announcement—with press releases and conference calls ready to go—they realized they had no choice now but to mentally switch gears. It seemed appropriate to quaff a couple of overpriced Bud Lights after such a demoralizing day. The following morning, Tom Santel switched off all of his electronic gadgets—a deeply symbolic move for someone so tethered to the office—and hopped on his road bike for a long, contemplative ride out into the St. Louis suburbs.

That Monday marked a critical pivot point. Some Anheuser staffers and advisors had walked into the day's meeting expecting that the board would endorse a bid for Modelo by the time it adjourned. Instead, the board issued a sobering set of instructions and agreed to reconvene two days later to weigh the results. August IV would contact InBev to request its best and final offer. And he would have emotional and legal backing from the two men InBev had secretly targeted as its likeliest allies.

■ ■ ■

Modelo's entire team—from Carlos, María, and the other family members on down to their bankers, lawyers, and hired PR guns—waited in suspense that Monday, anticipating that at any moment they would receive a phone call that would change their lives. It never came.

Instead, Anheuser's board told Goldman to raise some modest clean-up issues with Modelo to help stall the process, under the guise that a deal was still happening. "It was 'Go tighten up a few of these things that need to be tightened up with Modelo that the board wanted a little bit more clarity on," said one person involved in the matter. "But in truth, it was mostly going to Modelo and saying, "Modelo, sit still for a week. The board will make a real decision next week."

Fearing that their client would end up as the odd man out, Mercado and Kindler had already scheduled a meeting with InBev's advisors for the following day at Lazard's offices at 30 Rockefeller Plaza, the Manhattan skyscraper that houses the NBC studios and the famous Rainbow Room restaurant. They had a fully negotiated deal with Anheuser-Busch—the documents were ready to be signed. After getting stood up the day before, though, they wanted to nail down a treaty with InBev in case the Anheuser deal lost traction altogether. InBev, for its part, wanted to keep Modelo from striking that deal. Antonio Weiss and the rest of InBev's team didn't know that Anheuser and Modelo had come within inches of a merger, but they knew the talks were still on.

The two sides sat down in a conference room that morning at 8 A.M. and began diligently chipping away until an assistant ducked in to tell Weiss he had an urgent phone call—something that was important enough to pull him out of the discussion for a few minutes. The Modelo's team's minds started racing as they watched Weiss walk out.

"We're sitting there thinking, 'You know what? We'll see what happens with A-B. We have the agreements ready to go," said one person close to Modelo. "But we're not leaving this room either, because if it doesn't happen, we want to get our agreements done with InBev." Weiss eventually returned, and by the time Modelo's team left that afternoon, they had negotiated for five hours.

It was already too late. As Fernández, Kindler, and Mercado swung out through the revolving door exits of marble-laden Rockefeller Center, where cell phone service is spotty, they connected with Goldman and received word that Anheuser's board had just asked InBev for a higher offer.

"We literally knew that it was over," said one person close to Modelo. "There was zero chance our deal was happening once they told InBev, 'Give us your last bid, because we're going to do something else.'"

Kindler turned to Carlos Fernández, shook his head, and said, "Let's just all go home."

The fact that Anheuser-Busch's board was stalling in order to talk to InBev didn't escape Don Antonino and the rest of Modelo's controlling family members. Don Antonino was nearing the end of his rope and threatening to pull his support altogether.

It put Carlos in a precarious spot—he was trying to bridge the gap between Modelo and Anheuser-Busch, but the space between the two companies was growing wider by the hour, and he could only stretch so far. If Anheuser-Busch didn't press "go" soon, it was going to lose Modelo altogether.

Sandy Warner, sensing Carlos's predicament, called his former colleague to confirm that the board was indeed reaching out to InBev. He offered a few words of support to Carlos, who sensed that Warner was still open to a deal.

"Hang in there, Carlos," Warner said. "We'll be back."

Chapter 14

Put Up or Shut Up

The story here is that Anheuser-Busch really played the game fairly well. Everybody assumes they got rolled. They didn't. They played the game well by making enough noise to force Brito to go beyond his comfort zone.

—Anheuser-Busch advisor

InBev's executives and advisors woke up on the morning of Tuesday, July 8, to find that the tectonic plates underlying their takeover attempt had shifted overnight.

Before leaving the office the evening before, they set the agenda for a strategy meeting that had been scheduled for the following morning at Lazard. That evening, August IV sent an e-mail to Jorge Paulo Lemann saying that Anheuser—for the first time since the take-over saga began—wanted to talk. It was the overture InBev had been hoping for, and it came less than a day after InBev publicly released its slate of nominees. Their attack must have hit the Anheuser board of directors right in the jugular, the InBev team deduced with a sufficient dose of pride, just before realizing that their agenda for the morning meeting was now moot.

InBev wasn't shocked that Anheuser was reaching out, but they were surprised it was happening so quickly. They had expected their American rival to stall for a few more weeks. InBev's top coterie of executives and advisors brought with them a palpable level of excitement when they assembled at Rockefeller Plaza that morning. "People thought, 'This may finally be the breakthrough,'" said one InBev insider. "Because obviously, we knew we had come out with a blockbuster slate the day before. We were pretty proud of ourselves."

Brito, as usual, was reluctant to read too much into Anheuser's outreach effort. He wanted to be sure it was an olive branch, not a riding crop. "People were optimistic and hopeful, but at that point, all we knew was they wanted to have a phone call," said a person close to InBev. "We didn't know whether it was a phone call to tell us, 'We're merging with Coca-Cola' or 'We have a deal to go private.'" Anheuser-Busch could just be looking to cover its bases before heading off in a completely different direction.

After a brief discussion over how to react to the overture, the Brazilians responded to August IV with an e-mail of their own. The two companies quickly agreed to hold a telephone call just a few hours later, with three designated representatives on the line from each side. Squaring off against Anheuser-Busch's Whitacre, Warner, and August IV—all three, businessmen who had led emblematic American companies—would be a triumvirate of Brazilians: Lemann, Brito, and Telles. The call was bound to be the takeover fight's most critical moment so far, no matter what Anheuser planned to say. And InBev was eager to listen.

August IV, Whitacre, and Warner each dialed in that day from separate locations. August IV broke the ice with a few words as the call began, but Warner and Whitacre took over once The Fourth hit the most critical points in the script they had agreed to use. "The board picked us to do it because Ed had done a lot of it in one capacity at AT&T, I'd done a lot of it as a banker, and August had never done any of it," Sandy Warner said. "We just brought different perspectives to it, and we brought those perspectives to the call."

The two elder board members got to the point quickly. Anheuser-Busch was close to pursuing a different option, Warner said, and a critical board meeting was scheduled for late in the day on Wednesday. If InBev was still interested in owning Budweiser, the board wanted its best and final offer on the table by the time that meeting started. And they wanted more than just hard cash. They wanted assurances that any deal InBev proposed had a high likelihood of closing. If Anheuser's board didn't hear from InBev by then, he said, it would assume InBev was sticking with its bid of $65 a share. And at that price, Anheuser could easily justify opting for another transaction instead.

"Before we do any of that, and this disintegrates into a very negative contest, you may want to go back and consider whether $65 a share is your best and final offer," Warner said. "If you get back to us within the time frame we've given you, we'll get back to you promptly with an answer."

Reports of Anheuser's talks with Modelo were all over the newspapers, but Whitacre, Warner, and The Fourth refused to reveal any details about Anheuser's second option. "We decided that if they wanted to go to bed thinking that we were doing a merger of equals with SABMiller, God bless them, and if they wanted to go to bed thinking we were doing a recap (which would have loaded the company with debt), God bless them," said one person close to Anheuser-Busch. "We weren't going to tell them point-blank what was going on."

Anheuser's threat of a "Plan B" mildly unnerved InBev, but it wasn't particularly convincing. "While it was something they were thinking about, I got the sense that this was something maybe their advisors or management had come up with, but not something that these two guys really wanted to do," said one InBev insider. "They basically told us, 'You misread everything. We never said we wouldn't sell the company. You misunderstood our rejection on the 26th—this is really escalating and becoming hostile, and it doesn't need to be. We're going to do the right thing by the shareholders. We need your best and final."

Before Tuesday's call had started, the Brazilians had agreed that if Anheuser-Busch made any sort of overture toward a deal, they would try to steer the matter toward their bankers rather than delving into specifics over the phone. "What they were going to do is say, 'Well, why don't we have our bankers get together, and maybe you can show us that there is more value. We want to understand this exactly,'" said one person close to the matter.

That's precisely what they did. And as word spread in InBev's camp that the two sides had talked, moods lifted significantly. "People started to think, 'This thing is really going to happen,'" one insider said.

■ ■ ■

InBev's newfound hope was matched by an equal, if not greater, sense of inevitability and dread on the part of Goldman's Ingrassia and Gross. The pair still had no clue what had really gone on behind the board-room's closed door at the previous day's pivotal meeting in St. Louis. They knew that Modelo had been put on hold and that Anheuser planned to put in a call to InBev, but they had flown back that night with scant visibility on what might transpire next.

Gross picked up the phone when it rang on his desk on Tuesday and was greeted by Whitacre, Warner, and August IV, fresh off their call with InBev. The Fourth stepped in first to act as emcee, quickly greeting Gross and Ingrassia, who had also been looped in, before Warner and Whitacre delivered the blow.

The board wanted Goldman to drop what it was doing and schedule a meeting for later that day with Antonio Weiss and the rest of InBev's bankers, Warner and Whitacre said. "We want you guys to go negotiate with these folks. We've told these guys that we have other opportunities and that they need to increase their bid. Now, you need to go to talk to Lazard."

"Holy cow," Gross thought, his jaw dropping in astonishment. Hadn't they just spent three straight weeks racing to save the company by inking a deal with Modelo and finding $1 billion in costs to cut? The board clearly hadn't been too impressed by the effort. "This is over," he thought. "This is *over*."

He and Ingrassia dutifully picked up the phone to rouse Weiss, who had been waiting for the handset on his own desk to ring, and then summoned a car service to shuttle them up to Lazard's offices. It didn't take long for the two bankers to assemble the materials they would need to make their case for a higher price—they had already presented them to Anheuser's board several times. They exchanged a doleful glance as they settled in for the ride, motoring through a burgeoning sea of Manhattan commuters who were ending their workdays and starting for home.

The ride was surreal. It seemed way too early to be racing uptown to strike up a deal. What would happen next seemed obvious to the two seasoned deal makers. They would engage Lazard in some variation on the same elaborate mating dance that preceded most corporate mergers. Goldman would start off by stating that Anheuser deserved a bigger price. Lazard would counter that InBev didn't want to pay more. The two sides would lay out their respective cases and set the next day's board meeting as a deadline. And unless InBev fell completely out of character, it would then bump its offer high enough to satisfy Anheuser's board.

The past month had been filled with wrenching twists and turns, but the next few days were threatening to become sadly predictable. Anheuser's team had been just a hair's breadth away on Modelo only 24 hours earlier, and now the board had yanked the tablecloth out from beneath them. After decades of dominance as America's best-known brewer, Gross and Ingrassia thought, Anheuser-Busch's goose was cooked.

■■■

The two teams met at Rockefeller Plaza for a few hours and then adjourned, each returning to their home turf with the other's arguments on what Anheuser-Busch was worth. Ingrassia had talked Lazard through the same script Warner and Whitacre had used over the phone with InBev. The board was facing an actionable decision, he said. "If we make that decision, you will have lost your opportunity to do something. Based on that, we need to know your best and final price by Wednesday evening." The ball was now in InBev's court.

Brito was concerned about paying too much, especially because he was bidding against himself. No other companies had the level of interest and financial wherewithal to buy Anheuser-Busch at the moment. He also feared that being too cheap might derail an acquisition that was just inches from his grasp. He wasn't InBev's ultimate arbiter—the board would rule at a meeting the following morning on whether to raise the offer. He would need to recommend a price and course of action, and that recommendation would carry the weight of his entire career behind it.

As Brito weighed the matter that night, the two people who seemed to have the most articulate and persuasive impact on his decision were Lazard's Antonio Weiss and David Almeida, the internal M&A head for InBev. Both appeared to favor raising the bid. They played up how well Anheuser's business fit within InBev, and said Brito was never going to get any closer to buying Anheuser-Busch than he was at that very moment. Did he want to lose the chance to make the acquisition of his career, to do the type of game-changing deal Lemann and Telles had lusted over since their days at Brahma in Brazil, over just a few extra dollars per share?

True to form, Brito wanted numbers. He wanted to know how the deal would play out financially if InBev's final offer were any one of a range of prices: $68 per share, $70, $72, and beyond. When InBev's team adjourned that night, planning to reconvene early Wednesday morning to prepare for the most important board meeting they had ever had, Brito still hadn't tipped his hand to indicate the price he'd support. It seemed highly unlikely that he would recommend more than $68 or $70 per share. The numbers, as InBev crunched them, simply couldn't justify paying anything higher.

There was magic to the notion of offering $70 per share. It was the biggest number that InBev still believed made sense. It was also the number August III and some other Anheuser-Busch board members had appeared to indicate they would support behind closed doors in St. Louis. Whether InBev received a quiet, back-channel indication that Anheuser's board could be reeled in at $70 per share has been hotly debated on both sides, and many people involved in the deal believe InBev was guided to that number by someone on Anheuser-Busch's side.

Back-channel communications in M&A deals tend to ruffle the feathers of those who are circumvented, and they don't uphold a high standard of transparency. They are certainly permissible, however. Anheuser's board didn't feel confident using August IV as a conduit between itself and InBev, and there weren't any other obvious executives they could enlist without violating the usual orders of engagement. If they wanted to let InBev know that $70 a share would yield a done deal, and didn't want to involve their bankers, the board's independent directors had few choices other than taking matters into their own hands. With all of the connections they had on Wall Street and in corporate America, several of them could easily have ensured that the right message reached InBev.

"If you thought there were outside-the-arena communications, it probably made sense," said one person close to the deal. "Somebody may have had that contact—to say that if the deal could be done on a friendly basis, that was the way it could get done. I don't see how anybody could say that it is not consistent with one's fiduciary duties to go explore and be informed."

On Wednesday morning, once InBev's board was debriefed on the call with Anheuser and the meeting with its bankers, debate quickly fired up over whether they should raise their offer. They weren't eager to pay more, but they also sensed that a sufficient bump in their bid might be enough to seal the deal quickly. An extra five dollars per share was manageable from a financial standpoint, but they didn't want to pay a penny more.

"The view was, 'You know what, we're going to raise to $70, we're prepared to pay $70, but this is it,'" said one person involved in the matter. "We'll do battle at $70, and we feel confident the market will take $70." It was more than Brito had hoped to pay, but he was tantalizingly close to seizing the brewing industry's most desirable asset.

"I think he swallowed very hard and said, 'When you're on the carousel, there's only one gold among the brass,'" said one person involved in the deal. "This is the golden standard. I go for it even if it means I take what I now have and get rid of it to pay my debt to J.P. Morgan."

Brito had grown tired of negotiating through Goldman Sachs and members of Anheuser's board, and wanted to deliver the new offer straight to August IV himself. Anheuser, though, wasn't willing to budge. They had been burned at that game before, and this time they weren't playing it.

"The board wanted to control this thing themselves, and they were not interested in having The Fourth go out and control it for them," said one person close to the company. Now that the two companies were entering into a negotiation, InBev's board was going to have to talk to Anheuser's board if it had something to say. "The board was trying, independent of anyone with the last name of Busch, to orchestrate how this was going to go," this person said. "Sandy and Whitacre wanted, as the board, to make this more about the board deciding it than about any one party deciding it." So Brito picked up the phone on Wednesday and contacted Warner and August IV—Whitacre wasn't able to make the hastily scheduled call.

"We're highly confident we can get this deal done at $65 a share," Brito told the pair as he launched into a somewhat antagonistic preamble, suggesting he was willing to push forward in a hostile manner if necessary. "It's a full price, we intended it as a full price, and it's a compelling proposition for Anheuser-Busch's shareholders."

"But we'd prefer for this deal to be a friendly one," he continued. "In order to make that happen, we'll tell you that our best and final offer is $70 a share."

At $70 a share, InBev's new offer now totaled a whopping $52 billion. The response from Warner and The Fourth, though, was disappointingly muted. "They really didn't talk about it," said one person on InBev's side. "They said, 'Fine, we'll take it back to the board.'"

Brito's end of the line went dead, and August IV started to speak, knowing that Warner was still patched into the call. "We can do better than that," The Fourth fervently professed, referencing the efforts that were underway to slash costs and boost the company's share price. "We've got a great team; we've got a great company. We've got to fight this!"

Warner felt sorry for The Fourth. The young CEO desperately wanted a chance to prove he could save his family's company. "I know how much he wanted to do this, I know how hard he worked for it, and he and his father were struggling," Warner said. It was too late, though. The clock had run out.

"I don't think the board is on the same page," Warner carefully replied. "It's a full price, it's low-risk, and it's a terrific payday for our shareholders. It's going to be tough to fight. But let's go into the next meeting with an open mind, we'll hear what you have to say, and then we'll talk about it."

Warner hung up the phone and then sat there for a moment in silence. "This is going to happen," he said to himself.

■ ■ ■

At 4 P.M. New York time on Wednesday, Warner and August IV delivered InBev's $70 per share offer to the board of directors. With so many meetings in such a compressed period of time, the board had opted to discuss and rule on the matter that afternoon by telephone rather than scrambling Anheuser's jets so they could convene yet again at the hangar. They expected their decision to be relatively clear-cut, anyway. They would start talks with InBev if it raised its offer to an acceptable level, and turn back toward Modelo if it didn't.

When they heard InBev's new number, the board—and particularly its inner circle of independent directors—displayed no hint of surprise. It seemed as if they would have been more taken aback if InBev hadn't come through with $70 per share. "It was totally expected," said one Anheuser advisor. "People knew that that was the number. I think they were totally, totally expecting that. The issue was whether they wanted to go back and fight for more."

The Modelo option had served its purpose—for Anheuser's board, at least. It helped them make a strong case for the $70 bid its directors favored. "Having Modelo got them to $70," a company advisor said. "It allowed them to show some leg. A-B played it very well, because they had heard that $68 was the maximum amount Brito wanted to pay. They got him to bite the bullet and pay more."

With InBev's new bid now in front of them, the board wanted to know whether the Brazilians could be trusted. They didn't want Brito trying to squirm his way out of the purchase six months down the road. After a good amount of back and forth on the topic, the board decided it was comfortable enough to move on to the last issue that remained up for discussion—but it was probably the biggest.

The Brazilians had stressed that this was their best and final offer. But who wouldn't say that in a negotiation? They had only made two offers, and some takeover fights progress through a handful of successively higher bids before the target finally acquiesces. With InBev dangling out there for the world to see, its desires for global domination now laid bare in front of everyone, would it really not consider tossing in another dollar or two to seal the deal? Goldman and Citigroup had agreed prior to that afternoon's call that they should at least advise the board to consider the option. So when a chance to address the matter presented itself, Ingrassia spoke up.

"There is still the option to go back and ask for more," he said, suggesting in his typical measured fashion that InBev might have a few extra dollars stashed in its pocket. The Brazilians knew their fingers were closing around the prize, he explained, and they weren't likely to walk away over the request. The worst-case scenario was that they'd say no.

Ingrassia's point was well-articulated, and not out of school. Several other people on the call shared the same sentiment. But he got a startling slap in the face as a voice that sounded like Whitacre's gruffly interjected and commanded—using language more appropriate for the deck of a ship—that Ingrassia shut his trap.

"I remember a very, very stern, and not entirely articulate, response to that, which was 'No way, we're not doing anything else,'" said one person who heard the rebuke. The comment was "both an attack on the idea and a little bit of an ad hominem attack on the 'foolishness' of trying to do that. And I remember being very stunned by it, because I thought it was an entirely fair thing for him to have said. And I completely agreed with him."

No one countered the rebuke—the rest of the board stayed silent, and the discussion moved on. InBev's new offer looked plenty rich compared to Anheuser's own plans for boosting its share price, some of them thought. "There was a feeling that you don't want to push your luck here," said Jim Forese. "Certainly Ed would not have been alone." Ambassador Jones had drawn his own line in the sand at $70, and was debating whether to accept a bid that just barely cleared the bar. He was also warily watching the news for details on Fannie Mae and Freddie Mac, two U.S. government-supported mortgage lenders that were verging on collapse that week. If they imploded and sent shock waves through the markets, InBev might abandon its interest in a takeover and Anheuser's stock could drop to the low $50s.

A $70 per share payout from InBev "basically gave the shareholders in cash on day one what we hoped to deliver them over three years, after a lot of hard work and a fair amount of risk," Sandy Warner said. "So you say to yourself, they are more confident than we that they can get the costs out, and they're really good at getting costs out. That sounded like something we had to think very, very seriously about."

There was also the question of propriety. Brito had held up his end of the bargain. He had responded with a substantially higher offer in the time frame Anheuser's board had given him, and the board had promised it would get back to him promptly. "Do we go back and jerk them around, say, 'Well, we want $72 and you've got a deal?'" Warner said. "Or do you say, 'We will proceed to see if we can negotiate a contract to do it at $70.' That's what we voted to do. We owed them a 'yeah' or 'nay.' That's what we told them we'd give them."

Some people close to the board, however, were angered by the biting remark toward Ingrassia and the rest of the board's muted reaction. "One of the things that is deflating is when you're in the room with these supposedly iconic guys, and they're either silent and not participating more robustly," said one Anheuser insider, "or you saw The Third being so heavily biased, and always trying to interpret information to fit his own preexisting view as opposed to really trying to step back and think about some of these things."

"Whitacre sat there mostly silent throughout. Which made you feel that he had already kind of decided on something and just didn't want to be explicit about it."

"It was a board that was essentially rushing and wanting to get a deal done. That's why, to be blunt, any narrative that InBev had orchestrated 'The Great Takeover' . . . it really had a lot to do with a board that was looking to go to the fire exits on this thing."

The angry outburst pricked up the ears of some Anheuser insiders who had already been wondering whether someone on their side had quietly promised InBev a "yes" vote if InBev offered $70 per share. The new offer seemed too efficient to be accidental.

"One of the things I immediately thought was that maybe somebody somewhere told somebody else they could deliver the board at

$70. The ferocity of the comment was so strong," said one Anheuser insider. "You couldn't help but feel in a little way that 'Wait a minute, this felt a little strange.'"

"It was uncanny to me," agreed Ambassador Jones, "but I have no idea what went on in those discussions."

Conspiracy theorists who swore there was a high-level overture behind the scenes had at least one easy target to point to: Sandy Warner. As former CEO of J.P. Morgan and then former chairman of the merged J.P. Morgan Chase, Warner had an obvious connection to Doug Braunstein, the J.P. Morgan banker who pulled together InBev's huge financing package. Each time InBev had issued a press release that coincided perfectly with an Anheuser-Busch board meeting, Warner had gotten a few sideways glances. When InBev came back at $70 a share and Anheuser's board jumped on it, the glares turned downright suspicious.

Warner's connection to Braunstein wasn't helpful in either case. "In fact, it was unhelpful," Warner said. "It rendered my position in all of this somewhat awkward, I would say. I can tell you I had not a single conversation casually, on the phone, in person, in any way, with anybody at Morgan while this was going on."

If InBev had offered just $68 per share, which would have put its bid at parity with the plans Anheuser had developed on its own, or if it hadn't raised its bid at all, the board's phone session that night would have been much more interesting. "They could have bluffed us and said, 'We're sticking with $65, and then we would have had to decide what to do," said Jim Forese. "All of those get to be the great 'ifs' of history."

"What if they hadn't" [raised the bid]? asked Warner, who found it interesting to speculate—even though he had assumed InBev would toss in a few more dollars. "We might then have bought the other half of Modelo."

Instead, the two sides came to an acceptable price without much of a scuffle at all. "By the time InBev bumped their price to $70, I think the board was just tired," said one person close to Anheuser. "I think they were also scared." InBev's budding effort to eject them from their positions wasn't the main thing that had motivated them, but it certainly had a degree of effect.

If anything caused Anheuser's directors to breathe a sigh of relief once InBev's new offer rolled in, it was the realization that selling the company would let them escape a mess they had helped create. It would put an end to the debate over whether The Fourth needed to be replaced, and it would quell the need for argument about why the board had bowed to The Third's wishes and put him in charge to begin with. One of the biggest advantages to selling the company, aside from the money they were set to make, was not having to admit they might have made a mistake.

Back in 2006, when The Fourth had interviewed to become CEO against a couple of other candidates, he professed to the board that he planned to emulate his father. He'd be a hands-on executive, The Fourth said, just like his dad was, and his reputational problems were well in the past. Yet after the board promoted him into the position, they started hearing complaints that August IV wasn't on the job enough—that he was often absent and tough to find. "It was always hard to get him in the mornings," said one advisor to the company. "It was hard to get him, period." He was great at motivating Anheuser-Busch's beer distributors, but there was more to being CEO of Anheuser-Busch than giving rousing pep talks.

"I just can't imagine, unless there was a negative personality transformation, how they could have ever made this guy the CEO," said one Anheuser advisor. "It's one thing if the family had 40 percent of the business. It's just another example of, ultimately, a corporate board having done something that didn't make that much sense. Certainly among the positives of selling the company was not having the world know about the management issues, not having that glaringly in front of them."

Whitacre had attested in a press release issued on September 27, 2006, the day of August IV's appointment, that he was the individual who was most qualified to lead the company. "The reason he was qualified is because he had done a pretty robust job running the U.S. operation, and he had been quite good at sort of tearing down the walls of history," said Jim Forese. "He was an advocate of making fundamental changes, given what was going on in the industry. And he had a pretty good record. He had a pretty good team around him."

"Certainly, no one ever called me and said, 'How stupid could you be to name The Fourth as the CEO?'"

"If anyone had been groomed for that position, certainly he had," said General Shelton. "I mean, marketing, sales, running the brewery, being a German-qualified brewmaster—he seemed to be the full package. We had watched him for quite a period of time, and I think the board felt very comfortable with him moving up to become the CEO."

Years later, the decision remained contentious. "I tell you, if I were August III and I wanted to continue family control or dominance of the company, I wouldn't have put The Fourth in there," said one person who has served on a number of high-profile boards. "The behavior pattern didn't make any sense. That was a bad mistake by that board. If a board has one thing it has to do right, it's to get the CEO right."

The board was basically stuck with the consequences of their actions. They were leaning in favor of InBev's offer in part because "nobody had confidence in The Fourth, and the one who had the least confidence in The Fourth was The Third," said another advisor. "If they didn't sell the company, they didn't have the gumption to shoot August IV in the head."

"This was sort of a nice way out after letting The Third convince them to put The Fourth into the top job, which never should have happened in the first place."

The Third's decision to support his son's CEO candidacy seemed particularly puzzling to those who were now watching him endorse a sale of the company to InBev. It represented a backtrack of epic proportions. "August the Third vouched for him in a very strong way, and August the Third was very persuasive with the board," said Ambassador Jones.

"He put his son in place. Quite frankly, I think he had hoped that his son would have been more quiet," said an Anheuser advisor. "But his son then had ideas of his own, and they weren't necessarily the ideas he liked. That really was a problem for him. It's very sad. When August [IV] came into the job, I think he had every intention of trying to get that company turned around. Different people might have different views on what his ability was or wasn't to do that, but certainly, I think his intentions were all very, very good."

"He got in the role, and his father immediately started to go against any initiative he had. And as a result, I think August became increasingly despondent because of . . . his father leading the board against him and openly criticizing his ability to lead."

■ ■ ■

With everyone in agreement on InBev's $70 bid that Wednesday night, Sandy Warner called Brito to relay the news. Brito was ecstatic—it was evident over the phone—and he started blazing straight into the specifics of how the companies would negotiate their merger contract, who would work on it, and where. They'd crank all through the night to get the deal done as quickly as possible, Brito pledged.

"Let's turn this over to the people who are actually going to do that work, and they can set the schedules," Warner replied. He had done enough brokering already, and had no plans to get stuck burning any midnight oil negotiating the merger's intimate details. The two men circled back to their teams of advisors and instructed them to start talks immediately over a deal at $70 a share.

The decision to reject Modelo was a massive disappointment to several exhausted members of the strategy committee, who had cranked relentlessly through the holiday weekend on the belief that they had the board's backing. They had walked into the boardroom on Monday thinking that while the session would be long and difficult, The Third and the rest of the board would ultimately support the Modelo deal. They had certainly spent meeting after meeting talking about it. All they needed to do, the executives had thought, was pull everything together in time.

"We, quite frankly, thought that was one of the great Herculean efforts of all time in the middle of a vortex," said one person involved in the talks. "To have negotiated it and then to all of a sudden have the board say 'Nah'—I think the management team in particular probably felt very betrayed.'"

"We were told on Saturday night and Sunday night that the Modelo deal was done," one strategy committee member said. "It was like, 'Yes, we have a chance!' The guys who were working that deal . . . were just devastated to the point where they can't even talk about it. They're so bitter. They were led to believe that Mr. Busch and the board were finally agreeing to do the deal."

It was impossible not to question the board's intentions after that. Had they ever really considered approving the Modelo purchase? Or had it been a bluff—nothing more than a trump card to use against InBev the entire time? At most companies, top executives and board members work closely in sync. It had become painfully apparent that there was a significant gap of information and intention between The Fourth's team and the Anheuser board. It seemed they were firing in opposite directions. That had never been more clear than it was now, with Anheuser's executives still pushing for the Modelo deal while its board was favoring InBev.

"I think people understandably felt very used and misled," said one advisor. "We had a very full negotiation, got there, and then the board wanted to see if that deal was possible as a fallback in case InBev didn't pay up more."

Not everyone was as sympathetic toward Anheuser's executives, however. "I think they were a bit naïve about it," said one person close to the company. "I mean, we looked at it, we worked at it, but I never expected it would be the thing to do."

Sandy Warner, even after wading deep into the Modelo talks as the board's representative, wasn't surprised that The Third had been so vocally opposed to the deal. "Modelo was a big price, so you could expect August would not be in favor of that," he said. "And he had trust issues over the years with some of the players in Mexico, so he was worried about it."

The concept of Fernández leading the company had proved divisive, and nixing the entire Modelo purchase over those concerns would have had all the hallmarks of The Third's classic deal-avoidance strategy. Despite their close relationship, "Fernández was a deal breaker for The Third," one strategy committee member said.

Yet by the time the board decided to reach out to InBev, Fernández had already agreed to take a lesser role, and the issue had been put to rest. "He was going to be head of international, and he was totally fine with it," said an Anheuser advisor. "In light of what we were going to do, in terms of the premium they were going to get, it really wasn't what things hinged on. He was willing to give that up."

Modelo lost its momentum instead for a different set of reasons—the most important of which was that it wrongly believed Anheuser-Busch was desperate to stay independent. Modelo saw a chance at redemption and went for it all: a huge price, continued autonomy in Mexico, multiple seats on Anheuser's board, a potential CEO candidate, and even a potential announcement of the deal in Mexico City. It had no idea that The Third and other key board members would favor a deal with InBev.

"Modelo's view was that they should be opportunistic—that Anheuser-Busch didn't want to be sold at any price, and therefore they could charge an exorbitant price to help A-B stay free," said an Anheuser-Busch advisor. "I just think that strategically, they misunderstood the dynamics of the situation."

It was too much to swallow in the end for Anheuser-Busch, a counterparty Modelo had known all along was going to be skittish. The Mexicans ultimately gave Anheuser a reason to knock on InBev's door.

"The Modelo people should have realized that the deal would never hold water," an Anheuser advisor said. "They shot themselves in the foot."

"The family was so greedy," another said. "Their demand was priced so high that it gave good cover to the notion of selling the company."

Put more bluntly by a third: "They over-negotiated like crazy. And the board was like, 'Fuck you.'"

If the deal had come together just one week sooner, it might have actually happened, one Anheuser advisor said. "I bet they drive themselves nuts with that question. But it's hard to criticize a $15 billion transaction that from birth to execution took three weeks. Saying they took too long is kind of Monday morning quarterbacking." Furthermore, Anheuser's board might have decided to reach out to InBev for a higher offer no matter when the Modelo transaction had grown ripe.

The deal's failure was rough for Carlos and María, who met with a big group of other controlling family members that weekend to discuss why things didn't pan out. And as blame was distributed on Anheuser-Busch's side after the fact, some of it fell upon Goldman Sachs's shoulders. Goldman's team had negotiated the transaction and vocally supported it at times in the boardroom. Rival bankers immediately surmised that Goldman had intended to sell Anheuser-Busch all along, however, in order to win bigger banking fees.

"I've got to tell you, I've seen this movie before," said one banker at a rival firm. "I know the modus operandi. This is something I've been saying for I don't know how many years. You want to get sold? Hire Goldman Sachs. At the end of the day, Goldman was never going to be able to deliver this deal because they didn't want to deliver this deal."

"I think Goldman thought they'll do the Modelo deal, and then they'll do another deal down the road," said another competitor. "They thought they'd get two things out of it."

Ultimately, however, the decision about whether to sign Modelo up that day wasn't up to Goldman Sachs, Citigroup, or any of Anheuser's other advisors. It was up to the board. And the board's choice was quite simple. Modelo came with lots of execution risk, and it gave them no way to fix one of the company's key problems: a CEO and management team who had proven lackluster. The board could endorse a risky plan to buy Modelo and integrate the two businesses, or it could shunt Modelo into a holding pattern and see what InBev had to offer. They had known that Modelo wasn't likely to walk away during the short time in which they waited for a higher bid from InBev—Anheuser-Busch, after all, had the big checkbook.

"It's a simple discussion: shareholder value," said board member Jim Forese. "We didn't get confused. Which is why the independent board decided, not the family members or the management."

"We made the decision, not August Busch III. He had his views, but he was just one member of the board, and he was not an independent member of the board," he said. "We concluded that the overall risk, including Modelo, was perhaps not worth the returns given that we could get $70 per share. It was all about the economics."

■ ■ ■

The board's gamble worked. They never had to find out whether their dalliance with the Mexicans would have yielded a successful defense. "I don't to this day know whether InBev knew how serious we were about trying to do Modelo," Sandy Warner said.

"So much time and effort was spent on the whole Modelo side of this—it was almost like the secret plan to get out of Vietnam," said one Anheuser-Busch advisor. "It was going to be this trump card we could play whenever we wanted to prevail."

"If the Modelo deal had happened, this company would not have been sold," said another. "We could all wonder whether the stock would be higher or lower today, but if the Modelo deal had happened, I can state with absolute certainty—100 percent confidence—that it would not have been sold to InBev."

"The more those risks were laid out, the more it made it almost impossible to pursue one angle that had so much risk versus another angle that didn't have much risk at all," concluded another.

Chapter 15

A Long Way
from St. Louis

At that point, the war was over. It was a very difficult thing for him to do, and it's something no one ever sees, but he walked in there, held his head high, and played the role he needed to play despite the obvious personal disappointment of the moment.

—Advisor to Anheuser-Busch

Anheuser's verbal acceptance of an offer sprang both sides into action, and the two companies started cranking away almost immediately on the deal's specifics. Merger agreements can take weeks, if not months, to draft and negotiate. However, Sullivan & Cromwell attorney George Sampas had been racing to fine-tune a detailed merger document all along, just in case Anheuser-Busch capitulated earlier than they had expected.

Sampas sent a draft merger agreement over to Anheuser's lawyers at Skadden on Thursday, and on the morning of Friday, July 11, hordes of advisors from both sides descended on 375 Park Avenue, the imposing steel skyscraper that housed Sullivan & Cromwell's midtown Manhattan conference center. InBev alone had about 50 lawyers camped out onsite, who, after first prepping their materials on Thursday at the firm's main office downtown, started scurrying back and forth between the uptown conference center's carpeted rooms and were soon buried in documents. August IV was destined for Park Avenue that Friday morning as well, but his mindset was decidedly less enthusiastic. His role as chief executive of Anheuser-Busch—which had already been diluted by his father, by his board of directors, and by his own lack of professional vigor—was verging on extinction. The Fourth was scheduled to meet face-to-face that day with Brito, his business partner-turned-foe. It would mark the first time the two men had seen each other in person since rumors of the takeover bid erupted in late May, and it would probably represent The Fourth's last chance to dictate the fate of his own career and those of his colleagues.

The Fourth and Pedro Soares stepped out of their jet in Teterboro, New Jersey, and settled into a car for the traffic-clogged 12-mile drive to Sullivan & Cromwell's conference center, which was spread across half of the eighth floor of the Seagram Building. It was the same building that housed the Four Seasons restaurant where August IV had dined a year earlier with SABMiller chief Graham Mackay, back when Anheuser-Busch's options had looked wide open. Peter Gross, who had been touching base with Soares intermittently to track The Fourth's progress toward Manhattan, stood waiting to meet the pair as they strode across the steel skyscraper's granite outdoor plaza and toward the lobby entrance. They were an hour late.

"August, how are you?" Gross asked as The Fourth finished up a conversation on his cell phone and switched off his earpiece. He had eschewed his favorite green suit and cowboy boots that day in favor of an East Coast suburban commuter look: a simple button-down shirt and pair of dress pants. The Fourth shot Gross a look in response to his loaded question that made it clear it had been a rough day.

"You know, look," Gross said, hoping to reassure his client and friend. "You're obviously playing an important role here." He had hoped that seeing a familiar face might ease The Fourth into the right mindset for what was bound to be a difficult encounter upstairs.

The Fourth needed to act as an ambassador for Anheuser-Busch as it approached the end of its run as an independent entity. While he had seemed detached and checked out at times during the past few weeks, he seemed, to his credit, to know what he needed to do that day.

Gross spent a few moments arming The Fourth with the points he needed to emphasize. He needed to make it clear to Brito and InBev's lawyers, who were pushing for more flexibility and less risk in the merger contract, that Anheuser-Busch wasn't going to budge. With that established, the men swung through the building's revolving doors.

Security was heavy at 375 Park Avenue, particularly in the wake of the September 11, 2001, attacks on the World Trade Center downtown, and visitors were required to check in at a security desk in the lobby with proper identification. InBev, on the assumption that August IV might be distressed upon arrival, had Sullivan & Cromwell pull a few strings to ensure that he could reach the elevators without being interrupted by a team of muscle-bound bouncers in mid-stride. The law firm had told its lobby attendants that someone would arrive at that allotted time who was too important to be stopped for identification. August IV certainly wasn't asked for his driver's license in St. Louis, where his recognizable face was plastered on billboards and in the newspaper, and InBev figured it was only right to remove a few administrative hurdles for him in New York. So The Fourth and Soares walked right past security and toward the building's elevator banks for the ride upstairs.

As the elevator's doors opened onto the eighth floor, Anheuser's team was pointed toward a conference room where Brito was stationed. August IV nodded toward his colleagues and then headed back to the room alone.

The Fourth was cognizant when he first greeted Brito of the points Gross had stressed. There was another important task at hand, though, and he aimed to address it before momentum was lost. He wasn't about to leave his subordinates hanging out to dry in the merger, with their professional futures subject to the impressions of strangers who lived half a world away. The Fourth's own fate was secure. He was already rich, and his advisors and lawyers were working up a lucrative consulting deal at that very moment that would last at least a few years and probably give him a seat on the merged company's board. If there was one last thing he could do to salvage potential losses, it was to lobby on behalf of his colleagues, some of whom had spent their entire careers at Anheuser-Busch and were now staring into a foggy abyss. Within minutes of entering the room, August IV had Brito hunkered down with him at a boardroom table, ticking through photographs of Anheuser's top managers as they discussed the merits of each executive.

"I think August went in there, quite frankly, to try and go to bat for members of the management team to highlight their skills and ability," said one person close to the matter. The Fourth wasn't overly optimistic about what the result would be. He made it clear, however, to Anheuser's advisors and to Brito that he was going to do what he could.

The Fourth and Brito spent about four hours together, perusing Anheuser-Busch's lineup and talking about other matters. They were cordial and respectful. "It was clear to everyone what had happened and who was taking over whom, and there was no reason for Brito to gloat," said a person who was there that day. "I think August was doing his very best to put up a good face."

The Fourth's remaining meetings on Friday were relatively procedural. By the time he had arrived at 375 Park, a raft of bankers, lawyers, and executives from both sides were already running at full tilt at the law offices to negotiate the merger agreement. If they could get it done and approved by both companies' boards by Sunday night, InBev could announce the deal either late that night or on Monday morning to gain maximum exposure before the European and U.S. stock markets opened for the week. Knowing that their respective teams were about to head into a long weekend of negotiations, August IV, Gross, Ingrassia, and Soares sat down to stress a few key points in Anheuser's favor to Brito, Lazard's Antonio Weiss, and J.P. Morgan's Doug Braunstein.

The minute that box was checked, August IV clocked out. InBev's public relations team had asked for a quick photo shoot of the two CEOs smiling and shaking hands to symbolically close the deal. It would send the right message to both companies' workers, they argued—and of course, it would give InBev an image it could circulate around the world as proof of Anheuser-Busch's capitulation. The Fourth refused to agree to the photo, and with that, he was gone.

It was a rough day, perhaps the worst of his life. Just 19 months before, he had been named CEO of one of America's most prized companies. His work at Anheuser-Busch was a big part of how he defined himself, and the same went for the team of executives who had ascended with him, some of whom were close comrades. This had been their opportunity to make an impression—to build the company into a global powerhouse—and they weren't going to get the chance. Even worse, the city of St. Louis would suffer for it.

"I think it weighed heavily on him that he was the guy in the seat at the time this went down, despite the fact that little of this coming to pass was on his shoulders," said one of the company's advisors. "I think he was very conscious of what this meant for St. Louis and for all of the other employees, and I think it probably weighed very heavily that on his watch, this happened."

After those difficult few hours with Brito, The Fourth headed back to the airport to catch a company plane to St. Louis that evening. He wasn't eager to stay in New York any longer than he had to. His deputies and advisors could pick up the slack. From that point through until early Monday morning, as Anheuser's lawyers, bankers, and a few top executives burned the midnight oil to complete their negotiations with InBev, The Fourth receded into the shadows in St. Louis and played essentially no role in the discussions in New York.

"I think The Fourth was self-aware," one Anheuser-Busch advisor said. "I think he carried himself as well as he could carry himself through all of this. He desperately wanted to do the right thing. It was clearly a crisis. It was his opportunity to step up and prove in a crisis that he could get things done. But long before any of this came up, I think he wished that he wasn't the CEO."

■ ■ ■

With the company's official leader out of commission by choice, Anheuser's scepter fell into the hands of its vice president of marketing, David Peacock, a St. Louis native whose father had worked in marketing for the company for 15 years. Peacock had been hired during

The Third's tenure but had become a trusted ally of The Fourth's, and he ultimately survived The Third's attempts to wipe key members of the management slate clean as his son took over.

"He's good, and The Third knew that. It was loyalty," said one person close to the company. "'Three' knew that Dave was loyal because he knew his father was extremely loyal to the company, so he trusted that. He protected [August IV], and he served as a buffer."

To outsiders, Peacock—who was just a few years younger than The Fourth—was viewed as the man who knew Anheuser's operations best. While he had an MBA, he wasn't an expert in financial matters. He had morphed into something of a brewer's "Jack-of-all-trades," exactly the kind of executive Anheuser had always tried to cultivate by shuffling up-and-comers between various divisions. Yet his most significant work—which was not surprising given Anheuser-Busch's proclivities toward the profession—had been on the marketing side of the company, where August IV had promoted him to vice president in late 2007.

Peacock had always handled a good deal of The Fourth's business, and had already been acting as Anheuser's senior ambassador for the past day or two in New York. When August IV left, that role quickly fell back into his lap.

"He was basically there and then took off," said one of InBev's advisors in reference to The Fourth. "He didn't stick around. I think it was just too painful and he wanted the hell out of New York. So Dave was really the only representative walking around, which was a little weird. Usually at that stage there are troops from both sides. But it was really just Dave and a bunch of InBev people."

In a way, August IV's scarcity during the meatiest part of the negotiations was a boon to Peacock, whose bright future as The Fourth's right-hand man had suddenly grown uncertain. This would give him plenty of exposure to the InBev team and give both sides a chance to see how well they could work together. Still, Peacock's job, for the time being, was to represent Anheuser-Busch and its shareholders as determinedly as he could and to battle InBev on important points when necessary. It was a fine line to walk.

He wasn't soft or overly deferential toward InBev, nor were Anheuser's M&A head, Bob Golden, or its top lawyer, Gary Rutledge, who, after laboring for weeks on Modelo, also played important roles in the negotiations with InBev that weekend. No one had any assurances that they'd have jobs with the new company, no real indications that their best efforts would amount to much of anything. They were too young to have accumulated the monstrous piles of stock options some of the older executives had, and they were in a position to continue working. If they played their cards right, there was a chance they could preserve roles for themselves.

"Dave Peacock had a very close relationship with The Fourth—would take a bullet for him," said one Anheuser advisor. "But he was a pragmatist."

The vacuum of leadership at Anheuser that week "caused Dave to take on an excess of responsibility," said one of his fellow strategy committee members, who noted that he worked "until 5 A.M." to manage the process. "He was the bridge to everybody," said someone involved in the negotiations. "He was in everything—he was the one sort of handling their employee communications. There was someone on the ground doing it, but everything was funneled through him. I don't know how he got it all done."

The amount of responsibility resting on Peacock's shoulders wasn't entirely out of proportion to the stakes the whole group was up against. They were trying to structure the biggest all-cash deal in history in a matter of days, and both sides wanted to emerge looking victorious while maintaining the perception that talks had been "friendly" in the end. For the most part, the tenor of the negotiations that weekend was amicable. "Everybody was there to get the bloody thing done," one advisor said, "and everyone was working toward that."

Yet after the public scrap the companies had had with each other, a few moments of friction were unavoidable. Anheuser's wounds were still raw after the stab in the back it had suffered at the hands of its former joint venture partner. The Anheuser-Busch team found it particularly tough to watch InBev's lawyers and bankers swagger into the conference room every so often with a request to alter the merger contract in a way that would reduce InBev's risk. Knowing how close they had come to striking a completely different deal that could have preserved their independence, it was all the Anheuser team could do to keep from losing it.

"The toughest thing, sitting down with InBev to negotiate that deal, was that I just thought, 'For the love of God, we beat you! We had Modelo done, and you just have no idea,'" said one Anheuser advisor.

InBev's team certainly had a sense of the strange social and familial undercurrents that ran through Anheuser-Busch, but they didn't have a real understanding of how much those factors—and in particular, The Third's eagerness to sell—had played into their hands. If InBev could see the full picture, the Anheuser team stewed, perhaps they wouldn't be so quick to take credit for orchestrating the perfect takeover campaign.

"They had no idea how those forces would work to really deliver this company to them," the Anheuser advisor said. "We had you beat! We just had a board that didn't want to beat you."

"The bottom line is that if the board had wanted to beat them, they were beaten," said another advisor. "If we had announced the alternative transaction, this deal would not have happened. Full stop, guaranteed. You didn't need fourteen winning strategies, there was one. And it was a big price, but it was a great deal."

■ ■ ■

As the two sides began negotiating their actual merger agreement at noon on Saturday, most of the friction between them revolved around InBev's repeated attempts to lessen its risk. Many merger agreements include a clause that lets the buyer cancel the deal if, despite all of its best efforts, its bank financing falls through. Anheuser, however, wasn't willing to allow for that possibility. Skadden and Goldman made it clear from the start that there was no way Anheuser-Busch would walk away from its other options—namely, Modelo—unless it had complete legal assurance that the merger with InBev would close. They felt Anheuser had a powerful alternative to the InBev takeover, and its board hadn't even chosen to play hardball and push for more than $70 a share. Plus, the markets were growing more and more uncertain by the day. They had no intention of giving InBev a chance to walk away from the contract using one loophole or another. InBev had come pounding on Anheuser-Busch's door, not the other way around, and Anheuser's advisors didn't care whether every single bank InBev had recruited to finance the deal suddenly collapsed. If Anheuser-Busch was going to sign on the dotted line, the contract needed to be airtight.

"This was really us saying, 'Okay, you guys want to take us over? There's no way in the world you're taking us over unless there's zero risk to us,'" said an Anheuser advisor. "God knows what's going to happen here, and there's no way we're going to give these guys essentially an option on buying this thing."

"It was, 'How many times do we have to tell you no?'"

The back-and-forth grew exhausting, and Anheuser's refusal to budge made for some tense moments. As Saturday wore into the wee hours of Sunday morning, the conference rooms at Sullivan & Cromwell took on a peculiarly ripe odor—the commingled scent of stale sweat, takeout Chinese food, and the occasional free InBev beer. Not everyone made it back to their homes or hotel rooms that night to shower and change, and some of the people involved in the talks later found that they had images burned into their memories of certain people wearing specific ensembles—a particular red blouse, or the same wrinkled khakis and polo shirt.

"I would say this as a joke but it's true," said one banker who spent the weekend holed up onsite. "The lawyers did not change their clothes, but the bankers were certainly changing their clothes. I changed my clothes. The guys from Lazard—it would be against their culture not to change clothes and put on new cologne."

During one particularly rough go-round with Anheuser's side, an associate from Sullivan & Cromwell lost her composure and left the room in tears after Tom Greenberg, a Skadden partner working for Anheuser-Busch, yelled at her over a relatively trivial detail. She hadn't slept in days and InBev's team rallied around her, threatening to tell Greenberg off, but cooler heads prevailed after a few minutes.

"There were, like, a lot of people in the room, and she just lost it," said one person in attendance. "It was clearly just exhaustion."

Tensions reached their most dramatic boiling point during a late-stage conversation between Antonio Weiss and Tim Ingrassia. One of the very last issues the two brewers needed to settle was how they should handle Modelo's threats to sue over the deal. The Mexicans were loudly claiming that the merger should only happen if they approved of it. Neither Anheuser-Busch nor InBev felt Modelo had half a leg to stand on, but that wasn't a clear certainty, especially since they were dealing with convoluted Mexican law.

InBev wanted to be sure that if it paid $52 billion to buy Anheuser-Busch, it was going to get the Modelo stake as part of the deal—Modelo was one of Anheuser's best-performing investments. To try to protect itself, InBev wanted a legal guarantee that it wouldn't lose Modelo or run into a situation where Modelo's controlling families could sell the stake to someone else. The scuffle over the issue stretched well into Sunday night.

Modelo's attempts to play both sides of the coin over the previous few weeks had been no secret to Anheuser-Busch. Modelo had deliberately told Goldman, in fact, that it was holding talks with InBev in an effort to maintain pressure on Anheuser. As the InBev and Anheuser teams argued over who should take responsibility for Modelo's threatened lawsuit, Ingrassia directed a pointed comment toward Weiss.

"Look, we know you've been talking to Modelo, so you should have an informed point of view about it. We can't take the risk," Ingrassia said. "The only way we're doing a deal with you is if we have absolute certainty."

Weiss bristled sharply when Ingrassia stated in front of the whole room that InBev had talked to Modelo—even though he and other InBev advisors had just met with Modelo earlier that week at Lazard's offices a few blocks away.

"That's wrong, we haven't met with them," Weiss countered.

"You're a liar. We know you've met with them!" Ingrassia shot back. Weiss boiled over at being called a liar and for a minute, the derailment looked like it might threaten the bankers' ability to negotiate the deal in good faith.

"That was a modest setback for a moment," said a person who was in the room. "I think Antonio didn't appreciate it."

"It was very clear that Tim and Antonio didn't like each other," said another witness to the argument. "Everybody was under tremendous tension. It was one of those things, boys being boys." Ingrassia left the room and walked up to Gross, who had stepped out as the conversation grew heated. He spent a moment ranting to cool off. After agreeing that the way Weiss characterized InBev's talks with Modelo was beside the point, Ingrassia apologized for calling Weiss a liar, and the two men set the uncomfortable exchange aside.

Brito and Ingrassia came to loggerheads at one point as well. It was hard to hold it against Brito, but his extremely confident nature irked some members of the Anheuser team. "You recognize when you do these deals that there's a tendency for everybody to kind of see the worst in the other guy," one advisor said. "What you realized with Brito is that this is a very entrepreneurial, very hardworking guy who had attained an unbelievable dream. And the thing you felt a little bit when you were looking at him, and people on their side, is that whatever self-satisfaction they had, they had no idea what was in the pot on the other side that made the thing possible and really had nothing to do with them."

"If anything, InBev got unbelievably lucky that they went after something that was vulnerable for reasons that were totally outside of what they truly understood."

In the end, InBev didn't get the protection it wanted from a Modelo lawsuit, nor did it win much flexibility in case its banks attempted to cancel the deal. The banks protected themselves by making it clear they would only finance the deal if InBev's debt maintained an "investment grade" rating, which signaled it wasn't overly risky. Whereas they could push the "eject" button if InBev's ratings dropped, InBev itself couldn't.

"If the ratings disappeared by closing, the banks didn't have to fund," said one Anheuser advisor. "But the amount of risk InBev took was mind-boggling. InBev was still obligated to close. Which meant they would have had to go find money that couldn't have been found." InBev's legal liability to Anheuser-Busch could be so significant that it would have to essentially hand the company over to Anheuser to pay damages.

"This was the strongest contract you can possibly imagine, but with this one real risk for InBev," the advisor said. "The net result is if they had lost their ratings, Bud and InBev would still be one company, but Bud would have gotten InBev in damages for violation of the contract."

It was clear how badly InBev wanted to own America's brewing crown jewel. It represented the fulfillment of a career-long dream for many of its executives and board members—not just the felling and seizure of an American icon but the conquering of the global beer market—and they were willing to put nearly everything on the line for it. They were way past the point of looking back now. By making their bid public, they had essentially told investors they needed Anheuser-Busch. And it was true. InBev's growth was slowing, and Anheuser-Busch was the only business in the world that completed the picture. If the company ran out of assets to buy and improve, it was going to have to face into the wind and deal with the same stagnant beer market that had been plaguing everyone else.

"This was InBev's lifelong dream, to do this," said one Anheuser-Busch advisor. "InBev never wavered for a moment in their interest in doing the deal. If you had had a buyer who wavered, it would have fallen apart. But they never wavered. This was their dream deal, and they knew they were going to make money on it. That made all the difference in the world."

Anheuser knew it was in a position to turn the screws on InBev because it had opted not to publicly malign its rival during the takeover fight. If Anheuser's team was going to sell such an iconic American institution to a foreign competitor, the least they could do was make one last stand and demand the very best terms possible.

"I credit Anheuser for being thoughtful enough not to preclude an agreed deal by doing something drastic," said one InBev advisor. "They didn't do anything rash, and they left open the possibility that they would have their moment too, at the end, where they could push for what they wanted."

With the deal's price already locked in place, Anheuser turned its focus toward smaller points of contention—some of the same issues InBev's board had originally weighed as being of likely importance from a psychological standpoint. A few seemed trivial, and were, from a financial perspective. But they gave Anheuser's employees a boost and secured the company a few desperately needed patriotic and public relations victories.

InBev had already said when it made its offer that it would keep St. Louis as its North American headquarters and integrate Anheuser-Busch's heritage into a new name for the company. After some back and forth, both sides agreed to subordinate the "InBev" moniker and name the merged entity "Anheuser-Busch InBev." InBev also agreed, as it had pledged, to keep all of Anheuser's U.S. breweries open and to stay committed to Anheuser's sales and distribution system. To do otherwise, at least up front, would have been foolish—InBev needed the support of Anheuser's powerful wholesalers if it wanted to make the deal work.

Anheuser won concessions in two areas that dragged InBev into uncharted territory. InBev's record of corporate philanthropy was paltry in comparison to that of Anheuser-Busch, which gave $13 million to St. Louis area organizations in 2008 and underwrote everything from local Christmas carol festivals to St. Patrick's Day Parades. So InBev agreed to support Anheuser's charitable causes in the area and to pay millions of dollars each year to maintain the costly Clydesdale operations and Grant's Farm, where admission was still free despite the hundreds of people it employed and roughly 1,000 animals it housed. InBev, whose name meant next to nothing to sports fans, also agreed to honor the all-important naming rights for Busch Stadium.

"We knew from the outset we were going to have to agree to all of this stuff," said one person close to InBev. "At that point, people were relieved we were getting the deal done. Everybody was willing to accommodate."

Anheuser's wholesalers were concerned about how much support they'd get from the new company, and Anheuser tried to get InBev to spell out its commitments to marketing. The frugal Brazilians, however, shied away from making any promises over that aspect of their budget.

"They recognized that Anheuser-Busch was a superior marketer— it's just that they felt some of the stuff they did was a waste of money. All those sponsorships were a huge cost," said one person close to InBev. "They had a hard time with the things that were actually beneficial versus those that were just huge ad spends that didn't actually support the brands. I think they felt that they'd use a much better, more targeted approach to marketing."

■ ■ ■

InBev's takeover of Anheuser-Busch was worth tens of millions of dollars apiece to some of the banks and law firms working on the deal, and as talks progressed that weekend, their efforts to win as much public credit as possible ramped up in stride. With the financial markets as treacherous as they were and merger activity falling through the floor, even bankers who played no measurable role in the deal were pushing for their firms to be listed as prominently as possible on the press release that would announce the transaction. It seemed as though Brunswick's public relations team spent more time drafting the list of banks involved in the transaction than they did on any other section of the six-page press release, as mid-level staffers stood watching over their shoulders, constantly questioning the order in which their firms appeared.

Several banks that were listed on the document did little to nothing and got paid accordingly. Merrill Lynch, for example, was named as an advisor to Anheuser-Busch, and Deutsche Bank as an advisor to InBev. Their inclusion, however, mattered for the industry's all-important "league tables," which measure which banks advise on the most deals each quarter. Wall Street firms' reputations hinge on the perception that they provide sought-after merger advice, and league tables, as flawed as they are, serve as the most useful measure bankers can point to. The bankers who milled about at Sullivan & Cromwell's offices that weekend knew that it could be months before they saw another deal this big, so they had to make sure they were associated with it.

Despite the size and significance of InBev's purchase of Anheuser-Busch, the vast majority of the two companies' merger agreement was negotiated between noon on Saturday, July 12, and the wee hours of Sunday morning—an infinitesimal period of time relative to most merger deals. It took just 16 hours to cobble together the basic legal document underlying the entire massive merger.

"From the date of InBev's public offer to the weekend after July 4, we had a fully executed, complex as hell merger agreement to buy Modelo, and a week after that we had it with InBev," said one Anheuser insider. "It was just 24/7. The speed at which this thing happened is mind-boggling."

Most of Anheuser's team left the Sullivan & Cromwell offices at around 4 or 5 A.M. on Sunday. They didn't fill InBev in on the specifics of what was happening next, but the Brazilians knew that Anheuser's board had a meeting scheduled for later that day in St. Louis. Unless something went disastrously awry before then, they would hold a vote that night on whether to grant final approval to the deal that had just been negotiated.

After taking a much-needed break for a couple of hours, InBev's team reconvened for a critical but, they hoped, largely ceremonial board meeting of their own. Brito and a few other key executives, who had finally had time that morning to grab showers back at their hotel, filed into a conference room at 375 Park Avenue alongside their closest advisors and shut the door.

The conference rooms were jammed with dozens of lawyers who were still cranking away on the Anheuser-Busch deal, but one room had been vacated and cleaned for another highly confidential meeting between two titans in another industry. H. Rodgin Cohen, Sullivan & Cromwell's influential chairman, was advising Lehman Brothers' chief executive Richard Fuld at the time on how to right Lehman's ship, which had started listing dangerously over the summer. He had arranged for a meeting that afternoon between Fuld and Bank of America over a potential deal between the two companies. Lehman's proposal fell on deaf ears that day at Bank of America, which ultimately bought Merrill Lynch instead, over a particularly disastrous weekend in September. On that Sunday in July, in two adjoining conference rooms, the fates of two of America's best-known companies were on the line.

■■■

As InBev's team in New York took their seats around the conference room table, board members started dialing in from all around the world and engaged in a bit of small talk before the call began. It wasn't a celebratory moment yet—InBev's band of Brazilian and European directors had questions about the merger agreement, the dynamics between the two companies, and what would happen next in the takeover process. Most importantly, they wanted to know whether it was clear that Anheuser-Busch's board would actually approve the deal. Several people took turns speaking—Brito helped answer the board's questions, as did the teams from Lazard and Sullivan & Cromwell.

Roughly two hours later, InBev's satisfied board agreed that signing a deal to buy Anheuser-Busch for $52 billion was worth the financial risk. They were upbeat but anxious.

"Everybody was like, okay, we're going to keep our fingers crossed," said one InBev insider. "We just didn't know what was going to happen on the other side."

Chapter 16

A Toast on Both Sides

I think we were blindsided by our conservativism.
— Anheuser-Busch board member Henry Hugh Shelton

By the time Anheuser-Busch's team assembled at Teterboro on Sunday for their 12:15 P.M. departure to St. Louis, they looked like a ragtag bunch—for a bunch of millionaires, at least. Anheuser's board needed to approve the deal that day if it was going to be announced by the next morning, so just a few hours after many of them staggered out of 375 Park Avenue at the crack of dawn, representatives from Goldman, Citigroup, Skadden, and Kekst climbed wearily back onto an Anheuser-Busch jet, bound yet again for the airplane hangar's upstairs conference room.

After the longest night of his life, Tom Santel had stumbled out of Sullivan & Cromwell's offices and over to the New York Palace hotel at around 6 A.M. He caught a half-hour nap and then, numb to his busy midtown Manhattan surroundings, crossed Madison Avenue to

attend mass at the landmark St. Patrick's Cathedral before heading to
the airport.

Dave Peacock, who wanted to make it back to headquarters
before the deal was announced, had also headed for the airport,
leaving the lawyers to hammer out the merger's final terms. He
felt it was more important to be on the ground in St. Louis when
employees got word that their proud company had been sold out
from beneath them. The media were already all over the situation,
and the whole world was expecting a deal to be announced within
hours. Anheuser's operations could quickly become paralyzed by
dread and uncertainty if key leaders weren't there to quell the fear.

Peacock ran into a few members of the New York contingent in
the waiting room at the airport as they prepared to board their plane.

"I guess I'm supposed to say congratulations," Kekst's Larry Rand
said to him in greeting.

"I guess you're supposed to, but please don't," Peacock replied,
looking utterly spent from the all-nighter he had just pulled. He had
been given a chance that weekend to prove his mettle to InBev, which
could bode well for him professionally. It was clear by that point that
August IV wouldn't continue on as an executive at the new company,
but Peacock, with his deep family ties to the company and blood that
"bled Budweiser," according to a colleague, might get that chance.

That afternoon, though, Peacock looked too broken up to care.
He hadn't showered or changed his clothes following Saturday's all-
night negotiating session. Most of Anheuser's executives drove home
once they touched down in St. Louis—or had their wives pick them
up—so they could grab a few hours of sleep, scrub down, and grab
something to eat before the board meeting began. "Quite frankly, we
all looked like hell," said an Anheuser-Busch advisor.

Vanities aside, the group set off for St. Louis on a jet that, as always,
carried plenty of Budweiser but almost nothing to eat. They had been
plied with free beer now for weeks. It was the kind of professional
assignment aspirational college fraternity boys dreamed of—getting
paid huge amounts of money to shuttle back and forth across the
country on a beer-filled private jet. No one felt like drinking, though.
That had been the case ever since Anheuser's board threw in the towel.

As the directors arrived from various corners of the country for their scheduled 3 P.M. meeting, conquering the logistical challenge that had become ritual in recent weeks, some were surprised to see that Ed Whitacre wasn't flying in to attend the meeting in person. He planned to dial in by phone instead to register his comments and make his vote. Whitacre was a busy man by all accounts, but it seemed strange to have him absent from the final independent board meeting of a legendary American company he had helped direct for decades—a company he had also helped hand over to a rival.

"I do remember, because he played such a prominent role in everything, that it raised an eyebrow when at this storied company, with this the last board meeting to approve it being sold, he wasn't there," said one Anheuser-Busch advisor. "I remember thinking, 'This is the biggest moment in the company's history.'

"But God knows, he could have had an extraordinary event he had to deal with."

The board's final crisis meeting was steeped in regret and sentimentality, but it was fairly perfunctory. Anheuser-Busch's fate had already been sealed, and the pivotal point had come six days earlier, when the board turned its back on Modelo and decided to approach InBev. The realization that it was all over was devastating to some in the room, but none seemed to be taking it harder than Pat Stokes. "I can't believe I dedicated 40 years of my life and it came to this," he said several times to no one in particular. "He's a really honorable guy," one Anheuser advisor said. "I think he was really disappointed. I felt really bad for him, [and] I felt bad for Randy. I felt bad for these guys who had busted their asses the whole life of the company and saw this happen, and felt, I think, somewhat powerless to prevent it."

After days' worth of negotiations that had pushed the deal to within a millimeter of success, all the board needed to do now was formally acquiesce. Companies tend not to enter into in-depth talks with their bitter rivals only to jettison a tie-up at the last moment.

So the teams from Goldman and Citigroup were justifiably surprised when, not long into the board's discussion, a murmur arose that perhaps Anheuser's board should spin around and ask InBev for more cash. Gross and Ingrassia, in particular, were incredulous. When

Ingrassia had suggested asking for a few extra dollars on Wednesday, before Anheuser and InBev had started negotiating, the directors had let him be chastised as if the concept was utterly ludicrous. Now, with the companies' merger fully baked, the board wanted to flirt with the idea of demanding more money? They had to be kidding.

"Guys, we had an opportunity and you chose not to take it. Why are we discussing it now?" Gross questioned tersely, briefly losing his cool out of sheer annoyance more than he would have allowed himself to a week or two earlier. "You talked about not wanting to worry about risk before, and now you'd have much more risk, completely backtracking on a deal that we've now negotiated!"

It seemed to be suddenly hitting some of the company's directors that Anheuser-Busch was going to lose its longstanding independence while they were in charge. "We had this flirtation with going back and negotiating, and there was just some strange, last-minute punting that was going on," one advisor said. "I think at that point, people realized what they had set in motion and it felt a little too real to everybody." The board quickly dropped the idea and rededicated itself to the matter at hand.

Skadden's team walked the directors through the merger document line by line to ensure they knew what they were approving, and the bankers gave a brief rundown that explained why they thought the transaction's price and terms were fair. The Third and The Fourth were businesslike and professional and showed no hint of emotion, but the rest of the board knew it had to be heart-wrenching for both men—for different sets of reasons.

"I could only imagine what August III probably felt like, because he had built the company," said General Shelton. "Having taken over from his dad in a coup, to continue leadership and then build that company into the great conglomerate it was, to him that had to be awfully tough. I just can't imagine. And of course living right there in St. Louis . . ." The Fourth, as far as anyone can remember, didn't speak a word.

After roughly two hours of procedural box-checking that seemed like an eternity, the board finally signed off on the merger. It was time to head home.

Their professional dalliance with St. Louis now over, Anheuser's advisors gathered up their things and headed out of the hangar toward a large jet that was bound for New York. It wasn't the last time some of them would set foot in the hangar. While that Sunday marked the announcement of the transaction, there was plenty of work to do in the coming months before the deal could become official.

The group didn't make it back to New York as smoothly as usual. Some members of the local St. Louis media had finally uncovered the board's hiding spot and had come armed with television cameras. Tom Santel had received a message on his BlackBerry during the board meeting that said there was footage on television of him getting out of his car, so he left through a back exit when the session wrapped up. Citigroup's Jeffrey Schackner wasn't so lucky—a cameraman shoved a lens in his face as he walked out the door and toward the jet bound for New York. He put his head down and vaulted up the steps into the safety and obscurity of the airplane, but the image ran repeatedly on local television, prompting some of Schackner's other St. Louis clients to joke that he'd be persona non grata in town for a while.

"I won't say that everybody was disappointed," said one person who attended the board session. "Yeah, there was disappointment that this iconic American company that had been independent for all of these years would no longer be independent. But they all said, 'We have a fiduciary obligation, the price was fair, and the execution risk was no longer with us but with somebody else.'"

"I just remember getting on that plane and being in this unbelievably pristine hangar, just shaking my head that the thing never needed to have happened," said another. But "at the end of the day, we're all businesspeople, and they received a good premium."

That premium was enough to significantly enrich members of the board who held a bunch of Anheuser-Busch stock—and August III and Pat Stokes in particular. A good handful of the board—Taylor, Warner, Jones, Loucks, Martinez, Payne, and Roché—held stock that was worth $1.25 million upon completion of the merger. That paled in comparison to the $427.3 million haul August III pulled in, a combination of stock he controlled directly and stock that indirectly benefited him through various trusts and through his wife. Stokes walked away with $160.9 million.

"It came to a point toward the end where I believe August III and Pat Stokes finally looked at how much money they were personally going to make and said, 'Let's do it. It's over, let's do it,'" said Harry Schuhmacher. "I think August IV still had an emotional tie to the company that he had not overcome yet, and it wasn't about the money. So he was trying to prevent the deal at any cost. I think I remember August even telling me that 'Pat and Dad have sold out.' It became hard for him to really do anything at that point."

■ ■ ■

Anheuser-Busch's capitulation was particularly frustrating to some of the Wall Street advisors who wanted to win for competitive reasons. They felt the board had pulled the rug out far too soon, leaving InBev's team able to claim credit for a masterful takeover campaign.

"The InBev side all throughout this thing had a perspective on what they thought we were doing—what they thought the story was—that couldn't have been more off," said one Anheuser advisor. "One of the greatest parts of this story was the disparity between what they assumed was going on and what was really going on. There was this view on the InBev side that somehow they and their bankers had orchestrated this inevitable push towards a deal, and that the sheer weight of the thoughtfulness of their tactics lead to a deal happening. I'll just tell you, that could not have been further from the truth."

InBev's ability to pull together a slate of alternate board members had "literally nothing to do with it," the advisor said. The board's decision came down to its view of the company's alternatives. Instead of taking more risk than necessary, whether by throwing their weight behind The Fourth or by trying to execute a deal with the Mexicans, they opted for the lowest-risk option.

"They were just incredibly, incredibly conservative in doing that," the advisor said. "It was nothing so much about any great tactics of InBev. There was nothing about their alternative board that did anything. No one was so intimidated by that at all. There was nothing about what Adolphus Busch did that mattered. This was very much just, 'What's the number they're putting up, what's the value we can do on our own, and do we feel like taking any risk at all to get there?' And the board saying 'No, we don't want to.'"

Once they had all piled on the plane, the group of New York–bound advisors settled into their seats for the flight back, deflated, hungry, and—with the company's fate sealed—eager to get home to bed. Some toasted the bitter occasion by finally cracking open a few free beers. They had no clue that Brito and the rest of InBev's team were doing the very same thing in a document-strewn conference room in New York, though in far more celebratory style.

Joe Flom, who seemed to have been itching for battle from the start, hadn't cooled off and began pacing like a caged tiger. "He was just running up and down the aisle of the plane," said one person who was on the flight. Out of Anheuser's entire pool of advisers, Flom was "probably the most disappointed that they didn't want to go to war," said another member of the group. It was Flom who had argued earlier that week that they should call attention to InBev's relationships in Cuba, where U.S. companies were mostly barred from doing business, in an effort to cast a pro-American shadow on InBev's operations. Anheuser had taken his advice and issued a statement that chided InBev for not explaining how its distribution partnership with Cuba's government would impact Anheuser's customers. The effort went over like a lead balloon. It was too little, too late, and too desperate. Many media outlets neglected to even note the Cuba angle in that day's news coverage. For a hostile takeover with such significant implications, that small shot across InBev's bow was as messy as the PR battle between Anheuser-Busch and InBev ever got. And to Flom, it seemed to be a disappointment.

"I remember sitting next to Joe on several of these flights, and I remember him being pretty upset, thinking that we could have fought more, we could have gotten more, and that we had been quick to take a bid," said one Anheuser-Busch advisor. "I think that Joe passionately cares about this stuff."

"He clearly was upset by some of these things, because he felt the board had moved quicker than he wanted it to."

Eventually, though, Flom's pragmatism won out. He and Larry Rand shared a car back home that night after their plane landed in New Jersey, and by that point, he had turned his preternaturally energetic attentions toward the future—he was planning an elopement in Europe.

"While all this is going on, he meets and marries a girlfriend based, I think, on a blind date," said one person on Anheuser's team. "That's impressive."

"When you're my age, you can't waste time," Flom liked to say as he told the story.

■ ■ ■

On another Anheuser-Busch jet that evening, this one bound for Washington, D.C., Jim Forese, Ambassador Jones, and General Shelton commiserated as well. They had boarded the plane in St. Louis with an emptiness in their guts and weren't particularly eager to drink, though Shelton wouldn't have tipped one back even if the mood had been sunny. He never imbibed while flying—private or commercial—to keep his senses sharp in case something went wrong. It was a habit he picked up in the Army's airborne special operations.

Anheuser-Busch was a global icon, and the last major beer maker in the country that was still American-owned. "When you look at A-B and Harley-Davidson, and Ford Motor Company, these are companies that represent America," Shelton said. Anheuser's era as a member of that dwindling club had ended in the blink of an eye, and the trio's sense of loss was overwhelming. "It was almost like 'This can't be happening,'" he said.

Feelings of self-doubt nagged at Ambassador Jones the entire flight back. "Could I have done something else?" he thought. "Could we have prevented this?" It was hard not to second-guess the board's decisions. Those pangs never really subsided, even after wild gyrations in the market in the months that followed made the board's timing look brilliant.

"We had some opportunities to buy some quality companies in Europe and we didn't—this was when August III was CEO— because he thought they were overpriced. And in the presentations that were made, it sounded like they were overpriced," Jones said. "So we may have missed some good opportunities overseas. That might have made a difference. That might have made us somewhat invulnerable."

"If I had to put my finger on any one thing, I would say we probably were too conservative," agreed Shelton, who found himself wishing there had been someone on Anheuser's board who would have pushed harder to do deals. "When you live in a world of either 'buy' or 'be bought,' you've got to be growing faster than we were growing externally. We should probably have been more aggressive in pursuing other opportunities."

"When you watch a company like Molson buy Coors, and SAB buys Miller, in the back of your mind you think, 'If we had been willing to maybe accept a little lower credit rating and been less risk-averse, would we not have fared a lot better in the long term?'"

Not a single move was made to pay tribute to what had just happened before the directors walked to their jets that evening—not one speech in honor of what Anheuser-Busch had accomplished over the past century and a half, not one note of formality to mark the end of an era. Anheuser-Busch wheezed its final breaths in the fluorescent-lit makeshift conference room of a St. Louis airplane hangar. It was a far cry from the rich, evocative imagery the company had always projected.

"That was it," Shelton said. "We got on the plane and flew back and it was all over."

■ ■ ■

Back in New York, InBev's core handful of executives, bankers, and lawyers prepped for what they hoped would be the biggest day of their professional lives. There was still a great deal of work to be done— legal disclosures that needed to be reviewed, press materials that needed to be vetted. It was hard to concentrate. They were waiting anxiously for a call from Anheuser to confirm that its board had approved the deal. If that call never came, their efforts would be pointless.

As the summer sun set that evening, the team grew nervous. Anheuser-Busch's board was bound to take an hour or two to fully vet and approve the deal. As two hours stretched into two and a half and then three, still with no phone call, the tension on Park Avenue intensified. Anheuser's board wouldn't dare hang InBev out to dry after wading this deeply into merger talks, would they? Up until that Sunday, the deal had progressed at a shockingly rapid-fire pace. Were they suddenly getting cold feet? Did they want more money? Were the Mexicans back in town? With Anheuser's whole team now in St. Louis, InBev could no longer cajole them into submission face-to-face.

Everyone in the room seemed on edge. This takeover bid was about to make or break each of their careers. They put their heads down and concentrated on the piles of antitrust filings and press materials in front of them. Brito, in particular, refused to loosen up. As he repeatedly made clear, the deal wasn't done until he got word from Anheuser-Busch firsthand. He wasn't the type to celebrate prematurely.

At around nine or ten o'clock that night, Brito's cell phone sprang to life. He put up his hand to quiet his colleagues and answered the phone.

August IV's lilting drawl came through from St. Louis on the other end of the line. His board had capitulated, he told Brito wearily. Anheuser-Busch was InBev's for the taking. Brito's dark eyes lit up as he disconnected the call, and the InBev team devolved into a round of whoops and back-slapping hugs. A few moments later, they gathered around a table where a round of Budweisers had been laid out on ice a few hours earlier in anticipation, next to some of the Stellas and Beck's they usually imbibed.

"Nobody touched the Bud until Brito had gotten a call from The Fourth," said one person who was there that night. Once that call finally came in, though, InBev's team cracked open the King of Beers for a toast, pulling out their cameras to document the moment as they knocked the drinks back with the exhilaration that comes with a hard-fought victory.

"There aren't that many deals where you literally get to drink their products in toast when you win it," said one person close to InBev.

■ ■ ■

It took an extra handful of hours to finalize the merger agreement once Anheuser's approval came in, which proved excruciating for both sides. InBev's camp couldn't wait to publicly declare victory, and the exhausted Anheuser-Busch team was ready to reclaim their lives. Anheuser-Busch had pulled many of its legal documents together in just 48 hours, so the delay was not surprising. It was like watching paint dry, a frustrating lull before a hugely anticipated moment.

As Skaddden combed through the merger agreement one last time, and as InBev pored over the reams of documents Anheuser-Busch had hastily submitted over the past two days, Brito took up residence in a separate room to be briefed for the following day's press conference. Mid-evening melded into late night and then early morning on Monday, the day InBev had hoped to announce its coup before markets opened in Europe. Some of the lawyers had been onsite on Park Avenue by that point for nearly two straight days, and many hadn't caught a wink of sleep. A few had holed up for catnaps in dark nooks and crannies, spread across or beneath rows of chairs.

"You'd sort of walk into a conference room, the lights would be out, you put the lights on, and there would be somebody sleeping in the corner," said one InBev team member.

Then, to InBev's great relief, Skadden finally announced that it was comfortable enough to let InBev issue its press release. Brunswick's Steve Lipin, who had repeatedly reviewed each line of the release to make sure everything was in order, conducted one last run-through with InBev's top two PR staffers. They were just about to press the button to send it to the news wires when they realized that while the document was still dated Sunday, July 13, the clock had already flipped over to Monday in New York and Belgium. For a few seconds, yet another administrative obstacle looked like it would delay InBev's moment of glory.

"It's still Sunday in St. Louis!" someone suddenly blurted out. The team digested the statement for a few seconds and then nodded in agreement, breathing a huge sigh of relief. They made sure that their press release included a Sunday dateline from St. Louis. And with that, they pushed the button.

Chapter 17

Cash Out or
Hunker Down

Everyone is a multimillionaire in the top management. I can assure you they were not unhappy, let's put it that way. I don't know that I hear too many complaints from them.

—Anheuser-Busch board member Jim Forese

On Tuesday morning, after giving the news of Anheuser-Busch's capitulation a day to sink in, the victorious Brito arrived at headquarters in St. Louis to address the troops. InBev had held a global conference call on Monday to coincide with the announcement of the merger, and Brito spent more than an hour waxing poetic about the future and detailing his plans. That public showing, however, had been tailored for the media, analysts, and investors on Wall Street. He needed to keep Anheuser's engine fires burning by engaging staffers in St. Louis, and he felt that showing up in person would help.

InBev was hoping The Fourth would pitch in to keep his employees' despair at bay, but his performance on the Monday call had suggested he was too distraught himself to be useful. When Brito turned the podium over to Anheuser's executives to see whether they had something to add, The Fourth remained completely silent, leaving Dave Peacock to fill the void with a few quick comments. August IV had prepared a series of remarks to make to his employees that day in St. Louis, but they were so dour that InBev's PR team edited them to inject them with some optimism. It was hard to blame The Fourth. He was being forced to act as the public face of a takeover he didn't support.

To honor Brito's visit and pay him the respect it felt he deserved as the soon-to-be new chief, Anheuser-Busch arranged for him to stay in a suite at the cushy Ritz-Carlton. The Ritz wasn't Brito's style, though, especially since he was just about to start indoctrinating Anheuser-Busch's staffers to InBev's frugal way of life. He had flown commercial into St. Louis from New York's LaGuardia Airport.

"He had someone call back and say, "No, no no, I've already reserved a room at such and such a place—like the Holiday Inn," said one InBev insider. "I think that's when it probably, for the first time, hit home in St. Louis that things were going to be different." Rather than hitching a town car or helicoptering in to Anheuser-Busch headquarters from his hotel on Tuesday morning, Brito accepted a ride from Dave Peacock.

Brito had been to St. Louis before. His first big business trip early in his brewing career had been a visit to Anheuser-Busch, where he learned about how the legendary American giant brewed and distributed beer. The coin had certainly flipped. He was now about to instruct Anheuser's staffers on how he did business at InBev as their new boss.

■ ■ ■

When Brito sat down in Anheuser's ninth floor boardroom with the strategy committee that day, most of the committee's members were still digesting the fact that they had become obsolete overnight. It was surreal.

"It all happened so quick," said Tom Santel. "It was only, like, 51 days. We thought it would last a lot longer."

"I don't think that early on, people really understood whether this thing was going to really happen," another strategy committee member said. "There was to a certain extent some denial that this was really true. Up until the day that the board agreed to sell, there was a lot of hope—anxious hope—'We're going to fight these bastards,' blah, blah, blah."

In an awkward presentation that elicited a few polite questions, Brito pledged to the strategy committee that InBev and Anheuser would do great things together and take the global beer market to a new level. His comments seemed highly scripted, but they helped convince at least a few staffers that he wasn't the devil incarnate.

During a brewery tour that day led by brewing head Doug Muhleman, a group of workers who manned one of the bottling lines presented Brito with a T-shirt—part of a tradition that particular team had for greeting special guests and VIPs. The contrast between globe-trotting Brito and the bottling line's blue collar workers was high-lighted by the fact that Brito walked around that day with his passport in his shirt pocket. Nonetheless, he was friendly and very approach-able. "He must have been trying to convey the sense that they weren't monsters, that he was a good guy," said one former Anheuser execu-tive who had never met Brito before that day. "I remember after that, thinking he was not so bad."

There was still plenty of anger and frustration to go around in St. Louis. Anheuser's top staffers spent the next few months repeatedly running over what they could have done differently. It was easy to point to the distant past, when most of them hadn't been in control, and to blame things on The Third's arrogance. They had also allowed certain more recent initiatives to be shelved rather than pushing for them aggressively, however, such as the talks with SABMiller or the long but fruitless flirtation with Modelo. Now, InBev was pledging to squeeze $1.5 billion in savings out of Anheuser-Busch within three years, another half as much as the $1 billion target Anheuser had just announced on its own. It was bound to be painful.

The hand-wringing grew worse as employees who wanted to keep their jobs realized they would have to fight for them. Anheuser had already announced plans to reduce its workforce by up to 15 percent on its own, and InBev was likely to slash even more.

It didn't take long for the layoffs to start in earnest. On December 8, 2008, three weeks after the deal was officially completed, InBev said it would cut 1,400 salaried workers in its beer-related divisions, about 6 percent of its U.S. workforce. Seventy-five percent of those cuts hit the St. Louis area. And they came on top of the 1,000 workers who took buyouts or early retirement. Peering out the front windows of Anheuser's headquarters became a painfully demoralizing exercise.

"I'd look out and there was yet another person standing by their car, carrying a box, sobbing uncontrollably," said Bob Lachky. "And there would be a security guard with them. They'd just run their butt right out the door. To watch it is vividly etched in your memory. It was just awful. And the phone calls and the networking afterward, people just begging for a job. It was not a good time for that. It's gut-wrenching."

The company's decision to announce the biggest chunk of its layoffs just a few weeks before Christmas sparked a great deal of anger, but the alternative seemed just as bad. "We didn't want to send people away over the holidays with 90 percent of the company afraid for their jobs," Dave Peacock told the *St. Louis Post-Dispatch*. "I just didn't think it was fair to people to send the whole company away with a lot of people afraid for their future."

The winter of 2008—just before the start of a year in which America's unemployment rate hit 10 percent—was a horrible time to be laid off in the hard-hit Midwestern United States. And the reverberation of those big initial job cuts stretched on for more than a year. One executive sent out a blast e-mail in early 2010 saying that his job had been discontinued. Some of the company's salespeople were told long after the deal closed that they needed to fire a layer of staffers beneath them. They did so, only to discover that they were being demoted into those newly emptied positions.

As Anheuser's employees realized their jobs were at risk in the immediate aftermath of the merger, their collegial behavior devolved into a fight for survival. "It was like *Apocalypse Now*," Lachky said. "The further and further up the river you got, the more chaotic it was. People were turning on each other. People were just taking each other out. But in the end, everybody got theirs. We were all going to get it."

Saying good-bye was slightly less painful for the strategy committee, many of whom drafted lucrative exit packages and left before the end of the year. "I just couldn't wait for everything to be over, because I knew I wasn't staying," said Tom Santel, who left the company on November 20, right after the merger officially closed.

Santel sat down with his staff the week after the deal was announced to detail what had happened and explain what might be coming down the pike. The loss of Anheuser-Busch was going to feel like a death, he told them, and they'd probably go through similar stages of mourning. "It was like a four-month funeral," he said. "It was sad, seeing all of the people there and all of the heartbreak." Santel, who was paid $26.5 million for his stake in the company, didn't get the final word on his dismissal until October. It was obvious well beforehand, though—InBev had no plans to replace his job. "I knew even if they wanted me, I wouldn't want to stay," he said. "I wouldn't have fit in there."

InBev asked Lachky, however, to stay on longer so that he could spearhead the merged company's first-ever Super Bowl ad campaign. After some coaxing from Dave Peacock, Lachky decided to take one last crack at the big event. He made sure to get assurances on an exit package of his own, up front and in writing.

"I never felt so lonely as I did doing Super Bowl creative for the last year, because nobody cared. Nobody really wanted to work on it," he said. "If you were relying on internal people to be motivated to get some Herculean task done, you might as well forget it. Because from that point on, it was all about self-survival and people counting their stock options every day. Everybody quit working mentally, quit putting in the extra hours."

"It was like anarchy. Mentally, everybody had checked out and they were fighting for themselves. The secretaries were crying in the hallways."

After a decade-long winning streak, Anheuser-Busch did not win USA Today's Ad Meter ranking for the best Super Bowl spot in 2009—even after luring comedian Conan O'Brien into his first-ever TV commercial for one of its spots. Anheuser's crackerjack marketing team finished second and third instead, losing out to two unemployed brothers from Indiana who created a Doritos ad as part of an online contest. "We beat the king of commercials," 32-year-old Dave Herbert, one of the brothers, proclaimed to *USA Today*. Lachky retired at the end of February, a few weeks after the game aired. He stood to earn $20.6 million.

■ ■ ■

Out of Anheuser's pool of top talent, only three executives kept their jobs. Peacock, thanks partly to the goodwill he built with InBev during merger negotiations, assumed the highest-profile role of any "old Anheuser" executive. As president of the merged company's U.S. division, he became the new public face of Anheuser-Busch once The Fourth dropped out of sight. The job wasn't particularly enviable, though. His new employer was pressuring workers, vendors, and wholesalers to slash costs, and he was stuck reporting to Brazilian Luiz Fernando Edmond, who had moved to St. Louis and was put in charge of InBev's North American operations. Gary Rutledge stayed on as general counsel for the company's North American business. And Bob Golden, Anheuser's former acquisitions head, eventually moved to New York after being named global head of the merged company's mergers and acquisitions effort. Golden's appointment dredged up at least one bittersweet irony: He was tasked again with trying to buy the remaining stake in Modelo, the same deal he had already brought to within an inch of completion while trying to defend Anheuser-Busch. One analyst predicted in March of 2010 that the two companies would strike a deal valuing Modelo at $10.8 billion, well below the price The Fourth's team had been willing to pay.

The large number of high-level departures left few who were willing to fight on behalf of the old Anheuser-Busch. Brito's qualms about keeping InBev's North American headquarters in St. Louis ended up being misplaced, at least in the executive suite. There wasn't much emotional or institutional baggage to wade through as InBev worked to remake Anheuser-Busch in its image, because nearly everyone who might have caused a problem packed those bags and left.

As one of the terms of the takeover, InBev pledged to put two Anheuser-Busch representatives on its board of directors—August IV and one other current or former Anheuser director. Two years after the deal was struck, it still hadn't made good on its promise. Some industry watchers assume that was because the spot had been set aside for Carlos Fernández in the event that the Brazilians could finally strike a deal with Modelo. Others attributed it to a lack of political will by anyone with ties to the old company.

"It's like they didn't give a shit," one advisor on the deal said. "Once they sold it, they didn't give a shit."

Frankly, though, many of Anheuser's former top executives had better things to do. While the deal dealt a crushing blow to their psyches and cut short their careers, it certainly padded their wallets. Those who didn't have stock options didn't get much, but those who did got rich instantly. And many did.

"All of these guys got lots of money," said an advisor to the company. "We were quite surprised. They had obviously been loading up for years."

"It almost made you a little uneasy, because it was like 'Oh my God, the day has come,'" said one former executive. "It's, like, unbelievable that you could go home with this kind of money."

Chief Financial Officer Randy Baker, one of The Third's original "eaters," pulled in $72.3 million upon leaving the company. Lauded by other Anheuser insiders for his even-tempered dependability during the takeover mess, he chose to recede into the shadows "and has kind of gone off to get away from everybody," one advisor said. "I thought Randy handled himself phenomenally through this whole thing," said another. "To have lasted and been trusted in that environment for as long as he was was really, really impressive. He did it by not ever taking sides—he was kind of all business."

Some of the company's former executives, upon winning the corporate equivalent of the lottery, used their new financial freedom to pursue the types of dreams that can only be chased by the rich. Anthony Ponturo, who had been the company's sports marketing head and one of the most prominent marketing executives in America, collected $16.8 million. He launched a New York–based consulting firm and threw a bunch of money into the production of Broadway shows. For a man who used to spend more than half a billion dollars each year promoting beer, financing *Hair* probably seemed like a steal.

Doug Muhleman, who pulled in $38.3 million when the deal closed, made a logical choice given his brewmaster credentials and moved back to his home state of California to grow wine grapes in Sonoma. Ensuring a good harvest can be stressful, but it doesn't hold a candle to Anheuser-Busch's long workweeks and treacherous internal politics. As one former executive said in reference to the BlackBerry he once carried and clicked through all day long, "I'm so glad I don't have one anymore."

One Anheuser staffer broke the mold, however, and went on the offensive less than a year after the merger closed. Francine Katz, who had been Anheuser's chief communications officer, sued the company after claiming that she learned through merger-related regulatory filings that she and Marlene Coulis, the other woman on Anheuser's strategy committee, earned less than their male counterparts. She said Anheuser-Busch maintained a "locker room, frat party" atmosphere, and claimed that while she complained about pay disparities to The Third and to Dave Peacock on multiple occasions, her requests were "ignored or met with hostility and misinformation."

InBev's takeover put August IV in a particularly uncomfortable spot. Between the day the deal was announced in July and the time it legally closed in November, he remained head of Anheuser-Busch. His responsibilities, however, were whittled down with each day that passed, and he had no real say on the new direction in which the company was heading. It was all about Brito from that July forward.

The day after the deal was made public, just a few minutes before Brito joined him to speak with a group of employees, The Fourth sat down for an interview with the *St. Louis Post-Dispatch* and unwittingly illuminated how difficult the transition would be. As he walked into the conference room outside his office and grabbed a chair at the head of the table, he paused, looked down at the chair, and said, "I don't know if I should put Brito here or not." The Fourth acknowledged that day that it was "a difficult feeling, needless to say," to weigh the impact of the sale of Anheuser-Busch on his family's legacy.

The Fourth's efforts during the merger talks to negotiate a consulting deal that would ease his transition paid off handily. He didn't exactly need the cash—thanks to the stock he held in the company, he made out with more than $91 million when the merger closed. Still, he accepted a seat on InBev's board for a three-year term, and agreed, at Brito's request, to advise InBev on new products and marketing programs and meet with the company's stakeholders and the media. In return, InBev handed him $10.35 million up front with the promise of an extra consulting fee of about $120,000 a month, and tossed in a personal security detail as icing on the cake. The deal tied The Fourth and InBev to a mutual "non-disparagement" covenant, which has limited what they can say about each other and bars them from uttering anything negative.

It makes sense to wonder why a man who was incredibly wealthy—and had just become much, much more so—wanted to be involved with the new company at all. He certainly wasn't tight with Brito and his crew, and it quickly became apparent that the services and advice he'd be providing would be minimal.

"There's a lot of emotion tied up in something like that," said one person close to The Fourth. "I don't think that his involvement in the company, post-deal, has been incredibly robust. I think, if anything, the opposite. But at the time of the deal, he probably had a lot of mixed feelings." A seat on InBev's board gave The Fourth a chance to stay associated with a company that meant a great deal to him, and he may have thought his presence there would provide useful continuity. More than anything else, though, the consulting deal looked like an expensive effort by InBev to keep up appearances after it wiped out Anheuser's entire board and most of its executive team. Busch was a no-show at industry events in the year following the deal, according to analysts and media outlets, and wasn't quoted in papers or photographed at meet-and-greets.

■ ■ ■

The names and faces of Anheuser's ninth floor occupants weren't the only things that changed once the companies' marriage was consummated. For decades, Anheuser's executives had roamed the halls of their headquarters in respectable coats and ties. It didn't take long for InBev's casual dress code to infiltrate their ranks, however. Most of the company's staffers now march around Anheuser-Busch's St. Louis campus wearing some variation on the decidedly unfashionable InBev uniform: jeans with tucked-in button-down shirts, their employee IDs clipped to their belts.

"If he was still there, I don't think he would feel too good about going to work in blue jeans," Lee Roarty said as she nodded toward her sartorially savvy husband, Mike, her mouth pursed in distaste.

Brito got to work quickly on a slew of other physical and cultural changes that caused almost as much consternation in St. Louis as the takeover itself. Rather than chipping away slowly at Anheuser's layers of waste and making gradual shifts to keep employees from panicking, the Brazilians decided to blow everything up all at once. They took sledgehammers to the cushy, private offices that lined the hallways of Anheuser's executive suite—offices that had allowed staffers to go days at a time without encountering their colleagues—and supplanted them with a sea of community tables and tightly packed desks. Brito had no quiet office, or even a desk, of his own, and he wanted his new North American operation to reflect that team-oriented mentality.

"It looked like they had thrown a bomb on the 9th floor," one top executive told a Brazilian publication. "There was mahogany everywhere." Secretaries were fired, the company's luxurious furniture was auctioned off, and 40 percent of its employees' 1,200 BlackBerries were taken away.

Within months, perks like free tickets to St. Louis Cardinals games and Busch Gardens disappeared, as did the free beer that Anheuser-Busch had distributed to employees and handed out to customers at its theme parks. "I don't need free beer," Brito had said. "I can buy my own beer." The soccer park was signed over to the St. Louis Soccer United organization. A range of sports sponsorships were tossed to the curb. Even expenses like color printing and shipping kegs of beer via FedEx were curtailed. And Brito showed no qualms about tinkering with Anheuser-Busch's holiest symbols while looking to make an extra few dollars. Roughly a year and a half after the deal closed, the company confirmed that it had quietly started to charge $2,000 per day for Clydesdale appearances, reversing Anheuser's longstanding practice of absorbing most of the horses' costs itself.

Employees began to complain that morale in St. Louis was suffering, and InBev acknowledged that the moves might disenfranchise staffers who didn't appreciate its startup mentality. It shrugged off the criticism, however. InBev's performance demands were simply higher than Anheuser's had been, and staffers needed to be held more accountable.

With the rich price it paid for Anheuser, InBev gave itself no option but to cut deep toward the bone. It wasn't going to slash costs the traditional way—by ridding itself of overlapping operations—because the two companies had very few of those. "To pay off this thing, Brito is going to have to turn the company inside out," said one longtime Anheuser advisor. "They're already selling off big hunks of the business."

InBev used Anheuser's Blue Ocean plan as a road map and then pursued that agenda even more aggressively. "There's probably not a nickel of Blue Ocean they haven't delivered at this point," said a person close to Anheuser-Busch. "I would bet you they've gotten literally every nickel of that and more. . . . It would have been harder, I think, for Bud to do it."

The new company sparked an uproar from its suppliers when it announced it would take 120 days to pay its bills rather than 30 days, affording itself time to use that money for other purposes. Local electronics giant Emerson, whose executives had always had close ties with the Busches, launched a boycott in protest and stopped buying Anheuser-Busch beer for its headquarters, conference center, private jets, and even, ironically, its suite at Busch Stadium. One vendor of beechwood chips lost out when the company consolidated its vendor roster and closed up shop entirely.

St. Louis had fought Milwaukee for decades for the right to call itself the "beer capital" of America, but thanks to the Brazilians, that critical claim to fame vanished overnight. Residents who had always compared St. Louis to larger Chicago as an important Midwestern nexus began to worry that without an independent Anheuser-Busch, it could tumble down the roster toward the likes of Des Moines, Iowa.

It didn't take long for St. Louis's citizens to make their distaste for the new regime apparent. Anheuser-Busch's market share in the once loyal town, which had hovered at nearly 70 percent, fell in 2009 as sales at Schlafly, an independent local brewery, shot 38 percent higher. Schlafly's founder said nearly a thousand resumes from former Anheuser-Busch employees piled into his mailbox in 2009.

Brito's effort to tackle the most conspicuous example of Anheuser's excess, however—its fleet of corporate jets—moved much more sluggishly than many analysts had expected. Coach-class airfares quickly became the rule, and the company attested that it planned to eventually sell every plane in its fleet. Yet, more than a year after the deal closed in late 2008, it still owned a few planes and employed several pilots. When a local newspaper latched onto the apparent hypocrisy, InBev said it was "not in a rush to sell them" into a rough resale market, and a spokeswoman refused to address the exact number of planes that were either being sold or still being used. InBev still used the Anheuser jets "when it is a cost-effective option," she said.

InBev put several large assets on the auction block to help pay off its massive debt to the banks that financed the merger. It sold Anheuser's 27 percent stake in China's Tsingtao, sold a few beverage can and lid making plants to Ball Corporation, and sold its own South Korean beer business for $1.8 billion to private equity firm Kohlberg Kravis Roberts & Co.

More critically for American consumers, InBev put the 10 heavily trafficked theme parks in Anheuser's Busch Entertainment unit— including its three SeaWorld locations—up for grabs soon after the merger closed. Just less than a year later, it announced it would sell the enterprise to private equity firm The Blackstone Group for up to $2.7 billion.

"It killed me to see they had sold those theme parks," said one former ad executive. "The Busches were such outdoorsmen, and they were so committed to preserving the environment and working with and helping animals." The Brazilians timed their sale well, however. Two months after the sale closed, an orca attacked and killed a female trainer at SeaWorld in Orlando, sparking a renewed round of protests over shows that feature such animals in captivity.

Brito's decision to cut Anheuser's top marketers loose also generated plenty of scorn. InBev needed to cut $1.5 billion in costs, and it was clear that Anheuser's massive advertising budget would come under scrutiny—particularly in such a rough economy. Brito had never hid the fact that he favored shooting far fewer commercials each year and employing fewer ad agencies than Anheuser-Busch used. Experts argued that chopping at Anheuser's ad budget and sticking gum in the gears of its creative process could permanently snuff out the fire that made Budweiser an American icon.

"What other brewer has gotten to 50 percent of the market?" said Charlie Claggett. "What's that worth, and what did they spend to get there? To me, that's how you do it. You can't do creative in a research laboratory. You can test stuff until you're blue in the face, and you end up with work that P&G does." Some of InBev's success in selling Budweiser will forever be based on the global political climate, which puts it outside of InBev's control—a fact that its data crunchers may find difficult to stomach.

"The beer is such an American flag, it's such an icon, that your sales into each country really depend on what people think of America," said Claggett, who worked on the Budweiser account in England for a while. "When America's stock goes up, sales of Budweiser go up. To talk about Budweiser as an international brand, like Heineken or Beck's, is a little bit naïve because none of those brands are as iconic as the red, white and blue Budweiser label."

In one regard, InBev actually decided to lay out some cash. It signed a 10-year lease on 31,500 square feet of office space on Park Avenue in New York, pouring fuel on the speculation that Brito would eventually abandon St. Louis and shift Anheuser-Busch InBev's North American headquarters to the East where he was now based. Anheuser's St. Louis employees took particular offense to the news and ramped up their anti-InBev rhetoric, calling Brito "Carlos Burrito" and rechristening the company's famous One Busch Place address as "One Brito Place."

■ ■ ■

InBev's executives and their advisors, unsurprisingly, made out quite well. Brito moved with his family to a tony Connecticut suburb north of Manhattan, joining a wealth of other top staffers who eagerly relocated from sleepy Leuven to New York to set up shop in the company's new Park Avenue digs. A bar to serve their expanded roster of beers was quickly installed at the office. A better lifestyle in the Big Apple paled as a motivational tool compared to the pay deal Brito and InBev's other top executives cut in the wake of the merger. The company's top 40 executives set themselves up to reap stock options worth nearly $1 billion, if not considerably more, if they were able to shrink the company's debt levels back to normal levels by 2013. Brito was poised to pull in more than $200 million in options alone if the value of the company's shares doubled. The company quickly shot well ahead of schedule on its debt-slashing campaign, an indication that those sums wouldn't remain hypothetical for long.

The deal marked the pinnacle of success for ambitious InBev board members Jorge Paulo Lemann, Marcel Herrmann Telles, and Carlos Alberto da Veiga Sicupira. Out of their estimated $50 million investment in Brazil's Brahma in 1989, they cultivated a 25 percent stake in Anheuser-Busch InBev worth roughly $9 billion by mid-2010, making relatively few cash injections along the way. A little less than two years after the deal closed, in September of 2010, an investment firm backed by Lemann, Telles and Sicupira called 3G Capital—which also happened to employ Marc Mezvinsky, the man who married former first daughter Chelsea Clinton that July—announced plans to buy Burger King, another iconic American company, for $3.3 billion. 3G said it would open more restaurants in Asia and, to no one's surprise, Latin America to try to boost Burger King's sagging performance. Antonio Weiss's work as InBev's most trusted advisor pushed his star straight to the top at Lazard. He was named as the investment bank's global head of mergers and acquisitions in March of 2009 and, months later, when Lazard chief Bruce Wasserstein unexpectedly died, as global head of investment banking. Weiss relocated from Paris back to New York, taking up residence with his family along the western edge of Central Park; in 2009, he was identified as the banker who worked on more deals that year than anyone else in the world. Frank Aquila and George Sampas brought home huge fees for Sullivan & Cromwell, as did Doug Braunstein for J.P. Morgan. In June of 2010, Braunstein was named chief financial officer of the bank, which was paid handily both for financing InBev's deal and for providing advice to the company.

Compared to the long months of late hours and last-minute travel most takeover battles require, the level of involvement on both sides was relatively painless. The work didn't end when the deal was signed in July, however. Both companies had a gargantuan amount of effort to put forth before the merger actually closed, and the global financial markets had started crashing down around them. As the pillars of credit that supported Wall Street grew increasingly fragile in the fall, stress levels at both companies ratcheted higher. "I bet we had as many board meetings on 'Is this deal going to close?' as we had on "Are we going to do the deal?'" said one Anheuser advisor.

Pat Stokes flew to New York at one point and questioned Tim Ingrassia over lunch about the worsening liquidity crisis. Stokes had a good view on how hard the Midwest was getting hit by the housing crisis and credit crunch, and he was worried that the odds of the deal's collapse were rising.

"On a scale of one to ten, Tim, where are you?" Stokes asked.

Ingrassia said there was an eight-out-of-ten chance that the deal would still close as negotiated—decent odds in his view, given the carnage he was seeing on the Street. Stokes looked as though he had been punched in the gut. To him, a 20 percent chance of failure sounded mortifyingly high.

No one could have predicted that just months after the Anheuser sale was inked, the global financial markets would collapse and one of the 10 European banks that agreed to finance the deal—Dutch bank Fortis—would flat-out fail. InBev had deliberately chosen a pool of banks that looked strong enough to withstand the market's battering. Anheuser's share price hovered roughly 7 percent below the agreement's $70 price that September, however, as a slew of banks imploded, a reflection of how wary investors had become over the deal's chances of success. In mid- and late September, right after the collapse of Lehman Brothers and the rapid-fire sale of Merrill Lynch to Bank of America, one analyst warned that "should the credit environment deteriorate further, the proposed $52 billion takeover of

A–B could fall apart. At this point, we think the deal is likely to go through," she said, "but with new uncertainties unfolding almost every day, we think it is important to be cautious."

"The banks must have been nervous," said an Anheuser advisor. "I guarantee InBev was scared to death." And it had reason to be. The airtight contract InBev had signed to get the deal done was threatening to come into play. If some of the banks that had agreed to cover the deal's nearly $55 billion in financing failed, and others tried to use that as an excuse to get out of their commitments, InBev would have to fund the acquisition on its own.

"There was no remedy. They had to close," an Anheuser insider said. "One way of closing was to give us their company. This thing could have really been a mess."

"When that contract was signed, we joked that one way or another, either they're going to own us or we're going to own them," said another. "And for the next five months to closing, there were plenty of points in time in that crisis when you really wondered which way it would go."

■ ■ ■

If InBev had made its offer just a month later, or if Anheuser-Busch had waited a month or two more to admit defeat, key players on both sides say the deal would never have happened. The takeover's perfect timing was a fluke that had little to do with planning or strategy.

"One of the things that enabled all of this was that the credit markets were willing to shower them with loans," said Sandy Warner. "It wouldn't have been possible to do this a month or two later."

InBev and its banks did close the deal, however, slightly ahead of schedule, on November 18. The stock of the old Anheuser-Busch, known for its "BUD" ticker symbol, stopped trading, and shareholders were paid $70 for each share of stock they owned. Modelo kept InBev tied up in arbitration for more than a year and a half over whether it could block the deal, but in July of 2010, a panel ruled that the takeover did not violate Modelo's original agreement with Anheuser-Busch. The ruling confirmed that InBev could keep its half-stake in

Modelo and sparked new talk over whether the rest of the Mexican brewer would finally be sold.

Despite Anheuser's missteps and its arrogance over the years, Bob Lachky said ruefully that he couldn't help but feel like a victim of America's cutthroat and, later, fractured business climate. "What's really amazing is how merger mania and the weakness of the American financial system really did us in," he said. "Yes, we could have done all of those other things . . . but we were doing so well in our own little world."

As more time passed following the deal's closure, however, Anheuser's newly minted former executives turned thankful that it happened precisely when it did. Had the merger been signed up earlier, they might have sunken their new piles of cash into the stock market just before it tanked. And had Anheuser-Busch come up for grabs later, the chances of convincing InBev or anyone else to pay $70 per share would have been slim.

They were lucky to cash out at all—several other takeovers had already fallen apart by the time the Anheuser-Busch deal occurred, and many more collapsed soon afterward. Nearly a year beforehand, in the late summer of 2007, the buyout of Home Depot's wholesale supply unit was renegotiated to cut $1.8 billion off the price. That kicked off a slew of other broken or nearly broken takeovers, including the $15.3 billion purchase of chemicals maker Rohm and Haas by Dow Chemical and the failed mega-buyout of Canadian telecommunications giant BCE. All together, a scrap heap of $660 billion worth of deals fell apart in 2008. Thanks to its bulletproof contract, the InBev takeover of Anheuser-Busch was one of the few transactions that survived.

"At the end of the day, this deal looked phenomenal because the whole world fell apart and the Anheuser shareholders got $70 a share," said an Anheuser insider. "Who knows what that share price would have been if the deal had gone away and the markets collapsed?"

"Could we have maybe gotten a couple more bucks? Maybe we could have. In hindsight, in light of everything that happened in the financial markets and everything else, the premium that was attained—in the biggest all-cash bid in the history of U.S. companies, right at the crash of the financial markets—was a remarkable thing for the shareholders."

"It makes the board look like heroes for reasons totally outside of anything they ever did. From a shareholder perspective, they can be heralded as heroes for things that they really don't deserve."

The debate over whether to ask for more than $70 per share had seemed logical on Wednesday of the takeover battle's final week. By the time the companies announced their deal that Sunday evening, though, the U.S. government had announced that it would take emergency measures to rescue Fannie Mae and Freddie Mac—two mortgage lenders that owned or backed a combined $5 trillion in home mortgages. Both companies' share prices had lost nearly half their value the previous week, which had factored into some Anheuser directors' decisions to take InBev's offer while they had the chance in case the market spiraled downward.

"The banks were telling us, 'You guys could get $75, you could get more,'" said Bob Lachky. "We couldn't have gotten that. We were lucky we got $70. They had one bank fail. We were lucky."

"These guys would be like, 'You guys are only in the first inning at $70, you've got nine innings to play.' And I was like, 'You're talking about people's lives here. You guys can just jump in a lake.' Because in the end, you were wrong. $70 was the perfect place. If you're going to talk about the cold reality of the takeover price, we were fine. Glad we didn't listen."

In commendation for his efforts to broker the "hotly contentious, then widely praised" sale of the company, Sandy Warner was named "2009 Outstanding Director" by the Outstanding Directors Exchange. Ed Whitacre was quoted as saying that the board was "very fortunate" that Warner had rotated into the lead director position by the time of the deal. "Sandy was the perfect guy to be in that role when InBev approached," he said.

"We got one of the best deals in the history of business when we finally completed the transaction," said Forese. "It's just one of those things that happens in industry in general. People get acquired. People move on."

Epilogue

The way this played out was Shakespearean in nature. I haven't decided which play.
The dynamic between father and son was just Shakespearean and tragic.
—Advisor to Anheuser-Busch

The wisdom and success of each U.S. presidential administration tend to be viewed through a lens that grows more and more prismatic as the years pass. Popular decisions that seemed brilliant at the time morph into dead ends down the road, and others that looked ill-advised at the outset prove lucky. The same can be said for the reign of August Busch III.

Perhaps, rather than coldheartedly selling his company out from beneath his son, August III was actually fighting to make sure Anheuser-Busch survived in some way once it was irretrievably backed into a corner. He helped secure a high price for the company as beer sales started flagging and the economy turned south, and then traded off all of its risks and responsibilities to InBev—which couldn't have closed the deal at a worse time as panic gripped the world's markets at the end of 2008. Anheuser-Busch InBev's sales slid 2.2 percent in 2009 and then started to drop off even more significantly. The company's cost-slashing effort "was already running out of steam in the first quarter of [2010]," said Benj Steinman, publisher of *Beer Marketer's Insights*. "North American earnings were down, and the volume declines early this year were like nothing we've ever seen."

Some former executives argue that handing the company to InBev was a necessary end to Anheuser's story after the string of wins it posted through the 1980s and early 1990s. "The things that made us great when we were growing from 10 percent market share to 48 percent are not the same things that make a company great when it's going from 48 percent share to 55," said Jack Purnell. "It's the difference between the winning ingredients in consolidation and the winning ingredients once the industry has already consolidated."

"Fortunately for the company, InBev has some of those skills. Skills you need when you are not gaining share at a rapid pace. When you are gaining share, that's all you need. You can have relatively low pricing, but as long as you're gaining share rapidly you're going to be fine. But once you stop gaining share, you'd better have cost-cutting and pricing and focus skills, and these are three skills InBev brings."

To some, the obvious question is: Why couldn't—and didn't—Anheuser-Busch develop those abilities so it could survive on its own, without needing an acquirer to take the reins? It simply didn't prepare for the inevitable, and chose to press on for years with its insular growth strategies and profligate spending.

"The company was just so overstaffed, and always had been," said Harry Schuhmacher. When Anheuser-Busch executives made appearances, he said, "they brought 14 people with them. They brought a guy with a laptop, a guy with a spare laptop, and a guy with a spare for the spare laptop. They brought their own teleprompters, and five bulletproof Suburbans would pull up. It was just crazy expensive, whereas MillerCoors's Tom Long would just walk up by himself with a thumb drive. That kind of culture was ripe for the picking."

"Neither Pat nor August [III] did the really heavy lifting that needed to be done" to eliminate spending, Sandy Warner acknowledged.

"When August IV got in the seat, he and his team recognized that they had a ton of costs that they could and did need to take out, and developed a plan to do it. But this deal overtook them."

■ ■ ■

In the months that followed the loss of the company that brought wealth and notoriety to generations of their family, both The Third and The Fourth dropped out of sight. They did so separately—The Third to his secluded farm, and The Fourth splitting time between his home near St. Louis and a new place farther west, near Lake of the Ozarks. There was little need for communication between father and son without Anheuser-Busch to bind them together. The two hardly spoke in the immediate aftermath of the deal, and as far as anyone in St. Louis could tell, they hadn't picked up much of a dialogue in the months since. The status of their relationship gave locals plenty to chatter about.

Neither man seemed to have many close friendships to fall back upon. Both had always tended to turn to their love of the outdoors and of flying—of the tranquility and the feeling of unbridled power that comes with drifting alone through the air.

"They always lived a very isolated life anyway. Mr. Busch is out on a very secluded farm, so no one is there kissing his fanny," said one former top executive. "Mr. Busch is just very isolated from even those he would consider friendly associates.

"Young August always had a cult of people who wanted to be in his entourage, but he was always good about blocking that kind of stuff," the executive continued. "He just wanted certain people around him, so he didn't tolerate that. They were very, very suspicious about people trying to get close to them just because of who they were. But that suspicion cannot lead to many solid friendships."

The takeover forced The Fourth through some jarring life changes. In early April 2008, the month before reports of InBev's interest first hit, he had stood jubilantly in front of workers outside the huge Anheuser-Busch packaging plant in downtown St. Louis at a party to celebrate the 75th anniversary of the end of Prohibition. With his ancestors' perseverance through that difficult era on his mind, The Fourth gave a rousing and heartfelt address to the crowd.

"I love you guys, you ladies!" he said. "What an honor. An emotional day. Here's to our future," he said, lifting a bottle of Budweiser in a toast, "and another 75 fantastic years. Let's go get 'em!"

Exactly 14 weeks later, just a brief walk from that site, The Fourth faced his employees again and explained that Anheuser-Busch had just surrendered its longstanding independence. This time, Brito stood at his side as Anheuser's victorious new commander. The Fourth's reign as the last great American beer baron was up, just a year and a half after it began.

His life already in upheaval, he made a couple of other personal adjustments once the merger closed. Rather than pursuing a long lusted-after quest as some of his colleagues had, he seemed intent on withdrawing as much as possible from everyone.

He filed for divorce from the former Kathryn Thatcher on November 26, 2008—less than a week after the takeover closed, and after just two years of marriage. The couple, according to the filing, had already been separated for nearly two months, and Thatcher had moved to Massachusetts. Thanks to a prenuptial agreement she signed before the marriage, the case moved quickly through the courts and the divorce was made official at the end of January 2009. "She Was His Wife, But She Wasn't His 'Bud'" rang the pithy headline on one St. Louis news blog that covered the split.

"I felt badly about that, because the girl was a sweet girl," said Ambassador Jones. "I don't think she had any real idea of what it's like to be in a corporate family, and her responsibilities. She tried hard. I never knew whether that was a real marriage or one that was necessary" for The Fourth to become CEO.

Earlier that same month, The Fourth resigned as a director of FedEx Corp., relinquishing a position he had held since he started prepping for Anheuser's top spot in 2003. A gossip column in the local paper reported that he went on a car-buying spree, picking up a $160,000 Audi 10, an $84,000 Nissan, and a $350,000 black SL series Mercedes, which put the number of cars he owned at 16 or 17. People who knew The Fourth said he was spending most of his time out at his lake retreat, and gossiped that he had put on some weight for a while before paring back down. "He always said he liked wearing flip flops and T-shirts, and that's pretty much what he does," said Harry Schuhmacher. "The distributor there will still drop beer off at his house."

The Fourth's friends and former colleagues have made efforts to reach out to him and offer support, but they can only extend themselves so far. Many are still recovering from the loss of Anheuser-Busch themselves.

"In my discussions with young August since then, he's so beaten down, we don't even talk about it," said Bob Lachky. "He's just not reaching back out too much. He sent some beautiful flowers for my birthday a couple of weeks ago, and a beautiful note, and I knew Lisa [his assistant] didn't write it. I knew it was from August. That really was touching."

"The Fourth had a pretty wounding experience," said one of the company's advisors. "When I've tried to reach out to him, he does respond in a reasonable period. But I think a lot of those relationships represent, to somebody like him, a bit of a reminder of all that could have been. Those things become very difficult."

It's hard to write off The Fourth's missteps as purely his father's fault, however, admit some of those who know The Fourth and like him. His upbringing may have been emotionally complicated and unconventional, but he was born into immense privilege and squandered plenty of it over the years. At any other company, he might have remained a marketing executive rather than rising to the top.

"That was a very tough relationship. But he's an adult," said one person close to the company. "Everybody has to take responsibility for their actions at some point in their life."

"He's a very likable guy, and he's had a tragic life in a way that no one will ever be sympathetic to. And they probably shouldn't be," another said. "He was just over his head."

Jim Forese shrugged off the loss of the company during The Fourth's tenure as something he couldn't have prevented during the year and a half he was CEO. "This is just one of those things that happens," he said. "It happened on his watch. It's not the worst thing to have happen on your watch." The Fourth, however, might disagree. His devotion to Anheuser-Busch was about pride and a longing for approval—not about money or power. He had access to plenty of that.

People close to The Third and The Fourth unanimously hoped to see a renewal of their relationship. Given the divisive history of the Busch family's men, however, few said they expected one soon. Gussie and The Third didn't speak for roughly a decade after The Third forced him out as CEO, and The Fourth once said he remembered watching the two of them try to patch things up on trips with his father out to Grant's Farm.

"I think The Fourth, regrettably, hungered to have a better relationship with a guy who just seemed to lack the interest," said one person who has known him for years. "If you weren't a carbon copy of The Third, The Third just didn't want to have anything to do with you. And August was never going to be his dad. He's just a different kind of guy."

"It's a very sad story, really," said beer industry writer Benj Steinman. "It's living proof that money doesn't buy happiness."

■ ■ ■

The manner in which the takeover unfolded has left some people close to Anheuser-Busch mulling one critical—and perhaps unavoidable—question: Did The Third recognize that the company's days as an independent brewer were limited, and engineer things so that it would be sold on his son's watch rather than his? August III began supporting The Fourth's CEO candidacy once Anheuser's glory days ended, he blocked his son's efforts to resurrect the company after he became chief, and then, once Anheuser was firmly established as a takeover target, he steered it toward InBev. He had hundreds of millions of dollars personally at stake.

"At some level, The Fourth got totally thrown in front of the bus," said Buddy Reisinger. "Pat and August are not stupid. At some level, they probably knew. When The Fourth came in, even before this happened, I thought, 'These guys know there are no more levers to pull. This guy—his best-case scenario is they tread water.' I said, 'August IV cannot pull a rabbit out of a hat. It's not possible. There's not going to be another Bud Light. What's the guy going to do?'"

"He took the legs out from under his own son," said a former ad agency executive.

Not everyone, however, is convinced that The Third could stomach the thought of losing Anheuser-Busch to a foreign competitor, no matter who was in charge. Crediting him with the foresight he would have needed to see InBev coming years in advance might also be a stretch.

"I don't think that's viable at all, because knowing him, there's no way he would ever surrender," Bob Lachky said. "His personality and his drive and every bit of his wiring is based on winning. I don't think there's a way he would ever drop a hot potato and then scream when it was on the way down."

"Hindsight makes The Third look worse than he is," said one company advisor.

He certainly didn't make it easy for his son to succeed, however, which suggests the truth may lie somewhere in between. While he repeatedly dodged opportunities at global expansion, his intentions there weren't nefarious. It was his constant effort to dilute his son's authority that raises eyebrows and prompts other former executives to wonder whether The Fourth ever really had a shot at changing the course of Anheuser-Busch's history.

"I think it would have been very, very hard, because so many board members were vestiges of his father's group," an Anheuser insider said. "The only way he would have gotten more credibility is if the performance had been stronger. And the performance was just okay. So he wasn't doing things fast enough to build up his own credibility, and his father just seemed to take everything he wanted to do and talk about how stupid it was."

"If you had given him, say, five years as CEO, you could say, 'Well, the fate of the company was literally determined by the last five years of his leadership,'" said General Shelton. "But time ran out on us."

"The InBev offer came in before very much of the stuff he had working really started to pay dividends," Shelton added.

The Fourth had been head of the U.S. brewing business for several years before becoming CEO, however—it wasn't as if he parachuted straight into the CEO's spot. He had been given a good chunk of time to try to revive Budweiser's flagging market share, and his efforts had been largely fruitless.

Still, even people on InBev's side of the fence find it hard to peg too much blame on August IV. "You know honestly, the guy wasn't there long enough," acknowledged one InBev advisor. "If anything, the place was probably starting to turn around."

The Fourth opened a window into his tortured psyche in several e-mails he sent to Harry Schuhmacher during and after the take-over battle. Some were coherent; others weren't. Each suggested that he was wallowing in despair and felt he had let everyone down. He deeply regretted vowing to his distributors that the company wouldn't be sold on his watch. If he had known that his father and the board would turn against him and Modelo at the 11th hour, he wouldn't have opened his mouth.

In late 2008, Schuhmacher told The Fourth that he wanted to present him with an award at his annual beer summit. The Fourth was no longer in power, but it would give him a chance to break bread one last time with his former distributors and other friends in the industry. August waffled for weeks as he considered it, weighing the type of reception he thought he'd receive from the crowd. He finally gave Schuhmacher an answer in the last of his e-mails, sent late at night and, Schuhmacher said, probably under the influence.

"It was just a desperate e-mail of self-pity and regret. He decided not to do it," he recounted. Still, "I don't think the harm that came to that company was a result of anything he did."

While InBev was ultimately the aggressor, Anheuser-Busch fell victim to its own insularity and hubris. It was too risk-averse, too provincial, too hemmed-in to an aging strategy, and too unwilling to accept that the world was rapidly changing whether it liked it or not. The Third ran Anheuser-Busch like a monarch, and his loyal board of directors and subordinates were all too willing over the years to oblige him. It all contributed to an atmosphere of delusion in which Anheuser-Busch believed it was safe from a takeover not because it had actual protections, but because the sheer concept was simply unthinkable. In August III's case, one man's brilliance was his hubris.

In many ways, the script of what happened at Anheuser-Busch was written not by August Busch IV but by August Busch III, said people close to the company. August III ran one of America's most iconic institutions and was the lion of the brewing industry, but he also made it all but impossible for Anheuser-Busch to sustain itself and to maintain a strong headquarters in St. Louis. He knew how to operate a U.S.-centric brewery, they said, and he made some important forays into China. When the beer industry turned south, however, the insular strategies he had laid in place weren't enough to ensure Anheuser-Busch's survival.

"Do I believe that the guy was probably great at running a domestic brewing company?" questioned one company insider. "Yes. But as a great macrostrategist, thinking about what the future would bring and preparing them for it, the guy doesn't get marks there.

"I think history has to suggest that the guy was way too pigheaded and stubborn to do what he needed to do to put that company in position to have a future."

■ ■ ■

Plenty of forces afoot that summer helped to drive Anheuser-Busch into InBev's arms. A fleetingly perfect set of market conditions. An apathetic group of American beer drinkers. And a board that needed—and found—an escape hatch.

Anheuser's isolationist history drove the result in the end, and made everything that occurred during August IV's tenure a footnote to a much bigger story. Anheuser-Busch's fate was sealed not during his year and a half in office but during the decades-long span in which it was run by a man who couldn't fathom that anyone else could fill his shoes. He ultimately ensured that no one did.

"There were not enough people around him who would tell him when he was talking crap," said the head of a rival brewer. "He ruled by fear; he was megalomaniacal."

"Their strength became their weakness. They became extraordinarily successful pushing the formula of one man. But that's the problem with great men. They end up breathing their own smoke, believing their own stories."

Notes

Chapter 1   The Game Is Afoot

Page 7   "One newspaper report had included . . ."   Neil Hume, "InBev Targets Takeover of Anheuser-Busch," FT Alphaville, May 23, 2008.

Page 7   "The fact that we're going to be forced to listen . . ."   Robert Lachky, interview by author, St. Louis, Missouri, November 5, 2009.

Page 10   "Whoa! Over 100 results found . . ."   www.whitepages.com (accessed April 2010).

Page 10   "To keep "Air Bud" running smoothly . . ."   Todd C. Frankel, "A-B Jets Linger as Clipped Wings," St. Louis Post-Dispatch, January 10, 2010, A1.

Page 11   "They should feel very important. . . ."   Rick Hill, interview by author, St. Louis, Missouri, November 4, 2009.

Page 11   "During The Third's tenure . . ."   William Finnie, phone interview by author, October 20, 2009.

Chapter 2   Crazy and Lazy at Loggerheads

Page 24   "Born in St. Louis on March 28, 1899 . . ."   *New York Times,* September 30, 1989, Obituaries.

Page 24   "He started out in 1922 . . ."   *Encyclopaedia Britannica,* August Anheuser Busch, Jr.

Page 25   "Eschewing planes and buses . . ."   "The Baron of Beer," *Time,* July 11, 1955, Cover story. www.time.com/time/magazine/article/ 0,9171,807368−1,00.html.

Page 26   "All the pain was worth it . . ."   Ibid.

Page 26   "He owned a camel . . ."   Ibid.

Page 26   "Adalbert "Adie" von Gontard . . ."   Peter Hernon and Terry Ganey, *Under the Influence* (New York Simon & Schuster, 1991), 168.

Page 26   "If Diana was the People's Princess . . ."   Matthew Hathaway and Jeremiah McWilliams, "What Would We Be without A-B?" *St. Louis Post-Dispatch,* June 1, 2008, A1.

Page 27   "People liked to joke . . ."   *Under the Influence,* 335.

Page 28   "Edward Vogel, who had been a company vice president . . ."   *Under the Influence,* 233.

Page 31   "It served as a forceful reprimand . . ."   *Under the Influence,* 268.

Page 31   "The talk . . ."   *Under the Influence,* 268, citing *BusinessWeek,* "When You Say Busch, You've Said it All," February 17, 1986.

Page 31   "I couldn't give my secretary . . ."   *Under the Influence,* 271.

Page 31   "After Gussie's lieutenant . . ."   *Under the Influence,* 275.

Page 32   "Confident that he had the backing . . ."   *Under the Influence,* 287−289.

Page 32   "This should be the best thing . . ."   Walter C. Reisinger, Jr., interview by author, St. Louis, Missouri, November 4, 2009.

Page 33   "August has stabbed my father in the back, . . ."   *Under the Influence,* 287.

Page 33   "He and I had years of a great relationship . . ."   Outstanding Directors Exchange *Agenda,* July 14, 2008, 6, www.theodx.com/outstanding directors/Busch%20071408%20Agenda%20issue_fnl.pdf.

Page 33   "They didn't speak for roughly a decade . . ."   David Kesmodel, "Anheuser's Chief Must Fight for His Legacy," *Wall Street Journal,* May 27, 2008, A1.

Page 33   "For his work as executor . . ."   *Under the Influence,* 402−404.

Page 34   "The company ultimately paid . . ."   *New York Times* Abstracts, February 6, 1977.

Page 35   "One former ad agency staffer . . ."   Steve Kopcha, interview by author, Columbia, Missouri, November 5, 2009.

Chapter 3   The Colossus

Page 39   "He had been known to pick up the phone . . ."   Rick Hill and Walter C. Reisinger, Jr., interview by author, St. Louis, Missouri, November 4, 2009.

Page 40 "Now let's get to work . . ." John Greening, phone interview by author, October 6, 2009.

Page 41 "When he fixes his stare . . ." Ellyn E. Spragins, Marc Frons, "When You Say Busch, You've Said it All," *BusinessWeek*, February 17, 1986, 58–63.

Page 43 "He was known to take off his watch . . ." Hill and Reisinger, interview by author, St. Louis, Missouri, November 4, 2009.

Page 43 "If the restrooms are unclean . . ." Peter Hernon, "Going on 90," *St. Louis Post-Dispatch,* March 5, 1989, 1C.

Page 44 "He once demanded that a television commercial be reshot . . ." Patricia Sellers, "How Busch Wins in a Doggy Market," *Fortune,* June 22, 1987, 99.

Page 44 "He performed the same ritual . . ." Charlie Claggett, interview by author, St. Louis, Missouri, November 4, 2009.

Page 47 "He knew everything." William Finnie, phone interview by author, October 20, 2009.

Page 47 "Anyone scheduled to accompany him . . ." Rick Hill, interview by author, St. Louis, Missouri, November 4, 2009.

Page 49 "I never heard him say a braggy thing . . ." Finnie, phone interview by author, October 20, 2009.

Page 49 "You can't predict the likes and dislikes . . ." Thomas C. Hayes, "August Busch, King of Beer," *New York Times,* October 12, 1980, F1.

Page 49 "By August III's last year . . ." David Kesmodel, "Anheuser CEO Fights for His Legacy," *Wall Street Journal*, ay 27, 2008.

Page 50 "Peter pleaded guilty . . ." "Peter Busch Sentenced to 5 Yrs Probation, St. Louis, for Manslaughter in Shooting Death of Friend David Leeker," *New York Times* Abstracts via United Press International, March 1, 1977, 17.

Page 50 "Billy Busch, another of The Third's half-brothers . . ." Peter Hernon, "'Busch Blood' Plays Role in Custody Battle, Mother Says," *St. Louis Post-Dispatch,* October 16, 1988, 1C.

Page 50 "Billy ratcheted down his profile . . ." Christopher Tritto, "Busch Family Eyes Return to Brewing Biz," *St. Louis Business Journal,* August 14, 2009.

Page 50 "The Third married Susan Hornibeck . . ." Jerry Berger and John M. McGuire, "Near Beer: Decades After Their Much Talked-about Divorce, Susan Busch Remains on Good Terms with August Busch III; and, for That Matter, with All of St. Louis," *St. Louis Post-Dispatch,* June 13, 1995, 1D.

Page 50 "Following a wedding reception . . ." Ibid.

Page 51 "Amid rumors . . ." *Under the Influence*, 246.

Page 51 "She and The Third used to get together . . ." Berger and McGuire, "Near Beer."

Page 51 "She called Ginny, his second wife . . ." Ibid.

Page 52 "I learned in my 20s and 30s . . ." Hayes, "August Busch, King of Beer."

Page 52 "As part of the probe . . ." Robert Johnson, John Koten, and Charles F. McCoy, "State of Shock Anheuser-Busch Cos. Is Shaken by Its Probe of Improper Payments," *Wall Street Journal,* March 31, 1987.

Page 53 "The first time Schuhmacher met The Third . . ." Harry Schuhmacher, phone interview by author, April 27, 2010.

Page 53 "Although the company had a strict policy . . ." Johnson, Koten, and McCoy, "State of Shock."

Page 54 "He had been Anheuser-Busch's "inspirational leader," . . ." Ibid.

Page 54 "The Third's determination . . ." Stephen Phillips, "No. 2 Busch Official Quits Amid Turmoil," *New York Times,* March 26, 1987.

Chapter 4   Selling the American Dream

Page 58 "Many beer connoisseurs . . ." Budweiser's overall rating as of July 11, 2010, is "'D+' Avoid," with 1,207 reviews, representative adjectives pulled from reviews by top reviewers "feloniousmonk," "BuckeyeNation," and "mikesgroove," BeerAdvocate.com.

Page 59 "John Murphy, Miller's president . . ." Peter Hernon and Terry Ganey, *Under the Influence* (New York Simon & Schuster, 1991), 317.

Page 60 "And he meant every word of it . . ." Adrienne Carter, "Miller Brewing It's Norman Time," *BusinessWeek,* May 29, 2006.

Page 60 "I'm more direct . . ." Patricia Sellers, "How Busch Wins in a Doggy Market," *Fortune,* June 22, 1987.

Page 61 "By 1985, Anheuser-Busch . . ." "AdAge Encyclopedia Anheuser-Busch," *Advertising Age,* September 15, 2003.

Page 61 "In 1989, it spent $5 million . . ." Judith VandeWater, "Anheuser-Busch Super Advertiser," *St. Louis Post-Dispatch,* January 9, 1989, 5.

Page 65 "When the conventions took place in California . . ." Charlie Claggett, interview by author, St. Louis, Missouri, November 4, 2009.

Page 66 "Then he flipped off the projector . . ." William Finnie, phone interview by author, October 20. 2009.

Page 68 "He later dieted to lose 75 pounds . . ." Gary Prindiville, phone interview by author, October 26, 2009.

Page 69 "He doesn't approve of barbecue sauce . . ." John Greening, phone interview by author, October 6, 2009.

Page 70 "His plate was still bare . . ." Claggett interview.

Page 74   "What a bunch of thugs . . ."   Ibid.

Page 74   "The ad men turned to look straight at August III . . ."   Greening interview.

Chapter 5   The Fourth Abides

Page 77   "On June 15, 1964 . . ."   Callaway Ludington, "Bud Man Prince of Beers August Busch IV Pours a Little Dash into the Family Business," *Chicago Tribune*, June 14, 1991, C1.

Page 78   "By the time he was in second grade . . ."   Patricia Sellers, "Bud-Weis-Heir August Busch IV Is Rebellious, Risk-Taking—and (Nearly) Ready to Rule the World's Largest Brewer," *Fortune*, January 13, 1997.

Page 78   "By his senior year in high school . . ."   Ludington, "Bud Man," C1.

Page 80   "It wasn't clear they could prove . . ."   *Under the Influence*, 337–352.

Page 80   "She felt her son had been unfairly treated . . ."   Jerry Berger and John M. McGuire, "Near Beer," *St. Louis Post-Dispatch*, June 13, 1995, 1D.

Page 80   "He said alcohol was not involved in the crash . . ."   Melanie Wells, "Busch IV Likely to Pop to Top," *USA Today*, September 4, 1998, 2B.

Page 80   "The assault charges stemmed . . ."   "Busch Heir Arrested After Wild Chase," *San Francisco Chronicle*/Associated Press, June 1, 1985.

Page 81   "You get me out of this . . ."   *Under the Influence*, 350.

Page 81   "After a three-day trial . . ."   Ludington, "Bud Man," C1.

Page 81   "Yet even during the takeover battle . . ."   Andrew Ross Sorkin, "Chilling a Deal for Bud," *New York Times* DealBook, June 17, 2008. http://dealbook.blogs.nytimes.com

Page 82   "You have to do three times as good as the next guy . . ."   Ludington, "Bud Man," C1.

Page 83   "After dropping out of the University of Arizona . . ."   "Interview Heir Apparent," *Modern Brewery Age,* September 19, 1994, S10.

Page 83   "In February of 1990 . . ."   Ludington, "Bud Man," C1.

Page 83   "Budweiser's branding under his command . . ."   Barbara Lippert, *Adweek*, July 20, 1992, Critique.

Page 88   "August Busch III has always seemed . . ."   Bill McClellan, "To Sell Beer Takes More Than a Glare," *St. Louis Post-Dispatch,* July 7, 1997.

Page 90   "We just hope it doesn't come to that . . ."   Ludington, "Bud Man."

Page 90   "I don't know that it's true . . ."   Gerry Khermouch, Julie Forster, and John Cady, "Is This Bud for You, August IV?" *BusinessWeek*, November 11, 2002.

Page 90   "That wasn't something I was looking for . . ."   Christopher Tritto, "Brewery Heir Steven Busch Acquires Krey Distributing," *St. Louis Business Journal,*" December 8, 2006.

Page 90 "August IV's sister . . ." Matthew Hathaway, "History of the Busch Family," *St. Louis Post-Dispatch,* July 9, 2008, A6.

Page 91 "I don't think anyone can say . . ." Sellers, "Bud-Weis-Heir."

Page 91 "If my brother continues to perform . . ." Ibid.

Page 92 "Every senior Anheuser-Busch officer . . ." Al Stamborski, "Anheuser-Busch Chairman Undergoes Heart-Bypass Surgery," *St. Louis Post-Dispatch*, September 29, 1999.

Page 92 "He owned just 3.4 million shares . . ." Wells, "Busch IV Likely to Pop to Top."

Page 92 "Considering the history . . ." Sellers, "Bud-Weis-Heir."

Page 93 "I wouldn't operate under the assumption . . ." Wells, "Busch IV Likely to Pop to Top."

Page 94 "I'm not going to consider . . ." Ibid.

Page 94 "He's not a character . . ." Khermouch, Forster, and Cady, "Is This Bud for You, August IV?"

Page 95 "*BusinessWeek* called The Third's decision . . ." Ibid.

Page 95 "It's not a foregone conclusion . . ." Ibid.

Page 96 "The goal was for The Fourth . . ." General Henry Hugh Shelton, phone interview by author, June 10, 2010.

Page 98 "If this is successful discounting . . ." "Anheuser Profits Fall in Tough Market," Just-drinks.com, October 27, 2005.

Page 100 "He also added non-alcoholic drinks . . ." Greg Edwards, "Anheuser's New Chief Faces Challenges," *Wall Street Journal*, December 6, 2006, B3G.

Page 100 "The Third's eyes welled visibly with tears . . ." Mike Beirne, "A-B Marketing Ready to Rumble," *Brandweek* (online), March 25, 2005.

Page 101 "His home, which had once been owned . . ." Khermouch, Forster, and Cady, "Is This Bud for You, August IV?"

Page 101 "Their engagement was called off . . ." Ludington, "Bud Man."

Page 101 "I'm not making predictions . . ." Sellers, "Bud-Weis-Heir."

Page 102 "The Fourth spent a good amount of time . . ." Jason Horowitz, "The Complete Ron Burkle," *New York Observer*, April 12, 2006.

Page 102 "If I don't start seriously working on a relationship . . ." Wells, "Busch IV Likely to Pop to Top."

Page 102 "Where's the cutoff? . . ." Ellen Florian Kratz, "A Busch (Beer) Marries for the Corner Office," *Fortune*, September 15, 2006.

Page 102 "To the chagrin of some disgruntled locals . . ." Carolyn Kylstra, "Clydesdales Grace Green for Wedding," *The Dartmouth,* August 8, 2006.

Page 103   "The Fourth's decision to get married . . ."   Andrew Ward, "Anheuser Keeps Crown in the Family," *Financial Times,* December 5, 2006, 28.

Page 103   "It was 'August, until you settle down . . ."   Kratz, "A Busch (Beer) Marries for the Corner Office."

Page 104   "It also pledged . . ."   Christopher Tritto, "A-B Picks up Aircraft, Beer Tabs for Busch IV, Stokes," *St. Louis Business Journal,* December 1, 2006.

Page 104   "Stokes made a similar election . . ."   Anheuser-Busch Companies Securities and Exchange Commission Filing Form 8-K, December 15, 2006.

Page 105   "Beer's total share of the alcohol market . . ."   Edwards, "Anheuser's Chief Faces New Challenges."

Page 106   "Mr. Busch now has center stage for himself . . ."   Ward, "Anheuser Keeps Crown in the Family."

Page 107   "The Fourth said in one newspaper interview . . ."   David Kesmodel, "Beer Clan Anheuser CEO Fights for His Legacy—As Rival Weighs a Bid, Busch Heir Still Seeks Father's Approval," *Wall Street Journal,* May 27, 2008, A1.

Page 108   "Mr. Busch remains a bit of a mystery . . ."   Edwards, "Anheuser's Chief Faces New Challenges."

Page 109   "The Fourth spread his net wide . . ."   Ward, "Anheuser Keeps Crown in the Family."

Page 110   "He concluded, 'I honestly do believe . . ."   Kesmodel, "Beer Clan Anheuser CEO Fights for His Legacy."

Page 110   "He later regretted making those comments . . ."   Schuhmacher, phone interview by author, April 27, 2010.

Page 110   "In his first decade . . ."   Sellers, "Bud-Weis-Heir."

Page 110   "The Third, as usual, stayed silent on the matter . . ."   Kesmodel, "Beer Clan Anheuser CEO Fights for His Legacy."

Chapter 6   The Hunter's Frozen Trigger Finger

Page 113   "We made our share of mistakes . . ."   Ellyn E. Spragins, Marc Frons, "When You Say Busch, You've Said it All, *BusinessWeek,* February 17, 1986, 58–63.

Page 117   "The globalization of American culture . . ."   "The World Beer & Beverage Forum Power Brands Made by Power Men," *Modern Brewery Age,* November 10, 1997. www.entrepreneur.com/tradejournals/article/20216423_2.html.

Page 117   "He weighed the possibility . . ."   Rick Hill and Walter Reisinger, Jr., interview by author, St. Louis, Missouri, November 4, 2009.

Page 118 "Two gunmen had unleashed a torrent . . ." Simon Romero, "Cashing In on Security Worries: Bad Times Are Good Times for Car Armorers in Brazil," *New York Times,* July 24, 1999.

Page 118 "Lemann moved his family . . ." Tony Smith, "A Bet on a Brazilian Brewery Pays Off for 3 Investors," *New York Times,* March 4, 2004, W7.

Page 118 "They funneled a fraction of that cash . . ." Ibid.

Page 119 "Brahma won clearance for the deal . . ." "AmBev: Third Largest Brewer Created with Merger Approval," *Food & Drink Weekly,* April 3, 2000, 1.

Page 126 "The United States and China were well illuminated . . ." Jeremiah McWilliams, "Brito Begins to Brew New Company: CEO Meets A-B Chief with Eye on Bottom Line, Employee Angst," *St. Louis Post-Dispatch,* July 16, 2008, A1.

Chapter 9   Mr. Brito Goes to Washington

Page 162 "In Missouri, where McCain ended up beating Obama . . ." Election Results, *New York Times,* Tuesday, December 9, 2008.

Page 162 "But this is about something bigger . . ." Heidi N. Moore, "One Couple's Crusade to Save Budweiser," *WSJ* Deal Journal, June 2, 2008.

Page 163 "Cindy McCain, who was known to drive around Phoenix . . ." Susan Davis, "McCains to Profit on Anheuser, InBev Deal," *WSJ* Washington Wire, July 14, 2008. http://blogs.wsj.com/washwire/2008/07/14/mccains-to-profit-on-anheuser-inbev-deal/.

Page 165 "Its political action committee . . ." Jeffrey H. Birnbaum, "InBev, Anheuser Battle in Washington," *Washington Post,* June 28, 2008.

Page 165 "A team of eight Anheuser Clydesdales . . ." "Hey, Bill, This Bud's for You," *Seattle Times,* January 16, 1993, A3.

Page 166 "That put it ahead of other heavily active PACs . . ." The Center for Responsive Politics. https://www.opensecrets.org/pacs/toppacs.php.

Page 167 "It started paying operatives . . ." Birnbaum, "InBev, Anheuser Battle in Washington."

Page 168 "The meeting adjourned after half an hour . . ." Ibid.

Page 168 "I said, 'Not going to happen.' . . ." "McCaskill Questions InBev CEO about Anheuser-Busch," Associated Press, June 17, 2008.

Page 168 "We do not have a 'For Sale' sign on our front lawn in America . . ." Deirdre Shesgreen and Rachel Melcer, "InBev Chief Feels Heat," *St. Louis Post-Dispatch,* June 18, 2008, A1.

Page 168 "Brito called his meeting . . ." "McCaskill Questions InBev," Associated Press.

Page 168 "She issued a letter . . ." Senator Claire McCaskill, "McCaskill Urges Anheuser-Busch Board to Reject Offer," June 18, 2008. http://mccaskill.senate.gov/newsroom/record.cfm?id=299367.

Page 168 "It would mean job losses . . ." Birnbaum, "InBev, Anheuser Battle in Washington."

Page 170 "The strongest words spoken against InBev . . ." *The Colbert Report,* Comedy Central. www.comedycentral.com/colbertreport/videos.jhtml?episodeId=174853.

Page 171 "Brito wrote an opinion piece . . ." Carlos Brito, *St. Louis Post-Dispatch,* June 17, 2008, Commentary.

Page 177 "*Advertising Age* ran an article . . ." Jeremy Mullman and Michael Bush, "A-B Losing the PR War to InBev," *Advertising Age,* July 7, 2008.

Chapter 10 Angry Bedfellows

Page 181 "During a meeting two weeks earlier . . ." Anheuser-Busch 2008 proxy.

Page 184 "If Modelo's biggest rival was going to tie up . . ." Jack Purnell, phone interview by author, October 29. 2009.

Page 185 "In late 1996 . . ." William Flannery, "A-B Invests in Mexican Brewer; Raises Grupo Modelo Stake to 37 Percent," *St. Louis Post-Dispatch,* December 19, 1996, 3B.

Page 185 "Three months later . . ." Bloomberg News, "Anheuser-Busch to Increase Stake in Mexican Brewer," *New York Times,* May 23, 1997, 3.

Page 190 "By high school, he was working there part-time . . ." David Luhnow and David Kesmodel, "Modelo CEO Faces Limits of Family Firm," *Wall Street Journal,* June 27, 2008, B11.

Page 191 "Fernández was elected to Modelo's board . . ." "Who's News Anheuser-Busch Cos.," *Wall Street Journal,* February 29, 1996.

Page 191 "She decided to throw herself into the family business . . ." Ginger Thompson, "Daddy's Girl Turns Beer-and-TV Billionaire," *New York Times,* July 21, 2002, Saturday Profile, 4.

Page 191 "María proceeded to build a reputation . . ." David Luhnow, "Crashing Barriers," *Wall Street Journal,* October 1, 2001, R9.

Page 191 "Known by the nickname Mariasun . . ." Kevin Sullivan, "Bilaterally in Love," *Washington Post,* February 7, 2005, C1.

Page 192 "The "golden couple's" 2005 wedding . . ." Susana Hayward, "'Golden Couple' All the Buzz," *Miami Herald,* Knight Ridder News Service, February 8, 2005, 16A.

Page 192 "In 2007, just before the global banking system . . ." Luisa Kroll and Allison Fass, "Special Report The World's Billionaires," *Forbes,* www.forbes .com/lists/2007/10/07billionaires_The-Worlds-Billionaires_Rank.html.

Page 194 "He spent Wednesday night prepping . . ." Tom Santel, phone interview by author, June 26, 2010.

Page 197 "By the end of that year . . ." Corporate information provided on Modelo web site (www.gmodelo.com).

Chapter 11   The Board: August, August, and Augusta

Page 204 "The scare tactic worked well . . ." Robert Slater, *The Titans of Takeover* (Beard Books, 1999), 167.

Page 206 "But The Fourth said he wanted to push . . ." Matthew Karnit-schnig and David Kesmodel, "Anheuser-Busch Gets a D," *Wall Street Journal* Deal Journal, June 16, 2008.

Page 206 "They were trying to change the board . . ." James Forese, phone interview by author, May 26, 2010.

Page 206 "The Third had been one of the AT & T directors . . ." Tim Barker, "Loyalty of A-B Board May Be Put to the Test," *St. Louis Post-Dispatch,* June 20, 2008.

Page 208 "So I don't think there are any questions . . ." Outstanding Directors Exchange *Agenda,* July 14, 2008 issue. www.theodx.com/ outstandingdirectors/Busch%20071408%20Agenda%20issue_fnl.pdf

Page 210 "But on July 11 . . ." CNBC, Julia Boorstin interview with Warren Buffett from Sun Valley, Idaho, July 11, 2008.

Page 210 "They and other directors . . ." Margie Manning, "GenAm Board Settles for $30 Million," *St. Louis Business Journal,* January 17, 2003.

Page 212 "Citigroup was set to earn . . ." Anheuser-Busch definitive proxy, October 2008.

Page 212 "Anheuser's directors had known . . ." General Henry Hugh Shelton, phone interview by author, June 10, 2010.

Page 216 "Augusta is famous for its pristine links . . ." "Augusta National Golf Club Members List," *USA Today* Projects Staff, August 4, 2004.

Page 218 "At six-foot-four . . ." Roger O. Crockett, "The Last Monopolist," *BusinessWeek,* April 12, 1999, Cover story.

Page 219 "Loucks had become an Anheuser-Busch director . . ." Julia Flynn Siler, David Greising, and Tim Smart, "The Case Against Baxter International," *BusinessWeek,* October 7, 1991.

Page 223 "So he's seen all the deals . . ." Outstanding Directors Exchange *Agenda,* July 14, 2008 issue.

Page 224   "When August IV started . . ."   Douglas Warner, phone interview by author, June 14, 2010.

Page 230   "To show that they weren't stonewalling . . ."   Anheuser-Busch press release, June 26, 2008.

Page 231   "I believe that as directors . . ."   "Adolphus Busch IV's Letter to Busch Board," Reuters, June 20, 2008. www.reuters.com/article/idUSN2044456620080621

Page 231   "Andrew Busch, another half-brother . . ."   *New York Times* DealBook, June 22, 2008.

Page 239   "I was wrong on that statement . . ."   Call transcript, http://yahoo.brand.edgar-online.com/EFX_dll/EDGARpro.dll?FetchFilingHtmlSection1?SectionID=6019032–43754–68909&SessionID=C9W3We-yRPmMhz7.

Chapter 12   The Montagues and the Busches

Page 243   " [T]heir ability to come along with us . . ."   David Kesmodel and David Luhnow, "Anheuser Courts an Ally in Mexico," *Wall Street Journal*, June 13, 2008, B1.

Chapter 13   A Seller from "Hello"

Page 257   "Ahead of the previous year's July Fourth . . ."   The Beer Institute, "Fourth of July Ranks Tops in U.S. Beer Sales New Data Shows Beer Contributes Billions to National Economy," press release, June 26, 2007 via PRNewswire.

Page 259   "He had, however, been abruptly replaced . . ."   Alex Berenson, "A Long Shot Becomes Pfizer's Latest Chief Executive," *New York Times*, July 29, 2006.

Page 268   "He didn't push them in one direction . . ."   General Henry Hugh Shelton, phone interview by author, June 10, 2010.

Page 271   "Anheuser's team of dejected executives . . ."   Tom Santel, phone interview by author, June 26, 2010.

Page 271   "The following morning, Tom Santel . . ."   Ibid.

Chapter 14   Put Up or Shut Up

Page 282   "In order to make that happen . . ."   Douglas Warner, phone interview by author, June 14, 2010.

Page 283   "This is going to happen . . ."   Ibid.

Page 287   "He'd be a hands-on executive . . ."   General Henry Hugh Shelton, phone interview by author, 10, 2010.

Page 287   "Yet after the board promoted him . . ."   Ambassador James R. Jones, phone interview by author, June 1, 2010.

Page 289   "The two men circled back . . ."   Warner, phone interview by author, June 14, 2010.

Chapter 15   A Long Way from St. Louis

Page 307   "InBev's record of corporate philanthropy . . ."   "Anheuser-Busch's New Brew," *St. Louis Business Journal*, July 31, 2009.

Chapter 16   A Toast on Both Sides

Page 315   "Stokes walked away with $ 160.9 million . . ."   Christopher Tritto, "A-B Brass Catch Gold Ring from InBev," *St. Louis Business Journal*, November 21, 2008.

Chapter 17   Cash Out or Hunker Down

Page 324   "Rather than hitching a town car . . ."   Jeremiah McWilliams, "Brito Begins to Brew," *St. Louis Post-Dispatch*, July 16, 2008, A1.

Page 325   "The contrast between globe- . . ."   Ibid.

Page 326   "And they came on top . . ."   "Anheuser-Busch's New Brew," *St. Louis Business Journal*, July 31, 2009.

Page 326   "I just didn't think . . ."   Jeremiah McWilliams, "The New A-B 'More of What You Need, and Less of What You Don't,'" *St. Louis Post-Dispatch*, March 8, 2009.

Page 326   "They did so, only to discover . . ."   Walter Reisinger, Jr., interview by author, St. Louis, Missouri, November 4, 2009.

Page 327   "Santel, who was paid $26.5 million . . ."   Christopher Tritto, "A-B Brass Catch Gold Ring from InBev," *St. Louis Business Journal*, November 21, 2008.

Page 328   "We beat the king of commercials . . ."   Bruce Horovitz, "'Two Nobodies from Nowhere' Craft Winning Super Bowl Ad," *USA Today*, December 31, 2009.

Page 328   "He stood to earn $20.6 million . . ."   Tritto, "A-B Brass Catch Gold Ring from InBev."

Page 328   "The Fourth's team had been willing to pay . . ."   David Jones, "AB InBev to Buy Modelo This Year; Broker Evolution," Reuters, March 9, 2010.

Page 329   "Chief Financial Officer Randy Baker . . ."   Tritto, "A-B Brass Catch Gold Ring from InBev."

Page 329 "Anthony Ponturo, who had been the company's sports marketing head . . ." Ibid.

Page 330 "She said Anheuser-Busch maintained . . ." Jonathan Stempel, "Ex-Anheuser Female Executive Sues for Gender Bias," Reuters, October 27, 2009.

Page 330 "As he walked into the conference room . . ." McWilliams, "Brito Begins to Brew."

Page 330 "He didn't exactly need the cash . . ." Tritto, "A-B Brass Catch Gold Ring from InBev."

Page 331 "Busch was a no-show at industry events . . ." Jeremiah McWilliams, "Busch Slips Off Stage Despite Positioning for Role in InBev Spotlight," *St. Louis Post-Dispatch,* August 30, 2009, A1.

Page 332 "Secretaries were fired . . ." "Brazilian Style at the Largest Brewery in the World," *Exame,* February 2010.

Page 332 "I can buy my own beer . . ." Ibid.

Page 332 "Even expenses like color printing . . ." Jeremiah McWilliams, "The New A-B."

Page 332 "Roughly a year and a half after the deal closed . . ." Kelsey Volkmann, "Anheuser-Busch Adds Fee for Clydesdales Appearances," *St. Louis Business Journal,* April 12, 2010.

Page 333 "One vendor of beechwood chips lost out . . ." "Anheuser-Busch's New Brew."

Page 334 "Schlafly's founder said . . ." "Brazilian Style at the Largest Brewery in the World."

Page 333 "InBev still used the Anheuser jets . . ." Todd C. Frankel, "A-B Jets Linger as Clipped Wings," *St. Louis Post-Dispatch,* January 10, 2010, A1.

Page 335 "Anheuser's St. Louis employees . . ." "Brazilian Style at the Largest Brewery in the World."

Page 336 "Brito was poised to pull in . . ." Ibid.

Page 336 "Out of their estimated $50 million . . ." J.P. Morgan research, "Anheuser Busch InBev," January 26, 2009.

Page 336 "Weiss relocated from Paris . . ." Liam Vaughan, "Lazard's Weiss Is Year's Busiest Banker," Mergermarket, as quoted in *Wall Street Journal,* December 14, 2009.

Page 337 "At this point, we think . . ." "Credit Market Instability Rattles InBev's Takeover of Anheuser-Busch," *St. Louis Business Journal,* citing Ann Gilpin, Morningstar, October 3, 2008.

Page 338 "The ruling confirmed . . ." Clementine Fletcher, "AB InBev Wins Dispute Over Ownership of Modelo Stake," Bloomberg, July 12, 2010.

Page 339 "All together, a scrap heap of $660 billion . . ." Serena Saitto, "Goldman Leads in M&A as InBev Deal Fails to Add Fizz to Fees," Bloomberg, March 2, 2009.

Page 340 "Sandy was the perfect guy . . ." Heather Wolf, "Sandy Warner The Stalwart Director," Outstanding Directors Exchange. www.theodx.com/outstandingdirectors/WarnerSandy%20OD%20web.pdf.

Epilogue

Page 343 "They did so separately . . ." Jeremiah McWilliams, "Busch Slips Off Stage Despite Positioning for Role in InBev Spotlight," St. Louis Post-Dispatch, August 31, 2009, A1.

Page 344 "Let's go get 'em! . . ." Ibid.

Page 344 "She Was His Wife . . ." Riverfronttimes.com, January 30, 2009.

Page 344 "A gossip column in the local paper reported . . ." Deb Peterson, "Wonder What August Busch IV Has Been Up To?" St. Louis Post-Dispatch, September 28, 2009.

Page 346 "Gussie and The Third didn't speak . . ." David Kesmodel, "Beer Clan Anheuser CEO Fights for His Legacy," Wall Street Journal, May 27, 2008, A1.

Acknowledgments

A few people who aren't brewers or bankers nonetheless contributed immensely to my ability to get this book onto store shelves. My heartfelt thanks go to my agent, Andy McNicol, at William Morris Endeavor, and to Pamela van Giessen and Emilie Herman at John Wiley & Sons.

I'm boundlessly grateful to my husband, Micah Levin, for serving as baby bather, proofreader, chef, and cheerleader at various points during the book-writing process, and to my son, Miller, for his patience and joyfully sunny disposition right from the start.

I must also thank the rest of my family—James and Faye MacIntosh; Emily, Trevor, and Ella Fetters; and Kate MacIntosh, Karl Donner, Paul MacIntosh, Daniel Levin, Judith Karlen, Sherry Levin, James Friedberg, Brendan Levin, Tonya Fletcher, and Erin Levin—for providing such a tightly woven safety net. I hope I can return the favor. My profuse apologies go out to them and to all of the friends and colleagues I was remiss in contacting for a while.

I'm also grateful to the journalists at the *Financial Times* in New York (and to Francesco Guerrera in particular), who were willing to pinch-hit in my absence during my book leave, and to Dr. Jason Rothbart, for easing my family through an unexpectedly hasty transition to California living.

About the Author

Julie MacIntosh covered the takeover of Anheuser-Busch while working as a correspondent for the *Financial Times*, based in New York. Prior to her work covering mergers and acquisitions for the paper, she wrote for the *Financial Times'* influential Lex column. Julie studied as a Knight-Bagehot Fellow in business journalism at Columbia University and, upon completing the Fellowship and earning a Master of Science in Journalism from Columbia's Graduate School of Journalism, then earned a Master of Business Administration from Columbia's Graduate School of Business. Julie also spent six years as a reporter and correspondent for Reuters, in New York and Chicago. She received her undergraduate degree from the Medill School of Journalism at Northwestern University.

Julie, who was raised in the fruit- and wine-growing region of Traverse City, Michigan, always preferred the vineyards of Napa, Sonoma, and Tuscany to the breweries of St. Louis and Milwaukee, but writing this book instilled in her a new respect for brewers' pride.

Index

2020l